A Celebration of Poets

Great Lakes
Grades 7-9
Spring 2009

creativecommunication
A CELEBRATION OF TODAY'S WRITERS

A Celebration of Poets
Great Lakes
Grades 7-9
Spring 2009

An anthology compiled by Creative Communication, Inc.

Published by:

creative COMMUNICATION
A CELEBRATION OF TODAY'S WRITERS

1488 NORTH 200 WEST • LOGAN, UTAH 84341
TEL. 435-713-4411 • WWW.POETICPOWER.COM

Printed in the United States of America

ISBN: 978-1-60050-279-8

Foreword

Earlier this year I received a phone call from an individual who was sending in a poem written by a friend's son. Through the conversation it was revealed that the person I was talking to was the author, poet and playwright, John Tobias. His poem, "Reflections on a Gift of Watermelon Pickle Received from a Friend Called Felicity" is one of my favorite poems. Starting with the line "During that summer, when unicorns were still possible..." his poem takes me back to all the magical summers that I had where anything could happen. I was given a treat in that Mr. Tobias recited his poem and related the story that inspired it. What I gained most from the conversation was that the inspiration for any writing may seem to come from an event, but it is really written from a lifetime of experiences.

I also received a letter this spring from a young lady who was published in one of our anthologies in 1999. Now a published author working on her second novel, she took the time to write and thank Creative Communication for giving her the start for her writing career. The poets in this anthology are beginning writers. Yet, as they continue in their writing, the experience of being a published author will hopefully be an inspiration to them. As they gain a lifetime of experiences, I hope they will continue to write and share themselves through poetry.

As you read each student's poem, realize that every famous author started somewhere. I hope that I will continue to receive letters from authors who relate that we were the first place they were published. Will one of these authors become famous? Anything is possible.

I hope you enjoy this anthology and the poets who share their lives through words.

Thomas Worthen, Ph.D.
Editor
Creative Communication

WRITING CONTESTS!

Enter our next POETRY contest!

Enter our next ESSAY contest!

Why should I enter?

Win prizes and get published! Each year thousands of dollars in prizes are awarded throughout North America. The top writers in each division receive a monetary award and a free book that includes their published poem or essay. Entries of merit are also selected to be published in our anthology.

Who may enter?

There are four divisions in the poetry contest. The poetry divisions are grades K-3, 4-6, 7-9, and 10-12. There are three divisions in the essay contest. The essay divisions are grades 3-6, 7-9, and 10-12.

What is needed to enter the contest?

To enter the poetry contest send in one original poem, 21 lines or less. To enter the essay contest send in one original non-fiction essay, 250 words or less, on any topic. Each entry must include the student's name, grade, address, city, state, and zip code, and the student's school name and school address. Students who include their teacher's name may help their teacher qualify for a free copy of the anthology. Contest changes and updates are listed at www.poeticpower.com.

How do I enter?

Enter a poem online at:
www.poeticpower.com

or

Mail your poem to:
Poetry Contest
1488 North 200 West
Logan, UT 84341

Enter an essay online at:
www.studentessaycontest.com

or

Mail your essay to:
Essay Contest
1488 North 200 West
Logan, UT 84341

When is the deadline?

Poetry contest deadlines are August 18th, December 3rd, and April 13th. Essay contest deadlines are October 15th, February 17th, and July 15th. Students can enter one poem and one essay for each spring, summer, and fall contest deadline.

Are there benefits for my school?

Yes. We award $15,000 each year in grants to help with Language Arts programs. Schools qualify to apply for a grant by having 15 or more accepted entries.

Are there benefits for my teacher?

Yes. Teachers with five or more students published receive a free anthology that includes their students' writing.

For more information please go to our website at **www.poeticpower.com**, email us at editor@poeticpower.com or call 435-713-4411.

Table of Contents

Poetic Achievement Honor Schools 1

Language Arts Grant Recipients 7

Grades 7-8-9 11
  Top Poems 12
  High Merit Poems 22

Index 267

STATES INCLUDED IN THIS EDITION:

MICHIGAN
MINNESOTA
WISCONSIN

Spring 2009 Poetic Achievement Honor Schools

** Teachers who had fifteen or more poets accepted to be published*

The following schools are recognized as receiving a "Poetic Achievement Award." This award is given to schools who have a large number of entries of which over fifty percent are accepted for publication. With hundreds of schools entering our contest, only a small percent of these schools are honored with this award. The purpose of this award is to recognize schools with excellent Language Arts programs. This award qualifies these schools to receive a complimentary copy of this anthology. In addition, these schools are eligible to apply for a Creative Communication Language Arts Grant. Grants of two hundred and fifty dollars each are awarded to further develop writing in our schools.

Abundant Life Christian School
Madison, WI
Christa O. Palmer*

Boulan Park Middle School
Troy, MI
Fran Blatnik*

Bristol Elementary School
Bristol, WI
Cheryl Fowler*

Cedar Grove-Belgium Middle School
Cedar Grove, WI
Gail Gonwa
Laura Hatfield
Christine Huiras*

Central Middle School
Iron Mountain, MI
Grace Laydon*

Centreville Jr High School
Centreville, MI
Andrea Justus*

Chippewa Falls Middle School
Chippewa Falls, WI
Mrs. Toutant*

Christ Child Academy
Sheboygan, WI
Julie Scharenbroch*

Clarkston Jr High School
Clarkston, MI
Erin Shaw*

Clintonville High School
Clintonville, WI
Kevin Godfrey*

Core Knowledge Charter School
Verona, WI
Carla Bonsignore
Heidi Mondloch

Detroit Country Day Middle School
Beverly Hills, MI
Carla Chennault
Cheryl Duggan
Mr. Grubaugh

Detroit Country Day Middle School
Beverly Hills, MI (cont.)
Carol M. Tabaka
Stephanie Trautman

Edison Middle School
Green Bay, WI
Nancie Brennan
Amy Phillips

Elkhart Lake Elementary-Middle School
Elkhart Lake, WI
Patricia Van Duerm*

Fairview Charter School
Milwaukee, WI
Janelle Konkol*

Gesu Catholic School
Detroit, MI
Judy P. Kuzniar*

Grosse Pointe Academy
Grosse Pointe, MI
Lawrence DeLuca*

Hally Magnet Middle School
Detroit, MI
Karen Careathers*

Hartland High School
Hartland, MI
Karen Quinn*
Kent Wabel

J C McKenna Middle School
Evansville, WI
Kim Stieber-White*

Lake Fenton Middle School
Fenton, MI
Nicole Guiles*

Lakeview Christian Academy
Duluth, MN
Pastor James Joseph*

Langston Hughes Academy
Detroit, MI
Maxine B. Rushing*

Lombardi Middle School
Green Bay, WI
Jill A. Anderson*
Joelene Wentland

Luxemburg-Casco Middle School
Casco, WI
Judith M. Delain*

Manistee Middle School
Manistee, MI
Rick Gebhard*
Mary Hunter*

Messmer Preparatory Catholic School
Milwaukee, WI
Renee Larsen*

Middle School at Parkside
Jackson, MI
Samella Kendrick*

Montgomery-Lonsdale High School
Montgomery, MN
Tyne Brodenburg
Jen Davidson*
Jason Hebzynski

New Auburn High School
New Auburn, WI
Steven Renfree*

Northport Public School
Northport, MI
Kevin Skarnulis*

Northwood School
Minong, WI
Karen A. Duffy*

Oak Creek High School
Oak Creek, WI
Ms. Appel
Penny A. Kapitz*

Our Lady of Good Counsel School
Plymouth, MI
Nancy Carapellotti
Barbara Hecmanczuk*

Our Lady Star of the Sea School
Grosse Pointe Woods, MI
Alice Dandy*

Pennfield Middle School
Battle Creek, MI
Christine Jordan*
Amanda Zima

Perry Middle School
Perry, MI
Sharon Johnson*

Petoskey High School
Petoskey, MI
Glen Young*

Pilgrim Lutheran School
Green Bay, WI
Mrs. Strysick*

Prairie Lakes School
Willmar, MN
Cathy Erickson*

Ramsey Jr High School
Saint Paul, MN
Lisa Vogel*

Richmond Middle School
Richmond, MI
Ms. K. Schweiger*

Roosevelt Middle School
Blaine, MN
Tammy Gruenwald*

Saint Thomas More Catholic School
Saint Paul, MN
Brenda Wagner*

Sandusky Middle School
Sandusky, MI
Desiree Benavides*

Scranton Middle School
Brighton, MI
Gwen Lucas*

Seymour Middle School
Seymour, WI
Tanya Hashagen
Matthew Molle*
Mary Yaeger*

Shakopee Area Catholic School
Shakopee, MN
Kyle Metzger*

Sherman Multicultural Arts School
Milwaukee, WI
Nadine Emanuel*

Spring Hill School
Wisconsin Dells, WI
Roxanne Bartz*

Springfield School
Springfield, MN
Mark Buerkle*

St Andrew's School
Grand Rapids, MI
Jenny Lastfogel*

St John Lutheran School
Fraser, MI
Susan Machemer*

St Katharine Drexel School
Beaver Dam, WI
Barbara Kalscheur*

St Thomas More Academy
Burton, MI
Phyllis Cory*

St Mary's School
Bloomington, WI
Amy Bohman*

St Roman School
Milwaukee, WI
Rosemary Karnowski*

Suring Elementary/Middle School
Suring, WI
Stacy Stocki*

Trinity Lutheran School
Utica, MI
Ms. Bean
Mrs. Delmotte*
Jane Henwood
Deborah Wesenberg

Troy High School
Troy, MI
Meagan Foster
Dr. Goslin
Donna Guith*
Jo O'Brien
Linda A. Pavich*

Valley View Middle School
Bloomington, MN
Mary Moeller*
Stephanie Rollag*

Washington Middle School
Kenosha, WI
Melissa Jakubowski*

Washington School
Waterford, WI
Toby Thompson*

Washtenaw Christian Academy
Saline, MI
Eileen Wiersma*

West Middle School
Plymouth, MI
Nicole Lerg*

West Suburban Christian Academy
Waukesha, WI
Jessica Szaukellis*

Wheatland Center Elementary School
Burlington, WI
Cheryl Fowler*

Whitehall Jr High School
Whitehall, MI
Mary Dykstra*

Language Arts Grant Recipients 2008-2009

After receiving a "Poetic Achievement Award" schools are encouraged to apply for a Creative Communication Language Arts Grant. The following is a list of schools who received a two hundred and fifty dollar grant for the 2008-2009 school year.

Acushnet Elementary School, Acushnet, MA
Benton Central Jr/Sr High School, Oxford, IN
Bridgeway Christian Academy, Alpharetta, GA
Central Middle School, Grafton, ND
Challenger Middle School, Cape Coral, FL
City Hill Middle School, Naugatuck, CT
Clintonville High School, Clintonville, WI
Coral Springs Middle School, Coral Springs, FL
Covenant Classical School, Concord, NC
Coyote Valley Elementary School, Middletown, CA
Diamond Ranch Academy, Hurricane, UT
E O Young Jr Elementary School, Middleburg, NC
El Monte Elementary School, Concord, CA
Emmanuel-St Michael Lutheran School, Fort Wayne, IN
Ethel M Burke Elementary School, Bellmawr, NJ
Fort Recovery Middle School, Fort Recovery, OH
Gardnertown Fundamental Magnet School, Newburgh, NY
Hancock County High School, Sneedville, TN
Haubstadt Community School, Haubstadt, IN
Headwaters Academy, Bozeman, MT
Holden Elementary School, Chicago, IL
Holliday Middle School, Holliday, TX
Holy Cross High School, Delran, NJ
Homestead Elementary School, Centennial, CO
Joseph M Simas Elementary School, Hanford, CA
Labrae Middle School, Leavittsburg, OH
Lakewood High School, Lakewood, CO
Lee A Tolbert Community Academy, Kansas City, MO
Mary Lynch Elementary School, Kimball, NE
Merritt Secondary School, Merritt, BC
North Star Academy, Redwood City, CA

Language Arts Grant Winners cont.

Old Redford Academy, Detroit, MI
Prairie Lakes School, Willmar, MN
Public School 124Q, South Ozone Park, NY
Rutledge Hall Elementary School, Lincolnwood, IL
Shelley Sr High School, Shelley, ID
Sonoran Science Academy, Tucson, AZ
Spruce Ridge School, Estevan, SK
St Columbkille School, Dubuque, IA
St Francis Middle School, Saint Francis, MN
St Luke the Evangelist School, Glenside, PA
St Matthias/Transfiguration School, Chicago, IL
St Robert Bellarmine School, Chicago, IL
St Sebastian Elementary School, Pittsburgh, PA
The Hillel Academy, Milwaukee, WI
Thomas Edison Charter School - North, North Logan, UT
Trinity Christian Academy, Oxford, AL
United Hebrew Institute, Kingston, PA
Velasquez Elementary School, Richmond, TX
West Frederick Middle School, Frederick, MD

Grades 7-8-9

Note: The Top Ten poems were finalized through an online voting system. Creative Communication's judges first picked out the top poems. These poems were then posted online. The final step involved thousands of students and teachers who registered as online judges and voted for the Top Ten poems. We hope you enjoy these selections.

Top Poem Grades 7-8-9

Under the Stars

In cool summer nights
we lay out under the stars
beside a quiet bonfire
the coals are at their hottest,
with colors of purple and deep red
We lay out under the stars
holding each other, speaking just above a whisper
as not to disturb the peace of the cool night
We lay out under the stars
and speak of dreams, love, and problems
yet it all melts away, as we lay out under the stars
you and me, not a care in the world
So why should we?
We are young, and beautiful and oblivious
to the terror of this world, the hate, the pain
we won't worry about tomorrow
As we lay here, out under the stars
and whisper I love you
our lips meet
I look up, under the stars
and smile

Ashley Booth, Grade 9
Clintonville High School, WI

Top Poem Grades 7-8-9

Hostilities

Gunfire explodes into the man's ears
All around him his friends are lying dead
He closes his eyes and sees his worst fears
He can't escape the things in his head

Ten years later, the man sits on a chair
Reminiscing on the past and crying
Looking at the leg that's no longer there
Listen to the sound of his voice sighing

Oh how he wished he could do it again
Go back in time and maybe fix the past
Perhaps he could have saved those other men
It's too late now — it all happened so fast

He cannot return to his life before
Because humans insist on having war

Angela Bumstead, Grade 8
St John Lutheran School, MI

Top Poem Grades 7-8-9

A Walk to Remember

Along the beach I walk
With sand between my toes
A scuttling crab I stalk
The fresh sea breeze wafts to my nose

With the sand between my toes
The seagulls caw and crow at me
The fresh sea breeze wafts to my nose
Oh I love the great blue sea

The seagulls caw and crow at me
The sun upon the water gleams
Oh I love the great blue sea
This walk seems like a fulfilled dream

The sun upon the water gleams
A scuttling crab I stalk
This walk seems like a fulfilled dream
Along the beach I walk

Hannah Byrnes, Grade 8
West Suburban Christian Academy, WI

Top Poem Grades 7-8-9

America

From the oceans so blue,
To the plains all so green.
There is a place,
Where miracles are seen.

People live together,
All different ethnicities.
From all our small towns,
To our largest cities.

My home is free,
It is equal and right.
Where colors and looks,
Are not in our sight.

We live together,
In peace and in love.
All over this great land,
As seen from above.

For our goal is simple:
Do the right thing.
God bless America,
Let freedom ring.

Michael Francis, Grade 8
Our Lady Star of the Sea School, MI

Top Poem Grades 7-8-9

Red

Red is the taste of strawberries on a hot summer day
And the watching of a butterfly flutter away
The torture of the heat as the sun sets low
The fire sirens that put on a show
For the gather of children that love to play
And the fire ants that run around all day

Red was the apple that poisoned the girl
So is the cinnamon that glides with a swirl
Red are the roses and tulips in spring
And red are the lips of the girl who shall sing
Red is the cherry, perfect as a pearl
But red is the anger and hatred of the world

Red are the curtains that open so slow
They make you so eager to watch the show
Red can be happy, deadly too
Red can be me, red can be you
Red can be anything and everything in sight
Red can even be the whispers you hear in the night

Carley Gordon, Grade 7
Gull Lake Middle School, MI

Top Poem Grades 7-8-9

Listen

Listen just listen to the raindrops ting tang ting tang on the
roof top swirling down the drain spout thunder
booming like a marching band shaking
the house lightning flashing down like
an old light bulb flickering on
and off listen the rain has
stopped listen you can
hear the new baby
birds chirping
listen

Shane Grant, Grade 7
Valley View Middle School, MN

Top Poem Grades 7-8-9

Wolf Song

The stars glitter in the blackness of night
They're near the moon, a sliver tilted slight
It reflects upon the silver coat dashing through brush
Air wisps by the keen ears with a silent rush

The muscles stride with ease, over the cool damp earth
The legs travel on, with all their might and worth
Eyes are dancing as they look up to the sky
Smoky breath seeps through, as the mouth lets out a sigh

The head tilted back, the muzzle in open air
It points to the clouds and stars that are there
A cry is let out that could make the world shiver
As the wolf is howling, to that radiant sliver.

Anna Meier, Grade 7
Northstar Middle School, WI

Top Poem Grades 7-8-9

Hands

Hands
Softly flowing over the ivory keys;
Strands
Of memory passing in thought;
Bands
Of emotion raging, though unseen;
Sands
Of time falling slowly, unnoticed.

Tears
Flowing silently with the memory;
Fears
Of another loss filling the room with darkness;
Years
Of waiting restlessly are destroying, then
Appears
The awaited angel of divine inspiration.

Because
Of her savior, her gift of song,
Does
She cry no more.

Katie Meshew, Grade 9
St Thomas More Academy, MI

Top Poem Grades 7-8-9

Not How It Looks

The sky turns black as he rolls by.
Shimmering droplets fall from the sky.

He grumbles and moans and yells to be heard.
To look up at him your vision is blurred.

He lets down his pride at things below
Most hide in fear from this amazing show.

His pride is jagged, rough and sharp to the tip
Yellow and white this bright long strip.

His voice grows louder you cover your ears
No one realizes these droplets are tears.

For he is not scary this dark rolling cloud
There is a reason for his pride and being loud.

He's crying and wailing about
For his pet lightning bolts have gotten out.

Jocelyn VanPay, Grade 7
Luxemburg-Casco Middle School, WI

Top Poem Grades 7-8-9

Praying

Look into my eyes, tell me what do you see?
I see a strong man deep inside of me.
A man that has picked cotton and a man that has been beat.
As blood drips down my body, and with sores on my feet.
I'm praying to be free!
I'm praying that daylight I now will see,
I'm praying for that day I will be set free.
I'm praying that there would be no master, hoping that it will come faster.
My prayers have finally come true, the last hundred years have been a shame.
Freedom is finally here, but is it?
Brothers of today need to take advantage of that freedom.
Learn from our ancestors, who just wanted to see the light,
Young brothers of today get educated and take flight!

Jaelen Wilson, Grade 7
Sister Academy/Harvest Prep School, MN

Dog/Cat

Dog
Independent, smart
Running, sleeping, barking
Dog Chow, toys, bells, Cat Chow
Meowing, purring, loving
Soft, cuddly
Cat

Hannah Quigley, Grade 7
Northwood School, WI

The Window

Staring out the window
On a rainy day
Looking for the sun
Right over the bay.

You can see people
Animals too
The birds chirping
As the snail moves.

I can hear voices
Whether it's people or wind
As the breeze goes by
Why are you so grim?

In the dusty water
With sand all around
The sand was smooth
I then felt like a clown.

After looking through the window
I understand
That life is surrounding us
In any way it can.

Justin Piotrowski, Grade 7
Gesu Catholic School, MI

Elements

Water, sweet water
Cold, wet and moist sweet water
Water is the best.

Fire, harsh fire
Golden, cruel, burning fire
Fire has its rage.

Earth, very calming
Wonderfully moist soil
Earth is our own home.

Wind, refreshing breeze
Blows around and through the trees
It helps sailing ships.

Gaby George, Grade 7
Core Knowledge Charter School, WI

Sometimes You Need Something

Sometimes you need someone to talk to.
Sometimes you need a friend. Maybe a best friend,
Someone that you can trust or maybe someone you can hold.
You always need something sometime.
Sometimes you maybe just need a little love or maybe just a hug.
Every living thing needs something sometime.
It never hurts to say what you need at any given time.

Starsha Nicole Taylor, Grade 7
Sherman Multicultural Arts School, WI

The Freedom and the Will

I am the freedom and the will.
I wonder when I will belong to all.
I hear the cry of the oppressed.
I see the agony of the afflicted.
I want to give my gift to all.
I am the freedom and the will.

I pretend I am not needed, but I am.
I feel the tear of the people that long for me.
I touch the invisible barrier that separates me from all in desperate need.
I cry because I cannot be where you are.
I am the freedom and the will.

I now understand why I am needed.
I say that I am not the only one.
I dream of the day I will be with you all.
I hope that I am received as everything you have ever hoped and dreamed for.
I am the freedom and the will.

Taylor Seegert, Grade 7
West Suburban Christian Academy, WI

Is Your Love True?

The day we met is a day I will never forget
You always managed to put a smile on my face
Just the thought of you makes my heart race
You give me a feeling I never felt before
A feeling I want more of and more
Your smile is a smile I will always remember
And the way your eyes glowed in the snow in December
You told me how you felt about me
And I wanted to tell you the same words back
But we never seem to have time to talk
But I have to say
My head can't seem to decide if it wants to come to you or walk the other way
A lot of people tell me no, he's a player and he's got to go
My heart tells me they're wrong
I wish you could tell me which path to walk on
I guess this would be known if a couple of questions were answered
Like do you really love me?
Or will I just be another work of art in your gallery?
Will there be a future where we are together
Or will this be a relationship that would end sooner or later
Will there be a meaning for this love and joy or will this just be a game for you to play?

Ismahan Ali, Grade 9
Universal Academy, MI

Wisdom

The question is how to know.
Years and years of practice.
It is the only way to grow,

Or the only way to glow.
Then your inner soul will explode of pleasure.
The question is how to know.

When to let your heat flow.
When to let your mind departure.
It is the only way to grow.

Your sorrow will be low.
Your life will be full of leisure.
The question is how to know.

Answers will be found below.
Enjoyment does not have a measure.
The question is how to know.

Then you will be able to melt the snow.
Your freedom will not be captured.
The question is how to know.
It is the only way to grow.

Rocio Riillo, Grade 8
Pilgrim Park Middle School, WI

Loving Yourself

Before you can love anyone else
You should always love yourself
You should love the way you act
When you look in the mirror
  you should love what's looking back

Love the way you think and the way you feel
Love yourself and always be real
Don't let others change who you are
If you love yourself you will go far

Gabrielle Johnson, Grade 7
Hally Magnet Middle School, MI

Research Paper

Permit me to tell you about a research paper:

Looking at the screen
Waiting for it to do it itself
Nothing happens
Keys tap slowly
Some pages more to go
But the research paper
I remember most
The Saturday that was wasted
The Sunday that was gone
Time is almost up

Hampden Meade Maxwell, Grade 8
Grosse Pointe Academy, MI

Brokenhearted Girl

I never thought this day would come
When you would have me broken down
You promised me that I was all you'll ever need
But I see that promise was broken
I made a promise to myself
That when I see you with her that I wouldn't break down
Thank you for making me known as the
Brokenhearted girl

Alexis Turner, Grade 8
Gesu Catholic School, MI

Remember

Do you remember the first time we met?
Longing and loving for the other,
Though we couldn't see in the night,
We knew we had a desire to take flight.

Can you fly to the sea with me?
I will keep you close to my heart,
Wandering, strolling without my troubles
As we ignore the piles of rubble.

I may love you to the ends of the earth,
But I cannot follow to places you may go,
Please help me ignore the pain and sorrow,
That follows us from yesterday to tomorrow.

Now you've passed on I see what has happened
Your love acted as a shield against the world,
Shielding me from the past and the present,
Without you I'm somebody new who's filled with resent.

Harrison Grittinger, Grade 8
Core Knowledge Charter School, WI

March Madness Time

M arch Madness is the best time of the year.
A ll the fans dressed up in their gear.
R ushing home to watch the games, eating out of a bin.
C heering on the teams they picked to win.
H aving lots of parties, laughing at the drunks.

M aking amazing plays, jams, and dunks.
A thletes work harder than ever.
D reams come true, when they work together.
N o one ever wants to fail.
E veryone wants to tell their game winning tale.
S weet sixteen to the elite eight to the final four.
S omeone will be the champions, before we walk out the door.

T ick-tock, March is almost over.
I 'm holding my lucky clover.
M arch Madness should end in a parade.
E ndless, marvelous memories made.

Carli Peters, Grade 8
Seymour Middle School, WI

What I Remember!

I remember
The time I was in Florida and
I was on a
Roller Coaster and I was going so
Fast I was like lightning.

I remember
The time I was riding my first bike
And I Fell.
I remember the time I was sleep walking
And I Fell
Down the stairs I hurt myself really
BADDDD!

I remember
The time I first started playing guitar
And I was so
Bad I could not do anything with the
Guitar!!!

Cody McShane, Grade 7
Manistee Middle School, MI

Nature Is Easy to Love

Nature is easy to love,
the sun rises up above.
The birds, bees and bugs awake,
the wind makes the trees shake.
"Wake up," says the sun,
get ready for a day of fun.
Spring is here and winter has past,
this year is going by too fast.
The snow is no longer here,
"Food," yell the deer.
The flowers sprout,
a bit hungry from the drought.
"We are hungry," says a flower
get ready for an April shower.
The squirrels hurry to get seeds,
from the gardeners pulling weeds.
Little kids run and play,
all day every day.
The day move along,
humming nature's song.
Night begins to fall,
"Good night," says all.

Tayler Karinen, Grade 9
Hartland High School, MI

Horse with a Tail

There once was a horse with a tail
He was best friends with a whale
It swam out of sight
Because they got into a fight
Goodbye said the horse to the whale

Alex Grinn, Grade 8
St Patrick Catholic School, MI

The Window

As the sunlight streams in and brightens the room,
the window sparkles with sunlight
The window on the wall is my opening to a whole new world.
A world that cannot be held inside a home
nor can it be recreated.
The beauty that comes from nature,
is one of a kind.
The kind of beauty no one should ever take away from the world.
As I sit and I think about the true beauty of nature,
I gaze through the window.
I see the small animals scamper by
and I watch the birds soar through the bright blue sky.
I see the wind blowing lightly through the tree branches
and I see patches of snow covering the grass.
I sit and I gaze out the window,
my opening to the beauty of the world.

Kimmy Kendzierski, Grade 8
St Roman School, WI

Good Night, Good Night

The rusty leaves wave to me,
Dancing blissfully in the afternoon breeze,
I can see the sunset sinking beneath the Earth,
It stretches, and yawns then finally drifts away.
Mother nature puts a black sheet over the sky,
And draws in the stars that shimmer, and twinkle in the night.
The moon springs up and casts a faded light overhead,
For the moment the whole wilderness is hushed,
Softly whispering to me,
Good night,
Good *night.*

Rylee Smeriglio, Grade 7
Roosevelt Middle School, MN

Oh How the Times Have Changed

Oh, how the times have changed, my friend, oh, how I let you go.
Where did our friendship break off, my friend, why did you have to go?
Oh, how the time has flown, my friend, oh how I miss your face.
I used to see you every day, my friend, but that memory starts to fade.
Oh, how we've gone our ways, my friend, oh, how we rarely cross.
You used to fill my life with laughs, my friend, without you my days are cold.
Oh, how we've grown apart, my friend, oh, how I miss your smile.
All the adventures we had, my friend, I wish to be with you for awhile.
Oh, how we used to laugh, my friend, oh, how we used to talk.
All my secrets were safe with you, my friend, my trust with you you'll never know.
Oh, how naive we were, my friend, oh, how we loved the world.
The simple things that made us smile, my friend, would never be understood.
Oh, how much fun we had, my friend, oh, how I miss it so.
All the days and nights we spent with them, the memories I'll never let go.
Oh, how you understood me, my friend, oh, how you knew me well.
You read through my spoken words, my friend, to know how I really felt.
Oh, how the times have changed, my friend, oh, how they will to come.
Why must you move away, my friend, why must I let you go?

Lizzie Benzik, Grade 8
St Joseph Catholic Middle School, MI

What Is Pink?

What is the color pink?
Pink is the color she turns,
When a boy gives her a wink.
Pink, like a ribbon in your hair.
Pink, the Pink Panther pouncing on a pear.
Pink, the pink lip gloss begs for attention,
Pink, the color slip for detention.
Pink, the Kool Aid you slurp from your glass,
Pink, the flowers you surpass,
While walking in the grass.
Pink is so many wonderful things,
Like a topaz on a wedding ring.

Dakota Hitchner, Grade 7
Luxemburg-Casco Middle School, WI

Love Is Not Money

There was this boy
short, shy, and shines in the light
He bought this girl a diamond necklace.
She BROKE it
He bought her a ring
She BROKE it
He bought her a bracelet
She BROKE it
The next time he bought her something she said
she didn't want it.
She said I don't want your MONEY
I want your LOVE.

Carissa Maynard, Grade 8
Adams Friendship Middle School, WI

Every Night

Resting my head and closing my eyes.
The feeling is unbelievable,
I love it so much.
As a teenager,
I'm growing up way too fast.
I have sports, school, friends, and family.
One thing goes wrong, it's hard to fix.
As a 14 year old girl,
I balance everything and try to make it perfect.
Through it all I cry, smile, yell, and laugh.
It's one huge rollercoaster.
Putting my head on the cloud,
When I fall, it's there for me.
A rectangle, my favorite color, customized for me.
Worn out colors from multiple washes.
I have three of them I use,
Every single night it's those three.
Laying my head, closing my eyes.
I think of so many things.
And at the end of my restless day,
My pillow is there for me, every night.

Mary Hannosh, Grade 9
Clarkston Jr High School, MI

Just One Year Ago

Just one year ago, I started Middle School
Couldn't wait to save the date
For that first day of school
I walked into the great brick place
On that special date
Excited as can be
Just couldn't wait to see
All the adventures
That they call middle school

Jordyn Salerno, Grade 7
Scranton Middle School, MI

The Argument

Every day it's the same thing.
The two opponents step into the ring.
One is dark, and one is light.
Neither ever gives up the fight.
Darkness always wants to stay,
But the sun is itching to start a new day.
You think that they could get along
And work it out, but you're wrong.
Night pushes down like a weight on the sun
Until she submits, and the day is done.
The sunset bleeds orange, pink, and red.
Twilight leaks the stars and moon instead.
Yet the sun never accepts defeat.
She's back in the morning and can't be beat.
Endless their quarrel might be,
But it's a beautiful sight to see.
Their problem seems big and diverse,
But how much does it matter in the whole universe?

Emma Sutherland, Grade 8
Our Lady of Sorrows School, MI

Summer's Day

It was a cold winter day,
When summer came along
And claimed that day hers,
Where nothing could go wrong

The clouds were overjoyed,
The sky a bright blue
When the sun began to shine,
Everyone knew

Summer's Day has come,
It is finally here.
Have fun in the sun,
And never fear

For summer's sweet wrath
Has fallen upon us
Cherish these days,
And celebrate with us.

Melina Washington, Grade 8
Messmer Preparatory Catholic School, WI

Bright Eyes

Bright eyes are like the sunset,
So beautiful and so delightful,
Peaceful and almost just so rightful,
The sun sets in the middle of the day but,
Bright eyes stay bright all day,
That's why I love to say I love bright eyes,
All day.

Aniyah Pitts, Grade 7
Sherman Multicultural Arts School, WI

The Coffin

You dress in black
And walk through the grass
And you stop and find
The coffin.
You walk up slowly
And everyone's mourning
And leave a lily for
The coffin.
The one who you loved
Resting in peace
To be found inside
The coffin.
She lifts up the top
Everyone stops
To find him not in
The coffin.

Ashley Tindall, Grade 8
Washington Middle School, WI

Dreams

I can be anything, anything at all
I just hope that I don't fall
Into a nightmare
A realm so deep
That might put me in a terrible sleep

I can be a knight with shining armor
In a battle fighting for honor
With victory
And freedom
Because I will always defeat them

I can be a dragon firing flames
With a very accurate aim
At quaking gargoyles
Making every one
But when they come to life, it's no fun

Remember this is just a dream
Even though it may seem
Like it's real
Even beyond belief
But never give up what you can achieve

Catalina Kenney, Grade 7
St Thomas More Academy, MI

Too Much Darkness

These words that I speak are the truth
Only that and nothing but
The darkness hurts
And so does the loneliness

There's no one here it's just me
I can't stand the pain inside
I try to hide it and not to let it show
But it's just not working
And pretty soon, I'm going to explode
I don't know what to do

There's too much darkness inside
And not enough light
It's an ongoing fight
Between darkness and light
Who will take over my life?
I need the darkness
I need the light
But who do I need more?

It's eating me from the inside out
I better enjoy life while I'm alive
There's too much darkness on the inside

Ahmad Hicks, Grade 7
Gesu Catholic School, MI

I Love You

The way you kissed my cheek
When you tucked me in at night,
When I was sad and broken
The way you held me tight.
The way you would always tell me
Everything's all right.
The way you called my name
When it was time to eat,
The way you picked me up
When I had fallen off my feet.
The way you'd smile so big
When you came to greet.
There is only one person
That I have ever missed this way,
I can't tell you how much this hurts
That I didn't get to say…
I love you.

J.C. Gilmore, Grade 8
Spring Hill School, WI

Anger

Anger
Is a hated puma
Clawing and ripping to get what he wants
Deep down in a dark den
Ready to get his revenge

Autumn Cooper, Grade 8
Anderson Middle School, MI

The Frog

C rawling out under a
R ock, she finds supper
O n her lily pad
A waiting more to come
K atydid goes into her mouth and
S he is satisfied!

Kyle Baldeshwiler, Grade 8
Chippewa Falls Middle School, WI

He Never Quit

Hair dark as the midnight sky
All smile when he passes by
Boy of twelve, sweet as can be
Always cared for my family and me

Not knowing the future tragedy
All pass with happiness and glee
Until one day he hears the news
Without there being any clues

Waiting for the doctor's answer
He was diagnosed with cancer
Struck with sadness and disbelief
The family's words were brief

The young boy took it well
Although we could never tell
The cause of his happiness and joy
He was an extraordinary boy

No one can forget his cheerful charm
Even at the end he showed no harm
His spirit lives within my heart
Until the day I depart

Anne Mackowiak, Grade 8
St Thomas More Academy, MI

Comerica Park

Under the lights,
Smelling the fresh baked peanuts,
The Detroit Tigers win the game,
They limp off the field,
Into the locker room,
Where the manager starts yelling,
Back on the field,
Batting practice,
With wooden smooth bats,
At 11:00 p.m.,
It's dark,
The moon shines down,
Back to the locker room,
Getting changed,
Go to the car,
Go to bed.

Noah B. Robart, Grade 7
Whitehall Jr High School, MI

New Found Freedom

Up off the ground,
My feet danced through the air,
As my sisters' toes edged back towards Earth.
Trying to fly,
Knowing that gravity would suck us back down
To the trampoline's elastic ground.
Just us three
Laughing and bouncing.
Trying to keep balance and poise
In front of my big sisters and not let them see my inexperience.
They would tell me not to worry,
Just to let go,
But it was my first time not being on the calm, stable ground
Which I knew of,
And one wrong leap could send me flying
Across the sky.
Then, seeing their beaming faces
I knew I could
And my feet danced through the air.

Caylin Waller, Grade 9
Clarkston Jr High School, MI

It's My Future

My future is in baseball
Whenever I play, I play from the heart

My future is in baseball
I will also have a degree in science

My future is in baseball
Last season I was hitting over .600 after half the season

My future is in baseball
I playing in a clutch situation

My future is in baseball
I can clear off the bases with one swing of my bat

My future is in baseball
If I need to I can lay down a perfect bunt

My future is in baseball
I love the sport!

Alex Portner, Grade 7
Springfield School, MN

Patience

Patience is the color of calm in a mother's eye
Patience looks like a new mother with a crying baby.
Patience smells like fresh bread.
Patience sounds like a mother's calm voice.
Patience tastes like a warm cup of tea.
Patience feels like a big warm hug.

Elizabeth Meling, Grade 7
Northwood School, WI

Life

Life, life is good life is fine,
try to live yours before you try to live mine.
Life is a gift you should make the best of it
find your own person to be and not me.

Jeremiah McWilliams, Grade 8
Gesu Catholic School, MI

We Are All Unique in Our Own Ways

We are all unique in our own way I heard one day!
How are we unique I asked and they said to me
some are tall some are short
some are weird some are normal
some are special some are special but they can't notice
some are black some are white
some are hispanic some are asian
some are nice some are mean
some are helpful some are caring
some are sensitive some are tough
some are brave some have fear
some are shy some are not shy
some are happy some are sad
some are mad some are bored
some are selfish
I said wow yes we are all unique in our own way
even if we don't show it to everyone they say!

Andrea Lezama, Grade 7
Valley View Middle School, MN

Earth Savers

Reduce, reuse, recycle
Is what we Earth Savers do
We're a group of four girls
Maya, Olivia, Kira, and me (Tracy)

The Earth screams with delight
When we help pick up trash
The starving kids are very glad
When we have food drives for them

We donate every cent we make
From our lemonade stand
To pet stores and charities
We're as happy as clams

We feel like goddesses when we help the Earth
We hear the sparrows tweeting away
They sound happy and filled with laughter
Sitting on the brown skinny branches

When it's time to clean
We never go mean
We just shout
GO GREEN!

Tracy Xiong, Grade 7
Ramsey Jr High School, MN

Suddenly

I thought my life was swell
Until in my head rang a bell
And suddenly I was aghast
Amazed at how life had flown by so fast
I've never made time to play
Reported to work every day
Haven't stopped to play since I was four
I don't want to be like this anymore
Its time to start over again
My new life is about to begin

Courtney Kilbourn, Grade 8
Perry Middle School, MI

My Grandfather

Even though I never got to know you,
You're always in my thoughts.
Even though I never got to know you,
I feel as if I did.
Even though I never got to meet you,
I've always wished I could.
Even though I never got to see you,
I feel as if I had.
I've heard so much about you,
I wish I knew if it were true.
If I could ever meet you,
I would ask you so many questions.
Would I be like you?
And would you love me?
Who's your favorite person?
What do you do in your free time?
I wish I got to know you, before you left.
Even though I never got to know you,
Thank you for being you!!

Jason Walburg, Grade 7
North Rockford Middle School, MI

Summer Blossom

Nature blooms a little bit
every day.
Swaying in the soft,
sweet summer sky,
Or in a tall, cold vase
in a cottage nearby.
The gentle breeze carrying
the sweet, warm fragrance
towards an open window,
bringing people to a slow
to savor nature's nectar.
The baby pink blush
of the soft petals,
floating across the lush green grass,
inviting for you to pluck
the slender stem of
summer home.

Laure Bouret, Grade 7
Our Lady Star of the Sea School, MI

A Result of Hope

I held on to his hand and looked into his eyes,
and thought these simple words: "I don't want him to die."
Last year, he had been diagnosed with a tumor of the brain.
Even though he'd been in remission, it was now back again.
The doctors and the nurses said there was some hope;
If he stayed positive and took his medicine, maybe he could cope.
The knowledge of the doctors and talents of the nurse
Helped the little boy overcome the worst.
All through it he stayed happy and never had a pessimistic thought;
Instead he played games and met with friends, and not once was he distraught.
A long year later, he finally began to be better.
When released from the hospital, he sat down and wrote a letter:
"Dear God," it read, "Thank you so much for saving me.
Now I am a normal boy just like my friends and can even climb a tree!
Now I can celebrate Father's Day and Mother's Day too.
I can even teach my baby brother how to tie his shoes!"
What a happy day this was for him, when he knew he was not sick;
His positive attitude, and friends' support gave him the strength to give cancer a kick.

Carolyn Gearig, Grade 8
Boulan Park Middle School, MI

Lie

I am dishonest and never ending
I wonder how big I will turn into
I hear the joyful sounds of dishonesty and crying
I see broken-ness in people's lives but never in me
I want to be on the tips of everyone's tongue
I am dishonest and never ending

I pretend I'm something I'm not
I feel pain and sorrow
I worry if someone finds me out, I will break
I touch the hearts of many in deceiving them
I sometimes cry because I am something I'm really not
I am dishonest and never ending

I understand that if I'm never ending, more people will accept me
I say things that are not true
I dream that I will be carried on mouth to mouth
I try to convince as many people as I can
I hope that I will turn into something huge
I am dishonest and never ending

Hannah Johnson, Grade 7
West Suburban Christian Academy, WI

Storm

Did you hear that I asked as the low groan of the wind pierced my ears
I looked out the window and I saw the trees dancing in the wind
The leaves were struggling to hang on their branches
The birds were forced to leave their homes
A storm was brewing
The waters were jumping up higher and higher
The warning sirens were screaming at us
Everyone was running away from the rushing waters

Taylor Tomczak, Grade 8
Washington Middle School, WI

Beach

Walking to the
beach, seeing the
blue water, the
seagulls making
noise, people
swimming, surfing,
barbecuing chicken and
burgers, later in the
afternoon it's 90°, people
putting on suntan lotion,
the burning hot sand
on your feet, when the sunset
is going down, you can see that the colors are
so beautiful, from such a great day.

Katlin Cagney, Grade 7
Whitehall Jr High School, MI

Clouds Can Cry

Clouds can cry big blue tears
And shout shouts that put pain in the ears.
Over the ocean they cry
Sometimes wishing to die.
They carry a deep pain,
That's what makes them rain.
Then, they cloud cities with mist
As they make the sound hiss.
Until they are happy with sun
You should watch out and run.

Ian Davidson, Grade 7
Luxemburg-Casco Middle School, WI

From You

There's teardrops on my notebook
Take a look,
They are from you,
You want to be friends but have no clue,
I want to be more than friends,
But last time it had to end,
Couldn't concentrate on school,
Parents didn't think it was cool,
I want you back,
Why'd I have to slack?!
You moved on,
Reminds me of a sad love song,
Now you like another girl,
She gave the thought of you a whirl,
Now you are dating,
It's just frustrating,
She made me think I could trust her,
I can't help but think I won't find another,
You were a great boyfriend,
Why'd it have to end?
Why'd it have to end?

Tori Roberts, Grade 8
Spring Hill School, WI

Forever Mine

No matter where you go, no matter what you do,
I'm always going to love you.
You might not love me back or remember me in a few years.
But one of these days, we're going to run into each other.
You're going to reminisce about everything we went through —
the good times and the bad.
So, goodbye for now, forever in my heart.

Victoria Farnam, Grade 8
McKinley Middle School, WI

I Am Depressed and Lonely

I am depressed and lonely.
I wonder when my day will come.
I hear the cries of sad children.
I see the people that are like me.
I want the day when I won't be depressed.
I am depressed and lonely.

I pretend to be happy.
I feel my day coming around the corner.
I touch the cold lonely hearts.
I worry my friends will leave me.
I cry my heart out every day.
I am depressed and lonely.

I understand that I shouldn't think the way I do.
I say I'm not depressed and lonely.
I dream about the day I won't be lonely.
I try to stay on God's path.
I hope to live a life of happiness and love.
I am depressed and lonely.

Abigail Schieber, Grade 7
West Suburban Christian Academy, WI

Math

So many problems so little time
Can't figure out the equation of 1,099
Got to multiply by 7, and 3

Got a calculator but you do not want to cheat
You are so frightened you cannot feel your feet
You sweat and cry but tears are dry
You think you would rather die

you run across the hall with fear
Because you know that math is near
You need to do the problems quick
But you can't find your pencil stick

It's time for math you have to go
You get to class with so much fear
But then he tells you it's not due today
Because you were sick yesterday
So then you get an extra day

Emiliano Suarez, Grade 7
St Roman School, WI

Nighttime

Nighttime is when evil lurks, when Satan's spirits are unleashed.
To do what they do best they, scare, hurt and kill the innocent. But the worst of all, make more evil.
All of any ages are or should be frightened, even the wise who think they know better, know not to look under the bed.
But it doesn't matter who you are or what you're like. Young or old, smart or dumb it can still get to you.
If you want to save yourself. Don't check under the bed or in the closet because it's everywhere no matter where you are.
Most hear that the real evil is unleashed on Halloween. Now I am not saying that it isn't but you still need to watch what you're doing. Because it won't take pity on the innocent like you.
Those who do not believe, all I am saying, all I have is five words for you. BEWARE it can get you!
Oh and one last thing don't go out at nighttime. Don't ask questions just trust me.

Sophie Kuntz, Grade 7
Saint Thomas More Catholic School, MN

Change*

Instead of another door opening all of them close instead, it makes everything seem dead everybody tells me what to do and how to act, and for a fact I feel inside like a flower without water that slowly but surely slaughters. The big sign of "do not enter" in the center of the door to happiness makes me heartrending and cheerless but then even so I tried to go in. There was this figure made out of tin. Change that's what it was called, my happiness door was fire walled. U.S.A., pointing the finger at that door which meant to say. I really had to break in, taking another path from the happiness where I have been. In the room there was a mirror, the picture became even clearer; U.S.A., that's where you'll have to stay! Stand tall, stand proud, you have to believe without a doubt! So here I am standing proud and tall, like a painting on the wall. I should be proud of going here, but all I can give is a tear. I am a painting on the wall sitting there with a plastic smile like a doll where someone painted a face that looked happy with lots of grace that's how people want to see me however I am perceiving however behind the paintings wall I was not at all those pretty though fake happiness that was holding up my success I left all my friends and happiness overseas, though my tears do please. And when I cry I remember home, though now here I am all alone. I was hunting for another way, but there was no doubt I had to stay. Then suddenly one came up to me, trust in yourself that is the key! I tried to open up myself like a fallen book from a shelf I started reading between the lines and saw past the stop signs that were holding me up but now I can reach the top I remember back in times that sometimes you have to believe in yourself to not be a lonely book on the shelf to rather stand up in front of the challenge and master it with lots of balance the key to life is the belief in change even though it seems so strange sometimes you have to think of the future instead of the past which will surpass the anger deep inside otherwise you will collide.

Friederike Haag, Grade 8
West Hills Middle School, MI
**Dedicated to my sister Caroline Haag*

My Dear Sun

My darling sun shines day after day.
Day after day in L.A.
Day after day in Rome and Dallas and even Canton too.
The sun is truly one of my best friends.
It knows my secrets, my fears, my strengths.
It knows my ancestors, Cleopatra, Reagan, even Elvis.
That same sun will someday know my great-grand children.
Day after day the sun and I become better friends.
Even though I'll never know the secrets deep hidden in my golden sun, we still remain close.
My sun lives with me but sadly, at night we part.
My sun leaves me and goes to its beloved land of stars and planets.
Hearing me long for my best friend, the sun returns to me in the morning.
Someday, I'll meet the sun and we'll be everlasting friends.
My sun never questions me.
Never lies to me.
Never talks to me.
Yet its golden magic solves all my problems, comforts me, and gives me the wisest advice.
My dear sun has done so much for me, I wonder how, simply how, I can repay it.
God Bless my sun.

Amy Bhullar, Grade 8
Discovery Middle School, MI

Running

I was running faster and faster
The trees blurred as I ran
It felt like I was trying to fly
But the burden I carried was too heavy
But what was I running from
Why was I running
I didn't understand
Every step I took seemed to make me lighter
Every step seemed to make me forget
Forget the reasons why I'm running
Forget it all
It was done the dagger was plunged into my heart
But every step I took seemed to make it looser
I saw him and the dagger finally broke free
I was finally done running and the pain was forgotten
He embraced me and all the pieces fell into place
It was all over and done
It was all forgotten

Jocie Scherkenbach, Grade 7
Calvin Christian School, MN

In 15 Years...

Someday I will head off to college,
And there I will get even more knowledge.
When I am all done, I'll travel afar,
Driving around in my new shiny car.

I'll still kick around a soccer ball,
But I won't become a professional after all.
Instead, my hobby could be to save the planet,
Then later maybe have a daughter named Janet.

I would like to meet a millionaire,
When everyone sees us, they'll stop and stare.
I truly love the U.S.A,
But maybe one day I'll move away.

I'll hopefully still have all my good friends,
There to tie up all my loose ends.
So much could happen in just 15 years,
I'll build my own bridges and overcome my fears.

Nerissa Zoller, Grade 7
Royal Oak Middle School, MI

Summer Days

When rain falls, and the wind hauls.
You can feel the summer breeze,
Like trees and their leaves.
When clouds are white, and the sun is bright,
You can see the green grass grow tall,
By the flowers that fall.
When trees are green, and they're in the scene.
You can smell the flowers, after April showers.
When summer is here, it's filled with fun and cheer.

Rebecca Tran, Grade 7
Valley View Middle School, MN

I Never Know

My life is like a box of chocolates
I never can predict what will happen next
I never know if I'm going to smile or if I'm going to cry
I never know if I'm going to laugh or if I'm going to sigh
I never can tell if I'm going to fall or if I'm going to crawl
Things happen that would never be expected to happen
One day I might wake up and cry
The next day I might wake up and die

Jessica Paschke, Grade 7
Power Middle School, MI

Volleyball

It was the game of my life
My turn to serve
Please don't mess up
The ball curves and went out of bounds it goes
I yell "Oh No"
The other team cheers
The other team's turn to serve
She throws the ball up
I spring into action for the ball
Right up to the setter it goes
The setter sets and our team makes the play
We won the game
We all yell Hip Hip Hooray!

Megan Mueller, Grade 7
St Roman School, WI

Yea, I'm Dreaming

They say you look like her and you look like her,
But all you say is that's not really me.

Yes, we may look alike,
But who's she?

No, I'm not who I want to be quite yet.

I'm gonna be big.
No! Not just in this small town or state.

The whole world will know my name...
Somehow.

I don't care what you say,
I'm not gonna be passive anymore.

I'm gonna do myself a favor;
Do what I want for once.

I know I can do it.
Just give me my chance.

Haven't I done enough for you.

CharLee Mathieu, Grade 9
Lincoln High School, MN

The Championship Game

The championship game
15 seconds left tied 2-2
I move like an eagle
I pass, he passes back.

I have an opening I go for it
I take strides, digging the
Skate into the ice, passed center ice
Move, move, move, dig, dig, dig.

I'm free as a bird heading south
As if I could not stop
Breathing faster, and faster
Heart rate rising, rising

5 seconds left
Deke once Deke twice
Deke's one last time, BOOM
The puck shoots, goes in
RRRnt buzzer rings
Titans win, Titans win.

Lucas Ailport, Grade 7
Ramsey Jr High School, MN

The Forgotten Book

Your whole brain,
Mashed into one book.

Your true feelings,
Written on one page.

Your fulfilled heart,
Combined into one word.

Your entire soul,
Left as one space.

Your never-ending pain,
Forgotten like one stitch in the binding.

Your self,
Your entire self,
Left to stand alone

In a world of selfless,
Criticizing bodies.

Caitlyn Norman, Grade 7
Ramsey Jr High School, MN

Footprints

I feel my footprints in the sand
It feels so good against my hand
Soft and wet, so very warm
On the beach such a swarm

Lisa Donskey, Grade 8
Spring Hill School, WI

Wind

The wind blows and sways with the early spring day.
I never had wondered about the wind.
So silent and stealthy it moves like an anaconda in the night.
So brisk it comes so brisk it leaves.
It means so much to the world it means so much to me.
Wind sways and shifts, it bends and swirls.
It is so mysterious and still lovable and as soon as it came it goes.

Matthew Foster, Grade 7
Manistee Middle School, MI

I Don't Want to Lose You

I am sad I don't get a chance before he leaves
I wonder if he thinks about me as much as I think about him
I hear him in the hallway laughing and talking
I see him in the halls and sometimes say "hey"
I want to date him
I am sad I don't get a chance before he leaves

I pretend he doesn't blow me away
I feel excited when I see him
I wish he wouldn't move
I worry he sees right through me
I am sad I don't get a chance before he leaves

I think he looks good in white
I understand he's moving and I can't change that
I say I really like him and I want a chance
I dream that someday I will get a chance and I dream about him all the time
I am sad I don't get a chance before he leaves

Ashley Ralston, Grade 8
Riverview Middle School, WI

I Am

I am loving and caring
I wonder about Heaven and what it's like
I hear my grandma's voice during the night
I see her lying in a casket
I want to go and visit her in the assisted living again
I am loving and caring

I pretend to make cookies with her
I feel her holding my hand as we cross the street
I touch the warm cookies as I break it to let it cool before I eat it
I worry about my future
I cry some days missing her so
I am loving and caring

I understand everyone has to die
I say I'm fine to others, but sometimes I'm really not
I dream to see her in Heaven and relive some of our memories
I try to remember most of the good memories that we've had
I hope she remembers the good memories that I remember
I am loving and caring

Ashley Dindorf, Grade 7
West Suburban Christian Academy, WI

Clouds

The clouds sway in the light warm breeze
They look as soft as velvet.
I begin to dream.
I begin to dream of riding them,
As they move as silently as an ant.
They begin to turn into a big puff of cotton candy,
And my dream starts to quiver.
The clouds become a dark black shield that blinds my sight.
The clouds rumble like an angry lion.
I lose my balance and fall from the furious black shield.
My dream starts to shake and crack into a nightmare.
I keep on falling, falling, falling
Into emptiness that never ends.
I begin to open my eyes
And I feel the light warm breeze
And see the snow white clouds sway.

Debbie Nitka, Grade 7
Luxemburg-Casco Middle School, WI

Baseball

Every time I play baseball it's fun.
Even though I get sweaty when I have to run.
Whether you're just playing catch,
or in a game sitting on the bench.
It's a game for people of all shapes and sizes.
There will always be a lot of surprises.
Sometimes when I play I get hurt,
but at least I'm doing it for baseball.

Tony Biggs, Grade 8
Washington Middle School, WI

At the Lake

Fun all year round
Boating in the summer
Snowmobiling in the winter

Always something to do
At the lake
Biking, walking, swimming
Ice fishing, sledding

Friends always welcome
Anywhere, any time
Frying out for supper
Eating yummy cheeseburgers

Fun continues into the night
Having parties with friends and family
Telling stories around the campfire
Roasting s'mores and hot dogs

Never a dull moment
Always fun at the lake

Kim Hertel, Grade 7
Elkhart Lake Elementary-Middle School, WI

Recycled Dreams

The road was bleak
It did not have the light that used to set underneath my feet
The glowing life that had been staged on my face vanished
Now a flurry soul ignored everything dear
I burnt bridges that I want back
I composed a past I want packed
As the light ignites in my eyes again
There is still a flicker of past sins

As I try to build bridges that I destroyed
I am told there is no hope
As I move on from boxes of tears
They will come back even more clear

Today I open my eyes to a new sky
I drink new water
And I inhale new air
I neglect what relinquished me in tears

One day very soon
I will be able to state I'm new

Kate Rolka, Grade 9
Clarkston Jr High School, MI

Heartbeat of a Hoof Print

The heartbeat of a hoof print
is the squeal of a young child
as he discovers
how to sway
with his devoted horse.

The heartbeat of a hoof print
is the smile of a volunteer
as she listens
to the steady shuffle
of her beautiful horse.

The heartbeat of a hoof print
is the shared pulse of affection
between loving horse
and gentle master.

The heartbeat of a hoof print
is the throbbing ache
as one witnesses its long time companion
depart from our world and arrive in the one
of pure freedom.

Erika Anderson, Grade 9
Clarkston Jr High School, MI

Snow State

Cooling, the cheese state
No cows in the long tall grass
Wisconsin's all white

Sarah Groth, Grade 7
Elkhart Lake Elementary-Middle School, WI

Ode to Glacier National Park

Waterfalls,
snowballs in June
shrinking glaciers
can see the moon

A winding road
going way up high
over a pass
the continental divide

Hiking trails
go everywhere
but a single road
goes through

Huckleberries, thimbleberries
for grizzly bears
restaurants far and few
for you

The land is wild
barely touched by humans
but marked forever
by God

Kayla Niccum, Grade 7
Pilgrim Lutheran School, WI

The Holocaust

They took our houses
They killed our family
We won't give up
They pushed us in trains
Took us to camps
We won't give up
The gases hugged the elder's lungs
The young ones too
We won't give up
Most of us died from starvation
Or even lack of cleanliness
We won't give up
Screech the train's stop
Thinking we are home
Yet we are sad to see
It's not the place we want to be
We won't give up
O what it took to survive this tragedy
We did not give up

Abigail Haughie, Grade 9
Hartland High School, MI

Ocean

The ocean is huge.
The ocean is very fierce.
The ocean can calm.

Dennis Birkley, Grade 7
Washington School, WI

Starting All Over

Leaving behind the mess I made
cleaning up everything and
starting all over
Getting on with the life
I once knew
No more feeling alone
No more feeling unloved
No more anything but,
the person I once knew

Jazmine Ecklor, Grade 8
Riverview Middle School, WI

ATV/Snowmobile

ATV
dirt, mud
drifting, riding, handling
wheels, suspension, skis, track
skipping, skiing, fixing
snow, water
Snowmobile

Robbie Volz, Grade 7
Northwood School, WI

Wolf

Wolf as dark as night,
howling through the night,
gives me fear tonight

Dan Monahan, Grade 7
Centreville Jr High School, MI

My Role Model

Through the dense forest
I am following my dad
Stepping carefully over fallen branches
I am hiking soundlessly
Just like my dad.

He kneels down and so do I
Looking at the ground he
Points to footprints along the trail side
We follow the direction they go
I am walking
Just like my dad.

I am still trying
To be oh-so quiet
I am proud of myself
For being
Just like my dad.

And he turns around to see
If I am still behind him
A smile comes to my face
Just like my dad.

Daniel J. Byrne, Grade 9
Clarkston Jr High School, MI

Summer Vacation

When school is out
Then summer vacation starts
The sky is clear like crystal
The giant, green grass is in the backyard
And the wind sounds like a whistle
Rain, thunder, and lightning
But then the next day
The rain trickles away
And the sun always comes out
School is out
So scream and shout!
Summer vacation has started
First comes June, then July
Last comes August, then bye bye
To my summer vacation

Hope Dalebroux, Grade 7
Luxemburg-Casco Middle School, WI

Blind

We, as humans, see the outside,
But not all that is in.
We, as sinners, see the bad,
And everything as sin.

We are blind to ourselves.
We should be lovers.
God would never judge us,
Yet we judge others.

We are blind to the truth,
We have been since forever.
Just forgive and forget.
Learn to love together.

Jenna Hayes, Grade 7
Trinity Lutheran School, MI

Day of Days

The hum of engines
In the midnight air in the skies
Over Normandy.
You see flickers of light
Down below.
You jump out of a craft
Falling
Just falling.
You hear a pop
And softly hit the ground.
A chatter of fire
Rings out in the air.
You run hard and fast as
The ground flies up in stacks of smoke.
You clamber into a hole with friends.
Today you survived
June 6, 1994.

Joe Mocol, Grade 7
Shakopee Area Catholic School, MN

A Voice in the Hall

I heard a voice come from the hall
Swiftly coming to my door.
The voice sang a song so sweetly;
I never heard it before.
As it crept closer I heard it say,
"I have come for my love forevermore."
Never before did I hear the voice in the hall
Screaming my name more and more.
The voice screamed, "I seek revenge
For the one I love, forevermore!"

So it was revenge the voice wanted,
Not me, which was what I had hoped for.
"Remember what Mother said to you
When you were a child," nevermore!
The thing came pounding on the door
"Go away!" I said, it was fear I used more.
My fear fed the feast of that awful beastly
Voice that now arose from the floor.
I screamed as it came for me,
As I froze with terror next to the door.

Amie Winfield, Grade 7
Bristol Elementary School, WI

Washed Away

The water laps gently against the sand
It washes over the sparkling grains
The sun rises lazily
The golden rays gild the crests of the waves
The wash of the waves gropes up the shore
Birds sing softly, breaking the silence
All is peaceful for a time
Soon to be washed away forever

Jeff Woolstrum, Grade 8
Grosse Pointe Academy, MI

Great Barrier Reef

I reach for the goggles,
Breathing tube sticking out of my mouth
Getting ready to immerse myself in a world of amazement.

As I look in the depths of the glimmering blue water,
I see the corals,
Coming in all shapes and sizes.
Some like slingshots,
Sticking out of the ground.

Fish surround me,
Pushing me around
As if they were fans,
Pouring out of a stadium.

Something of such wonder
Can only be seen in the "Land Down Under."

Mihir Dekhne, Grade 7
Detroit Country Day Middle School, MI

War

Bravery and assassination, honesty and elimination,
Heading to the safe house.
The captain assigns you a mission
And you leave.
You see the enemies in front of you,
And feel terrified.

You look around,
And everything is moving in slow motion.
You can hear the war cries,
The enemies are letting out.
You hear yourself panting,
Trying to keep up.

They get closer and closer,
When you hear the clash
From the opposing forces.
From side to side you look,
Seeing your friends being killed.
You then know, that we don't have a chance.

Bobby Klabunde, Grade 7
Springfield School, MN

Family

We're playing outside on a sunny day,
when Dad says, "Feed the horses some hay."
Inside the barn Dad is working hard,
while sister and I are playing in the yard.

Greyson Wolf-Dixon, Grade 7
Washington School, WI

Hunting

On a special day
I go hunting with my dad
We get on our orange vests
We get our guns loaded
We see the leaves flying on the wind
Under our boots we hear the leaves crunch
I smell the forest pine trees
I stop and hear a something
crunching the leaves
To my surprise I see a deer
I pull up the gun
I shoot
I miss
I took another shot
I hit it in the heart
I gutted it dragged it to the truck
It looked lifeless, It didn't blink
It was staring at me
I unloaded my gun and left
I accomplished something
Yet I took a life of an animal

Tyler Elwood, Grade 7
South Middle School, WI

Day and Night

Day is beautiful:
Sunny and warm.
Flowers blooming,
Bees that swarm.
Grass is greener,
Breezes are blowing.
Birds are singing,
Clouds are glowing.

Night is beautiful:
It is dark.
The stars shine bright,
The fire has a spark.
Wrap yourself tight,
With meteors flying.
You never know what's coming,
The sky might be lying.

Taylor Huwatcheck, Grade 8
Pilgrim Park Middle School, WI

Skiing

I'm sitting on a ski lift,
this is my favorite ride.
I'm ready to get off,
and show my skiing pride.

I'm glancing down the slope.
I want to have a race.
I'm fastest on the hill,
with snow flying in my face.

Down I go on steeper slopes,
on moguls with no pain,
gliding on the icy spots,
and jumping the terrain.

I'm coming close to the end,
and skiing with all might.
I'll get up on the lift again,
and stay here until night.

RJ Michielutti, Grade 7
Our Lady Star of the Sea School, MI

Swimming

Gliding, soaring through the water
Hold your breath
As you jump into the pool
Water, where everybody can be graceful
Pride as you accomplish and defeat
A brand new stroke
Speeding through the water
If only it were never time to leave
The comforting smell of chlorine
Swimming breaks all barriers

Emma Wallander, Grade 7
Luxemburg-Casco Middle School, WI

Humor

A life without humor is like a crayon without color
We all laugh and if we didn't, this world would be stale
Some people prefer a stale world but they wouldn't if we had one
Kind of like a world without a sun
There's no purpose
When I think of humor I think of the color yellow
Fun and happy
Some jokes go back a long way
Some jokes just stay
Jokes can be personal
Some you wish you hadn't of said

Travis Matusik, Grade 9
Hartland High School, MI

My Brother

My brother likes to watch lots of television
He really gives it a lot of attention
He gives it so much attention he wouldn't notice if one of us died
Being with my brother feels like detention
He also likes to listen to songs on the television that he plays loud
The music is so loud that the neighbors start complaining
His favorite shows are; *Family Guy*, *Family Matters*, and *George Lopez*
When he talks on the phone he turns our bill into $2,000
Most of the time he likes to watch sports, like his favorite teams,
Championship games or Super Bowls, and Finals
My brother has a voice like my dad
He is taller than my mom and dad
My brother needs television and video games like I need air
When he sat on the couch his butt left a permanent print

Abdirashid Hassan, Grade 7
Cedar Riverside Community School, MN

Life

I am from light shining in my eye from the cool air from the fan blowing in my face
From clothes thrown everywhere and footsteps on a light wood floor
I am from laughter of kids running in the yard playing baseball
From a round fire pit in the middle of the sidewalk
From big red strawberries growing on the vines on my house
And air blowing the rocking chair on the porch back and forth
I am from home, white snow melting, the water running down the sidewalk
I am from craft stores on Main Street, from people planting and growing produce
From a clean and healthy state, a cheese state
I am from the country where the Statue of Liberty stands tall
From a country that has presidents to fight for what's right
From soldiers fighting in wars to protect us
From a country where the seals are made into souvenirs
I am from Mount Rushmore where each president represents something special
I am from Wal-Mart workers, from delivering babies
From people that take care of veterans, from Panama City, Florida
I am from better lives for children
From a future working with babies
From better and cleaner houses
From a cleaner community to stay healthy in
I am from the United States of America

Courtney Shearer, Grade 7
Robert Kupper Learning Center, WI

Life

I was so happy when you smiled,
your smiles breaks through the clouds of grey.
Far from the sunny days that lies in sleeps,
waiting with patience for the springs,
when the flowers will bloom renewed
again knowing there's more beyond
the pain of today,
Although the scars of yesterday remain,
you can go living as much as your heart believes.
You can't be born again,
although you can change,
Let's stay together always!

Joe Vue, Grade 7
Achieve Language Academy, MN

Jesus' Sacrifice

Jesus died on a tree
to save people like me
and he gave us life
for eternity
He died on Good Friday
it was a day of great sadness
He went down to defeat the devil
and his mission was a success
death could not hold Him
and He rose three days later
He appeared to his disciples in a room quite dim
and forty days later ascended into heaven
Jesus is the savior of man
and saved us from the devil's plan.

Tanner Viegut, Grade 7
Pilgrim Lutheran School, WI

Tear

It slides down your face
With such a slow pace
It happens when you're sad
Or even mad
Your eyes get clear
But there's nothing to fear
Do you think it's a tear?
You might get embarrassed,
But shouldn't get embarrassed,
There's nothing to be afraid of
Learn to rise above!
It can happen any time of the day
But that's o.k.
Now show you're letting go!
It'll happen because of family,
However sad that may be
You'll get through it!
You will soon admit that this thing is no big deal,
Eventually your heart will heal, and your heart will be Free!

Tabitha Wilson, Grade 7
Manistee Middle School, MI

Friends Forever

Friends forever is what we will be
Rosa and Sandra always with glee
Laughing all day and texting all night
Our friendship has grown to new heights
Always together even when we're far apart
Always in each other's heart
We can tell when something's wrong
Because our friendship is so strong
Friends forever is what we will be

Shayla Ferguson, Grade 8
Spring Hill School, WI

Caught

The crisp grass tickles my bare feet
As I wander through it
The hot summer sun beats down on my back
I bury my face in my arms
Counting aloud slowly to 10
I tiptoe silently around the yard
Turning my ear to the slightest sound of movement
Pacing back and forth with my eyes fully alert
I hear a faint snicker from behind me
Turning quickly but quietly on my heel
To follow the sound
I crouch in front of a small bush
Hesitantly reach out my hands to grab two branches
In one quick motion I snap them back
To see the innocent little face of my kid sister
In shock she covers her face with her hands
As if that would make her invisible
She giggles as I say with a proud grin on my face
"Caught Cha"

Morgan Sego, Grade 8
Perry Middle School, MI

For You

Gazing up at you
Counting your shining sparkling stars
Life going faster than the light showing the way
Wondering —
What, who, why
Life is —
Wonderful with you
But awful at the touch of your hand
Wondering —
What, who, why
Lying on your blanket of grass
It feels like you're next to me
Beneath your streaming shooting stars
That are falling like warm rain
Crushing life as we know
Wondering —
What, who, why
I may never understand

Emily Pelky, Grade 8
Seymour Middle School, WI

Weapons

W elded iron turns to steel
E nforces law and order
A ir and air soft guns
P recision aiming
O utlaws and bandits
N on lethal and lethal
S oldier on a roof top.

Colin MacLellan, Grade 7
Northwood School, WI

Life's Journey

I'm beginning my journey,
It shall be a long one,
I see the stones ahead,
I see the bends and curves,
I see the light of happiness.

I'm approaching the halfway point,
I've made it this far,
I've encountered some beauty,
I've encountered some sorrow,
There is more to come.

The end is near,
I've had a good run,
I've hit countless stones,
I've walked through the darkness,
I've had my share of pain,
I've had my share of love,
That's life.

Alli Kremers, Grade 8
Holdingford Secondary School, MN

I Am an Eagle

I am strong and graceful
I wonder how far the sky can go
I hear the rushing water
I see the fish swim through the rocks
I want to eat the fish below
I am strong and graceful

I pretend I can fly anywhere
I feel the wind flow through my feathers
I touch the tops of all the trees
I worry I won't find enough to eat
I cry out my mighty cry
I am strong and graceful

I understand the beauty of the forests
I say the rivers are strong and powerful
I dream of flying around the earth
I try to fly higher each day
I hope that I will reach the sky
I am strong and graceful

Travis Mentch, Grade 8
West Suburban Christian Academy, WI

Mother's Kisses

Mother comes scampering when she hears the call.
She opens the door which slams the wall.
She looks at me with a worried look as she sees my finger like a little hook.
The worried look goes away as relief is back to play.
She walks slowly over and wipes the tears and gets rid of all my worrying fears.
She gentle kisses it the way that makes it clear.
Then all the sadness goes away and happiness is here to stay.
When all is said and done the jumping, running, skipping has begun.
So, I wait for another rainy day to come and play, but fear not 'cause mother's kisses can't be too far away, for the call to be heard again.

Amber Lucas, Grade 8
Oakview Middle School, MI

Freedom

It is what America fought for in the Revolutionary War,
When faced with anger and sadness.
It is the choice of what a student will do after school,
When they have nowhere they need to be.
It is a woman saying yes or no to a man,
When he proposes to her.
It is your fate resting in your hands,
When you are faced with a hard choice.
It is a man turning left or right on a street corner,
When it leads to fame or happiness.
It is an environmental activist having a calm demonstration in front of a store,
When polar bears might go extinct.
It is a family moving from Minneapolis to Saint Paul,
When their children need to be closer to school.
It is whatever you want it to be,
And more.

Erica Wilczynski, Grade 7
Saint Thomas More Catholic School, MN

Ode to Shark

O Shark,
Your rough, sandpapery skin
Scrapes my side when you glide through the water.
Your mystical eyes are an enigma to all who surround you.

O Shark,
As you begin your hunt your beautiful pupils are restless.
They scan the water with the fierceness of a true hunter.
Your eyes are black coal that have an endless depth.
You stalk your prey silently until it has no chance to discern that you are there.
The *rip* and *tear* of your feeding is so rapid that it's hardly noticeable.

O Shark,
Many see you as a mindless man-eating machine.
I see you as a misunderstood creature.
Your eyes tell me that you are not purposefully harmful.

Shark, tell me
What makes you so irresistible to me?

Caris Bing, Grade 7
Japhet School, MI

To You

I wrote a ten page letter to you,
Saying how I feel.
Starting all over, feeling so new,
It's the one written in our color, teal.
I'm not sure if you got it,
I left it in your locker, and there it just may sit.
Every night I wish upon a star,
Hoping you feel the same as me.
Remembering that night in your car, not going too far.
Thinking every night,
About if I was permanently gone, what would you do?
Would you even care?
I'm not trying to start a fight,
But would you even have a clue?
You had me at hello,
But you don't know how much it meant to me.
There is more, but you read that letter,
That letter,
To you.

Makayla Eick, Grade 8
Seymour Middle School, WI

Saugatuck Indians

Strong
Determined
Won't back down from a challenge
Indians, that's what we are
Never going to end, never going to change
We don't need a blue ribbon to tell us how good we are.
And to tell other people that we are good.
People already know.
The Indians don't back down from a challenge.
We are orange crush
We are and always will be
The Saugatuck Indians

Meaghan O'Brien, Grade 8
Saugatuck Middle/High School, MI

Swirled Tip Shell

Smooth like a rolling hill,
A nose that swirls around,
It's spotted like a Dalmatian,
I hold it to my ear,
But I don't hear a sound.

Flip it over and you'll see a smooth inside,
You will also see a rough edge to protect,
When it needs to hide.

The smell inside is kind of drab,
Reminds me of my cousin's hermit crab!

This shell does not have much to say,
Kind of like talking to my uncle Ray.

Bennett LeDuc, Grade 8
Chippewa Falls Middle School, WI

The Shining Soldiers

On the 12th of January
All asleep and no one wary

Millions of soldiers fell
On the ground but did not yell

They lay there in the cold dark night
But alas they did not fight

They kept on falling to the ground
But still they did not make a sound

Piling up on houses and streets
The last one falls and all doth greets

The sun rises up from under ground
All the soldiers have been found

Look out the window and you'll see
The millions of soldiers are filled with glee

Shining in the sun they glow
For the soldiers are the snow

Alison Ford, Grade 7
Core Knowledge Charter School, WI

Skate

There are a lot of kids that like to skate.
They grind the benches and the rails.
They get together with all their pals.
A lot of people decide to hate the kids that like to skate.

Tyler Fassett, Grade 7
Robert Kupper Learning Center, WI

My Beliefs, Straight Up

I believe in strength in many, but wisdom in few,
In the ease of speech, but difficulty in action,
In patience before persecution,
In the idea that each day is not a given right,
In the integrity of liberty.
Honor, Freedom, Perseverance

But I don't believe that just because you have a chance to get
something for free, you shouldn't have to work for it.

I believe that people have the power to persevere,
That there is a reason for everything, even the bad,
That every day is another chance to get life right.
Strength, Determination, Success

And I believe that if you don't have time to do something
right the first time, when are you going to have time to do it
the right way a second time?

Robert E. Stippich, Grade 8
West Suburban Christian Academy, WI

Stars

"Oh my! Oh my!" As night grows nigh, I cry, I cry to the moon in the sky.
"When can I see those twinkling, blinking stars in the sky?"

"Soon! Soon!" the moon cries, from way up high in the pitch-black sky.
"Tomorrow after the sun goes down, I'll take you up there, show you around."

"Oh why! Oh why!" As day draws near, I yell to the sky.
"Can't I see the stars, my friends so dear?"

"My, my!" said the sun in the sky, who is so high. "They whisper to you, wish you were near."

"Oh my! Oh my!" As night once more draws nigh, "Now may I see my friends in the sky?"
I cry, I cry to the moon, way up high.

"The stars, the stars, they are so far!" the moon as pale as can be tells me.
"They called you once they spotted you, and they called you here."

So here I fly, up in the sky, drawing close to my friends so near.
I join them in the cry they issue in my ear.

"Now you're home, now so near, come to us brother, sister dear!
Come stay with us now that night is nigh,
Breathe your last breath here, in the sky."

Monica Czuprynko, Grade 8
Spring Hill School, WI

The Empty Bed

The day started out rainy and gray.
But somehow we knew that this was a day to be celebrated.
We stood there, staring as if we were statues, forever frozen in time.
A single note floated through the air continuously.
This was not a pure musical note though.
This note sounded as if one had come and took all joy and happiness out of it.
When that note sounded, we knew that we would be hit with a wave of emotion.
But this was no single emotion, it was what one could describe as being devoid of hope, yet overly joyous at the same time.
We still stared, only this time, it was as if everything turned into chaos.
All around me people were filled with an agony that happens upon folks way too often.
Yet for me, among the agony, I saw a what appeared to only be a thread of light.
For all of those around me saw a family member who had been lost.
But I saw an empty hospital bed.
For I knew, that he had gone home to spend some time with his father.

Alex Castle, Grade 9
Lakeview Christian Academy, MN

Dear Daddy

I remember the day I woke up to your voice telling me it was my first day of kindergarten.
I remember the first day you took me fishing and I ended up falling into the water.
I remember the first time we were fighting and I told you I hated you.
I remember the time I cried in your arms telling you to never leave me.
I remember the good times we had before they told us you were sick.
I remember the day the flames almost took you away.
I remember the last time you turned and looked at me and said I loved you.
I remember the day I had to say good bye forever.
I remember the other day when I was told you're still talking to me and mom even though we weren't talking to you.

Jordan Sartin, Grade 8
Washington Middle School, WI

Joy

The color of joy is the flickering glow of golds,
oranges, and reds of the flame.
It looks like the newborn filly,
trying to rise off the soft straw bed.
It smells like the wafting aroma of a fresh apple pie
sitting on the windowsill.
It sounds like the cheers of the crowd
after their team was victorious.
It tastes like your birthday cake
as you grow another year older.
It feels like the warm summer breeze across the lake
as you spend a day of fun with your family.

Shannon Stone, Grade 7
Northwood School, WI

Tree Life

To be a seed is to be fragile
But I can only grow to get protection
As I grow, I get stronger and taller
However, I attracted much more attention
Once in a while, my fellow trees are uprooted
I stuck to my rule, and growing I did do
One day I hear rumbling and crashing
Then I see yellow shiny things running over trees
To see the breaking of old, strong trees was terrifying
Unlike that thing I couldn't move or run away
Eventually it got to me and I heard myself dying
In the end, I was like the others who fell

Alfred Santos-Braceros, Grade 7
Core Knowledge Charter School, WI

A Magical Adventure

Walking up to the looming intimidating building,
A deep scared nervous feeling found my heart.
As I bravely strode through the big doors,
Loud unrecognizable voices clashed in the air.
Then one warm smiling face leads the way,
To my incomplete advisory.
Inside, everyone sits in their chairs listening attentively.
All too soon, the bright red ball screamed its ominous shriek,
So all my fellow associates leapt,
And started for their first stop on their mission.
We climbed treacherous stairs,
preparing to enter lands of difficult learning.
Finally, we returned back to headquarters,
To report back on our findings and experiences.
Our spirits calm and relaxed,
As we recited our newly found knowledge.
The nervousness I once contained,
Turned into eagerness,
As the first day of school comes to a conclusion.
The doors of the utterly magical world close,
Waiting for me to open them once again.

Angela Yim, Grade 7
Detroit Country Day Middle School, MI

Fishing

Awakening early in the morning to fish,
To get a big one is only a wish.
I throw on some clothes and run outside,
To get in a boat and take a boat ride.

By the time I arrive at that perfect spot,
I hope my old worms would not rot.
I cast out a line and hope for a bite,
Then try it again to cast it just right.

The sun starts to come out after a while,
The warmth from it I start to feel.
I feel a bite and my heart starts to pound,
The fish tries to get away by swimming around.

I reel it in with all my might,
But the fish put in a pretty good fight.
Finally, the fish is reeled in,
Then I throw it into my bin.

The fishing trip was really great,
But now I'm glad it is on my plate.

Daniel Kudwa, Grade 7
St Thomas More Academy, MI

They Say I'm Their Friend

Every day, it feels the same
Little friends, their little games
They laugh and giggle and have lots of fun
Not really with them. I just look on
Sure they talk about each other
But me as well, for I'm a bother
They squeeze me out, till I'm no more
Out the room and out the door
I'm not like them, I care a lot
But they don't mind, I have no spot.

Jordyn Myhran, Grade 9
South View Middle School, MN

Spring

A bright time of the year,
it comes and goes,
there's rain that clears all the dirt and grime away.
Spring,
a time when new things bloom,
animals come back from hiding,
in their hidden homes.
The season of spring renews the world,
creating new ideas of beauty,
wherever you look.
Spring is a time when the world seems to be happy,
showering everything with new life,
people are given new ideas.
Spring.

Reina Gomez, Grade 8
Saint Thomas More Catholic School, MN

Chains

I feel chains —
Chains on my voice
My emotions my energy
They'll go away
After my final round

Most people say
What of it?
It's a phase she needs to speak louder
And it will pass
But it won't

It's something —
Something I was born with
Something that will never go away
Never be taken away
No matter how hard you try

They don't limit me
They tell me that I'm me
And the chains that —
That you say limit me
Actually help

Hallie Bates, Grade 8
Falls High School, MN

Hearts and Love

A heart, as fragile as the sea,
A tiny heart, traced a tree,
A love as kindness, sees you through,
As love a mirror, points back to you.

A heart as lovely as rainbows,
A tiny heart, with love, it shows,
A love as kind, as is true,
A tiny heart from me to you.

Samantha Polonis, Grade 8
L'anse Creuse Middle School East, MI

Spring

While the blue birds sing,
the ice fishers cry.
The flowers bloom,
and the snow plows die.

While the sun comes out,
The snow melts, hurray!
Get your umbrellas out,
put the snow shovels away.

The time seems to fly,
as the cold season closes.
It's springtime now,
sit back and smell the roses.

Meg McGuire, Grade 9
Montgomery-Lonsdale High School, MN

Thinking the Worst

If you only
Think the worst
Of people
You could end up
With no friends.
Or anyone to look up to you
If you only think
The worst of people
They will think
The worst of you too.

Alisha Hendricks, Grade 7
Luxemburg-Casco Middle School, WI

Class Clown

The class clown is the
funniest in the class.
They make you laugh,
then you fall on the grass.
The teacher sees you,
first you get quiet.
She begins to get closer.
You start to play
the blame game and
begin to make a riot.

Alex Aviles, Grade 7
Valley View Middle School, MN

The Sky Bleeds Blue

The sky bleeds blue
As the trees hide in the background
Like children playing a game
As the moose walk around

The moon shines like silver
On the knit blanket of white
For the moose who are wandering
In the middle of the night

The trees' crack is like thunder
As it falls to the ground
If no one hears the boom,
Does it make a sound?

The snow sees the tracks
Of the long gone moose
And to its surprise
They are very big hooves

Mike Passint, Grade 8
Chippewa Falls Middle School, WI

Gothic Thoughts

The strike of lightning
The darkness of the black sky
The end of the world

Ryan J. Geydoshek, Grade 7
Christ Child Academy, WI

Oppression

The oppressors sit in the center,
Comfortable in their dominance.
The rest flit around the edges
Trying desperately to survive.
Walls hold them back.
Immovable, implacable barriers.
Cutting them off from the ones in power.
Separation creating resentment.
The rulers sit high on their perch,
Held aloft by ideals.
Arrogant in their ways,
Horrifying in their actions.
The oppressors stand tall in tyranny,
Towering over those beneath them.
But the walls are the only defense
Against the hungry crowds.
When the walls come down
They are left unprotected.
At the mercy of the people
They once ruled over.

Kyle Gruebnau, Grade 9
Clarkston Jr High School, MI

Just Shooting

In the empty field
And in my backyard
My father's hand holding mine back
He turned my hands left and right
He was right next to me
Giving me advice
So I wouldn't miss
Just shooting
I avoided the hay stacks
And maneuvered the arrow to the deer
I began to see a pattern
He said
Bring it back to the same spot each time
Every so often I would miss
My father retrieved them
I never will forget
Those skills I learned
As long as I can
Hunt.

Zachary Scott Proper, Grade 9
Clarkston Jr High School, MI

Sad Story

I wasn't sure about what we said,
Your words I keep replaying in my head,
Lost hearts and hidden feelings,
It's over now, and our song,
Continues to play, on my radio,
Memories of us make me think,
It wasn't supposed to end like this.

Chelsey Clark, Grade 7
Robert Kupper Learning Center, WI

'Till the End

All laugh and cry all live and die
Life the dream worth dreaming
Day by day I'll find my way
To look for the soul and it's meaning

I will always be your lady
You will always be my man
When you reach out to find me
I'll be there when I can

Even though there may be times
It seems I'm far away
Never wonder where I am
'Cause I'll be by your side to stay

And when you say you see, every time you look at me
The reason you love life so
I'll try my best and do all I can
To never let you go

We're heading for something that's new to me
Somewhere I've never been
Please promise to hold me oh so close
And love me 'till the end

Amanda Bechler, Grade 9
Winnebago Lutheran Academy, WI

Angel

He was my best friend
Diagnosed when I was two
They thought it was the end
But he made everyone smile
He was a great man
But it wasn't his plan
When he was in the hospital
We all started to mourn
When he took his last breath
Our angel was born
My eyes started to swell
But I know he's better and well
For my best friend's in heaven
Who passed away on 8/11

Paige Springer, Grade 8
Iowa-Grant Elementary-Middle School, WI

Ice Cold

As cold as Alaska as hard as a brick
The cold ice heart of a cruel person.
The person whose face you see in
Every want-ad in the newspaper
They do the unthinkable to get to the top
But to me where they are trying to go is the bottom
To me the world is a cruel place but it can always
Be changed

Kamau DaaJa-Ra, Grade 7
Gesu Catholic School, MI

A Serene, Instinctive Sort of Feeling

Through the hills
and down the beaten path
I try to comprehend
this beauty

I scan the trail and I glimpse
brown dirt, swimming around my shoes
green trees, contending a war with my elbows
blue water, darting down the creek

It is a serene, instinctive sort of feeling
gliding through nature at a pace
undeniably, uncontrollably, unsuspectingly
fast

Yet it is slow in the same
hearing, the clap of my feet
watching, the trees whiz by in awe
feeling, my muscle ache in pain

Michael Culver, Grade 9
Clarkston Jr High School, MI

Drums

Loud, like thunder
Banging, booming, kicking
Loud amplified riff, Les Paul
Strumming, solo picking
Colorful, smashed
Guitar

Jake Shovan, Grade 7
Elkhart Lake Elementary-Middle School, WI

Remember

When filled with sorrow and strife,
It makes you move on in life.
Hope.
When the whole nation has a celebration,
A celebration of sheer jubilation.
Joy.
It becomes more than trust,
Having it becomes a must.
Faith.
When it settles on the world, like darkness onto day,
We hope that it is here to stay.
Peace.
When you risk your life to help another,
No matter if it's a neighbor or brother.
Love.
Do always what you believe is right,
Follow your heart, don't put up a fight
Remember, as you go on in your life,
That faith and hope will overcome strife,
Peace, love, and joy, will lead you to right.

Cecily Linsenmeyer, Grade 7
Immaculate Heart of Mary School, WI

One Window Is All I Need

One window is all I need
To see what the road ahead lies for me
To find out who I really am
To seek the wonders of adventures
To see the troubles that I will face
One window is all I need

Molly Spencer, Grade 7
West Suburban Christian Academy, WI

Stormy Seas

Blue to brown ocean waves pound
Against the weathered shore.
Crashing, screaming, sobbing waves.
They fall, hit me hard.
Black boundaries.
Stormy seas.
Flustered feelings.
Nowhere to turn.
Walls pushing in.
Falling apart, breaking…
Sinking am I
No one to guide me.
Like a bird flying.
First time, plummeting.
Frigid earth, pain.
Arctic waters, sucking in…
No help.
Drowning.
Reaching…
My end.

Brittany Hoffman, Grade 9
Clintonville High School, WI

Future

I sit here in class
Figuring out my future
Expecting great things

Eli Schwartz, Grade 7
Centreville Jr High School, MI

M

His name was Little M,
For M is all he knew.
For instead his actions,
Spoke louder than his words.
Little did he know,
Something big,
No,
Bigger than he would ever,
Imagine,
Began to grow.
Mistaken M thought,
For the trouble he had caused,
On that dreadful day.

Jonah Pollard, Grade 7
Gesu Catholic School, MI

I Remember

I remember when I first learned how to ride a bike.
I remember when I went to Florida to go camping.
I remember the first time I ate at the Outback Steakhouse.
I remember when I fell down the stairs at my grandma's house.
I remember the time my uncle ran me over with a golf cart.
I remember when I almost drove my dad's car through the garage.
I remember when I wrote this poem on things I remember.

Tommy Morin, Grade 7
Manistee Middle School, MI

One Second Left

Bravery is the last shot with one second left
You, the ball, and the basket
Either win or lose
All you
Everyone shouting, trying to mess you up
Pressure and discouragement come into play
Just like the players itching for you to shoot the ball
The voice inside their head screaming at you to shoot the ball
The butterflies fluttering inside everyone's stomach longing to see what will happen
The players eager to touch the smooth leather of the ball
Will I miss?
Will everyone hate me after this?
Bend your knees, relax, ignore the people, and let it fly
Whatever happens is for the best
SWISH!!!
The buzzer sounds
You just won and overcame the fear inside of you and the questions thrust upon you
Bravery is what you show for not letting the screaming fans get in your head
Bravery is the last shot

Alyssa Schmitt, Grade 8
Cedar Grove-Belgium Middle School, WI

I Am a Child

I am lonely and afraid
I wonder if I will live to see the dawn
I hear the cries of my sister and the others around me who are starving
I see my friends dying day by day
I want to hope that life will go on
I am lonely and afraid

I pretend to be a mother
I feel the hard, cold, dirty cement floor that we sleep on
I touch the tears running down my face
I worry about what we will eat the next day
I cry because my parents are dead
I am lonely and afraid

I understand there is nothing I can do without God's help
I say He will provide for us when we need it
I dream of a perfect life
I try to make the best of each passing day
I hope that my sister will grow up strong in faith
I am lonely and afraid

Bekah Schamens, Grade 7
West Suburban Christian Academy, WI

Summer

I feel the cool breeze blow gently around me as I walk
Around in my flip flops and shorts.
I lay down my towel and shake off my shoes.
I love the sand between my toes.
Mostly everyone goes to the beach.
You hang out with your friends
And eat lots of s'mores.
Have all the sleepovers you possibly can.
Don't worry about school or the bedtimes that drool.

There's never a day when the sun doesn't shine.
Flowers and fun, smiles and love.
I hope the summer sun and the never ending fun
Never dies down and turns into a frown.

Kelsea Buchanan, Grade 7
North Rockford Middle School, MI

Hockey Is

Hockey is
my stories, my memories, my thoughts.

Hockey is
my trips, my adventures, my hotel stays.

Hockey is
my struggles, my experience, my glory.

Hockey is
my happiness, my disappointment, my questions.

Hockey is my life.

Zach Tavierne, Grade 7
West Middle School, MI

Never Alone

Sometimes I feel so full of anxiety,
not a pinch of anything else.
I wander through the crowded halls alone,
and I don't ask for any help.
I don't mind being alone at all,
people find it concerning.
I think to myself, wonder in silence
and experience what it's like to be learning,
But other times I'm energetic,
and full of unanswered questions.
When I'm in the moment
people say "pay attention to your lessons"
So…
I pay attention, and push myself
to read the bible book.
Now, I know I'm never alone
He's really there! All I need to do
is look.

Vannessa Saccoman, Grade 7
Shakopee Area Catholic School, MN

I Am a Traveler and a Farmer

I am a traveler and a farmer.
I wonder how this world can be improved.
I hear the seeds crying.
I see the earth nurturing.
I want to assist others.
I am a traveler and a farmer.

I pretend I am back on Loch Ness.
I feel the wind blowing, almost knocking me over.
I touch the dark water.
I worry that I will never see it again.
I cry at the thought of the friends I'll never see again.
I am a traveler and a farmer.

I understand there will always be struggles.
I say that agriculture will always be important.
I dream of people getting along.
I try to help my community.
I hope others will see the importance of getting along.
I am a traveler and a farmer.

Rachel Kirchner, Grade 9
Clintonville High School, WI

Hunting

It is quiet in the woods
I see bright orange everywhere
The sound of gunshot
My coat is jingling with bullets
My sling is tight across my chest
The crunch of leaves beneath my feet
Wide open fields on the side of the woods
Deer running every direction

Roger Thiry, Grade 7
Luxemburg-Casco Middle School, WI

Water

I dive in,
The water surrounds me.
It whispers to me as I sink.
The weight of the world leaves my shoulders,
And I relax as I float on my back,
And an indescribable peace overwhelms my body.
When I resurface I take a deep breath,
And feel nothing,
Just a silent numbness.
The sun looks down in despair jealously.
As I float silently along,
The water comforts me as I listen to it.
The sun begins to set,
My world of serenity comes to an end.
As I leave I feel happy,
Calm and understood,
Finally at peace with myself,
And my insecurities.

Alexa Jeans, Grade 8
J C McKenna Middle School, WI

Dreams

Dreams come when you sleep at night
Dreams can be beautiful sights
Not all dreams last
Some can be a blast
You must not go in too deep
Soon they'll go away and make you weep
Dreams can be a nightmare
And just leave you standing there
Dreams may always be around
You just never notice they sneak
Without making a sound

Daniell Deitrick, Grade 7
Luxemburg-Casco Middle School, WI

Betrayed

You cut my heart
With a piercing blade
If only you knew
I felt so betrayed
You took my trust
And threw it away
I can't believe
I loved you just yesterday
I don't want you
To apologize
All you ever wanted
Was to take the prize
I wasted thousands
Of kisses on you
You were untrue
So I will take this lesson
With grateful hands
Maybe one day I will learn from
This mistake
And never again
Feel this heartbreak

Julia Young, Grade 8
Perry Middle School, MI

Forgiven There

Jesus Christ died upon the cross
We can't understand the cost.
We can try, but we'll never succeed
He died so that we could be freed.

Do you know what He went through?
He was battered and bruised.
The world's suffering He had to bear
By His pain we were forgiven there.

It doesn't matter what you do
He will always love you.
He loved us enough to care
All sins were forgiven there.

Michaela DeVaney, Grade 9
Lakeview Christian Academy, MN

Price of War

Four generations of veterans in his family's past,
Thinking when he goes to war it will be over fast.
Head'n off to battle in the middle of the night,
Knowing when he lands on the beach there's gonna be a fight.

His unit's already taken heavy casualties,
as his company tries to push on to the enemy cities.
Knowing that he has family back home makes his will strong,
and makes him fight the battle no matter how long.

Knowing it's hopeless his unit backs up in retreat,
He now relies on the swiftness of his feet,
Bang! A bullet goes straight through his chest,
Wishing he could have done better, but he tried his best.

As he slowly drifts farther away,
Trying to keep his ever creeping death at bay,
Thinking of his folks back home, while laying on the body strewn shore,
Then he drifts off and wonders if this is the price of war?

Parker Gayan, Grade 7
St Roman School, WI

The Sun

The sun sends its light from above
Showing off her wonderful beauty
Streaming down like a beautiful painting
She surrounds us with her warmth and comfort

Showing off her wonderful beauty
She warms our bodies but also our spirits
She surrounds us with her warmth and comfort
She falls down into the horizon, painting another magnificent picture

She warms our bodies but also our spirits
She rises up out of the darkness of the night
She falls down into the horizon, painting another magnificent picture
She makes this world go round and round

She rises up out of the darkness of the night
To wake us up out of bed
She makes this world go round and round
The sun sends its light from above

Ben Meleski, Grade 7
West Suburban Christian Academy, WI

Alone Time

It's early morning at the beach. The sand is now cold in my hands.
It's my alone time before anyone awakes.
Every morning I look out the tent at the big, expansive ocean.
I see dolphins on the horizon as the sun rises.
It starts gray then to a pale orange.
The colors change rapidly before my eyes.
It's late morning and the others are stirring. My alone time is done.

Sarah Harley, Grade 8
Spring Hill School, WI

The Outstanding Misfit

I'm the outstanding misfit,
Because I don't fit in.
I'm the one I notice
Not fitting in.
I cry and cry almost every day,
Because there are no friends coming my way.
They form cliques, not inviting me
I'm the misfit you see.
They have best friends and I don't,
I'm their best friend, oh no, no, no.
Stickup and put down is all they do,
They think I don't know, but I'm no fool.
I'm not just the misfit, I'm the outstanding misfit
Because I don't fit in with any of the other girls.

Chidimma Okoroh, Grade 8
Gesu Catholic School, MI

Home Is for Me

A house is a house until you make it a home.
Wonderful family makes it hard to go roam.
Be it a warm meal waiting for me.
After a hard day I look forward to see.
My parents and dogs who greet me with a kiss.
They all show just how much I was missed.
The evenings are homework, chores, and some fun.
And I crawl in bed satisfied when the day is done.
There's no place like home, so the saying does go.
I can tell you it's true because I really do know.

Nicole Rydzewski, Grade 7
Luxemburg-Casco Middle School, WI

Just Do What You Do*

Teachers in my face askin'
a million questions
like Dontae where you stay
I tell 'em Twin Lake
where we get cake
eat 20 grand spend a grand at the lakes
I'm just in the zone forces on my feet
on dat apple juice so get like me,
13 and I'm cutlass with the rusted seats
food in my trunk for
yall who wanna eat

Catch me in Whitehall posted at wesco
Cappuccino mocha sittin in the espresso
If I like a girl I let her do her thang
Be like T-pain flirt with her and buy a ring
All the dudes hate me because I am so fly
They don't throw the deuce every time I walk by
I know they wonder why I am so cool
Don't ask me
Just do what you do

Dontae Burks, Grade 7
Whitehall Jr High School, MI
**Inspired by Yung Joc*

Snowing, Snowing

Snowing, snowing down it falls,
blocking all the entrances to the malls

Snowing, snowing it won't stop,
I need to shovel until my shoulder "pops"

Snowing, snowing it's everywhere
filling up the town square

Snowing, snowing heat come soon,
but don't flood the town, or I'll have to ride in a pontoon

Taran Bemis, Grade 7
Shakopee Area Catholic School, MN

fastur

i remember the kool air raseing thru my hare
my feat lined with fore weals
fastur fastur fastur
i remember the waey the clowds rased by as i flu
down my vary familiar streat
fastur fastur fastur
i remember the adrenuhlin rush thru my boans
howses spedd passt me
fastur fastur fastur
i remember the waey my bak waz hunchd ovur
laping peepul on bikes
fastur fastur fastur
i remember the rok wateing fore me on the rode
my weal smashd aganst it
fastur fastur fastur
crash

Riana Mefferd, Grade 9
Clintonville High School, WI

Poetry Block

She stares at the paper, but doesn't know what to write
She imagines her grade, and looks down in fright
She counts in her head, one-two-three
Thinking of how to write perfect poetry
Suddenly an idea enters her head
She's about to put this poem to bed
The poem turns and exits the way it came
She's starting to think this idea is lame
The door is locked, and she doesn't have the key
She doesn't think she'll ever write poetry
She looked at the paper one last time
She thought to herself, "What's the crime"
She starts to think, now she's climbing the tower
She feels like she has all of the power
She looks over what she writes
She's reaching up, reaching new heights
She counts to herself, one-two-three
She just wrote perfect poetry

Rebecca Spleas, Grade 7
West Suburban Christian Academy, WI

Rhythm

th-thump!
Time stops
As the wheel rips itself from your hands
Dragging a ton of metal into the ditch
With you inside
th-thump!
Your pulse dances
Under the fingers of the paramedic
Carrying you from the wreckage,
Back to safety
th-thump!
A mask falls
Drowning you in instant calm
You let it take you away from the world,
Forgetting pain
th-thump!
You awake
Staring at the faces floating above
Painted with joy from your recovery
Bringing the rhythm back
th-thump! th-thump! th-thump!

Robert Brennan, Grade 8
Oakview Middle School, MI

I Love You

A silent movement,
Deep within the shadows,
Quiet heartbeats surround me,
You silently emerge.

I wait in anticipation,
My heart begins to race,
We suddenly see each other,
And I smile.

Warmth holds us tightly,
One feeling we have both missed,
Whispered words pull us together,
I say the words.

Brief silence filters in,
You smile and say it too,
We both embrace one another,
I love you.

Tina Foote, Grade 9
Sandusky High School, MI

Summer/Winter

Summer
Sunny, luminary
Swimming, rollerskating, surfing
Hot, stormy, cold, windy
Freezing, snowing, skating
Winter

Maritza Lopez, Grade 7
Edison Middle School, WI

The Tree

The tall figure
Barren
Winter just withdrew
It had taken the leaves with it
Right now the figure is
Bald, void
And will be until
Bestowed with rain

Its arms extending
In all different directions
Snatching and grasping
Nothing at all
It can't move
It can't take
It can't grow
Until it's given…
Its water

Parker Higgins, Grade 9
Clarkston Jr High School, MI

Thankfulness

I am thankful for God,
who made light.
I am thankful for nature,
And everything that's right.
I know He loves me,
and gives me blessings and food.
I know He cares for me,
So I should not be rude.
He shows me peace, kindness,
cheerfulness and gratefulness.
So we can go to heaven,
and we couldn't want less.
I pray for my family,
So we'll all have faith and hope too.
For all that God's given us,
I want to say thank you.

Logan Arndt, Grade 7
Abundant Life Christian School, WI

Football Shell

It is smooth as silk
It has smooth skin just like
The pigskin of the ball.

IT has the shape of a football
An oval.

This shell has a point
At one end just like a football.
The tan on this shell looks
Like sand on the beach.
The shell is bruised and worn.

Nathan Insteness, Grade 8
Chippewa Falls Middle School, WI

Snow

The wind blows oh so harshly
The snow is pouring down
All I can say, I wish the snow a way
And for spring to come around.

The roads are covered in ice
Everybody is sliding
The ice is gone and I'm singing a song
Spring is coming around.

Danny Vaughan, Grade 7
Shakopee Area Catholic School, MN

Computers

Wires burning,
Gears are turning,
Electrical energy flowing,
A computer is ever-knowing,
Pixels lighting,
Forever igniting,
The images we see,
Will always forever be,
Tapping clicking,
Ever ticking,
Time is wasted away,
Lost beyond the fray.

Charles Schooler, Grade 8
Centennial Middle School, MI

Gentle Words

She is quiet, but always heard
And you are lost, but never lonely
Because you'll hear
Her gentle words

Hailey Carl, Grade 7
St Patrick Catholic School, MI

My Life with Diabetes

I only have one life
But it's my life
I suffer the pain
But it's not in vain
It's so I can continue to live
I have so much love to give
We never know
How much we will grow
I want to be free and to love
Like the freedom of a dove
I don't have a choice
But I do have a voice
I don't think it's fair
But I do care
That they find a cure
So I'll take as much pain as I
Can endure

Alexandria Ruiz, Grade 7
St Roman School, WI

Grandfather*

Gathering me up in his arms,
He would lift me up as high as the sky
And give me a hug so big I could barely breathe,
Then set me back down to Earth with a thump
So I could gaze up to his grand stature.

His gray white hair and twinkling eyes
Would tell stories all their own,
As he plays with me all day
Running around in the backyard.

Now I go to where he rests
To show my love for my grandfather gone,
And maybe, just maybe
Remember the love of a grandfather I used to have.

Ryan Linak, Grade 7
Assumption BVM School, MI
**In loving memory of Patrick Linak.*

It'll Never Happen

What if there were no tomorrows?
There were todays
There were yesterdays
And many days before
But there was no tomorrow.
There would be no reason to dream
To make plans for the future
Or just wish on a moonbeam.
If there were no tomorrow
There would be no birthdays to celebrate
No Christmas trees or gifts
No plans for vacation or special little trips.
If there were no tomorrow
Life would soon be ending
A scary part for sure.
I'd hope for lasting friendships
And great love to endure
If there were no tomorrows…

Nick Karow, Grade 8
Wheatland Center Elementary School, WI

Davannis

I enjoy the chatter of the cooks,
the ringing of the register,
and the sound of pizza baking

I enjoy seeing the tables, the booths,
the pizza, and my fellow customers
I enjoy the taste of the cheese and the sauce

I enjoy feeling the warmth of the pizza
and the coolness of the soda
I enjoy the rich aroma of tomato sauce

Tim Hart, Grade 7
Valley View Middle School, MN

March Madness

It is everyone's favorite time of year
The NCAA tournament is here
All 64 teams have made a good run
But the trophy could belong to anyone

Everyone I know fills out a bracket every year
Do not be surprised if down your cheek runs a tear
Because a lot of us pick our favorite teams
But they never win as it seems

Many have gone home after this long journey
But four still remain in the NCAA tourney
All four teams want it; you can see it in their eyes
The team I picked lost to my surprise

All four remaining teams have a great chance
To win this tournament they call "The Big Dance"
With only three games left, the end is near
I wish this tournament came twice a year!

Chris Hughes, Grade 8
St Roman School, WI

Shadowed

Ghost,
Why do you haunt me?
In my dreams, you pace with me
Through the empty streets of my memories
Your words
The wobbling flagstones
That pave those narrow, treacherous roads
I do not want to tread on those insubstantial steps
But I must, in order to go forward.
Nightly,
You lead me into the city
I long ago walked away from
Presenting me with the beautiful things
I once loved,
And alone I am forced to remember
The darkness
That made me turn away.
Specter,
Cut these chains loose
Set me free
I cannot dwell in shadowed memories.

Hannah Frame, Grade 9
Clarkston Jr High School, MI

Morning Dreams

I awoke, the sun smiling and radiating warmth,
A plate of dreams in the kitchen,
Baked banana bread buried beneath bacon.
A stomach full, and a mind filled,
With thoughts as bright as the sun.
Boom! The dreams fade as I awoke.

Kevin Marvin, Grade 9
Hartland High School, MI

The Person Who Did Not Sleep

There once was a man named Fred
who never slept in a bed
his wife said you snore
and I can't take it anymore
so he slept on the floor instead

Robert Heise, Grade 8
Fairview Charter School, WI

My Best Game

Baseball is what I do best
No doubt, I am better than the rest
Every time I take a swing
The ball will stay in the air
Until next spring

When I am pitching
I throw it so hard
It will break right through the fence,
Into the next door neighbors' yard

I can scoop up a grounder,
So very clean
Many people I talk to
Say I'm the best they ever seen

Later in life,
I will be in the pros
So get out of my way
Or I will step on your toes!

Colyn Buss, Grade 8
Spring Hill School, WI

Dreams

In dreams
You can do anything
And anything can happen.
You can fly,
Surf,
Or explore a cave.
You can climb mountains,
Be a millionaire,
And own a thousand mansions.
In dreams
You can do anything
And anything can happen.
You can hang out with your friends,
Swim with dolphins,
and bungee jump.
You can ride on horses,
Sleep on clouds,
And be royalty.
In dreams
You can do anything
And anything can happen.

Rachel Jungbluth, Grade 7
Abundant Life Christian School, WI

What's the Point

Filling out papers,
Sometimes it's a force.
Going against something you hate.
Or maybe something you want to pursue.
Sometimes getting drafted
To others it's an excitement!

Saying goodbye to loved ones.
Not knowing when you will see them again.
Or not knowing if you'll ever come back.
Finally arriving after a long ride-the airplane takes a sigh.
Getting prepared and ready to train.
Getting haircuts learning, running. Hard work.
Practicing shooting, trying to defeat the other team.
After months and months the day has come.

All hidden and prepared, like a game of hide 'n' go seek.
All guns screeching out, ready to be used already.
The battle begins! Gun shots everywhere! It's a riot.
Shooting and dodging bullets. Some people are fortunate enough.
Others get shot. Some die.
War…why do we fight? Just to prove our side?
And because of this we lose the willing and the innocent.

Kim Fairbanks, Grade 8
Saugatuck Middle/High School, MI

Blest

Why were we born in a country, where freedom is more than just a dream?
Yet in other parts of the world, people are killed by the regime.
Why are we fortunate enough to have as surplus of food in this great nation?
While small children in Africa are dying of starvation.
Why do we complain about schoolwork and fake sick on a day of a test?
While many aren't given the opportunity, but still consider themselves blest.
Why do we need to spend a thousand dollars on the newest designer bag?
While some children can't afford clothing much nicer than a rag.
When we die and go to Heaven, the place where all will meet,
God won't be judging at the brand of shoes on our feet.

Alexis Abee, Grade 8
Our Lady Star of the Sea School, MI

For What?

I tell you all my secrets
For what
So you can spread them even though I tell you not to
I share all of my emotions with you
For what
So that you can make mean and heartless comments
I tell you everything that is on my mind
For what
So you can make jokes and laugh about the personal things I share
I try to be the best best friend I can be
And for what
So you can continue to "hurt my feelings" even though
I'm always nice to you

Tori Tysinger, Grade 7
Hally Magnet Middle School, MI

Water

Water's rushing, stopping, flowing.
Peaceful one minute, harsh the next.
A savior of all, a killer to others.
Slow, then the speed of a cheetah.
Soft tranquil, a rock wall later.
Cloudy on dark days, shiny with bright waves.

Alex Mott, Grade 7
Valley View Middle School, MN

Dear Daddy

Dear Daddy,
One day I hope you can see,
all that it is that you do for me,
that you've loved me unconditionally,
and let me fall, but was there all along,
to help me up and remind me,
that mistakes can be forgiven,
and that you love me.

Dear Daddy,
I'll show you how much I love you,
and live my life the way you've exampled,
by giving and not receiving until the deed has been done.

Dear Daddy,
You've been there for me always,
were the first hand I held,
and you'll be there for me always,
like when you walk me down my aisle, and give me away,
Daddy don't cry and know,
you'll always be my hero,
and I love you!

Victoria Carter, Grade 7
Centreville Jr High School, MI

Friends

Side by side or miles apart
Friends are forever close to your heart.

Some friends are real. Some friends are fake.
My friends have my back, with no precautions to take.

There's stuck-up, shy, safe friends,
And there's brighten up your day friends.
Some friends talk on, and on, and on.
My friends sound like a cat singing a song.

My friends are monsters, they say Boom! Crash! Roar!
Then people that don't know them run out the door.

At the end of the day you're all worn out.
You sit around and pout, pout, pout.
When you're with your friends everything's better.
Just always remember that friends are forever.

Cyanni Andrade, Grade 7
Ramsey Jr High School, MN

Be Happy

Life can bring you down,
But don't wear a frown, be happy.

Though you did lose a race,
At least you kept your pace, be happy.

Though your day was very bad,
What a great week you have had, be happy.

Though today the rain may fall,
Tomorrow won't "drip drop drip" at all, be happy.

Though the sport you play is rough,
At least you prove you're tough, be happy.

The sun is smiling down,
So don't wear that frown, be happy.

Michael Wojciechowski, Grade 9
Hartland High School, MI

Biscuit

Biscuit is one of my favorite pets in the world.
Biscuit can be a good dog sometimes.
But she can also get in trouble too.
And also she loves to be by people.

Her tail is like a steal baseball bat.
She's blonde and a little white.
Her eyes are little puddles of mud.
Her ears are soft as feathers.

She is eight years old now.
It makes me sad that she has to leave soon.
I hope she knows she's special.
Biscuit will be happy in heaven as well as she is now.

Samantha Anderson, Grade 7
Manistee Middle School, MI

Roller Coaster Ride of Love

When I first met you,
I felt as if I was on a roller coaster.
That wouldn't stop —
Life was a little ride awaiting your arrival —
I've heard love seems always like a roller coaster —
That it's a distant journey to take —
Many are confused by this feeling —
But I promise you it's an amazing ride to have when it's true.
That yet it's never more terrific,
Sometimes love turns out fake,
Sometimes it's real —
The roller coaster is never always there —
But I told you it's amazing,
So you ignored me…

Samantha Rajewski, Grade 9
Petoskey High School, MI

Subway

Down from the noisy, bright, blaring streets. Into the dark, cavernous tunnel that is the subway.
Stuffy updrafts of stagnant air blast out as the escalator descends, the tiny hole of light shrinking above.
A swipe and a bleep from the card-scanning turnstile grants access to below.
Waiting on the platform. Neon lights illuminate the next Yellow Line's arrival.

3 MINUTES

Between the roars of passing trains and swells of gabbing tourists, tiny squeaks are barely audible.
Not from screeching breaks, but meek creatures dwelling in these caves.
Scuttling toes. Dark blurs with pink, furry tails disappearing and reappearing in and out of the shadows.

The yellow beast opens its mouth, spits out rush-hour businessmen and
Swallows its next meal of incoming travelers.

The rails too rusty for gripping, the benches too slimy for sitting, the journey too jostling for surfing.
The humming of overhead lamps and the rocking of the wobbly car lull even the stiffest into relaxation.
Awkward silence fills the car, as newspapers flutter and overhead lamps buzz enharmonically.
The stench of old coffee stains and body odor waft about the cabin.
Yellow-lighted window squares flash past, the Blue Line
Zooming in the opposite direction through the dark, narrow tunnel.

Vertigo ensues as the train rumbles to a halt.
The monster's yellow elevator-door lips uncurl, ejecting old customers and
Welcoming in the new evening snack.
A light breeze reawakens the city senses. The smell of home a returning memory from above.
Up from the dangerous, dark, dreary depths. Back into the lively, glowing haven that is the city.

Lauren Rodewald, Grade 9
Clarkston Jr High School, MI

My Favorite Noise

As I sit on the plastic leather bench
The keys call my fingers as if they want them home for dinner.
The tip of my nails gently rest upon the whiteness of the shiny keys and I close my eyes.
I open my eyelids, wondering what music is in my mood at the moment.
On the side, a stack of sheet music is so scrambled, I can't choose
To go classical or jazzy, or *piano* or *forte.*
I pick the top papers, the most recent.
I set it upon the stained fake wood holder right in front of my nose.
Ahhh… I sigh with a smile, my favorite noise, I again set my long fingers on the keys.
My left hand starts with the pick-up notes and soon my right hand joins in singing with the melody.
I know this song inside and out and I could hear its voice from a mile away.
I don't dare look up from my bouncing fingers because I don't want to ruin the sound.
I could play this piece forever, suddenly my fingers press softly, then loudly again.
The dynamics note that it's almost time to end my piece of heaven
Heart and soul, I fell in love with you, heart and soul…

Amelia Stecker, Grade 8
Japhet School, MI

I Do Not Understand

I do not understand why fish isn't considered meat and why Goofy can walk on two legs and talk when Pluto can't and they're both dogs.
I really don't understand why my sisters have such random mood swings. One minute they are mad at me so I leave for a while and when I come back they are all buddy, buddy with me.
What I understand most is that I can't do something bad and not pay for it.

Andy Breuer, Grade 7
St Mary's School, WI

The Man That Sneezed

There once was a man who had to achoo.
He tried to hold it in, until his face turned blue.
But he eventually sneezed.
He coughed and he wheezed.
And then someone said "Bless you."

Dylan Hoey, Grade 8
Fairview Charter School, WI

Hold

I need a hand to hold
To save me from these hearts so cold
I have a crazy wild heart
I knew that right from the start
All I did was give it away
But you stomped on it day after day
Finally I realized your love wasn't true
So I found someone who was better than you
He makes me feel safe, warm and all right
And when I'm scared he holds me tight
I have no fear when he's around
I know he'll keep me safe and sound
Letting out my feelings is easy with him
So now I don't cry when the lights are dim
Whether I'm filled with rage, comfort, or sorrow
He always reminds me there's always tomorrow
I know he'll save me from my fright
What can I say? He's the perfect knight
Even if you're rich, poor, or you just struck gold
Shy, sweet, gentle, or even bold
Everyone needs a hand to hold!

Sadie Nier, Grade 7
Pilgrim Lutheran School, WI

Lemonade

I'm tasty,
I'm yellow,
I'm sour and sweet,
I can make any scorching hot summer day neat.
I'm cold,
I'm tart,
I'm fresh from the squeeze,
I can turn anyone's frown upside down.
I'm cold,
I'm fresh,
I'm bitter as can get,
I will agree with your taste buds that I can tell,
I'm easy to take almost anywhere,
I'll quench your thirst,
I'll quench it good.
I'm a little bit of sugar,
A little bit of ice,
A lot a bit of lemons,
And a lot a bit of nice.

Jackie Koenig, Grade 8
Saint Thomas More Catholic School, MN

What Is Happiness

Happiness, what is happiness?
Happiness is hot cocoa on a cold winter day.
Happiness is a pair of fresh clothes after a cool swim.
Happiness the feeling of academic accomplishment.
Happiness is giving something to someone worth giving to.
Happiness is on the faces of people around the world.

Ian Thorpe, Grade 7
Valley View Middle School, MN

My View of Artwork

The artist of this painting here,
Must have been some kind of queer.
I believe I've heard more artistic farts,
Than this particular work of art.
If you look at the musicians there,
You cannot help but feel scared.
Their music must be moving though,
For all the artists to praise them so.
I believe this artist was disturbed,
To create anything this absurd.
What does it mean? I'm not quite sure,
But it's hard to write about what can't be heard.
The confusing colors and gigantic shapes,
Remind me of big, nasty apes.
When it comes to art I don't believe,
There's anyone as confused as me.

Max Holden, Grade 8
Abundant Life Christian School, WI

A Year Behind

It might surprise you
But I'm behind
A year to be exact
I'm one of the youngest in my grade
And it's a fact

I try to catch up
But I fall even further out of sight
I wait in the dark
No one hears me not even you
Even though you're so close to me

You've always known me unconsciously
And sometimes I come out
But only for a while
Then you go back to ignoring me
But why?
Why would you want me in the dark

So who, who am I you ask
Well I can tell you, I'm the real you
The one you've hidden away
Not many people can see through your disguises
But I'll always shine through, always.

Alisha Frohmader, Grade 8
Spring Hill School, WI

Spring

Spring is in the air,
you can see the grass turn green,
trees no longer bare.

Spring is in the air,
you can hear the sounds of birds,
chirping everywhere.

Spring is in the air,
you can taste the strawberries,
sweet like fresh cherries.

Spring is in the air,
you can smell the fresh flowers,
blooming in the vase.

Spring is in the air,
you can feel the bright, warm sun,
shining on your face.

Kayla Malecki, Grade 7
St Roman School, WI

Spring

Spring is a wonderful time of year.
It makes me want to stand up and cheer.
The clocks are slowly ticking.
The hour hand is always clicking,
counting down the days,
until spring will be here to cause a haze,
on all the students everywhere!
When spring arrives we get a pair,
of brand new boots on sale.
Sometimes it will rain and hail,
so boots will be fun, to play in the mud!
Then in the spring time, call up a bud,
and go outside and have some fun.
Now this poem is almost done,
Except for on more thing…
It's almost spring!

Dezarae Marshall, Grade 7
Centreville Jr High School, MI

Music Is…

Music is as loud as thunder,
As loud as a mountain,
Crashing down to the ground.
Music is as loud as a wave,
Deep down on the ocean's surface.
Music is as quiet as lightning,
As quiet as the wind,
Whispering through your ear.
Music is as quiet as a wave,
Coming up to the shore,
Then falling back down.

Aryanna Frinak, Grade 7
St Katharine Drexel School, WI

A Walk in the Fall

Yesterday I took a walk, while the rain was pouring down,
And even though the world was wet, I could not wear a frown.

The cars are crowded in the streets, but I don't mind at all,
All that I can think about is the beauty of the fall.

A little leaf, and then one more decide to follow down,
Then more and more soon pile up and put color on the ground.

The wind, it blows and then the leaves begin their lively dance,
Across the yards and parks and schools, they put me in a trance.

When I came home I wrote a poem about that dreamlike day,
So my memory of that autumn walk will never fade away.

Mary Kate Blondin, Grade 9
St Thomas More Academy, MI

My True Poet

My inner poet is a thistle. Protective, but soft on the inside.
My inner poet is the thunder roaring out feelings.
My inner poet is the rain falling and splashing the ground below.
My inner poet is a lullaby soothing and sweet.
My inner poet is a smile, affection in the simplest way.
My inner poet is a light sheltering and comforting.
My inner poet is a sigh, of joy, of fear, of sorrow.
My inner poet is a song, relatable yet special.
My inner poet is a painting, completely original.
My inner poet is a dance, expressive and fun.
My inner poet is a secret, held deep inside me.
My inner poet is a heart, beating softly.
My inner poet is a tear rolling down my cheek.
My inner poet is a book, the best part is deep in my soul.

Mackenzie Jade Strachan, Grade 8
Holmes Middle School, MI

Home

Lock clicks open.
I step through the doorway.
Look around.
Breathe in deep breaths, the smell of a smoker's domain.
About to sit on the pea green couch.
The itchy, scratchy, pea green couch.
When a flash of black, followed by a squeal of laughter, tear round the corner.
I forget about my rest.
Grab an Arizona tea, to revive myself, from the fridge.
The refreshing taste of summer in my mouth.
I follow the duo down the stairs.
Clomping and Stomping, with my big feet, down the stairs.
The touch of cold cement and the scratch of carpet greet me at the bottom.
I run, barefoot, across the basement floor.
I find Jazebella, the black streak, hiding on the topmost shelf of the cabinet.
Boo, the girl who squealed as she ran through the house, hanging from the rafters.
I am home.

Anna Goddard, Grade 7
Whitehall Jr High School, MI

Needed Rain

Raindrops fall filling lakes like hope fills the heart.
When raindrops stop falling they send clouds.
The lake turns to dark.
Deserts and everything stops,
To take a breath until it rains again.

Nikki Whiteaker, Grade 8
J C McKenna Middle School, WI

Smooth Shoreline

Rough waves crash into darkened shorelines
Foam hands reach out to emptiness, grabbing nothing
Heightened waves, scurrying animals
Water like a blackened wall separating land from sea
Staring out across the growing waves
Searching for something not there
Thousands of years wasted watching waves
Drowning tears, confusing answers
Crashing waves on last hopes
Washing away last dreams
Leaving behind a smooth shoreline

Heidi Krause, Grade 9
Clintonville High School, WI

Sheep in My Sleep

I just love to sleep!
So when I wake up I start to weep
I end up going down stairs to eat
Then I go grab my toy sheep and go back to sleep
Every time I sleep I dream about sheep
They are white and fluffy with little pink noses
They are very dramatic and do many poses
Each sheep is unique in its own way
Some are small, tall, large, and short
Some even snort!
All the sheep in my sleep have feet
Gross! The sheep sweat from all the heat
But I always love the sheep that I count in my sleep

Joanne Reiners, Grade 7
Bristol Elementary School, WI

My Star

My love for you is like the stars in the sky.
Always bright,
never fading.

Sometimes I stare at the stars,
and think, maybe you are too.
Maybe my hero is thinking about me,
just as I am about him.

My bright, never fading love belongs to you,
my father,
my hero,
my star.

Sydney Stordahl, Grade 7
Jackson Middle School, MN

Every Day

Mostly, I wander.
Opening new doors,
looking out different windows,
a curious child wondering what the world is.

Playing a game,
often making the wrong move.
Overall, life is like a puzzle,
every day.

My future doesn't always know where it's going,
but friends and laughter can help point it
in the right direction.
A right direction.

Everything changes once in a while.
First it's this and then bam,
it's that.

For now, I'll just enjoy what I have,
a beautiful, bustling, bright beyond.
Full of colors so bright,
I can't see my own tomorrow.

Molly Poole, Grade 7
Ramsey Jr High School, MN

Tell Her

Tell her you admire her.
When she's upset, hold her tight.
Pick her over all the other girls you hang out with.
Play with her hair.
Pick her up, tickle her and wrestle with her.
Just talk to her.
Tell her jokes.
Bring her flowers just because.
Hold her hand and run.
Just hole her hand.
Let her fall asleep in your arms.
Tell her she looks beautiful or cute.
Look into her eyes and smile.
Kiss her on the forehead or cheek.
Kiss her in the rain.
If you want to be with her…
Tell her.

Avyonne Wilson, Grade 7
Gesu Catholic School, MI

Thunderstorm

Lurking like a tiger the clouds move in slowly
The rain that follows hydrates the land on which it falls
The roar of thunder awakens the sleeping
Somewhere in the sky an unknown voice speaks
And it leaves with only puddles left as a reminder of its visit.

Addison Andonoff, Grade 7
Richmond Middle School, MI

My Friends

My friends are like family
They know everything
We have fun together
We dance and we sing
They know all my secrets
I know all of theirs
Our friendship is clear
With no rips and no tears
Sometimes we argue
And sometimes we fight
But in the end
It turns out all right
They are my brothers and sisters
I love everyone
We are wild and crazy
We always have fun
There are guys and girls
Who I always care for
They all love me
I could not ask for more

Reanne Sheppard, Grade 8
Shattuck Middle School, WI

Spring

The wind blows softly
Across the trees, I see the
Buds blooming in May

Tia Oakes, Grade 8
Langston Hughes Academy, MI

Sounds of Nature

Wind whooshing at my ears.
I hear wolves howling
At the moon, hwooo

Geese squawking in the sky
Rats running through the leaves,
The ground is freezing cold,

Frogs croaking by the lake,
Owls howling in the trees,
Bears growling in the distance

Trees brushing together
Rabbits hopping in
And out of bushes

Deer stopping in their tracks
Birds tweeting in the trees
Foxes wrestling in the distance

Every step I take
Leaves crunch beneath me
I love the sound of nature

Renee Janz, Grade 8
Seymour Middle School, WI

Good Morning Again

A tinkling yawn.
Off to start the day.
Drowsy and groggy,
Breathing loudly and with effort,
SL
OW
LY,
very
SL
OW
LY,
It's mind coming to, and
getting things back into
Rh-yt-hm.
A quiet steady hum,
To use when getting
Work done.
Eyes shining bright,
"good morning again." It says.
You know it means it because
It actually works today.

Christine Menge, Grade 7
Roosevelt Middle School, MN

Nature Is Wonderful

Trees are towers
that stretch up to the sky.
Vines are clotheslines
with clothes hung up to dry.
Birds are planes
when they stretch their wings to fly.
A rooster is an alarm clock
with its awakening cry.

The wind is a fan
that cools and soothes when it blows.
A firefly is a lantern
when it lights up and glows.
A stream is a road
when it twists, turns and flows.
Nature is wonderful,
and it really shows.

Lauryn Trautmann, Grade 7
Roosevelt Middle School, MN

Bowling

Bowling is my thing
When I throw the ball
Down the lane all it does
Is crush the pins
I don't even need to try
It just comes so easy
1, 2, 3 there's a turkey
It's just so easy for me.

Trent Uselmann, Grade 8
Spring Hill School, WI

What Am I?

I am a light
Shining long and bright
I am a magician
Disappearing when I'm done
I am a reflector
Reflecting the sunlight
I am trustworthy
Rising and setting every day
I am tired
Resting among the stars
I am always there
To start the night

I am THE MOON

John Davis, Grade 7
Washtenaw Christian Academy, MI

Halloween Night

For only one night,
The creatures will roam!

As the monsters crawl,
The goblins moan!

Under the moonlight,
The witches take flight!

All of this happens on
Halloween Night!

Devin R. Neumann, Grade 7
Scranton Middle School, MI

Beneath the Flames

As the bird chirps
The deadly smoke will move
Like a cat
With nothing to prove.

The sky is shrouded
In the darkness of gray.
As trees fall to the grips
Of human stupidity.
Forever and ever
The forest will pay.

Unwrongful death
Engulfs the air.
The creatures wonder,
Does no one care?

As the fire creeps,
The grove sleeps.
Forever and ever
The forest will pay.

Austin Buerkle, Grade 8
Sandusky Middle School, MI

Mother's Loss

the peaceful breeze
blows over the lake
everything seems calm
but that might not be true
up the river which feeds the lake
a mother hippo and her baby
not knowing what the crocodile will take
the baby wanders off
fascinated by the marine life and fish in its own little world
the crocodile stays low
waiting patiently
the baby senses danger
swimming faster
the crocodile closes in
one bite
and it is over

Micah Cheng, Grade 7
Abundant Life Christian School, WI

The Father I Never Had

We were at the doctor's office and you came in
you gave us a hug while crying it seemed like the end

I wanted to know what was wrong but you did not say
I wish I could help you take the pain away

We went outside and my mom held you in her arms
feeling as if your body was dead and gone
I got sad as I started to cry
I had to wipe the tears that came out my eye

As you walked away I never thought I would see you leave
now that you're back it is such a relief.
I love you like you're my own dad
to see you leave makes me so mad.

DashaNette Craig, Grade 8
St Joseph Catholic Middle School, MI

Roller Coaster

I strapped myself in
I knew that it was going to be a bumpy ride
It all started
It was fast, fun, and exciting
There were some bumps and loops on the track
But going on them was half the fun
Once it reached the top I dropped down
It was scary
But I knew I had a guardian angel watching over me
It slowed down
We reached the end
I got up
I thought to myself
How could I have thought a roller coaster was scary

Daniella Sinks, Grade 7
St Roman School, WI

Without a Trace...

Have you ever wondered
What the world would be
Without a trace of humans
Just like you and me?
There'd be no people to see
All the beautiful things God created for you and me.
The plants would wilt
And the clouds would cry
At the thought of no person being alive.
Soon God would see
That the earth was made for people,
People like you and people like me.
The churches' steeples would tumble and fall
When the mournful ground would rumble,
Trying to see if there was any human life left at all.
Then, God would finally see
That our world would not be such a happy place,
Without a trace
Of you and me

Awbreigh Slagle, Grade 7
St Patrick Catholic School, MI

My Best Friend

As your remembrance is very clear,
I hear you talking gently in my ear.
As you woke me up softly in the morning,
Saying get up you bum and stop moaning.
As we ran down the stairs
With the smell of a great awesome breakfast in the air.
As you packed us up for another day of school,
You ship us off saying I sure do love you.
As you picked us up from school all worried,
Saying how did you do.
As we come home and take a nice long nap,
I got to lay comfy on your lap.
As we wake up and cook dinner,
You say, all proud of me, you're my little winner
As we start the day over and over again,
I say, Mom, I love you and you're my best friend.
Even though today you aren't here with me,
I think about how you are so dear to me.

Rico Drewery, Grade 8
Oakview Middle School, MI

Dogs

Dogs have good personalities.
They will love you forever and ever.
The canine can kiss you if you'd like.
He or she will have a tail.
It will wag if it is happy.
But, it will drop between its legs if it is scared.
The animal wants to be fed.
Dogs may do tricks if they are taught.
Dogs are the best friends you can have.

William Lutzke, Grade 7
Luxemburg-Casco Middle School, WI

My Swing

Every time I climb upon its lap,
My whole body opens up,
And I feel free.
He spreads his wings,
And takes me to the sky.
He makes me feel alive.
I tell him my secrets,
And he listens.
He brings me back down,
To a gentle landing,
Feeling calm and awake.

Danielle Zurfluh, Grade 8
J C McKenna Middle School, WI

Aries

Aries is the god of war.
He is someone you will not adore.
If you want to bet
He is someone you'll regret.
Although you cannot see him
You would much rather be him.
For he controls the fire.
He does as he desires.
He is one you don't want to deal.
For thy soul shall conceal.
Now the god of war
Said there shall be no more.

Vincent Poe, Grade 8
Adams Friendship Middle School, WI

Love's Truth

Blood red, a sight of beauty
Like a pointed needle
Each petal soft as baby skin
Tightly enfolded upon itself
Waiting
All the best…unfurling
Petals cupping each drop of dew
All the best…
Shriveling into a milky brown
Love's lost

Danielle Benser, Grade 8
Suring Elementary/Middle School, WI

Football

Some people don't like football.
That I can really say.
Maybe it's because of the practice.
That goes on all day.

I really love football.
That I'm sure to say.
But the all day long practices.
Are just the price I pay.

James Kay, Grade 7
Luxemburg-Casco Middle School, WI

The World

When I look into the world I see,
People laughing, crying, jumping, running
Animals crawling, crouching, barking, chirping
Nature, living, growing, planting, eating
Cars honking, moving, speeding, screeching
Everything on one street, one city, one state, one country, one WORLD

Grace Arend, Grade 8
Saint Thomas More Catholic School, MN

Hallway

Clink, clank went the lockers of the busy middle school hall
Zip goes the backpacks of middle schoolers
Students start to rush to get to class
Students start muttering, trying to talk to their friends over all the noise
They are speaking about last night's TV shows
"Hush! Quiet down" say teachers stomping down from their classrooms
Some boys are wrestling with each other in the crowded hallway
"Ouch!" screams a person that was stepped on by the wrestling boys
"Ha-ha" laugh students about some joke
And I silently stood there thinking "Wow. This place is a jungle!"

Nasra Hussein, Grade 7
Cedar Riverside Community School, MN

Why Waste My Time

I really don't get it, why you acted like you cared
Why you said that you really liked me but you were never really there

I thought you were different. I thought you were my friend
But now I know that you're untrue. I still can't understand

We goofed around. It was all good and I thought that would be that
But then you said the same things to her like you were your own copycat

How could I fall for you? This happened to me before
How did you get away with all this? Why did I open up that door?

How could all your kind words make me feel so happy?
Why did I let you do this to me? And why did you if you could

I can't let you get to me anymore even though I thought you were mine
I have one last thing to ask you though, "Why did you waste my time?"

Trudie Bruce, Grade 8
Lake Fenton Middle School, MI

Manor House

I love the old Manor House in England.
The flowing gardens bring out beautiful colors.
The old tennis courts remind me how lucky I am to be there.
I adore the vines growing up the old, beautiful stone.
I love remembering how long ago the nobles lived there.
Walking in the huge fields looking for my favorite pond,
Exploring and getting lost in the huge mansion.
I love my grandparent's old house; I wish they would have kept it.
It is a favorite picture in my head and one of my greatest memories.

Izzy Sadiq, Grade 7
Elkhart Lake Elementary-Middle School, WI

School Is

School is like prison
We can't leave

School is like going to jail
You never want to go back

School is like an island
We are all trapped

School is like a baby
It always needs your attention

School is like a salad
You have to put something on it to make it better

School is like vegetables
You hate them but they're good for you

To some, school is like Heaven
They never want to leave

School is like a gateway
It leads to many places

Raelon White, Grade 8
Messmer Preparatory Catholic School, WI

Victory

The color of victory is a pink sunset.
Victory looks like a herd of triumphing
horses going to the pasture
Victory smells like a fresh-baked
apple pie coming out of the oven
Victory tastes like a pound of white chocolate
Victory feels like you are floating on a cloud through the air.

Jennifer Flamang, Grade 7
Northwood School, WI

My First Dog

I can remember that wet summer day,
We pulled into the farmer's driveway,
After months of begging I was getting a dog,
All of the puppies ran from me except for her,
She let me pet her,
Immediately I loved that tiny, precious, furry ball of love,
I told my dad that she was the puppy,
He said I'd have to wait just one more day for her,
We went to get all her supplies,
A cute little food dish was my pick,
A bunch of cute little toys for her to play with,
An itsy-bitsy pink collar,
That night I couldn't sleep,
The next morning we drove up to the house,
I grabbed her in my arms and walked back to the truck,
She was finally mine.

Courtney Mueller, Grade 8
Seymour Middle School, WI

Campfires

Crackling pops of fire
Smokey smell of hot dogs roasting
Buzzing noise of mosquitoes in your ears
Cool breeze away from the fire
Sticky marshmallows on sticks
This moment will last forever

Aubrey Reitz, Grade 7
Elkhart Lake Elementary-Middle School, WI

My Little Flower

I once saw you
like a seed.
You needed water and soil
to thrive in the world
as you grew.
I could see the stem getting longer
and the roots holding tighter.
You reached for the sun
as if you had a ladder.
Nothing,
ever stopped you,
even when somebody
stepped on you
your stem would take care of you.
But, that wasn't the best part,
I could see you in the morning
with your flower all abloom,
you had all you needed in that little garden.
Where I first saw you.

Kelli McCallum, Grade 9
Clarkston Jr High School, MI

Heart of the Sky

The long straight sticks shooting
into the vast open sky.
Barren, dead
and devoid of life,
some people might call it.
But it's really life standing still,
as if in decision of what to do.
Defy the laws of nature or do the easy
thing and fade until spring.
You can tell they want
to grow but can't.
You can see it in the
way they sway in the silent wind,
or in the tangle of their branches.
They look like the heart and veins of the sky.
Bigger at the bottom where life is
and their nourishment,
lesser when they're in the sky.
And the way they web.
This heart is how everyone survives.

Evan Gorgas, Grade 9
Clarkston Jr High School, MI

You-nique

I am a leopard without spots,
A bee without a stinger,
An ant without legs,
And a comedian without a zinger.

I am a bird without wings,
A cat with no meow,
A dog without a bark,
A magician without the "Wow!"

I am a tree without leaves,
A hurricane without an effect.
The wind without its gust,
And a politician who doesn't object.

In spite of all our differences,
Although our differences are fate,
We all have unique special gifts,
No one is second rate.

James Hendrickson, Grade 8
Boulan Park Middle School, MI

Feelings of the Sand

Feeling the sand
between my toes,
smelling that smell
of the salty sea air,
watching the waves
that wash the
shells away,
listening to the
birds soaring
through the clear
blue sky,
that all reminds
me how peaceful
the world can be.

Caleb Szopinski, Grade 8
Washington Middle School, WI

The World Today

You've just begun your long journey
You may hit a rock on the road
But keep going
All you need is to try to keep going
Life won't end until you end it
War won't make peace it'll just hurt it
Every step of the way
The dove keeps calling
While the bald eagle cries no
Colors aren't different
They're just different shades
Dreams won't end until you wake up
See you at the end

John Portillo, Grade 7
Valley View Middle School, MN

Hunting

Amazingly fun
Always have a joy doing it
Never have a disappointing day
Unless you miss a huge buck
Otherwise you always have a blast in the woods

You have to do about a half a dozen drives a day
You walk about 2 miles a day
The only time you ever stop is when you're in your tree stand
You shoot your gun usually once a day but most of the time it is a miss
Because they are running and are in pine trees and only get one shot
You look for deer in the woods all day

When it is time for lunch that is when you tell everybody what you see
Everybody in the whole camp is going to have a great story to tell
Sometimes it is how they shot a big buck or how they miss it
And sometimes they have the same excuse as the years in the past
Like the deer was running too fast for their bullet
But actually the deer was walking in front of their stand but they don't say that

Kegyn Steinmetz, Grade 8
New Auburn High School, WI

When I Looked into the World

When I look into the world I see war,
I see families doing several jobs to keep their family together,
And a roof over their heads,
I see families getting torn apart,
I see peace maybe as far as the moon, but it is getting closer every day.
I see love within families,
I see people who can grow a garden overnight,
I see people who can earn a living by playing music,
And I see people who can raise a family of five all by themselves.
I see babies being born with tears of happiness being shed,
I see people dying with tears of sadness being shed.
I see the lonely, the rich and the poor.
I see people caring for one another,
No matter if they are doctors caring for the sick,
Or just a random person helping an old lady with her groceries,
Or a woman with several kids trying to get them in the car and the groceries.
But they are running around
I see people inventing things to help the ordinary person,
I see the bad; they could have committed a murder
Or just not done something they were asked to.
All in all I see everyone no matter who they are.

Clara Hearst, Grade 7
Saint Thomas More Catholic School, MN

Soccer Player

To become a good soccer player
You have to train a lot,
You have to think that you are the best soccer player,
You have to believe in yourself it helps a lot,
In each soccer game you have to believe that you are the best soccer player.

Francisco Vargas-Alva, Grade 8
Spring Hill School, WI

Street Music*

The country
The *silent* road,
A car slowly creeps by
The wind,
Is about the only thing you hear!
Animals trudging around, just as if they were in the woods
Music, no such thing when you're on my street!

Kaitlyne Lynn, Grade 7
Whiteball Jr High School, MI
**Inspired by Arnold Adoff*

October's Colors

Dark skies of late October and their winds come calling.
Telling the leaves it's time for them to go.
At first, just one, a beautiful apple red.
Others follow orange and yellow soft as silk.
I raked the first layer, the work was
Breathtaking with beauty.
Quickly the rapid fire of fall had begun.
Leaving beauty upon the ground.
I am now surrounded by fall's last show of color.
That have gathered and piled upon my feet.
I jumped and I played, until the sun went away.
With big leaves more unique than snowflakes and
The trees now almost bare.
I placed the leaves in bags.
As the bags are holding colors and placed by the road.
The last days of fall are ready to be taken away.
Temperatures are dropping with snow beginning to arrive.
The leaves are gone, the winds turned crisp and cutting.
I feel like yelling, "Come back,"
Only there are no leaves to hear my cry.
The October's colors are now asleep.

Hailey Kociszewski, Grade 9
Clarkston Jr High School, MI

Never Again

Never again will I let you hurt me,
Never again will I cry over you.
Never again will I be the one to say I love you,
Without a Response back.
Never again will I play the fool.
Never again will I be so blind.
The clues were so obvious.
I think you've caused me to lose my mind!
So lost in this world.
Without Guidance.
Changed perception now.
My heart is a fraction.
Can you make it whole?
I doubt it.
Never again will I fall in love with someone so heartless,
Without a soul.

Elexus Spencer, Grade 7
Hally Magnet Middle School, MI

Kennedy Fast Pitch

Bigger Balls, faster speed
Hurt shins and banged-up knees.
Running, fielding, catching pop flies
Batting and bunting,
"Make sure you follow the ball with your eyes."
Scoring home runs and winning tournaments,
Talking to Coach Fred or celebrating special moments.
Varsity, JV or Freshmen Team,
Us girls definitely know what that means.
Play your hardest,
Don't Give Up!
Not until we've won the golden cup.
For now we may just get stickers,
That stand for a perfect game,
But when we step out on the field,
Everyone knows our names.
We're the Eagles
Blue and Gold!

Emma Jogodka, Grade 9
Kennedy High School, MN

Life

People walking down the street
People you see on a subway
People all around are glad to be free
People all around the world wish that they were you
You can walk down the street
We can't
You can have your own religion
We can't
You know that your family is still alive
I don't
You can wake up and breathe clean air
We can't
But what we can is love one another
Can you?

Baily Meine, Grade 7
Springfield School, MN

Beautiful Blue

Blue are blueberries, so squishy and sweet.
I love to eat them for a treat.

Blue are my jeans, so comfy and worn.
Some days I'm surprised they haven't been torn.

Blue is the lake, so cold and fishy.
When my feet touch the bottom it feels all squishy.

Blue is the jewel of sapphire, so hard and pretty.
To lose it would be such a pity.

Blue is the shirt I wear when I show.
When the sun hits it, it sends out a glow.

Angela McManus, Grade 8
Wheatland Center Elementary School, WI

Children at War

War is for people that can't get along war is for people that don't think that they can belong.
So you ask your self — why put children at war.
Children want to go out and play instead they grab weapons and begin to pray and hope for another day.
So why put children in harms way. Why send children to their grave even before they get to shave.
Why put a child in front of a grown man. That's as evil as the klu Klux clan.
They want to go out and play but instead they put out their hand.
And is given a gun and are told this is now your life. And from those words it feels like they where stabbed with a knife.
From then on life is all work put to the test if they don't succeed to do there best from then on it's a mystery.
So no longer can they be free grab their helmets and gun close their eyes and count to three.
Look at each other and say good-bye because this could be the last time.
As they stand alone at war they can almost hear their heart beating faster and faster.
Knowing this could be their last breath.
They remember what they had trained for and even if they do make it they still will remember blood and gore.
So please don't send kids to war.

Tannon Perry, Grade 8
Saugatuck Middle/High School, MI

Hollywood

I sit there, in the beautiful fall weather, watching the world pass on by.
Gazing at all of the people who wonder why they washed away
their amazing dreams by living in such a small, hopeless town.
I am curious.
I see the loneliness in the expression on their faces, the emptiness in every single beating heart.
As they fade away into the distance, I realize how they must feel.
I have been in their sinking depression before.
I write my hopes for a brighter future in a worn notebook as a leaf falls from the sky above.
It lands on my worried head.
I think that maybe one day, I will not live the life that I did in the past
and can actually experience the thrill of traveling to a place where the city lights never dim.
Where I can take a turn for the better with full potential.
Where I would be followed by the sparkling lens of a camera.
But until then, I'll keep sitting here watching the sun fall above the horizon.
Patiently awaiting the moment where I will shine in the spotlights of what we call Hollywood.

Jacqueline Maznio, Grade 8
Oakview Middle School, MI

What I Know

Live each day to the fullest,
and learn from your mistakes.
You can't go back to the past
so you shouldn't have regrets, but don't repeat the same mistakes.
Trust everyone to be exactly the way they are.
Laugh off those bad days, when it seems like everything has gone wrong,
and cherish each moment.
Hold onto your love, but know they can easily let go, slipping through your fingers.
A broken heart will take a long time to heal, and your first love will be the hardest to lose.
Society is built like the social ladder in high school, people will never change.
You may think that beautiful preppy girl has a ton of friends, but inside she may feel alone.
Never forget what is important to you and follow your dreams.
What is meant to be will happen in the end.
Share your knowledge with others.
But always remember to live each day to the fullest,
and if you do this,
you will always know you have made the most out of your life.

Colleen Napier, Grade 9
Clarkston Jr High School, MI

What the World Needs

Seemingly indescribable, yet distinctly transparent,
No color, no odor, no texture, no taste,
Rejected, like a flame refusing to burn,
For some it is sacred, others may be waste

A feeling that's just as cherished as ignored,
Both enemy and hero, it is needed to be shared,
Beyond the use of words of expression,
In many ways, it's not always fair

Indestructible, unbreakable, and understanding,
So caring, so incredible, and powerful at the most,
It can move mountains, clear waters, and stop war in its tracks,
Shows the right direction, as an angelic host

Blindly, we can't always see it for what it is,
Though it can make us whole, good, and kind,
It's our purpose, to receive and to give it,
The one thing we'll always have, forever yours and mine.

Hannah Seaman, Grade 8
Sandusky Middle School, MI

Thunder

Thunder comes in like a shotgun going off.
It answers the call of lightning.
It makes a loud noise to scare people in an instant.
It comes from invisible areas in the gray sky.
It leaves a blank trace like a crime scene with no fingerprints.

Austin Burnette, Grade 7
Richmond Middle School, MI

First Game

On a warm sunny day
my dad suddenly throws a softball to me.
The oversized baseball soars through the air,
just a yellow streak in the clear blue sky,
and drops into my outstretched hand.
He shouts
"Great job, keep it up!",
and I smile with pride.

The light silence was perfect,
no need to overwhelm it with noisy chatter.
The *swish* of the softball and the *clunk* of the catch
was enough for him and me.
My first game was tomorrow,
what was I going to do?
I glanced at my dad,
his face creased with worry lines too,
but he doesn't say much 'til it's time to go.
He looked at me with that reassuring face
I've seen so many times and said
"You'll be great,"
and we drove home in silence.

Kristina Ballough, Grade 9
Clarkston Jr High School, MI

Nature

The forbidden fruit of Adam and Eve
Hanging lazily on the wild tree
Scarlet and plump dappled with dew drops
Leaves like fairy wings sparkling
It calls my name
My mouth is sandpaper, yearning
Lurching forward, I pluck
Pearly whites split the fruit's skin
Cracks of agony
I crunch, chomp, and munch my way to its core
Sweet juice trickle
Satisfied

Liza Steffeck, Grade 8
Suring Elementary/Middle School, WI

always answers

i don't know how to feel
confusion is not my friend
jumbled feelings, lost thoughts, confused mind
i know answers are somewhere, just not here
the wind whispers,
trying to tell me answers
in some language i don't understand
lost, help, anyone
with questions like a desert and answers like rain
almost never together as one
murky waters may settle
and answers may become clear

Tisha Kenfield, Grade 9
Clintonville High School, WI

The Hate

Hate is the coldness,
It waits in the shadows,
It preys on the weak,
Stay inside and look through the windows,
It waits outside ready to creep,

Hold on to your sanity,
Once you start to hate your path is set,
The doors are shut on you,
It will get hard to hold onto the friends met,
Hate will keep you trapped like an animal in a zoo.

Gabriella Fantozzi, Grade 9
Petoskey High School, MI

Free

I sat and waited while I watched outside
Outside, outside where I can run and hide
Free, but till the time comes
When I can finally go out
But till that time I sit and wait
I watch the birds fly free
Just like I long to be

Katherine Belinky, Grade 7
St Patrick Catholic School, MI

Shadow

Bright sun glistens
I see someone
It looks like me, moves like me
Very different
Follows me
Mimicking my every move

In the shade
Man was gone
Nowhere to be found
Part of me is gone
My friend isn't there

Sun provides light and warmth
I feel its rays
And I can always see the black man
Mimicking me

Mike Schwartz, Grade 9
Clarkston Jr High School, MI

911

The sky was blue
Soon to turn gray
All I have to say
This is the worst day

Thousands of people died
No one knew why
All they did was pray and cry

The twins went down
With thousands around
Running and screaming
And people also bleeding

The Pentagon blew up
The world is now shook up
Now they were after the White House
The president was under attack
Route 93 hit the ground with a SMACK

They saved the president
They are our heroes
The world was left in horror
Wondering what was next in store

Zach Haack, Grade 8
Fairview Charter School, WI

Cookies

cookies
enjoyable
sweet and crispy in my mouth
freshly baked warm and soft at once
lovely

Nicole Frommann, Grade 8
St Patrick Catholic School, MI

I Am Not

I am not my glasses.
I am not my asthma.
I am not my parents,
Or grandparents,
Or aunts or uncles.

I am not the video games I play.
I am not the movies or shows I watch.
I am not the scars I have,
And I am not my past.
I am not how I write.

I am not how I dress,
Or what I am into.
I am not my doctors.
I am not the books I read,
But you don't know me,
So how would you know all this?

Alexia Dailey, Grade 8
Fairview Charter School, WI

Unique

I am unique and caring,
I wonder why people die,
I hear the music in my ear.
I see spirits flying around me.
I want to be free,
I am unique and caring.

I pretend to dream of my fears,
I feel my sorrows cry,
I touch my heart in fear,
I worry someday I'll die,
I cry to wash my fears away.
I am unique and caring.

I understand the sadness,
I say don't cry everything will be all right.
I dream about my tears inside,
I try to warm your heart.
I hope you fear too.
I am unique and caring.

Amanda Rogotzke, Grade 7
Springfield School, MN

Champion

C onfidence
H ustle
A ttitude
M VP
P ower
I ntensity
O ver achieve
N ever give up

M.J. Delmore, Grade 8
Spring Hill School, WI

Are Dreams Just Dreams?

Are dreams, just dreams?
Or can you grab them, by the seams?
Can they take you, to another place?
Maybe even, outer space?

Can they take you, away from here?
To another place, where there is no fear?
How would it be over there?
Until it, begins to tear.

Until you stir, and lie awake —
Deciding what, dream to take —
Thinking about, what's in that dream —
Is it more, than it will seem?

As you stay, lying in bed —
Almost sleeping, seeming dead —
Time for you, to go to sleep —
In that dream, for you to keep.

Nathan Manker, Grade 9
Petoskey High School, MI

The Playground

2nd grade
Playground
Cori and Evan
Walked over a stick
Pretended to get married
The old fashioned way

Nick Mabee, Grade 7
Shakopee Area Catholic School, MN

Music

Music is like chocolate
It can be soft
Or it can be hard
It can be sweet
Or it can be bitter
But either way it melts within you

Music is like the heart of life
It can tell a beginning
Or tell the ending
It can be depressing
Or be animated

Music can be a fun techno beat
Or a slow country song
Music can come from a bird
Or a violin

Music
Is
Life

Valeria Martinez, Grade 8
Washington Middle School, WI

Bella

Bella is our newest dog,
She tends to eat like a hog.
When we got her, she was quite small,
But we knew she'd be big, by the size of her paws.
We taught her how to sit and stay,
But she barks when she wants to play.
My other dog, his name is Billy,
He gets annoyed and thinks she's silly.
Bella loves to cuddle with us,
But Billy gets jealous and makes a fuss.
Bella likes to run and chase her tail,
I am glad we bought her when she was for sale.

Marisa Lindeen, Grade 8
St Roman School, WI

Brilliant Orange

A room full of orange, like an orange tree.
It feels calm, exciting, happy and free.
When I look around it's all I see, why not
purple, yellow, red or green.

Austin Teslow, Grade 7
Valley View Middle School, MN

Love, What Is Love

Love what is love,
Does anyone know what love really is,
If you do please tell,
Can love really be like happiness
Can it really be good or bad
As beautiful as a sailor's sunset or
As ugly as a natural disaster.
Is it only real in your heart and your mind.
Can love really be like the sun setting over a lake,
Or is love darker than the deepest part of hell,
And more painful than death.

Tianna Stackus, Grade 9
Petoskey High School, MI

Orange Is…

Orange is…the color of my background
Orange is…the color of fire in my eyes
Orange is…the color of a flavorful fruit named emotion
Orange is…the sunshine in my sky
Orange is…the glow of my beating heart
Orange is…the rebound of happiness
Orange is…the streak of an amazing sunset
Orange is…the burn of my sincerity
Orange is…the light of my life
Orange is…the birth of something new
Orange is…the amazement of my soul
Orange is…the mood of a relative who has past
Orange is…the play-book of my world
Orange is…me

Jack Krull, Grade 8
Seymour Middle School, WI

Break Free

a small soul yearning to break free
a precious face you'll never see
with little feet and hands to match
its a life you can easily snatch
without a second thought, or possibly with one
once you do it, it is done
in such short time you take a life
so easily with a surgical knife
will you regret it after the fact?
what's done is done, that is that
so think long and hard about what you've heard
for your babies' sake no abortion is preferred

Abigail Boll, Grade 8
Grosse Pointe Academy, MI

There's a Time

There's a time for everything,
Whether it's flying across the world,
Catching an oyster and finding a pearl
Maybe even designing a multimillion dollar creation,
Your time will come, you'll just have to be patient
Keep being the dreamer,
And when the time is right, jump in like a lemur.
There's a time for everything, I'll say it again,
Reach for the stars, because you can,
You can!

Donielle Lewis, Grade 8
Messmer Preparatory Catholic School, WI

B-Ball Banquet Blast!

What a chaotic day!
Full of joy and praise
It was nice to see all the smiling faces
even the black cases holding our awesome pictures

Oh, what a fun day!
It was full of laughter and fame
Even Kayla was there
with her beautiful long hair

While waiting for my name to be called
I felt a little shy
and then I went up there and I wanted to die
and even wanted to cry
because of all the good times I'm gonna miss
even the people like Mal, Yas and much more!

But let's put that aside
and talk about my big trophy prize
because there's no hurt in saying
we're winners even
if every tourny said different
I'm still gonna hurry
and remember this journey

Michaelle Nourse, Grade 7
St Roman School, WI

Ocean

I plunge into the water;
cold and refreshing
Millions of creatures swimming by;
fearful but curious.
So many things to see;
so little time.
I realize I'm out of air,
and reach towards the surface.
I burst through the waves;
the air cold on my skin.
I swim towards the shore;
the salty taste still in my mouth.
I wish to come back soon;
right back to the ocean's magical waters.

Christina Forcier, Grade 7
Valley View Middle School, MN

The Need to Succeed

Times are changing
Her determination is stronger
Why can't you see the girl she can be
She can't hold on much longer

Every year she tries out
And you always stand her up
And simply point the bench
Her skill is more than a tossup

You see the sweat on her face
The passion in her eyes
The shots that she shoots
Catches your surprise

That final night came
For that one girl to fulfill her dream
Just give her a chance
She won't break the team

Coach gave her a chance
She scored the winning shot
He learned that life's not about teaching
It's learning what was untaught

Rachael Conner, Grade 8
Sandusky Middle School, MI

Color Red

Bright red strawberry
Was picked by Mary
Rick gave Roben red roses
The campfire danced
In the moonlight
The sparks are fireworks in the sky
A fire truck turned on its siren
A fire truck is as shiny as glass

Cody Holtz, Grade 7
Luxemburg-Casco Middle School, WI

The Way of Death

The color of death is like the gray in the sky when the sun goes down.
Death looks like the sad faces of little kids after they drop their ice cream.
Death smells like the flowers at a funeral.
It sounds like thunder in the distance.
It tastes like salt tear drops out of a beautiful blue-gray dolphin's eye.
Death is like losing the one you love to cancer.

Alison Kosterman, Grade 7
Northwood School, WI

Where I'm From

I am from a place called school
Where my favorite subject is world history
Yelling and screaming in the halls
Banging on lockers is in
School lunch is what's out
And I have a best friend named Ashanti
Who keeps me laughing
I am from a place where there are lots of people
Family gatherings, exchanging Christmas gifts
Smelling the greens, ham and Mac and cheese from outside
My Mom yelling telling me to clean
And my little sister who wants to watch *High School Musical* all day
I am from a place where I am called mom
Where little foot prints walk beside me through the house
Little hands playing with toys
Little lips giving me kisses and hugs
And full of smiling, laughing, crying
I'm from a place called home
Where everything is purple
Food tastes spicy
And where I took my first steps

Shay'Toya Burks, Grade 9
Riverside University High School, WI

Can You?

Can you hear my cry?
Can you feel how time together just quickly flies by?
Can you feel the pain I feel?
Can you understand just how I feel?
You don't understand and I believe you never truly will.
I hate the way this is going.
No happiness, just tears can't help it, this is what I'm showing.
There's so much fakeness, hateness, going by and by,
I ask this question, time after time.
No one seems to understand or even hear my cry.
Can you hear it, so loud and clear?
Can you hear it, that's my fear?
You try and hide it, you try and fight it
Because you can't sleep with the pain.
Your heart hurts and feels so heavy because it never ever changes.
I'm so tired of asking.
So tired of the sighs.
So just please answer me this one question…
Can You Hear My Cry?

Daleshon Taylor, Grade 8
Hally Magnet Middle School, MI

Dark Cloud

I stood alone on the hill
The sky was calm and the earth was quiet.
The moon and the stars were gems in the sky
Until the dark cloud soared above.

I shook in terror as the world rumbled.
The cold wind chilled me to the bone.
The moon and the stars ran away
As the terrible storm came along.

The rain felt like cold stones upon my head,
And thunder brought me to my knees.
The world flickered in and out of sight,
Synonymous with the streaks of lightning.

But then the wind slowed,
The rain stopped falling and the earth stopped shaking,
And the moon and the stars came out of hiding.
Once again, the sky was calm and the earth was quiet.

Kevin Fortune, Grade 8
St Roman School, WI

23

I believe he was the greatest
Flying and leaping through the air
Throwing down monster dunks without a care
Numerous championships were won back to back
This made his legacy never fall back
Slam dunk champ in 1988
That's the year he told everyone he was great
He work his own hundred dollar shoes
Busting out his magnificent moves
Crossing over those sweaty dudes
This just made me think…
I believe he was the greatest

Chaz Miller, Grade 8
Oakview Middle School, MI

Old Friends

When I
used to watch
The Powerpuff Girls,
Pooh Bear,
and
The Little Mermaid,
I would always know
that the characters had
great friends.
The Powerpuff girls had each other
since they were sisters.
Pooh Bear, Piglet, and all the other creatures in the
100 acre woods had one another.
The Little Mermaid had her father, Flounder, Sebastian,
and her sisters.

Hannah Berg, Grade 7
Abundant Life Christian School, WI

Crazy Day

It was hot summer afternoon
There I was sitting and looking around
I thought to myself what shall I do today
As I thought many things were going
Through my head, that moment
It had finally popped into my head
The thing I will do today is just sit, relax,
And enjoy life
There were many things to do
But I chose this kind of idea
As the day went by friends and family came by
They were asking me to do stuff but I still chose
To take this day off and relax instead
Of running around
It was a good time but the day has come
To an end, that I was thinking I had really
Got some peace, this day was really enjoyable
Now here I am with my family talking about
The day, their day was really interesting
But I thought mine was better!

Kelechi Duru, Grade 7
Gesu Catholic School, MI

Fire

Infernos burning forests
Campfires cooking hot dogs and marshmallows
Embers and firewood warming houses
Wind blowing flames into scorching tornadoes
Fire can destroy
Fire can rebuild

Thomas Sweeney, Grade 8
Winter Middle School, WI

Grandma

My grandma is like a shining star
When she walks into a room,
She can change the mood completely

Since I am the one and only grandchild,
She does everything for me,
She gives me anything I could possibly want.

She is the kind of person
Who would give her last cent,
To help someone in time of trouble.

She taught me a lot of values,
That I'll use every day,
She is a very hard working person.

She told me I could be anything,
And never to give up
To take each star I grab.

Colin Hagert, Grade 8
Springfield School, MN

Back Then

I always looked up to my dad
And today I still do
I was sad the day he moved away
And found someone new

Even though he's far away
I know that he still cares
I wish he was here to tell me that
He says I'm in his prayers.

I still see him now and again
I wish it was so much more
I would do almost anything
For the way it was before.

Mike Dickman, Grade 8
Spring Hill School, WI

Mad Is

A mood that you get
like when you fight
why do we have moods
why do we get mad?

Fred Lett, Grade 7
Valley View Middle School, MN

Come Back

Some people say it'll be okay,
Others say stay strong through the pain.
It started out as nothing,
Nobody knew,
Not even the doctors had a clue.

I know you went through a lot of pain,
Just to keep me and Kyle in your game.
You tried your best to make it leave,
But the monster did a bad deed.

Even though you're not here,
I'll stay strong through every year.
It's hard to explain all the pain,
That's going through each of my veins.

I miss you,
You miss me,
Please Mom, come back to me.

Kassie Stowers, Grade 8
Spring Hill School, WI

Grandma

Grandma
Sleeping
Every day
In her bedroom
Because she's tired

Marisol Garza, Grade 7
Edison Middle School, WI

In the Middle of a War

my house is like a battlefield
with soldiers running across the treacherous, half ripped up carpet for ground
wielding nail guns, paint-grenade launchers, putty knives
and plaster trays as metallic shields
my dad is like the army's general
drawing plans of attack and leading us into battle
my mom is similar to the battalion's nurse
she's stationed in close proximity to the site of battle
ready to heal the injured with "Bob the Builder" Band-Aids
I on the other hand am like the army's soldiers
barely into this and already hoping for world peace

Chris Booker, Grade 7
St Katharine Drexel School, WI

For One Summer

Early July, given loud noises and bugs for a day
The fireworks would go off
At first, just a couple, erupting in the sky
Others of various colors, purple, green, falling to the ground
You saw the first one the colors so bright like a neon sign
Summer's memory sticking to your mind and longs for it again
The purple ones overlapping each other and that vision kept us watching
With our eyes, binoculars, and telescopes
Where the bugs bite and the soggy ground bled through our shoes
In backyards and parks and on the lake we watched and looked
Until they came to an end
Until everyone had packed up and left
With the thought of explosions in their heads
Our eyes could see nothing more than the colorful flashes in the sky
We did our best to remember but as time went by we found it hard
Only the faintest memory would stay

Emily Hawkins, Grade 9
Clarkston Jr High School, MI

The Faces of the Moon*

My three faces of the moon
came in my orbit in the summer of 64
when my whole life changed!

I realized running away from home was the best thing to happen to me!
Now I have more mothers than any random child of the street!
They are the moons shining over me!
They are strong African American women and they give me great strength.
To be up in the morning as a new day is dawning!

At night when life takes me back to guilt,
I remember the Mother Mary is always with me and when she rises from the heavens
She doesn't go further into the sky but further inside of me.

So truly the day my dad left me for good
I think he was saying you are better off with all these mothers
than plain old me they are "The Moons Shining Over Me."

Brandon Winn, Grade 8
Washington Middle School, WI
**Inspired by "Secret Life of Bees" Movie*

Jungle

Lush, wet, green leaves everywhere
Venom of the sweet, violet orchid in the air
Spine-chilling creak of a python's hiss
Small beads of sweat on my forehead
Fresh, delicious tropical water
I'm starting to love this place

Justin Miller, Grade 7
Elkhart Lake Elementary-Middle School, WI

MLK Jr.

M y dream was to end segregation
A nd today that dream has come
R iots, marches, and speeches just for my dream
T oday that dream has come
I had a dream
N obody could stop that dream

L ove for my people made me strong
U nderstand that your hate made me keep my dream
T oday they celebrate me in January
H onoring and remembering me and my dream
E very year I am celebrated
R elapsing to the time

K illed in Memphis, Tennessee
I may have been killed but
N othing could stop my dream
G etting along with whites and blacks

J ust before I have to go
R emember my dream is here to stay

Mohamed Abdi, Grade 8
Cedar Riverside Community School, MN

Blue

Blue is the color of the darkest night.
Blue is when the moon is shining very bright.
Blue is the color in another's cries.
Blue is the iris in one's eyes.
Blue is blood that is oxygen low.
Blue is the guilt which no one will know.
Blue is the ice cream and blueberry pies.
Blue is the dishonesty in another's lies.
Blue is the ice and all the snowflakes.
Blue is the depth in all of the lakes.
Blue is in one another's tears.
Blue is the shadow made in mirrors.
Blue is the rain when it pours.
Blue is the sorrow from someone who mourns.
Blue is the ocean with high tide.
Blue is the sadness that others have cried.
Blue is the death of a person adorn.
But, blue is also the joy of a baby being born.

Max Voss, Grade 8
St Roman School, WI

Friends

Friends…
Friends are like beautiful roses,
That you can always smell,
Friends are like them because they're always there for you!
True friends love you till the day you die,
Till you take your last breath,
They will always have a shoulder for you to cry on,
They're always right beside you when you need them
Whenever you need them,
Even when you don't need them and you're looking blue
They're there to ask you what's wrong?
Friends love you and are always there no matter what
You go through, they love you!
These kinds of friends are the kind we
Need in the society today!
And we need to be that kind of friend to others!
And did I say I love you, and my friends?
Well I do!

Cierra Crawfis, Grade 7
Abundant Life Christian School, WI

Pompeii Girl

There was a young girl from Pompeii,
Who liked to receive her own way.
She wanted some soy,
Instead got a toy,
And now she is doing ballet.

Haleemah Aqel, Grade 7
Harbor Beach Community High School, MI

Memories

Through church and swimming we met,
Laughing and enjoying ourselves

Through struggles and hardships
We've stayed strong,
Our bond never broken

Through the good times as well as the bad,
With sleepovers and fun, laughter and love

Through the many conversations
And jokes we've shared

Through the good and the bad,
Through the thick and the thin

You're always there, right by my side
To comfort me or make me laugh

Not knowing each other at first,
Coming together at last

Through all of this came a friend.

Allison Garland, Grade 9
Clarkston Jr High School, MI

Brownie

Brownie is furry
With brown and white hair.
She is very loving,
And will have fun curling up with you.
Even though she bites,
She is always there for you.
She is very talkative
Which can get annoying.
But I can't imagine life
Without her here by my side.
Brownie loves food
And eats a lot of carrots.
She needs a lot of care
And wants a lot of attention.
And I'll be happy to give it to her
Anytime she wants it!

Jennifer Staeglich, Grade 7
North Rockford Middle School, MI

Me

I am a twelve year old girl
who has lots of time to live in the world.
I'm going to be the best I can be
And no one is going to do it for me.
I want to become a lawyer
And basketball player too.
I hope to be known
whatever I do.
This is me
And what I want to be.

Candice Leatherwood, Grade 7
Gesu Catholic School, MI

If a Boy Was Free from All

I digress to the tainted tale,
Forgetting your faithful foundation,
And remembering only one winner.
Bemoaning the times towering tall,
Over all acclaiming actions.
You never knotted nooses,
While worrying wondrously,
About anarchist accusations.
Silently suffering,
Feeling frivolous,
Recalling rancor,
Emitting evil,
Everlasting energy.
Forever forgotten,
Renouncing reprobating reoccurrences,
Omitting all that was once wild.
Many memories escape ersatz entities,
All beyond our controlling caresses,
Living with Lucullan luxuries,
Life has never been better.

Kayla Skibbe, Grade 9
South View Middle School, MN

Garbage In — Garbage Out

Garbage in and garbage out
that's what school is all about
teachers teach us all we need
in life they help us to succeed

Nate Grodi, Grade 7
St Patrick Catholic School, MI

Twister

A tornado twists so fast bringing
dark skies, rain and thunder
so lowed, as it rips
through the sky
turning everything upside
down turning lives around
it ends up so fast in
a blink of an eye.

Brandon Shannon, Grade 7
Manistee Middle School, MI

What Becomes of Snow?

What becomes of snow?
Why, I don't know,
Is it water?
No, try harder.
How about H_2O?
No.
I have no clue!
Then I will tell you.
The answer to my riddle,
My very interesting puzzle,
Is when snow melts, my dear,
Never to be seen for another year,
It becomes spring!

Stephanie Mackley, Grade 8
St Edith Elementary School, MI

Dreams

Dreaming is life
Happens every day
You can dream in the night
but you can daydream in the day
You can daydream of a girl
with beautiful brown eyes
You can dream of a fire
running out of your mouth
Dreams are nice
but there's a kind of dream
that's not so nice
it's called a nightmare
and you wouldn't like that in your mind
but that kind of dream
only happens at night
so don't be scared
when you're daydreaming in class

Uriel Rios, Grade 7
Valley View Middle School, MN

The Love of My Life

T ough
H andsome
E ducated

L ovable
O ver protective
V ery cute
E nergetic

O utgoing
F un

M ale
Y oung

L aughable
I ntelligent
F unny
E verything to me

Leah Herrmann, Grade 8
Spring Hill School, WI

Shooting Star

Last night I saw a shooting star
It was very bright
From my window, it did not look far
It lasted only a few seconds of the night

It went away
Sorry to say
I did not make my wish

Dana Derenne, Grade 7
Luxemburg-Casco Middle School, WI

Summer

I love the summer
with all its sunshine.
the green all over
makes me happy and calm.

I love the summer
with fun things to do
like riding horses
and swimming in the lake.

I love the summer
when I get to
take care of my pets
and spend time with my friends.

I love the summer
with no school to go to
when my whole day is free
to do anything I want.

Nina Kahnke, Grade 7
Ramsey Jr High School, MN

Wohoo World

Wohoo World a grand place to be:
You can ask anyone from a he to a she.
The answer will always be the same,
Everyone knows Wohoo World is not lame.
From presidents to residents;
From yahoos to wahoos they're all the same,
Come in and join the Wohoo gang.

Wohoo World a better place to be;
You don't have to worry about taking your Wii.
There are plenty of games for you and me.
I don't know about you but I truly agree,
The Wohoo World is the place to be.

Wohoo World is the place to be;
I highly doubt you disagree.
You will have a very fun time I guarantee,
But if I'm wrong, you can kick me in the knee.
Come on in, to have some fun
The great adventure has just begun.

David Gorun, Dalton Gabris, and Jesse Auclair, Grade 8
Spring Hill School, WI

Man's Ultimate Downfall

War is a way of life,
That causes panic and causes strife,
And some people live their whole life,
With the burden of war on their shoulders,
War makes pleasant places miserable,
It replaces love and trust with hate and prejudice,
War is like dividing a number by zero,
When you're finished all that's left is nothing,
War brings out the worst in many,
But can bring out the best in some,
We all wish that war will be no more,
But it will continue forever more.

Shaun Quirk, Grade 8
St Roman School, WI

Brown

Brown is the dog that I keep.
It loves to run, and it loves to leap.

Brown is the dirt in my yard.
It is soft when wet and frozen when hard.

Brown is the coffee that I drink.
It gets me up in the morning and always helps me think.

Brown is the chocolate I hold in my hand.
The deliciousness fills me and is sold across the land.

Brown is the bell in my church,
Hung from a rope and is perfectly perched.

Sterling Grawe, Grade 8
Wheatland Center Elementary School, WI

Billy Bob

There was a young boy named Billy Bob
He liked the girl down the street
He showered her with flowers and gifts
Oh, that Billy Bob was so sweet

Over the years, they grew apart
Billy and his sweetheart went their separate ways
He looked, but couldn't find his soul mate
Oh, how long were the days

Billy Bob worked hard for many years
He often got home tired and beat
He deeply missed that lovely girl
Oh, that Billy Bob was so sweet

Katherine Woodward, Grade 8
Grosse Pointe Academy, MI

Friends

When you're blue, they know what to do.
By your side all the way through,
If the sky's gray or bright, there's no need to show fright,
There's the one who will be there through beginning to end.
Friends do come and go, but in the end,
There are those ones who will never let go,
There they will show.

Katie Rezac, Grade 7
Valley View Middle School, MN

Tears of Sorrow

He had a laugh that was contagious as the common cold
When God took him he was not so old
He loved to play and smile away
For him there was never a bad day

From crawling to walking to saying his first words
Whenever he laughed, everyone heard
If he tripped and fell he scarcely cried
He was a delight to us all, that tough little guy

He loved to help his mom and dad
His work was loved, good or bad
He loved to play with all his toys
His blocks and trucks with the girls and boys

We cherished him with all of our hearts
It's so awfully hard for him to part
To take him away, we say it's a sin
But now he's only a little angel in the wind

How did God pry him from our grasping hands?
To this day, I don't understand
We all still dry our tears of sorrow
Rest in peace Andrew Dean Morrow

Anthoni Morrow, Grade 8
Sartell Middle School, MN

Unhappiness

The tears roll down my face like razor blades of the sad sorrow in my mind I can't believe what is happening I will miss my family, friends and my hometown I will miss everything that is here. I will have to make new friends and leave my old ones behind. I hate the feeling every time I think about it because I might have to move. New school, new people, new house won't be the same as my hometown Manistee. I don't want to but it isn't my choice it is my mom and dad's choice my mom doesn't want to move but my dad sort of does. The sad sorrow in my eyes can be painful as I think about it. If I move I will miss my friends and family. I can't believe this is happening. Life isn't as easy as growing up and achieving at everything. I guess I have to move on So goodbye everybody in Manistee.

Garrett Kubiskey, Grade 7
Manistee Middle School, MI

The Hidden Shadow

I used to be you, one who hid her face behind the shadow of everyone else's.
Making yourself invisible by being a mime and disappearing from the scene
You want someone one to notice you but when they do,
You turn right back around with that same fatal shadow representing you.
Sometimes you wish if you could be a person you wanted to be and not this fake figure inside you
When you finally burn the figure out, it is too late
You have ruined the rest of your soul
Your shadow has vanished deep within you and now all you see is your deep dark tan awaiting you for anger and punishment.
You pray to God that you may renew yourself and have a new soul, but you only get one and it is gone
When you here in this cold stoned body you wonder about your ruined soul and you know that at that instant
God has been sending you signals from the very beginning and you are now devastated that you never took light of them
You ruined the very thing that God has given you
You ruined your soul by hiding your shadow

April Phillipi, Grade 8
St Andrew's School, MI

Cry

I smile on the outside knowing I want to cry, you can see the pain, the fear, the disappointment, if you take the time to look deep into my eyes. I want to cry deep down inside, until I realize I'm too strong, powerful, heartless. My emotions all built up inside, why not cry? Why lie saying I'm okay? Why not just break down and cry?

Alexis Luna-Walker, Grade 8
Messmer Preparatory Catholic School, WI

Rain

Rain.
Rain sounds similar to the pitter, patter when you drop colorful marbles on a wood panel floor.
I love the way it sounds against my window, at night to comfort me through a dreamless sleep.
Rain is what lets me stay inside, on a summer day to read an excellent book.
I also love to dance and play, in the rain as if I were dancing around a campfire and singing to campfire songs.
Rain is my comfort and joy, with its glistening drops against my bedroom window.
One thing I enjoy most about the rain is the spring-type smell before a big storm comes,
But I'm not too fond of the wormy smell, after it rains.
Rain.

Lauren Falicki, Grade 7
Cedar Springs Middle School, MI

Fall

I slowly run away from my home knowing that something is coming around the corner. I lay on the ground, cold and left behind waiting for someone to come and rake me up into a pile. The wind is getting more gusty and I shiver. I think about what is next for me. I know that I don't have such a bright future. I think that I'm going to be swept away, put into a big pile with my other brothers and sisters, and decompose into dirt. My skin color has changed. My skin has gone from a light green to mahogany. I have never figured out why I change colors right now. I scream wanting to not be raked up into a pile but I have no choice. There I go gone away from my friends. I yell good bye. Hopefully knowing I will meet back up with them.

Madison Gonsior, Grade 7
Roosevelt Middle School, MN

We Are One (Think About It!)

We are all from different parts of the world
Different origin, different ethnic groups
Yet we are all one people
Rich or poor
Slave or free men
We were all called to enjoy the fruit of one life.
A life that was put in place by the Creator
Of all that has come to being
So let us learn to love
Because if we let hatred and
Racial discrimination separate us
Then who are we if we are being
So loved by nature and yet keep hating
One another?

Emily Wallace, Grade 8
Messmer Preparatory Catholic School, WI

Acceptance

Acceptance is a child,
Eyes full of understanding.
Wrapping her arms around you
in your greatest times of struggle.
She needs you
and you need her
to keep you from falling apart.
She doesn't care what others think about you.
You are you.
In her eyes,
that's all that matters.
She believes that you can do *anything*
and trusts you. Even when you fail her.
She embraces you for who you are
and around her there is no fear of yourself.
Acceptance is a child,
Eyes full of understanding.

Kyra Flowers, Grade 8
Davison Middle School, MI

Beautiful Blue

BLUE is the lake where I like to swim.
It was discovered by an ancient friend, Pim.

BLUE is a blue jay, singing so sweet.
I love to watch it move on its cute, little feet.

BLUE is the description I use when I'm sad.
Instead of feeling down and blue, I'd rather feel glad.

BLUE is the sky, high and bright.
It makes me want to fly a kite.

BLUE is the rain at the end of the day.
Dancing in the rain is my favorite type of play.

Rebekah Varno, Grade 8
Wheatland Center Elementary School, WI

The Family Dog

The family dog has quite a life
She hangs around with no cares or strife.
The dog has no work or chores to do.
She lives her life easier than me or you.
Her favorite things are to sleep and eat
And play with toys or pull the socks from my feet.
She scratches the door, I let her out,
When she wants attention I get pushed with her snout.
When she's bored she barks for no reason
I tell her to stop but she thinks she's pleasin'.
Yuck!!! My dog does her job on the lawn
While I clean it up she gives a big yawn.
Truly my dog is the queen of the place
I thought I was king but that's not the case.
I can't help but asking, after seeing through my fog,
Who is the master and who is the dog?

Tyler Majeski, Grade 8
Seymour Middle School, WI

Late Night

In the darkness of the night
The moon shines bright
The midnight summer's breeze
Sways the branches of the trees

Watching the stars
Listening to the cars
The sun is starting to rise
It's very bright, and burning my eyes

Heading to the beach
Ocean out of my reach
I'm getting near
The beautiful water shining bright and clear

The clouds in the sky
Slowly pass by
Laying in the sand
Wishing I could be holding your hand

Taylor Minard, Grade 8
Sandusky Middle School, MI

Life

Well son, I'll tell you...
Life is not always a wide blue ocean.
It's more like a river,
Always changing as it flows.
Never knowing what's around the next corner.
Whether it be a rough current
With a rocky bottom
But no matter what obstacles you face in the river
No matter how dangerous the river may get
Always know that the river has to end.
And one day you'll find the ocean.

Justin G. Downs, Grade 8
Northwood School, WI

Like a Flower

People are like flowers,
Their petals are their beauty.
It's all we ever think about:
what we look like outwardly
And what other people think.
But soon the petals wilt away;
They become completely forgotten.
What the others remember, though,
Is where your roots remained.

Helen Feest, Grade 7
Abundant Life Christian School, WI

Rain

Drip, drop, drip, drop
It's so dark out.
Drip, drop, drip, drop
The moon is the only light out.
Drip, drop, drip, drop
It's so wet out.
Drip, drop, it's raining hard
As I put a rose on top of your grave.

Jaclynn Grenlin, Grade 8
Bloomingdale Middle School, MI

Where We've Been…

We'll never admit it,
How close we are,
But when it comes down to it,
We're more than stars,
We've known them since preschool,
They're more like sisters and brothers,
Loving is our rule,
They know us more than any other,
But when we leave to go our way,
We know they'll never forget,
When we met on that first day,
And our friendship was set.

Alexandra Hunt, Grade 8
Our Lady Star of the Sea School, MI

Reading

I love reading
it is so fun
to leave this town
for another one
I'm not sure
how it works when
a book traps you
in its own little world
Reading is escaping
from bad things in
your life
Reading is awesome
even if out of sight

Bailey Phillips, Grade 7
Shakopee Area Catholic School, MN

Images

The images in my head are shaking
I can't tell if I'm broken or just breaking
I just want everything I've seen to start retreating
But instead the images in my head keep repeating

I can't tell if all these images in my head are fake,
It gets harder to breathe after every breath I take,
In my head I hear, and feel thunder
It fills my mind with static and puts me in a blunder

The images in my head are making me lose my mind
It hurts me inside to know all the memories I have to leave behind,
I really wish you could understand
But I don't have much time, I'm holding onto one last strand

The images in my head are deceiving,
But the signals in my mind don't seem to be retrieving,
All these images in my head
I can't tell if I am alive or dead.

Kimber Perry, Grade 8
Sandusky Middle School, MI

A Soundtrack to Madness

Step out of the dreaming world
Hang the clocks back on the walls
Ring out your heart and fold up your dreams

Welcome back to reality…
The air is littered with un-pleasantry
It finds your ears and settles in your mind
It whispers softly like a lullaby
It screams profanities and you find yourself in a casual conversation
Who did wrong today?
And does the other have a finger to point the blame?
They stumble drunk and dizzy
They're walking contradictions
The floor is rippling from beneath their feet
And the sky is shaking fiercely
The moon and the sun have turned their backs and left you in the dark
Such a silly word wanders through your mind as stability…what does it mean?
You've heard this word before, though surely you have not seen it
Surely it does not exist in this world turned upside down
Where children scream for silence and find solitude in pain
And spinning round and round, that cannot be the world,
But the record player hard at work, playing the soundtrack to madness.

Sueann Campbell, Grade 9
Clarkston Jr High School, MI

Sports

Basketball, volleyball, softball
Cross Country, cheerleading, track, wrestling
Are all passions of sports that people may or may not have passion for.
They may also love to play the sport or not.
Any person could be different.

Stephanie Earl, Grade 8
Bloomingdale Middle School, MI

For His Sake

I have a shadow and a reflection
but the glass must be two sided.
What is on the other side of the mirror?
I see reflections of a girl I call me
but they produce nothing but
a little spot
in the back of my mind,
behind my ear.
Respond to this.
But we are just flames, walking and waiting
for someone to find us. Tell me
you wake every day half for your own good
and half for another's.

Stephanie Burnham, Grade 9
Clarkston Jr High School, MI

Love

Love is the meaning of life,
It can heal you, hurt you, find you, be with you.
Love can change you into a better person
Love is what makes your heart beat, and it won't be stopped.
Everyone finds love, but only few know what it is.
Your life will be great if you find that special person,
That will cherish every moment that you two are together.
Love cannot be found,
Love always finds you.
No matter who you are,
Love will always find you,
Until you and your love,
Are together forever.

Rachel Steffens, Grade 7
St Roman School, WI

Lucky

When we went out one summer day
We saw you wandering, helplessly
You only weighed three pounds
When you should have weighed thirteen
We took you home
We washed you and groomed you
We fed you, you loved us
Dad said we couldn't keep you, I fought
I wanted you to stay with me, forever
We knew something was not right — what could it be?
Weeks later, something happened
I woke up to your cries of pain
You ran to a closet, you laid down
You gave birth to four beautiful kittens
You washed them and groomed them
You fed them, you loved them
Two went to friends
One went to family
One stayed with you
And you both stayed with us

Ethan Rutherford, Grade 8
St Joseph Catholic Middle School, MI

Writer's Block

I have writer's block
I don't know what to do
The words are just not coming
They just aren't breaking through
Maybe if I thought a while
Something would appear
But I have to sit and write right now
And nothing will come clear

My brain feels like it's clogged up tight
And I just can't seem to think all right
Wow! Is this annoying or what?
My brain and thoughts are trapped up shut!

So as my eyes roam round the room,
Feeling bored, what else to choose?
They come to rest upon a sign, reading,
"It's not about the words you use,
It's what you feel inside."

Maddie Holtze, Grade 7
Rosemount Middle School, MN

The Turtle

The body is round and smooth like a man's bald head.
The shell is very very hard.
The colors of the shell look like a clown's costume.
It reminds me of an ocean.
The shell is green like grass and pink like a sunset.
Blue like sky and orange like carrots.
The sounds of waves crashing into shore is scary.
And hearing fish swim by gets old.
The body becomes a hard rock if its threatened.
Its wrinkly skin is like an old man's.

Quinn Miracle, Grade 8
Chippewa Falls Middle School, WI

Curse of the Verse

My teacher made me write a poem,
and I had to do it all alone
All my friends thought this was cool,
but I thought it was boring and cruel
I told her that I did not want to do it, but she didn't care,
she just looked at me and said life isn't fair
This made me angry and I shouted at her
but she stood her ground and didn't stir
My friends were shocked that I was acting this way,
but I was still able to keep my teacher at bay
My teacher and I argued throughout the day,
but in the end she made me pay
She asked me to write a poem one last time,
and I said no, because I can't rhyme
Since I did not listen, she called home
all because I wouldn't write this poem

Jon Austin Ferri, Grade 8
Our Lady Star of the Sea School, MI

Humming Bird

Oh beautiful humming bird
That dances with the flower,
And stands under a cute bell,
That works hard like a bee.

I do like your sweet humming
On a dark calm midnight scene
With beautiful colors like
Black, purple, white, and much more.

Hands reaching out to the bird.
Fingers poking a flower.
Like a person sucking a
Drink from a long bendy straw.

The many sounds of flowers
Rustling in the fast wind
Sends chills up my spine.

Megan Helland, Grade 8
Chippewa Falls Middle School, WI

The Pointy Tip Shell

A pointy tip shell
Sits on the grainy beach,
This shell is as smooth as silk,
Yet lumpy as the ground,
It is a peachy color,
Like a person's skin.
If you turn it,
It looks like a mole's nose.
It also has blush red in it,
Like if a person is embarrassed.
It's as small as the tip of your nose.

Kali Krumenauer, Grade 8
Chippewa Falls Middle School, WI

Band Class

A quick countdown
Then the melody begins
Sticks tapping
Cheeks puffing
Conductor's arms flailing wildly
Controlling the beat
"Watch me!" she bellows
Fingers flying over keys
Music fills the air

A pause
Whispers begin
Fidgeting
More yelling
A long treacherous cycle
Repeated
Over and over again

Stephanie Marani, Grade 9
Clarkston Jr High School, MI

Friendship

Friends may come and friends may go
Over time when the wind may blow
Some will make you laugh and some will create sorrow
Some will be there through the good times and the bad
You will get in fights but will always make-up
There's always a few bad friends but the good ones you'll know

You and your friend may be close, but you may separate as time goes by
You might travel together on a plane through the sky
You will always remember the good times you had
But you will always remember the fights you had over silly things
As the years go by you will look back and laugh at the fights you had
And no matter how close you are with your friends, they can end up telling you a lie

Samantha Nagle, Grade 7
Bristol Elementary School, WI

Waves

I paddle through the reckless, rebellious waves.
The waves came crashing down, bashing the boat 'round and 'round.
The lightning cracked the thunder roared.
The waves whispered, "Overboard, overboard."
The clouds grew darker, the waves came faster.

I could hear the waves coming faster and faster.
I could hear the wave's laugher in the wind.
Again the lightning cracked, again the thunder roared.
Again the waves whispered, "Overboard, overboard."
The boards on the boat grew weak.
Looking again, I saw there was land.
When I reached the land, my hopes flew.
The wind was cold and it blew my hair.
But then I realized I didn't care.
I gathered some food and began to eat.
The food was bland and the sky bleak.
But I was safe at last, for now at least.

Jessica Reiners, Grade 7
Bristol Elementary School, WI

Mellow Madness

This color makes you dizzy
It reflects from the shining sea
Looks like clouds or
Even the plain sky as you can see

It's the light from heaven
When you sense it with all your senses
It smells like blueberry muffins from the oven
Tastes like water that was locked in a secret place for a long time

The sound of crashing waves
Trying to put itself back to sleep
It's going deep in the ocean
But it might not return as you once seen

Rithdaro Phan, Grade 7
Valley View Middle School, MN

Super Bowl Sunday

S teelers and Cardinals will play
U nder the lights in Tampa
P layoff games they have won
E nding the hopes of the Eagles, Panthers, and Giants
R arely does a team make it this far

B olting out the tunnel they come like horses out of the gate
O utstanding players will play to win
W inners will go home a champion
L osers will go home disappointed

S unday will bring fans cheering
U p on their feet hoping their team will win
N ot a pass will be dropped
D efense will be at their best
A long the sidelines the coaches stand like statues in a park
Y ear after year teams compete very hard to make it this far

Brian Heiden, Grade 8
Seymour Middle School, WI

Memory

Dusty memories as old as time
They sit on a forgotten shelf —
the one way in the back of your mind
Old and forgotten, but so sweet and reminiscent
Hold on to those memories,
cling on tight!
Don't let them slip away…
old, forgotten, and unwanted
Think of the past
Live in the present
Dream of the future
As the sun sets, and the curtain of night falls across the sky
The present day becomes a memory
Tomorrow — the future
Yesterday — already fading away…

Emily Nghiem, Grade 7
Detroit Country Day Middle School, MI

Branson

Smelling the warm and a little bit spicy food
Smelling the chlorine water when hiking to stores

Seeing the pool crystallized
Seeing Yakov Smirnoff
Laughing at his jokes

All the cars rushing past us
People shouting and hollering
Everything overpriced

Hopping into the big pool
The water park as tall as a mountain

Will Schultz, Grade 7
Valley View Middle School, MN

I Am Fire

I am the energy and the warmth.
I wonder how long I will last.
I hear the food sizzling above me.
I see the people circled around me.
I want to heat the shivering.
I am the energy and the warmth.

I pretend to grow like the biggest.
I feel the fiery pain of Hell.
I touch the lifeless branches from trees.
I worry about liquids near me.
I cry but my heat dries the tears.
I am the energy and the warmth.

I understand why people must put me to an end.
I say that there must be a time to go.
I dream that I will one day spread harmlessly.
I try to satisfy the families around me.
I hope to bring life to those grieving.
I am the energy and the warmth.

Zach Tibbetts, Grade 7
West Suburban Christian Academy, WI

Angels

A white soft feather
A flutter in the sky
A halo over my head, someone watching over me
I know that no one can see but I still know is there
Always by my side
That soft feather and halo will always be over me, watching me
Angles are over my head that I know are there!

Bergindy Klaetsch, Grade 8
Spring Hill School, WI

My Dog

"That dog is crazy!"
I told myself
He jumps and runs and bites himself
He chews and scratches
Destroys the park
And keeps you up far after dark
He steals your socks
And eats a shoe
Not caring if it belongs to you
He sleeps on the couch
Instead of the rug
With a look on his face that surely is smug
He'll take all his toys
And tear them to shreds
Until left on your floor is a big pile of thread
But then he'll get tired
And lay on your lap
And I say to myself
"How long will this last?"

Becky Schultz, Grade 7
Core Knowledge Charter School, WI

Winter's

Winter's silent snow
The wind is howling back
As the white grass gleams

Meckeal Gates, Grade 7
Langston Hughes Academy, MI

The Day You Left Me

Wondering why you left me —
it makes me sad and angry
all at the same time.
But knowing you're in a better place,
makes me feel better.

Seeing you lay in the casket,
made me cry.
All the mixed smells,
like the flowers and perfumes,
burned my nose.
Everyone was crying,
missing you,
but wishing
they were you,
all the same.

I sure do miss you
Great Grandma,
and I can't wait
to see you again.

Amanda DeForest, Grade 9
Niles Sr High School, MI

Speak

Oh Holy Father,
Speak to me.
I am waiting here,
Just listening.

I want to know,
That You are there.
So prove Yourself,
Answer just one prayer.

I want to know,
What You are doing.
What You want me to say,
And what You want me to do.

I can't do this alone,
I need You right now.
So come to me Lord,
And let me hear Your sound.

I'm listening God.
I'm ready now.

Hannah Plys, Grade 9
Lakeview Christian Academy, MN

My Brother

He is silly and little,
Brown and funny,
He makes me happy,
When I am sad.
He makes me smile,
When times are blue.
He is always there,
When I need him
That's the reason,
The reason I love him so much.
I dedicate this poem,
To my little brother,
Davont'e Mercer.
Even though we may fuss,
and we may fight.
That doesn't mean anything.
I LOVE YOU!

Kachay Miller, Grade 8
Gesu Catholic School, MI

Sister Bay

Traveling to Sister Bay
Hope my father knows the way
If he doesn't mom will say…

Left my brother in Green Bay
All the week he'll be away
Without him I'll have fun and play

Cross the bridge at Sister Bay
Maybe dad does know the way
Getting close to where we'll stay

Found the cottage, by another bay
Swans in water, white and grey
I like this place day after day.

Anna Gergen, Grade 7
St Katharine Drexel School, WI

Life

For the first time
I feel wanted
For the first time
I've been invited
For the first time
I'm not standing all alone

I feel like I can spread my wings
and I can soar
through all the hate and all the war
there's still love in people's hearts
and kindness in peoples' souls

But if there's no one standing we all fall.

Denise Zahran, Grade 8
St Roman School, WI

where

I've looked inside and out
Where are you?
Traveling in space
Or just down the block?
My question has not been fulfilled
I am determined to find you
My eternal best friend.

Cali Sledge, Grade 7
Gerisch Middle School, MI

High and Low

High things are beautiful:
Airplanes racing through the sky,
And puffy white clouds on a sunny day.
The moon at night is up so high.
Birds fly by the snow capped mountains,
The luminous sun is always bright.
Monstrous trees,
And the stars at night.

Low things are beautiful:
Pebbles scattered on the ground,
A man's voice.
Snails creep by without a sound.
How someone feels when they're sad.
Shoes squeak on the floor,
Rugs spread across a house,
And mice creep under doors.

Danijela Krstic, Grade 8
Pilgrim Park Middle School, WI

Life

Live in the Flames
Dance in passion
Find a Heart

Live in the Water
Flow with the waves
Your guide to your dreams

Live in the mountains
Withstand your problems
Find your Strengths

Live in the Winds
Break through the barriers
Persevere

Live in the Elements
Find your heart
Guide your dreams
Find your strengths
Persevere
Life

Dominique Jones, Grade 9
Wabasha-Kellogg High School, MN

Turtle Ball

It is a ball
Or is it a shell
Like a butterfly in symmetry
Hoping not to hear the crack of bat and ball
Over the fence it might go

Resting like an unused ball
Lazy as can be
Waiting for a player
To throw it with a whoosh against the wall
Or simply set it down

Pale white shell
Bleeding through the stitches
Turquoise green body
Confused as if it fell
Only to see it as a dandy dream

Andy Snider, Grade 8
Chippewa Falls Middle School, WI

Mary

There was this girl named Mary,
Who had a husband named Gary.
He had twenty-eight toes,
a big, juicy nose,
and his body was really hairy.

Sammy LeMay, Grade 8
Wheatland Center Elementary School, WI

Frostbitten

A touch to the nose and I am frostbitten.
A thirty below winter night.
The telephone pole has two, three, four layers of ice.
Nothing else is in sight.

The wind gusts blowing snow, slate, and ice everywhere,
The sky dark, gloomy, and gray,
I take baby steps, my knees numb,
Three hours until the light of day.

The snow twirls and dances in the sky,
My scarf pulls and chokes my neck,
Without it I am frostbitten,
Every minute I check.

My gray hat flies off with the snow,
They soar and so does my mitten,
I look at my finger and it gets darker and darker,
Until it is frostbitten.

I get to my house and take off my jacket,
And throw away my one mitten,
I lay by the fire and look down at my fingers,
They had become frostbitten.

Abbie Chmelka, Grade 8
Seymour Middle School, WI

Mom

Anna
Thoughtful, supportive
Loving, caring, thinking
She helps me when I am in need of her assistance.
Mom

Makaiah Smith, Grade 7
Langston Hughes Academy, MI

Not Trusting

Dear Parents,
You say this, you say that.
You say yes, you say no.
You tell me I can, you tell me I can't.
You can't make up your mind.

Why would you tell all those lies?
Do you really think I'm that blind?
Did you think I wouldn't notice?
Is it that you don't trust him?

You don't even like me baby-sitting.
You won't even let me make cookies with him.
You can't stand me being there without her.
You think she'd stop everything.

When will you realize nothing is happening?
Can you honestly feel he would disrespect you?
How can I trust you if there's no way to?
Is it that you don't trust me?
— The Angry One

Kerilyn Elrich, Grade 8
Lake Fenton Middle School, MI

School

Some people say
School is fun,
Boring,
Bad,
Weird,
But the people that say,
It is bad,
They don't know,
What they are saying,
School is good because you can,
Meet new people,
Get into college,
Get jobs if you stay in school,
When people say bad things about school,
They don't know what they are talking about,
So when you think about school,
Make sure you think of good things,
And you should just stay in school,
So think before you say something bad.

Jasmine Long, Grade 7
Centreville Jr High School, MI

So Many

So many questions
not answered
so many lives
wiped away
so many pointless fights
take place
so many Men and Women
fighting
so many cries
for help
so many sighs
of pain
so much destruction
today

So many Americans
fighting
not for them
So many Americans
fighting for peace,
in Iraq.

Eric Wagner, Grade 7
Shakopee Area Catholic School, MN

9/11

Time to act quickly
Time to act fast
If they didn't
The opportunity would pass
A whole new enemy
A whole new threat
If the terrorists won
The whole country would fret
Hearts racing
Tempers flaring
Passengers fighting
A whole new threat, they are facing
The terrorists were defeated
At what cost
Oh, what cost
At least they succeeded
Now the time has passed
The passengers are praised
They may be dead
But at least their legend will last

Brian Jaskolski, Grade 8
Fairview Charter School, WI

School

School, School, School,
It isn't very cool,
The work is too much,
And, ugh, the school lunch,
Summer is gonna rule!

Lynnzee Hertzner, Grade 7
Northwood School, WI

Dreaming of Her

Thump, thump, the beat of her wings. Soaring, flying above the clouds.
Warm scales keeping me awake. Always going, never stopping.

Soaring, flying above the clouds. Unmatched beauty, radiant blue,
Always going, never stopping. Her thoughts, part of mine.

Unmatched beauty, radiant blue. Connected, part of me.
Her thoughts part of mine. Gentle giant, raging beast.

Connected, part of me. One with me, yet another person.
Gentle giant, raging beast. Protecting, watching over me.

One with me, yet another person. My heart aches without her here.
Protecting, watching over me. Emptiness without her.

My heart aches without her here. My companion, my protection.
Emptiness without her. My dragon forever.

My companion, my protection. And then I wake up from my dream.
My dragon forever. Thump, thump the beat of her wings.

Eric Busch, Grade 8
St John Lutheran School, MI

Forest Green

She cries emerald color crystals over the muggy forest and sharp, pointed rocks
Floating away in the swamp as the seagulls sing their song
Frogs rested on the stones floating through the olive colored lake
Jumping into the fog, landing with a plop
The dirt moves to fit the animal, the sun's reflection shining in the animal's eyes
As the day comes to an end, the leaves drip water on the still forest
Animals go to their homes, owls hoot looking for prey
Mice scurry away hiding under the tall grass
The ground, cold and wet, leaves still dripping
Branches lay on the ground blown away from their trees
Morning comes and brings daylight to the peaceful forest
Lizards lay on burning hot moss-covered rocks
The canvas over head keeps them happily shaded
Croaking begins as the girl in the sky cries more jewels

Amber Pajur, Grade 8
Centennial Middle School, MI

Love

Love can be
The color red like an inferno on top of water
Hot like a heat wave starting at my toe and ending at the end of my hair
Sounds like beautiful birds wiping their wings across the silent sea,
Tastes like the chocolate covered strawberry that dances in my mouth
Smells like the soft musk that fills my mind and never escapes.
Looks like the most beautiful fantasy with doves sleeping on clouds
Feels like the wind lightly brushing against my face like silk
Love moves like ballroom dancers
Perfectly in sync with each other
Perfectly graceful
Perfect

Destinee Russell, Grade 7
Manistee Middle School, MI

Simonelli

Cars racing down the street.
Dust rising up from the dirt road as it is fog.
Houses far apart.
B M Y
U P street.
As it rains, the ditches flood and mud is made.
P
U
Ditches b u b b l e
Quiet on the road.
Peace on this road.

Matthew Russell, Grade 7
Whitehall Jr High School, MI

Mother

O mother what have you done
You didn't think it was wrong
She's been gone for so long
Or has she
Her heartbeat still lingers
When you close your eyes, you see her little fingers
You see her face in the mirror
Every time you cry you feel her pain
The regret will always remain
Your baby's face stuck in your brain
Did you ever think about how she was slain
You thought it would be easy to let go
Like it never even happened
The smile on her face
Gone without a trace
O mother what have you done

Lee Rice, Grade 9
Kingsford High School, MI

My Life Has...

My life has love
When all my friends and family care
My life has anger
When times I just want to let it out
My life has bravery
When I feel like I can do it
My life has boldness
When I am told I stand out more than others
My life has happiness
When I see the sunshine smile at me
My life has sadness
When something tragic happens
My life has eagerness
When I am ready for something to happen
My life has hope
When I have it for my friends and family
My life has emotions

Kylie Combs, Grade 9
Hartland High School, MI

I Am a Sister

I am a sister
I wonder if EJ will ever talk
I hear silence
I see you all day long
I want to hear your voice
I am a sister

I pretend you can talk and I can hear your voice
I feel upset
I touch the air
I worry if you will ever be able to talk
I cry knowing you never will
I am a sister

I understand your pain
I say you are the best brother
I dream of the things you want to say
I try to help
I hope you understand
I am a sister

Emmie Mattson, Grade 8
Central Middle School, MI

Dreamers

The desire burns
As dreamers reveal their immense passion

It feels like something small,
Growing steadily

They own their destiny
For the path traveled belongs to no one else

It looks like innocent children,
Invincible to reality or reason

When given the fork in the road,
Hesitation is not touched upon

It smells like sweat
After the hard work that has been put in

Believing in themselves is key
For not even the sky is a limit for them

It tastes like the satisfaction
Of reaching a dream

They're young, and they're brave
And so very spirited

So is it a dream?
Or could it be just what it sounds like,
Determination.

Kelsey Smith, Grade 9
Clarkston Jr High School, MI

The Best Moments

The best moments in life,
are filled with happiness and joy,
heart pounding on fire,
proud family congratulates you,
and boasting to friends,
how special you are to them.
A ray of sunshine is upon you,
God putting a spotlight on you,
for everyone to recognize.
The day goes on,
the moment is savored,
this path comes to end.
Another path will come along,
and it will happen all again.

Anne Crowley, Grade 7
Our Lady Star of the Sea School, MI

To Move On

To feel the pain like there is no misery,
To hum a tune when there is no music,
To see something when it is not there.
To move on,
To love,
To be happy.

Lulu Gilmore, Grade 8
Spring Hill School, WI

Stars

Stars are like lights,
leading you through the night,
making sure you go the right way.
Stars are like lights,
they help you see,
that you can be anything you want to be.
Stars are like lights,
that twinkle in the sky,
making sure that you get by.
Stars are like lights,
shiny and bright,
they are like mini flashlights.

Brittany Sweeter, Grade 8
Middle School at Parkside, MI

Love

My heart says love is a funny thing
Sometimes it can really sting
Every time that she walks past
My heart starts beating really fast

Love is a special thing
Love is sweet candy
It makes you joyful and happy
Love has many meanings
Love is a special thing

Quinn Oteman, Grade 8
Jerstad Agerholm Middle School, WI

The Silver Lining

I believe in the kindness buried in people's hearts,
The innocence hidden inside tainted adults,
The humanity of unreachable murderers,
The simple solutions to complex problems,
The friendship shown between misunderstood enemies,
Joyous, distant, lonely

But believing in love at first sight is merely vanity.

I believe in gateways that will send you to other worlds,
I believe in dreams that will steal you away,
I believe in faraway places filled with kind people,
Adventure, love, hope

And I believe in the fact that the most beautiful of rainbows only appear
After the fiercest of storms.

Kazoua A. Yang, Grade 9
Oak Creek High School, WI

What a Fire Extinguisher Really Is...

The hefty, massive, and bulky case hanging on the corner of a wall
With the luminous fire extinguisher inside,
Like a friend, there when you need them,
Lost if they weren't there.

If you were to remove the extinguisher from the wall,
The extinguisher will perform its job,
Like a friend, when you are in trouble,
They are there.

Just hanging, day by day,
Frequently passing them by,
Until you need them the most
You never realize that they are there.

Taking them for granted
Seldom on your mind,
But always wondering
How long they will be there.

The mirror, unimportant, trivial case hanging on the corner of a wall,
With the incandescent fire extinguisher inside,
Like a friend, lost if they were to vanish,
But they will always be there.

Renee Morency, Grade 9
Clarkston Jr High School, MI

Snow

It comes in silent like the bird in the forest flapping its wings so softly.
Snow freezes the ground and covers everything in a layer of ice.
Over the winter the snow melts and refreezes over and over again.
In the north is where it goes like little diamonds falling from the sky.
When the early spring wind comes in, the snow disappears leaving only puddles.

Rosemarie Urban, Grade 7
Richmond Middle School, MI

Chains

I'm stuck in these chains that no one can see
They're invisible to everyone, everyone but me
They're holding me back from so much I can say
But here I am trying to get outta them every day
I tug and I pull with all of my might
But there they still are, they are on me so tight
I'm trapped inside these chains, with not a thing to set me free
And I know the only person to get me out of them would be me
I think so hard of what it could be
What's the simple thing that would set me free
Not love, not trust, not friends or honesty
Finally I know the one solution would be to believe
When I believe that I am found
I stand up proudly and the chains fall to the ground
But when I feel stuck with no way out
These chains make me miserable so I cry and I pout
There are times I feel trapped and, I forget to believe
But, when I remember I feel so relieved
Life can be tough, it can frustrate you and make you mad
But just live through it and, take the good with the bad.

Liz Garcia, Grade 9
Holland High School, MI

A Neighbor

A neighbor is someone you live by.
It's a second friend of mine.
Someone you can grow up with.
Someone that you can show up with.

They give you pride and a right mind
exactly at the right time.
Whenever you're down or need a pal you look
to the side and say, "There's my Second Friend of Mine."

Jordan Jones, Grade 8
Gesu Catholic School, MI

This Is True

This is good, this is true
It's something needed to be understood,
Get a clue!
This is what's important,
Someone you need to pursue.
This is the Lord.
He's always there,
Even when He's ignored.
When you laugh or cry,
When you're happy,
Or just want to die.
God is everywhere, and He sees every tear,
When no one cares, and you let no one near.
When no hope is there, you should know,
He listens to every prayer
So stop by to Him, and say "Hello"
He's there, no matter where you go.

Grace Schumacher, Grade 9
Lakeview Christian Academy, MN

When a Spring Day Comes

Slowly the snow will melt away
And the grass will poke through on a sunny day.
The trees seem to say that they're ready for spring.
If only the snow would no longer cling.

The flowers anticipate a colorful blossom.
To see such a sight would be awesome.
The icy lakes will soon defrost
Revealing the water that was briefly lost.

The robin is awakened by the morning sunlight.
I see his colors so pretty and bright.
He warns his friends of the new season sprouting.
They soon venture off on an enjoyable outing.

The children count the minutes on the clock
Until their imaginations unlock.
The sun enraptures the earth
With her brightness and mirth.

Before this first spring day ends
We must walk outdoors with our friends
To thank God for this heavenly day
For he has created this beautiful display.

Molly LeBlanc, Grade 9
St Thomas More Academy, MI

Betrayed

The notes so light they'd fly away
Became the notes of yesterday.
The tune that used to ease my soul
Grips so tight I lose control.

Sweet and smooth, beauty in each light
Darkness seems to win its fight.
My hands ache for something to hold
The fire you started is dead and cold.

So close I thought we'd never part
You left me here, you broke my heart.
Told you my secrets, every one
The day you went you took my sun.

I wish I'd never seen your face
Became addicted to your embrace.
If you had never caught my eye
If you had left me, let me die.

The pain that kills me wouldn't be
Death in your eyes I wouldn't see.
Suffocating; alone I can't live like this
Nothing without you, I accept death's kiss.

Christina Laidler, Grade 8
Perry Middle School, MI

The Bright Light at the End of the Barrel

roses are red, violets are blue, the world is cruel, and our contraptions crude, with diesel and corn, conflicts are bound, like an evil dark bomb, we wreck everything in our paths, who hurts the most, or what does the most damage, is not the question but they think advantage, 'tis not the bomb the atom or gun, 'tis not the person the rock the stick the string, 'tis the choice the hate the thought, no one is evil just mislead by an act, like the work of Hitler or Himler or Osama, the world can be scary, but we must help these people, not to destroy to wreck with fury, but to treat to love and show them so dearly, that life's always not fair happy or understood, but we must still try for the good, and this is the end, for I say farewell my friend, and please help others, for they're probably in despair, life is hard but doing right is harder.

Adrian Duczak, Grade 8
Washington Middle School, WI

Sitting Here Spinning Out of Control

Sitting here spinning out of control
Thinking of you and only you
How can I stop? How can I stay still and think of other things besides you
Trying so hard to stop spinning
I will not stop and, I will never stop
Spinning around and around is a good thing
I cannot find everything while standing still
I need to search for answers but, this answer I do not want to be solved
I will keep this problem to my grave and beyond my grave
I love this problem and I cannot go away
This problem has been chained to my heart
And these chains cannot break for they were formed by God himself
God was telling me not to solve this problem
I will fight for this problem
I will protect this problem from everyone who believes I should get away from this problem
This problem is good for me and I am good for her
Things always turn out good
I just need to wait for the time and the time will come
Soon the answer will come the answer will be good though it will be good for both of us
God only knows how she and I will be but before I know it she and I will be together forever.

Jacob Klusman, Grade 8
St Roman School, WI

My First Deer

It was a cool crisp morning as I got out of bed, I had thoughts of twelve pointers running through my head.
I crept downstairs to see if the others were awake, as I put on my orange and loaded my gun I started to shake.
We snuck outside all ready to go, said good luck, but kept it low.
My dad led the way out to the stand, he climbed up first and then gave me a hand.
We were sitting for almost an hour, just looking out of the tower.
When I heard a crack of leaves, I started praying, please!
I quickly grabbed my gun, but it started to run.
It ran to a tree and took a stop, I took the safety off, and then gave it a pop.
I thought I missed, so I just sat there and hissed.
Later on I saw it down, Oh man! I didn't frown.
I had a big smile, as I looked for a while.
On the way back to the cabin, I just couldn't stop gabbin'.
When I got inside, I had a big smirk, the others thought I lied so they called me a jerk.
Three of us went to look for my deer, we walked and walked so I knew we were near.
I saw it lying there on the ground, we took some pictures without a sound.
My dad and uncle dragged it out, they pulled and pulled and pulled about.
Everyone crowded around to see the big buck, they all said, "Geezz, girl you suck."
But I knew they were all proud, because they all were so loud.
It was the end of my hunting season, but next year a fourteen pointer would be my reason.

Shalyn Kuehnl, Grade 8
Seymour Middle School, WI

For Mom

Mom I am writing this poem for you
Because I know you love me too
The way you care the way you talk
The way you smile the way you walk
I love you even at your worst
Even when you take me out and put Annah first!
Just Kidding

You are my sun
You are my light
And knowing that you are Mommie
That means you are my life

I love you Mommie I say that all the time I know
Even when I act up and do bad things also
I want you to know that I appreciate you and love you till I die
And knowing that you love me makes me feel like I want to cry

This whole poem was to tell you that I love you
Have a Happy Mother's Day
Maybe one day I will be a mother as good too!

Mommie!
This is 4 you!

Summer Hunt, Grade 8
Gesu Catholic School, MI

The Light at Hiroshima

I was minding my own business
When a blinding light fascinated me
But a millisecond before my observations finished
This light I'd never again see

When a blinding light fascinated me
Thoughts were racing through my head
The light I'd never again see
For I realized I was dead

Thoughts were racing through my head
I wondered what would be in my legacy
For I realized I was dead
And the city's gates opened wide before me

I wondered what would be in my legacy
As my shadow forever imprinted on the tower
And the city's gates opened wide before me
The pearls shines like the grass after an April shower

As my shadow forever imprinted on the tower
But a millisecond before my observations finished
The pearls shined like the grass after an April shower
I was minding my own business

Stephanie Glyzewski, Grade 7
West Suburban Christian Academy, WI

Earliest Memory

On the couch
Sleeping
Dreaming, relaxed, quiet
Blanket of dreams
Ageless

Emerson Kuhn, Grade 7
Elkhart Lake Elementary-Middle School, WI

Nature's Beauty

I lay in the grass on a rainy morning
My eyes are closed and I'm just thinking
Above me the sun starts to shine
I hear birds chirping
I open my eyes and see a rainbow
I try and look for comfort
I look again and see life
I feel sad and happy at the same time
I am impressed with nature's beauty
I look again I see anger, happy, excited, bored, beauty, fun, sad
As if it represented people and emotions
Everything I see reminds me of myself
Contributing to the beauty above me
But I look again in hopes to find relaxation
In hopes God hears my prayers and in hope I find happiness
Yet I know life is a rainbow
There will always be ups and downs
And there might not always be that pot of gold waiting for me
I hope life takes me the way I want and
I hope the rainbow never disappears.

Kayla Holmes, Grade 9
Clarkston Jr High School, MI

Winchester

He is mine, a man's best friend.
A companion.
He is smelly, but warm like a burning fire.
He loves attention and good belly rubs.
He is my dog,
My best friend.

When times are bad, his warm coat surrounds me
Like an ocean of comfort and love.
He hugs me, he tells me everything will be okay.
He is sad when I am sad.
He talks with me,
He walks by me wherever I go.
His brown fur wraps me up tight, a blanket of kindness.
He begs to go out, I let him.
He leaps through snow,
He wants me to play too, that dog.

He whitewashes himself to show fun
He makes me feel better.
He always does.

Courtney Wilton, Grade 8
Paw Paw Middle School, MI

Forgotten

I am forgotten.
Lost within a crowd,
I want to be someone,
But I have given into the pressure.
Now I am no one —
A forgotten soul,
To whom it seems as if being original
Is a great challenge.
Thus, here I remain,
Waiting for the crowd to move
So I may follow them
To the ends of time.
My existence is diminished
To whatever the crowd will do —
Their decisions mine,
Their ideas mine,
Leaving me forgotten and
Lost within this crowd.

Ioana Grosu, Grade 8
Boulan Park Middle School, MI

Friends

Friends aren't just ordinary people,
They will always be there.
Friends are breathtaking.

They are there for you,
When you are broken.
Friends are breathtaking.

They care for you,
When you are ill or sad.
Friends are breathtaking.

They laugh with you,
When you laugh.
Friends are breathtaking.

They make you smile,
When you might not want to.
Friends are breathtaking.

They love you,
And always will no matter what.
Friends are breathtaking.

Heidi Veenstra, Grade 7
Springfield School, MN

The Beach

Walking along the shore,
Jumping in the waves,
Slathering on sunscreen,
And basking in the sun.
My day at the beach…

Claire Bouret, Grade 8
Our Lady Star of the Sea School, MI

Fishes

Fish swim in the lake
There's funny fish everywhere
Fishing from a dock

Blue skies overhead
I'm going to get a fish
Gonna feel a tug

My pole starts to bend
I'm straining to stay on land
Hope my line doesn't break

I'm starting to slide
My line is going to snap
Good bye giant fish

My line just busted
I am on my derriere
My dad is coming

I'm very depressed
But there's always tomorrow
Fish swim in a lake.

Robin Reedy, Grade 8
Seymour Middle School, WI

The Snowy Day

There is no school today,
I don't know what to do.
I just ate lunch and no one is home,
I think there's nothing to do.
The house is empty and I'm all alone.

The computer would be great to use,
If only I had a connection.
I could take a nap,
But then I would lose time.
The house is empty and I'm all alone.

I could go outside to play,
But the whiteout makes it hard to see.
I still don't know what to do,
At home on this snowy day.
The house is empty and I'm all alone.

Luke Reiner, Grade 7
Springfield School, MN

Silence

Silence is golden in the night.
Silence is a part of the world.
Silence is good when you sleep.
Silence is good at some moments.
We need silence in our lives.
We need it even if we think not.

Joseph Kruemmer, Grade 8
Roseville Jr High School, MI

Kid?

Why must we
Grow up?
Why can't we
Be a kid?

Not caring for
Things around us.
Not thinking
Before we act.

Not knowing what
We are doing.
Not having
A stressed out life.

So why can't we
Be a kid?
While we
Still are.

John Leja, Grade 8
Adams Friendship Middle School, WI

The Mark of Winter

One almost bare tree
Grasped at its final leaf,
But its strength was nothing
Compared to the
Frigid, stinging gust.
With one mighty, swift blow,
The aged and weary leaf
Swirled through the air
And gracefully floated
Down to join its siblings.
Once the final leaf
Settled down,
The long winter approached.
All things yawned gently
And sleepily
As a delicate blanket of snow
Covered them up
As if it was a mother
Covering up her children.

Annie Xiao, Grade 9
Troy High School, MI

Fishing

The boat rocks back and forth
All day on the water
Back and forth
All of the sudden wham
It's huge bass
All the waiting
Paid off

Justin Couturier, Grade 7
Assumption BVM School, MI

I Pretend

I pretend not to miss you
I feel sad and mad when I think about you
I touch your soft hands in my dreams
I worry about you still
I try not to cry…

Allison Edwards, Grade 8
Central Middle School, MI

Paint Strokes

A blank paper sitting on my desk
Waiting for me to give it color and light
Give it movement and make it come to life
I gently take out my soft brush
Wipe it in the cool paint
Slowly stroking it against the canvas
Swirling and twirling
Beautiful lines overflowing the page
Brightness and darkness
Depending on my mood
Gorgeous colors far and wide
Pink, yellow, green and blue
So many to choose from
It's hard to make a decision
I wipe my brush in the paint once more
Covering the sheet with an abundance of designs
Flowers and trees
People and animals
The images jump out at me
Birds are flying around my room
Then I remember, it's just my imagination

Emilee Anderson, Grade 7
South Middle School, WI

Hello! Goodbye…

It doesn't matter if you're pretty,
Or if you've got a commercial smile…
You're not getting any pity!
You've had it for a while.
You've taken your friends for granted,
And they're getting upset —
Your life is going slanted,
And you've got not rest.
Now I'm screaming and my throat's running dry,
My mind's a wreck, but my heart wants to try;
I want to tell you everything but with no lie,
But everything I say, I know you will deny.
I'm asking for your attention,
For you to listen please!
I'm asking for us to sit down,
To get through this with ease.
I'm too afraid to find out the outcome of my actions;
To figure out what you'll do;
But I'm eager to see your reaction,
Me, you'll never fool.

Tina Nguyen, Grade 7
Valley View Middle School, MN

St. Patrick's Day

S eeing green everywhere I go,
T elling myths about leprechauns,

P eople search for the pot of gold,
A ll the people look for the rainbow,
T ons of leprechauns dance around,
R eady for St. Patrick's Day,
I 'll see one coming my way,
C hasing the pot of gold,
K ids get ready for St. Patrick's Day
S o let's enjoy this day!

D ear leprechauns, all the children want a pot of gold.
A ll the kids sing with joy,
Y esterday was the best day ever!

Christen Tilkens, Grade 8
Seymour Middle School, WI

Headache

Grew up with a lot of fights
There were too many crazy nights;
While tears were running down my face
My mom kept tumbling and broke a vase;
Too much to drink:
Too much to say:
She wouldn't let us take her to the doctor anyway;

So I told my mom to stop this mess
I told my mom to stop this stress;
But she kept on doing it all the time
She said "Don't worry, I'll be just fine"
Too much to drink
This is too much I said
Then died alone with a headache in her head

Alicia Van Slyke, Grade 8
Spring Hill School, WI

Your Lies

Inside your eyes
All I see is lies
Your bitter selfish twisted truth
All I can see when I look at you is lies

You think no one knows
You think it is all a show
You think you're cool the way you push away what's right
You make everyone feel so low

When you look at me you burn holes in my head
All you ever bring is dread
You try to hide it but it's obvious
Your life will soon snap just like a thread

Abigail McLain, Grade 7
Centreville Jr High School, MI

Pudding

I like to eat pudding
It is really good
I like to eat pudding
All people really should

I like to eat it day and night
And all around the house
Some animals might like it too
Maybe even a mouse

Pudding can be chocolate
Or many different flavors
Just make it last forever
So you can really savor

Pudding is delicious
That's all that I can say
Everyone can eat it
Every night and every day

Brenna Sibley, Grade 7
St Roman School, WI

Ballerinas

Slip on the shoe,
instantly become a ballerina.
Tighten the gleaming pink ribbons.
The secure feeling around the ankle.
Stand up,
grow tall above all life's concerns.
Pushing the body to its limits.
Never to give up or back down.
Take off the shoes.
Bright red blistering toes,
but go on with life.
See those shoes another day.
Welcome to the life of a ballerina.

Hannah Jurcich, Grade 7
Whitehall Jr High School, MI

The Courtyard

The trees grow strong and tall
and house the birds that sing
The branches burst with color
announcing the arrival of spring.

The breaking of dawn
The sky bright blue
The shining of the sun
The green grass sprinkled with dew.

The sweet whisper of the wind
that blows my hair
I couldn't leave
wouldn't dare.

Jenna Shepard, Grade 9
Clarkston Jr High School, MI

The Seasons

Spring is here already
life wakes up, trees turn green, flowers grow, snow melts
Relaxing and warm

Summer starts faster
School ends, water warms, sun shines, it doesn't last long
Sunny, hot

Fall takes over
Vacation ends, leaves turn orange, life takes a break, ground freezes
Depressing, cool

Winter creeps in
People freeze, animals hibernate, some enjoy snow and some don't
Cold, crisp

Then spring is here again

Ethan Hau, Grade 7
Elkhart Lake Elementary-Middle School, WI

You

Deep in autumn, given lack of tire tracks and tiny cards
For three months: she sat in desperate silence
Then the tears — hard, fast, and angry
You bit your lip — shrank away.
She dug her nails into something no longer there
Leaving shredded hearts and shaking
Fingertips.
Her tears struck a chord
Where misspelled words were shouted
And hatred burned over a hundred miles
Until bitterness...ran itself out
Until your heart was dipped in guilt and mine in
Confusion.
Your words ricocheted around my head
Our minds touched, first with biting nails, then with careful fingertips
We lived for those brief moments
Carefully un-avoiding and breathing every moment for each other
Keys sticky with sweat and wait
I fooled myself into believing in forever
That I was worth what she was not.

Melissa Pavlik, Grade 9
Clarkston Jr High School, MI

Yes + Faith = Everything!

Yes, faith is a steady mountain lifted from its base!
Yes, faith is a turn directing a flowing river off its rough course!
Yes, faith is the firm achievement to an impossible race!
Yes, faith is a still lion as he roars!
Yes, faith is a tender baby as it giggles!
Yes, faith is a fawn as she leaps through the forest by her mother's side!
Yes, faith is the only thing!
Yes, faith is everything!
Yes, we got faith!

Dana Koch, Grade 8
Cedar Grove-Belgium Middle School, WI

The End of Something Special

The night we've all been waiting for
We'll remember forever

I hope things won't change if I decide to follow through
Bought the perfect outfit
This 1 and only occasion

Once it's over I'll have more decisions, more choices
But I'll admit I'm scared
My tears are like waterfalls

What hurts the most is saying goodbye
Although it's suppose to be a happy time
Balloons and music
A room filled with the ones I adore

But it's also the end
The end of something special
Once I walk across that stage it's over
And now all that's left are the memories

Dominque Murrell, Grade 8
Washington Middle School, WI

Colors: Black

There is no light to guide your way;
You start to wonder if it will ever be day.
It's as dark and eerie as a Halloween night.
There's only one feeling you feel; that's fright.
You feel as small as a mouse in the jungle.
You do not walk for fear you will stumble
Over something that is like this Halloween night.
Something that will fill you with more and more fright.
You ask yourself "Will I ever get out of this maze?
How long will this keep up? More than a day?
I will never get out of this as it may seem."
Until you wake up, and realize it was all just a dream.

Kalena Johnson, Grade 7
Roosevelt Middle School, MN

Rain

When our Earth gets touched by the rain,
We feel its effects very much so.
It brings us back to a level where we are sane.
Rain is calming, peaceful, and brings all of us to ease.
Rain trickling down a cool green plain,
Gives you a peace of mind.
Rain may also remind us of suffering and pain.
A lost loved one will bring much suffering.
So much that it will hurt to hear their name.
Rain is like darkness,
It may be unpleasant, but there is always an end.
It all leads back to Rain.

Courtney Welch, Grade 8
St Roman School, WI

A True Friend

Someone who cares,
A person who loves and shares.
Someone who is there for you,
To pull you back when you have fallen down,
Or to put a smile on your face when it is in a frown.
Someone who will stand up for you,
And never leave you hanging.
A person who will spend time to help you,
If you have gotten hurt.
Or someone who will protect you,
If you're in a bad situation.
Or someone who will fight for you,
Like lions fight for their prey.
And if that person leaves you,
You know they're not your friend.
But don't lose hope too quickly,
Because there are plenty to last 'till the end!

Emma Idzikowski, Grade 8
Fairview Charter School, WI

New Shoes

The best thing in my life to me is new shoes.
With a pair on my feet I can chase away my blues.
The best thing I love is that new shoe smell.
People say that's silly, so that I don't tell.
That new shoe sole and that new shoe shine.
My shoe's so fresh, they blow my bestie's mind.
I want new shoes all the time.
When you see me outside you better recognize.
I'm that new shoe queen and that's no lie.

Sarafina Scott, Grade 7
Langston Hughes Academy, MI

Have You Ever...

Have you ever,
Have you ever watched
As someone you loved was hurt?
Have you ever,
Have you ever felt
So useless, so naive,
When you watched as they
Slipped away?
Have you ever,
Have you ever truly wondered
If there was a place beyond earth,
For someone who was dying?
Have you ever,
Have you ever waited
Waited to find out if you'd have to get a new black dress
For the funeral of someone you watched die?
Have you ever,
Have you ever looked at a loved one
And remembered the time they nearly died before your eyes?
I have.

Rachel Martens, Grade 9
Hortonville High School, WI

The Fumbling Football Game

The fumbling fearsome figures ran down
The ball in midair did not yield
The clipping of the safety player
Left him at the bottom of the layer.

The quarterback he did call
That the receiver would catch the ball;
He ran and rushed and raised his arm,
The tackle came and did no harm.

Troy Garlock, Grade 7
Bristol Elementary School, WI

Smelly Shoes

I am sitting in this box
I don't know where I am
I think I'm on a shelf
In a store with a funny name
I see the light of day
I'm being taken out of my box
Something stinky is coming into my head
Someone is tying my laces
And taking me away!

Chris Wichert, Grade 7
Christ Child Academy, WI

I Am a Divorce Victim

I am alone and afraid
I wonder if you will come back
I hear the silence that used to be you
I see the empty space inside me
I want to fill it but with what
I am alone and afraid

I pretend that there's nothing wrong
I feel the hole inside me eating away
I touch the empty chair in which you sat
I cry for I know you left us
I am alone and afraid

I understand what happened
I say it isn't right
I dream to hug and be with my dad
I try not to let it show
I hope that Mom will stop crying
I am alone and afraid

Adolfo Castillo Canedo, Grade 7
West Suburban Christian Academy, WI

Thunder/Scary

Thunder
Loud, bright
Flashing, speeding, burning
Run away from thunder
Scary

Shia Lee, Grade 7
Edison Middle School, WI

Idil, My Idol

What can I say about sisters?
You can't live with them
And you can't live without them
Mine is a weird person when she talks on the phone,
She shouts on the phone like she is yelling at a person next door
She moves like a squirming eel
She is as silly as a clown
She jumps around the house for no reason
Did I mention that she creeps me out about that?
Sometimes I wonder if she is a bat
Because she sleeps during the day time
And is awake at night
She always talks in different accents
Like Asma when she tries to bug me
I said it once and I'll say is again,
You can't live with them
And you can't live without them.

Muhubo Mohamed, Grade 7
Cedar Riverside Community School, MN

I Used To…

I used to be short, but now I am tall
I used to like dinosaurs, but now I like wrestling
I used to go to a public school, but now I go to a Catholic school
I used to have a CD player, but now I have an iPod
I used to run around my house but now I walk from room to room
I used to watch Teletubbies but now I watch History and Discovery Channel
I used to eat my boogers but now I blow my nose
I used to ask someone to tie my shoes but now I can tie them

Ryan Fiol, Grade 7
St Mary's School, WI

My Cabin

As I lay on my bed,
I dream of being there,
My favorite place in the world.
My cabin,
I can picture the perfect water splashing up against the shore.
I can see the wonderful sunset, behind the lake.
I wish I was there,
Knee boarding behind the boat,
Hearing the splashing water,
And hearing the plops of worms hit the water when my dad is fishing.
I dream of being there,
Out by the fire, hearing the crackling of it.
I can hear the roar of the boat motor, as we go out into the lake.
I dream of being there,
In my room, humming as I lay and hear the chirping of the birds.
I can see the swings, and my friends playing on them.
I can see the inside of the cabin,
I can see the kids swimming in the lake,
I dream of being there.

Lilly Bjorkquist, Grade 7
Manistee Middle School, MI

Into the World

The tiny feet
The toothless smile
The hands that you never want to let go of
And to think we were once this small
Seems like a long time ago
As you take it all in
Something hits you
Can I trust the person next to me with something so precious?
Can I even trust myself?
To be there when this beautiful creature needs me the most?
To provide them with what they need?
To be the best that I can be?
Life will never be the same
You've just had one thousand pounds lift off your shoulders
And another three thousand added on
The life that you now have in your hands
Is depending on you
To love, care, and cherish it
And hoping it remains that way

Nneka Iroha, Grade 7
Gesu Catholic School, MI

Racing

R eally fast cars going
A round a small track with
C ars passing you on both sides with just
Enough space to get in front again just
I n time
N ot even knowing it's the last lap and then
G oing to Victory Lane and celebrate your win

Nick Miesler, Grade 7
Luxemburg-Casco Middle School, WI

A Real Man

When I become a man
I will have a successful life.
When I become a man
I will live a life that gives praise to Obama and Dr. King.
When I become a man
I will be acknowledged by everyone.
When I become a man
I will live a peaceful life.
When I become a man
I will do great things.
When I become a man
I will make all of my dreams come true.

After I've become a man
I will have done great things.
After I've become a man
I will keep forever the memories of our first black president
But most of all,
After I've become a man, I will be an old man
Who dies with no regrets.

Samuel Ewulomi, Grade 8
Dwight Rich Middle School, MI

Thank You

Thank you for being there.
Thank you for understanding.
Thank you for your advice.
Thank you for always having open arms.
Thank you for your honesty.
Thank you for guiding me down the right road.
Thank you for being my shoulder to cry on.
Thank you for being an amazing friend.
Thank you for being even a better parent.
Thank you is not enough to say it but,
Thank you Mom.

Elishia Garcia, Grade 8
Washington Middle School, WI

Betrayed

Betrayed
In this world of secrets and gossip
Barely any trust in sight
That one secret
That I shouldn't have told
That should have never slipped
Through my mouth
Into an ear that never should have heard
That one secret that everyone knows
From that one person
That took one minute to tell it to the rest
Within an hour my secret turned
To the next "Big thing"
My secret, now everyone's
One Mistake
A secret that has changed the way people look at me
A secret that has changed my life for eternity
Because of that one person
I thought I could trust
Betrayed

Reva Klein, Grade 7
Perry Middle School, MI

Rainstorms

Mist pricks at you
Thunder rumbles beyond
Bang, bang, bang
Lightning was loud like a furious lion
Horrifying images bounce before my eyes
I screamed for help but no one heard
That old grizzly bear yelped at me
Fire surrounded me and I thought it was the end
Over all the noise a warm sensation overwhelmed me
My rescuer came to the rescue
I hugged him with all my might
The storm became tired as a sleeping kitten
I was safe for now until next time

Julie De Jardin, Grade 7
Luxemburg-Casco Middle School, WI

Mommy Loves Me

Mommy love me,
Good morning Mommy,
Let's get dressed,
Breakfast is yummy,
Playtime is best,
My mommy loves me
Mommy makes me smile,
She keeps me safe and sound,
And loves me all the while.
My mommy loves me,
Mommy reads me a book
She even brushes my new teeth,
She sings me a lullaby,
Mommy always LOVES ME!!

Tyara Green, Grade 7
Gesu Catholic School, MI

Spring

Sweet smells fill the air
With hope for the new season
So snipes sing sweet songs

Colorful flowers
Fill the earth with vibrant color
To make the world smile

Baby animals
Emerge from the woods with life
Spring is here to stay

Becca Hlavaty, Grade 9
Hartland High School, MI

A Gaze

As I sat there I see you staring from afar.
You gaze off into the distance,
with an expression unknown
and unpredictable thoughts.
What is he thinking?
Does he know I can't tell?

When the sun sets
darkness covers the land
to hide that mysterious gaze.
Our time is running out
as the clock is winding down.
Will he stay for long?

The end is drawing near.
Before it does,
I get one last glance.
This time I know his face.
A face of love that disappears,
with the darkness of our ended day.

Lisa Lupient, Grade 9
South View Middle School, MN

Smoke

I don't know him
He doesn't know me
Cool morning air
In Chicago's streets
But it is clogged
By smoke
From an old man
Leaning against the cold hard bricks
With dirty clothes
And a strong smell
He is hungry
But I walk past
Because a mug with pennies
In his left hand
And in his right hand
A cigarette

Koree Holme, Grade 7
Shakopee Area Catholic School, MN

Try Not to Forget

I sat in our spot
Staring at the sky
Holding your last letter
Trying not to cry
Your life was taken
By an accidental fall
A splash in the lake
The noise was so small
I didn't hear you scream
I didn't really know
That you couldn't swim
I didn't have my phone
Your number was up
The minute you left home
You should've left
To wander and roam
Still, I love you
Whether here or in the clouds
Or sitting in our spot
Not surrounded by the crowds
Your last letter in hand

Monika Chroscicki, Grade 8
St Roman School, WI

Golden Days

During the golden days
The skies were vibrant blue
And the grass was fresh and green
The animals laughed
While the flowers changed their hue
And it would seem
That you were daft
If you did not dream of the golden days

Aaron Hayes, Grade 9
Hartland High School, MI

Ice Fishing

I ce cold pops
C oncentrated fisherman
E verything is cold

F amily time outdoors
I ce shanties on the lake
S lush from drilling holes
H undreds of minnows
I ce skating on the lake
N ever gets boring
G ood memories

Max Jensen, Grade 8
Necedah Middle School, WI

Home

A house is just a place
But a home is a place
Filled with love and memories
And family
And sometimes friends
Where you sleep and eat
A house is just a place
And a home is a place
For memories and love
A home

Jessi Lapczynski, Grade 7
Luxemburg-Casco Middle School, WI

Dream Catcher

The dream catcher,
Old and alone,
Watching over dreams,
Quietly living in someone's home.

Its circular shape is like a moon,
Like a parent it helps you sleep,
It hushes you,
Tells you not to weep.

It creaks when it's handled,
Its coarse, fragile frame,
Rough and circular
It makes you wonder where it came.

Its design is
Simple, yet complex,
Look at the spider web inside
So many of the letter "X."

The dream catcher,
Worn like an aged spirit
If you listen closely,
Maybe you can hear it.

Aaron Afdahl, Grade 8
Chippewa Falls Middle School, WI

The Soldier

The soldier
Running through the battlefield,
Trying to find some cover,
Seeing his friends get killed every day
Watching death take them away
"Why did I sign up for this?" he thinks,
Reaching into his pocket he grabs a picture,
The photo is now unwrinkled,
To see that familiar twinkle in his wife's eye,
He sees his children standing by,
One is four and one is five,
He now realizes this is why

Ryan A. Feldmann, Grade 7
St Roman School, WI

Real Me?

Don't you remember
What we used to be?
The real us
The real me?

This doesn't seem right,
This isn't who we are,
But what we have become has left a scar.

I'm hurt deep inside
You may not see,
What your "love" has done to me

I can't take the fake
This isn't who we are.
Or what we used to be,
Where is the real us,
The real me?

Katie Fritz, Grade 8
Washington Middle School, WI

Phantom Pantoum

This is the Phantom Pantoum
Gliding so fast you can't see him
He is as white as the new fallen snow
He stalks through the night without a sound

He glides so fast you can't see him
He whisks through the houses ever so quietly
He stalks through the night without a sound
He knows no fear, because he is fear

He whisks through the houses ever so quietly
No one has a chance as he glides through the house
He knows no fear, because he is fear
This is the Phantom Pantoum

Zach Reau, Grade 7
Manistee Middle School, MI

Sunflower

I am a sunflower
I wonder why I appear only once a year
I hear and feel the kids pulling my petals off me
I see faces smelling my beautiful scent
I want to grow to have the biggest bloom
I am a sunflower

I pretend to extend to the sky
I feel the sunlight heating my petals
I touch the earth
I worry that I may not last as long as others
I cry when the rain doesn't come
I am a sunflower

I understand that I must be patient
I say that one day I will be the tallest I can be
I dream that one day people will accept me for who I am
I try not to be the most perfect
I hope people see that
I am a sunflower

Grace Portz, Grade 8
West Suburban Christian Academy, WI

Embarrassment

Embarrassment is as red as frustrated faces
It tastes of rubbery braces
The smell is strong and reeks of rotten vegetables
It looks like blurry tunnel vision
Its sound is like a time bomb's tick
It feels like you're going to be sick

Brian Green, Grade 9
Hartland High School, MI

Time

Time is endless, ceaseless.
It is everywhere we are,
In everything we do.
Time is purpose, meaning, and life.
It can give life, and take it away.
Time is like a shadow, still, silent.
But ever present, and ever powerful.
Time is the space between Earth and stars
For with time, today is yesterday,
And tomorrow is forever.
Time is a story without an end.
A heart without a soul.
Tears with no pain.
If time could speak
It would whisper the knowledge of a thousand souls.
Each with their own story,
Their own life.
Brought together by time.
Time. The constant companion
To this journey we call life.

Laci Frazier, Grade 9
Home School, MI

People Who Love Skiing

They are people who love the adrenaline
And the feeling you get zooming down the hill.
They are the people who love the brisk outdoor air but rush in the lodge
To grab a steaming cup of hot chocolate
As if it were a million dollars.
Skiing through the fresh knee deep powder of snow makes them have the time of their lives.
When they ski down the mountain with the wind in their face,
It feels like they are flying and can do anything,
Their spirits soar like birds as they speed down the hill only to rest at the bottom.
They are people who love skiing.

Nick Cecconi, Grade 8
Central Middle School, MI

Where I'm From

Sometimes I want to forget where I'm from, but not where I originated.
Where I'm from, it's always cold and loud
Every night as I lie in bed, I hear sirens and people screaming and shouting.
When I go to sleep I have terrible dreams.
It would feel nice to hear laughter sometimes, but where I'm from that's never possible.
It's always crying and sorrow, heartache and heart break.
There's never birds singing in the morning.
Never the sweet sweet smell of fresh apple pie.
It's always the sound of gunshots in the morning and the fresh smell of blood and death.

Sometimes I want to forget where I'm from, but not where I originated.
Sometimes it's good to see happy faces and the sound of laughter as we talk,
But where I'm from it's never possible.
There's always hate and revenge in the faces I see.
It's always hurt hurt kill kill when I hear people speak.
There's no safer place to be, but in the mind.
Sometimes I want to forget where I'm from
Because remembering only brings harsh dreams and cold thoughts.
Where I'm from, the sun never shines, the flowers never blossom.
The sky is never blue, the birds never sing.
This is where I'm from

Charmane Ford, Grade 9
Riverside University High School, WI

Tornado

There was a night long ago, here things were scattered all around
There was no warning, not even a sound
But then something shattered the silence, a really loud pound
People all around cried, I just sighed
Thunder and lightning filled the sky; no one likes to hear that terrible terror of a sound
The trees swayed and never stayed
The wind was bustling and brushing upon my face.

The people were scared, they couldn't bear to see the mess
They all said they should go and never come back
But they couldn't escape the terrible mess
The moon was out, it was a crest
They wondered if they would make it, but they wouldn't
They wondered if they could rebuild, but they couldn't
They wandered, wondering.

Leah Birch, Grade 7
Bristol Elementary School, WI

Possibilities

Yesterday was once a today
Today was once a tomorrow
Tomorrow is...
What is tomorrow?

Tomorrow could be a today
Eventually it could be a yesterday
But today, tomorrow is
Well, just tomorrow.

Yesterday was a time of
Civil and Revolutionary Wars
A time of peace and flower power
A time of disco and bell-bottoms.

Today is the new age of
MP3s and iPods
Of high gas prices and finance problems
Being green and polluted air.

Tomorrow, however
Is a clean slate
It's just waiting to be written on
There are so many possibilities.

Sarah J. Burmesch, Grade 7
Wheatland Center Elementary School, WI

Blue

Blue is a sad expression
Blue is the sound of the tide crashing against the rocks
Blue is the taste of salt in the ocean wind
Blue is the soft glow of the moon, and the
color of a newborn baby's blanket
Blue is the sound of crickets chirping
and frogs croaking by a babbling brook
Blue is peaceful and exciting
Blue is serenity

Rachel Stoiber, Grade 7
St Joseph School, WI

Dreams

Sleeping and dreaming are such strange things,
With the fact that your consciousness is held by a string.
What exactly are dreams?
Well, they open many worlds in different doors.
Dreaming can take you to many different places,
Open new ideas, and maybe crack open new cases,
Which are full of mystery, puzzles, and wonder.
Your dream can take you to a world of peace,
Where all violence, and war shall always cease.
There are also nightmares, which are terrifying and scary,
Unlike the dreams, which are all so merry.
Dreams can be so happy, so bright,
But others can be as dark as the night.

Kaylee Tesch, Grade 8
St Roman School, WI

Hair Can Be...

Hair can be,

Hair can be stringy and preciously divine,
Hair can be on a fashion designer's line.
Hair can be curly and so very straight,
Hair can be horrible on the perfect date.
Hair can be long and so short,
Hair can be beautiful on homecoming court.
Hair can be purple and can be cherry red,
Hair can be called names like an ugly bed head.
Hair can be worn up and can be worn down,
Hair can be colorful on hilarious clowns.
Hair can be drawn in books in all different styles,
Hair can be a popular product found in grocery store aisles.
Hair can be cut or can be grown,
Hair can be an appointment dialed on the phone.
Hair can be seen so many times,
Hair can be guaranteed to last a lifetime.
Hair can be vanishing on people going bald,
Hair can be pulled out with people who's falled.
So next time you do something with your beautiful hair,
be careful you could do anything there.

Rachael Rienstra, Grade 7
St Gerard School, MI

Who Am I?

Who am I, I'm not quite sure,
Sometimes I'm as quiet as a mouse.
Sometimes I'm as loud as a motorcycle engine.
When I feel like I can be as strong as a weightlifter,
And as weak as a baby.
That is what I am.

Orissa Ramnarine, Grade 7
Valley View Middle School, MN

Blank Pages

Everything used to be visible
But now it's like a fogged-up mirror
I used to be able to understand
But now it isn't quite so clear
You start by telling me a story
One that I can't quite comprehend
But then you start to change it
You decide to get rid of the end
You can keep pretending
That nothing is really wrong
But if you go to the ending
You'll find out what went wrong
This story isn't what I asked for
It's ruined beyond repair
Close it, I can't listen anymore
Leave it blank right there

Miranda Rickard-Lindner, Grade 8
Iowa-Grant Elementary-Middle School, WI

Evil Pumpkin

It has a very evil look
And a mischievous smile
Like he's up to something
The hairs is a black cat
Eyes are blood red like good wine
Body silver like the moon
And is rippled wavy water
The smiles provoke a noise
The noise of a cackling
Little kid on Halloween
But trust me he is very safe
He is grown from a pumpkin
He sits perched in places
Front porches and living rooms
Harmless he may be
Kids run once they see him sitting there
They run screaming in fear
He's evil and eatable
He's just a decoration

Ivan Thull, Grade 8
Chippewa Falls Middle School, WI

Sadness Is September

Sadness is September
because we're going back to school
Happiness is summer
because we never have to learn
Anger is January
'cause you always catch a cold
Love is December
because of Christmas Day
Joy is the 4th of July
because it's the U.S.A.'s birthday

Anthony Caracci, Grade 7
Northwood School, WI

The Flood

A flood sneaks in secretly
Like a cat in the dead of night
It rips up the ground
And ruins everything in its path
With the thrashing of its whips of water
At every given object
Somewhere in the next storm
Where in it I am uncertain
When it leaves like a successful lion
It has just made its first catch

Alex Fuhr, Grade 7
West Suburban Christian Academy, WI

Calligraphy

Calligraphy
Beautiful hand drawn symbols
Japanese art work

Colin Gander, Grade 8
Spring Hill School, WI

Letting Go

Walking over the sand dunes
Our small hands hidden in your large ones,
Sheltered from the rest of the world.
The smell of salt water in the air.
I take a deep breath; my nose burns like I'd inhaled fire.
You had all the stuff crammed in a bag slung over your shoulder.
We made it to the sandy place where we would waste our day.
You watch us cautiously as we play in the sand,
Exploring and discovering all on our own.

You wrestled us into life jackets and floaties.
One tiny hand enlaced in one big one, the four of us head out to sea.
The waves crash all around us like I'm being pulled in every direction.
But you're there, holding my hand tight,
Watching over me like the moon watches over the darkness of night,
Still there but not overshadowing me.
We float around feeling weightless, letting the waves take us where they may.
I'm still close enough to shore and to you to know I'm safe
But, still far enough away to feel separate and independent.

Christie Campbell, Grade 9
Clarkston Jr High School, MI

Flying Then Falling

He was flying,
Then falling.
Once again flying,
Suddenly falling,
Every time he fell, he felt like he got locked in a prison cell,
But God would come and set him free,
And lift him up until he was flying with glee,
But he would keep falling,
Yet God stayed faithful.
Because he would come in and "Carpe Diem" seize the day,
God would come in and take his troubles away,
The man would be grateful to be flying again,
But some unexpected wind would send him plummeting back down,
He wondered why these tough falls kept happening,
Then he realized even though God would keep bailing him out,
Whenever he was flying he wouldn't put God as his King,
So he put God as his King and guess what,
No more falling, just eternal flying.

Elijah Isenberger, Grade 7
Abundant Life Christian School, WI

Werewolf Transformation

Above the trees was the glowing moon,
Under the moonlight was me,
I examined my reflection in the water as my veins pulsed with fear.
Through the water I saw all the fish swim away in fear from me,
I walked toward the dark forest,
I began to run swiftly through the trees.
I ran through them with my pace quickly increasing,
Upon the cliff I stood — looking up at the moon,
I welcome the other wolves around me on the hunt.

Sarah Peplinski, Grade 7
Beer Middle School, MI

The Symbol of the Dog

The symbol of the dog means
that the dog will always have loyalty to the owner
no matter what the owner is
happy
mean
sad
loving
the dog will always show loyalty
and love to the owner
and the dog is man's best friend
if you show respect to the dog
it will show respect to you
the dog will always be
the animal
of
the
house

Calvin Blackdeer, Grade 8
Spring Hill School, WI

Top Hat

Do you see that guy with the top hat?
With the tie and that crazy old cat,
Who looks a little chunky and maybe a little fat?
So, in a couple of hours
I will send him some flowers
And we'll see what he thinks about that.
I wonder what's underneath that top hat?
A bunny or even a rat?
I have a suspicion
If he's a magician
And he could turn into a bat.
All my question is…
What's underneath that top hat?

Tanner Chouinard, Grade 8
Central Middle School, MI

Enigma

I sit by the fireside
and I see the plans for an empty room.
I look to the sky outside —
I see faces looking back.
We humans are so pointless
is this all there really is to life?
But I look back
to the empty room
and I see my garden blooming
could it really be true?
I find the evidence of truth
staring me in the face —
just for me
it has come to this place

Stormy Hefko, Grade 8
River Crossing Environmental Charter School, WI

I Am

I am a girl who belongs at the coast
I wonder why the fish are gone
I hear waves tickle the white sand
I see the people engulfed by the surf
I want to be one of them too
I am a girl who belongs at the coast

I pretend to be walking, running, out to the middle of the sea
I feel a turtle brush against my knee
I touch the sky as I stand on my board
I worry that the sharks will finally get the best of me
I cry as the gulls do not far above
I am a girl who belongs at the coast

I understand I can't stay here forever
I say I will, however
I dream to be here for the rest of my life
I try to avoid the calling of my name
I hope I can come back
I am a girl who belongs at the coast.

Elaine Munn, Grade 8
Central Middle School, MI

Dinnertime Dreams

"Mom, what's for dinner?" asks Laura Lou.
There's ice cream, cake, and jellybeans too.
But where's the greens, proteins, and fruit galore?
Oh, honey, I just saw those walk out the door.
I had to think quick
To make sure this wasn't a trick.
Ice cream, cake, and jellybeans
No brussel sprouts, carrots, or any other greens
That's just a wish.
I've got to eat what's in my dish.
It's brussel sprouts, carrots, and those other greens.
Those were just my dinnertime dreams.

Laura Weisz, Grade 7
Central Middle School, MI

Alone

Alone in the dark
In the cold
Floating by a thread
Hanging in the blackness
Stars all around me
Nothingness pressing in
I work fast as I can
To repair the damage
I signal
I feel the pull
It's over
Back inside
Staring out the window
At the blackness.

Jason Wesseling, Grade 7
Hudsonville Christian Middle School, MI

Springtime Walk

I step outside,
And take a deep breath,
Ahh, the smell of spring!
As I am walking,
I hear the birds singing,
That new tune of spring!
I see the buds on the trees,
No more bare branches,
For it is now spring!
The flowers are blooming,
Bright and colorful,
All the colors of spring!
The gentle, warm breeze,
And the bright, hot sun,
Feels good 'cause it's spring!
The lakes are finally warming,
You can now see the grass,
But spring is just beginning!
There is lots to see on a springtime walk,
So step outside and take a breath,
Ahh, the smell of spring!

Kaitlyn Olson, Grade 8
Robert J Elkington Middle School, MN

Hated Things

Of all hated things
Wouldn't you agree?
Death is very unhappy.
It breaks your heart.
It's sorrowful, sad, and stupid.
Why, of all things,
Would there be death?
When people die,
More people cry.
It is the saddest of the sad.
I think death is bad.

Katie Lynn Barrett, Grade 7
Luxemburg-Casco Middle School, WI

Heaven!!!

Heaven is an eternal life
Opening the doors to a world unknown.

Going to Heaven is not a bad thing
God just needs you and He wants you.

Heaven is an eternal life
It gives you a second chance.

A second chance to do right
And give yourself to our Heavenly Father.

Heaven is an eternal life
You have a place to go.

Dustin Harbottle, Grade 8
Middle School at Parkside, MI

The Seven Stages of Me

All the world's a big fat book,
With characters who follow their own paths;
They have their opinions and beliefs with times for tears and laughs,
Seven stages is what they go through;
At first an infant, so cuddly and cute,
With their little pug nose and little toes, too!
The second stage comes along with terrible twos,
The wild, screaming toddler who is a monster;
Then comes the school life as our third stage,
With drama and boys, your mind in a haze;
College is next, responsibility knocks on your door,
You have to care for yourself and figure out what life is for;
At last there is love like a sweet-smelling rose,
So complex and confusing, but still it grows;
Then kids come along as our sixth stage,
You care for them dearly, and wish them the best, filled with happiness.
And finally there is death,
You start to age and get wiser but you have shortness of breath;
Life is short, I'm halfway through my story,
I have a lot to discover, has your life been perfect,
From cover to cover?

Allison Wallace, Grade 9
Northwood School, WI

Pink

Pass on the love. Pink is a little ballerina tiptoeing and twirling around.
Pink is a sunset melting into Lake Michigan.
Pass on the love. Pink is love floating around in the air.
Pink is a rose showing God's love and creation.
Pass on the love. Pink is Breast Cancer Awareness, supporting our women.
Pink is a pair of warm fuzzy bunny slippers warming us up on a cold winter day.
Pass on the love.
Pink is having comfort.
Taking the plunge.
Facing the world.
Pass on the love.

Ellie Brady, Grade 8
St Andrew's School, MI

True Love

Someone out there was meant to be the love of your life,
the one you can tell your dreams to and he'll smile at you when you tell him.
But he'll never laugh he'll brush the hair out of your face,
He'll tell you how much he loves you and hold you tight,
He'll stare at a movie that he paid $11 to see,
He'll call you five times a day to make sure his baby is ok,
He'll call to tell you that he was thinking about you,
But at the end of every conversation he never forgets to tell you he loves you,
He'll carry your books down the hall for you,
He'll stare at you and tell you you're the most beautiful young woman he's ever seen.
For the first time in your life, you'll believe it.
That's what I call true love.

Revin Gray, Grade 7
Gesu Catholic School, MI

Winter Wonderland

The moon is a golf ball, glowing
as if it were Earth's light in the night.
Glowing waves of green, red, and blue
help contribute to this beautiful sight.

Pine needles rustle under
the moose's feet,
he is like a shadow,
no warmth, no heat.

The trees stretch toward the night sky,
their branches like landing pods for snow.
The branches creak and moan
as the whistling winds blow.

Slowly and gracefully,
the snow is a pillow.
Protecting the rough pine needles,
but not the willow.

Jordan Hasenberg, Grade 8
Chippewa Falls Middle School, WI

Dreaming in the Backyard

With a dazzling smile and welcoming gifts,
I know she is there for me.

As I lie there on her green bed,
I can hear the sweet music playing through the air.

I can feel her as she speaks to me,
The warmth of her breath on my face.

She wraps me in a blanket of light and warmth.

And as I smell the freshness of the air,
I notice she has grown sad.

Her once gleaming face has now darkened.
But it is still as beautiful as before,
For now her eyes are twinkling with stars.

I tell her goodbye and she understands,
Because tomorrow will be a brand new day, full of surprises.

Karla Tinajero-Espinoza, Grade 8
J C McKenna Middle School, WI

Love

love is like an overgrown balloon,
the air inside so fresh, so soon,
love can be like the heat of a flame,
it can turn from blame to shame,
love is to feel a lover's passion, devotion, or tenderness,
love is the feeling that you belong,
love is the feeling that you're ready to bloom once again.

Christopher Evans, Grade 8
Middle School at Parkside, MI

Whacky Whales

Whacky whales whip their tails,
Wildly through the air,
Whacking, whumping, whipping wetness into the sky,
Whirling, woofing, simply without a care,
Wizened are those who watch this wild, witty spectacle.

Spinning, swirling, slicing through the surf,
Slapping, silly seals sporadically,
Slipping in and out of the sea,
They sing their somber songs,
Soaring, sinking, shredding the shrimp.

Twirling, twisting, a show of titanic proportions,
Tails tingling the whales slip beneath the surface,
Total Tranquility, is what describes life below the top,
Tortoises touring the long forgotten temples,
Traversing the treacherous deep, the whales spot tourists.

Whacky whales whip their tails, wildly through the air…

Chris Kollath, Grade 8
Seymour Middle School, WI

Dead Is the New Alive

What is a day without a blessed night?
What is peace without a blessed fight?
What is a day without a blessed night?
What is peace without a blessed blessed blessed fight?
A quick taste of the poison,
a quick twist of the knife
when the obsession with death,
the obsession of death becomes a way of life
Dead is the new alive,
So take me now or take me never,
I won't wait
You're already late,
I would give up my fame and fortune,
To fight your demons and your bloody wars.
I want to mix our blood,
And put it in the ground so you can never leave,
I want to win your trust, your faith, and your heart
You'll never be deceived.

Kaitlyn Keller, Grade 9
Webster High School, WI

Basketball

She's smart
He's very athletic
She loves to play many sports
He loves to play basketball
She's very encouraging to her team
He's everything anyone could ask for in a player.
They are just everything put together for a perfect team.

Elishia DeLong, Grade 8
Spring Hill School, WI

Tornado

Crackling filled the air
Like a train's piercing whistle
Debris strewn about.

Trevor Mauritz, Grade 8
Suring Elementary/Middle School, WI

Ice Fishing

Ice fishing, freezing, frosty, fun.
I sit on a frozen green pail.
I feel a pull on my pole.
I reel it in.
I get it up through the ice hole.
I throw the fish in the fish pile.
Be careful because ice could crack.
It was a 20 inch perch.
Ice fishing, freezing, frosty, fun.

Austin Estes, Grade 7
Luxemburg-Casco Middle School, WI

My Mark

Born
I was.
Defiant
I am.
To live without meaning
Is worse than to be damned
I, Myself, am planning
To leave my mark,
To be remembered
As a great man.
History shall be kind to me
Since I myself intend to write it.
So my spirit and soul will carry on.
I want to be remembered
As a kid who went to Harvard
And became a surgeon
Against all odds.
My parents say I am not smart enough.
I want to prove them wrong.

Marshal Chen, Grade 8
Boulan Park Middle School, MI

Rain

Rain is as soft as a pillow
Rain is as dark as night
Rain is as quiet as a butterfly
Rain is as hard as hail
Rain is my favorite
I like to watch it slowly come down
At night when it gently pounds
On the roof of my house
I gently close my eyes
And fall asleep

Tyler Zimmerman, Grade 7
Luxemburg-Casco Middle School, WI

Soccer Hero

Up and down
Side to side
Quick go around
Before you take that last stride.

You're about to reach your goal
You've seen it in the play book
You'll need all of your control
Lift your head up and take your last look.

Up and down
Side to side
Quick go around
Before you take your last stride.

You took your last look
Exactly what you saw in the book.
The shot was made
You're the hero of the day.

Kylie Ness, Grade 8
Seymour Middle School, WI

The Perfect Pop

P erfectly popped puffs
O ut of the ordinary snacks
P leasingly buttery
C runchy, salty bites
O utstanding goodness
R ighteously tasty
N early gone, in my stomach

Andrew Spryszak, Grade 8
Gesu Catholic School, MI

Just Walk Through, and Come Out

You can change your life,
if you think it possible.
But you can't change your destiny,
if you don't think it possible.
You might walk through the darkness,
and come out with the brightness.
You might walk through pain,
and come out peaceful.
You might walk through the evil,
and come out with the good.
You might walk through the loneliness,
and come out with community.
You feel bored right now,
but you might feel enthusiasm later.
Nothing is going to be bad,
if you don't try.
Don't complain with your density.
But be happy,
because you are still alive.

Phuong Trinh Nguyen, Grade 7
Ramsey Jr High School, MN

Lucy

There was once a girl named Lucy,
She ate an orange that was juicy,
In the car they hit a bump,
That really made a lump,
Which made Lucy really goosey.

Lori Herdic, Grade 7
Christ Child Academy, WI

O How I Miss My Life

O how I miss my life,
My days are filled with pain,
My nights agony,
I can't stop thinking about my wife,
Gunshots haunt my dreams,
Blood my nightmares,
My life is full of war and blood,
I fought in the battle of Saratoga,
And barely escaped with my life,
Sometimes I get wounded,
Sometimes not,
I lay awake trying not to think,
Of all the bloodshed,
I worry I won't come back,
So I write letters home,
In my letters I try not to,
Talk too much about my battles,
It might make her cry,
I don't want to make her sad,
I fight for freedom,
That is why I fight

Ross Lester, Grade 8
Sandusky Middle School, MI

Winter Wonderland

The illuminated purple sky
With tiny white sprinkles wandering
The snow is coconut
Fluffy, fresh, soft and white

A sparkling full moon in the night sky
Chunky chocolate moose mooing loudly
The clicking of their hooves
Rubbing of their antlers

The trees shivering in the cold night
Shaped like a rocky road ice cream cone
Covered in a layer
Of wet, cold, frigid snow

The sky is a lighted Christmas tree
Glowing with streaks of purple and green
Like a peacock feather
With moose tracks in the snow

Lisa Mayer, Grade 8
Chippewa Falls Middle School, WI

The Tornado

The wind is picking up,
Faster and faster the wind is coming,
Howling as if it were a wolf.
It is starting to rain,
The rain gets heavier and heavier,
Leaving puddles and ponds of mud.
The rain turns to hail,
The hail hits the ground with a thud,
The hail is as big as a baseball.
The waves on the lake are big,
Fish are getting thrown around like a ball
With children.
The wind, the rain, the hail, and the waves
All stop.
Everything is silent.
Then a cloud twisting down to earth,
It touches the ground and dust goes
Flying everywhere.
Everything is a blur,
Then it stops,
Everything is gone.

Tyler Fricke, Grade 7
Ramsey Jr High School, MN

Downtown

It's the city of sky-scraping towers,
And many nights of never-ending parties.
Almost every store has gorgeous flowers,
And maybe a little treat like Smarties.
For some it's a new experience,
But for others it's a stressed-filled work place.
So use the Park and Ride, it just makes sense,
Don't rush out too fast or you might forget your briefcase!
On a clear, brisk, night driving east to the lake,
The view is overwhelming, what a sight!
If you stay out too late your head might ache,
So get a good glimpse and enjoy your night.
Our lakefront is a treasure to behold,
So check it out before it gets too cold!

Rachel Schneider, Grade 8
Pilgrim Park Middle School, WI

Green

Green is weeds and algae and gemstones.
Green is the taste of pears.
Fresh grass and mints smell green.
When I'm sick it makes me feel green.
Green is the sound of frogs and bees.
Green is warm, itchy, and lily pads in the water.
Some tractors are green.
Stop and go lights are also green.
Green can mean a variety of things.

Tyler Kaiser, Grade 7
St Joseph School, WI

Fights

We are all friends why do we do this to each other
Do we even care about one an other?

He said, she said, look at her that's how it all starts
The gossip the lies and the broken hearts

What you tell me isn't the same thing you tell her
Is this the truth or a lie you can never be sure

Our stupid fights might last 5 minutes or 5 days
We don't think twice about what were going to say

We always have to be right
There's no reason for these stupid fights

We are all friends why do we do this to each other
Do we even care about one an other?

Elizabeth Golembiewski, Grade 7
Allendale Middle School, MI

A Special Place

Home is for free expressions
It's not for good impressions

Home is a place for fun and play
Please come sit and stay

Filled with memories you'll have forever
But maybe you'll move away from here, never

It's where you relax and put up your feet
Or where you and your siblings fight over a seat

Until the day in life when you move on
This is the place where you tan on the front lawn

It's where you might even have your first kiss
It's the place you'll most miss

Sometimes you regret ever wanting to run away
You always know you have a place for your head to lay

With all the ups and downs you might go through
You'll always know you'll have home to turn to
While God is right beside you.

Emily Webster, Grade 7
Shakopee Area Catholic School, MN

The Lost Sale

The sign said 'Get more bang for your buck'
but it appears I'm all out of luck
I missed all the sales
on pool and deck rails
and now all that's left is a duck!

Emily Philippon, Grade 8
St Patrick Catholic School, MI

Thunderstorm

Sheets of gray water
Roaring miles away
Awake; far away rumble, boom!
Thinking, "is this the end?"
Shaking, terrified
Nature's camera flashes
Drip, drop, drip, boom!
Who has angered you?
Rolling thunder escapes over the horizon
Silence

Lacey Streblow, Grade 8
Suring Elementary/Middle School, WI

Money

I like money
Yes I do
Money is good
But don't let it control you

I have money
How about you
I bless others with it
I hope you would too

God gives money to me
He gives money to you
I hope you bless others
Like God blesses me and you

James Stewart, Grade 8
Gesu Catholic School, MI

Language

L anguage arts class
A lways a due date
N othing but poems and stories
G etting frustrated
U nusual topics
A lways confused
G uessing
E verything getting lost

Michelle Knoll, Grade 8
Suring Elementary/Middle School, WI

Prayers

Everybody say your prayers
Thank God and rejoice
Love what He has done for you
Believe in Him
Thank Him
Love Him
Praise God every day and rejoice
God is your Savior
So just make sure
You say your prayers

Diamond Bush, Grade 8
Gesu Catholic School, MI

Mom

Before my eyes were open,
before my legs wobbled to walk,
before my ears could understand your voice,
before you walked me into my first day of school while I held your hand,
before you taught me to read and write with the deepest care,
when you said that I would do just fine
and before you said "you're on your way to anything you want to do,"
before your sweet, soft, soothing voice sang
"May There Always Be Sunshine,"
before you comforted me after I'd had a nightmare,
when you had been fast asleep at 12:15,
and before you told me to shoot for my dreams,
before we read "The Foot Book,"
and before your lips first kissed my head
and before you guided me on my first bike ride,
and at the park you pushed me on the swing,
before all illnesses were diagnosed,
before the good and bad and in-between
and before you became my shining star,
before all this, my heart was big
after all this, my heart exploded with the love you share.

Kelsey Runft, Grade 9
Clarkston Jr. High School, MI

Emotions of Life

Happiness is chocolate ice cream on a hot summer day,
Fear is trapped in a burning building with no way out,
Love is a field of flowers flowing in the wind and blooming in different colors,
These are my emotions of life.

Louden Grieser, Grade 7
Valley View Middle School, MN

Burst of Life

The large blank paper sits patiently on the table,
Waiting for the soft stroke of a paintbrush,
Anticipating the pleasant dampness of cool acrylic paint.
The thick, wooden brush trembles in my grasp.
As I stare into the whiteness, too scared to make a move,
My fear is marked with a tinge of horror.
Holding my breath, I lower my hand,
The rough bristles finally making contact with the paper,
Pulling a small yellow swirl across the center.
Soon more curves and arcs follow,
Filling up the space with luscious color and shape,
The motions becoming free, abstract, and careless.
As I scoop up heaping globs of red, yellow, and orange,
They morph into beautiful shades of rich crimson and gold,
Blending into brilliant hues of a sunset on the horizon.
The strokes form a figure that grows more and more apparent.
My multicolored brush picks up an earthy jade green,
Sprouting into even thicker rounded lines.
Persimmon orange, lemon yellow, and scarlet red burst into vibrant harmony,
Blossoming into a radiant rose,
Vivid, full of color, and alive.

Helena Chen, Grade 7
Detroit Country Day Middle School, MI

sunset

Your ways are similar to the rays of the sun
warm to many but too strong for some
the more you are needed the brighter you shine
watched for too long and your brilliance will blind the eye
of mortal men who threaten you
they regret to see you set but it's time for the moon.

Ashley Reed, Grade 8
Franklin Middle School, WI

The Surprise

An annoying sound roared in my ear,
Not knowing what it was not a cat nor a deer,
It almost sounded like buzzing in my ear,
Until someone kicked me right in my rear,
My rear hurt like I just got a bruise,
Like someone was trying to tell me some news,
I didn't wake up not then or not now,
But when I opened my eyes I saw a huge cow,
My uncle was visiting I didn't know,
I pretty much though he was putting on a show,
My aunt was yelling across the room,
Then she went to get the broom,
She swept up the mess that he had made,
Then she called for me…jade,
I didn't know what was happening no no no,
But then my aunt told us to go go go,
Off to the hospital on 8th street,
Someone smelled like stinky stinky feet,
We got in the hospital room 186,
My mother looked like she was sick,
But now in my hands I hold girl named Emily!

Shantae Harris, Grade 7
Brooklyn Jr High School, MN

Kingdom of Children

As you hit the edge of the sand,
You kick off your shoes and yank off your socks.
You step into the warm sand,
And she embraces you like an old friend.
The slides sing your name,
The bridge cries with joy,
The monkey bars laugh with glee.
They welcome you back to your kingdom,
Where princesses are rescued,
By handsome princes,
Where you ride dinosaurs,
Where the swings carry you higher and higher,
Until the ground is no longer visible.
That special place,
Where your independence was first found,
And friendships grew strong.
She's always been there,
And always will be,
Welcoming you back every time.

Maggie Jensen, Grade 8
J C McKenna Middle School, WI

Kindness

Kindness is sometimes compared to bunt cake
Small and sweet and fill'd with happiness
Most of us are mean and our joy is fake
But a select few are filled with kindness
They are nice and respectful to others
People of this nature feel good inside
Their hearts are full of joy like new mothers
But they had to take a very long ride
This road was bumpy and full of swerves
It curves and winds through valleys
When they come to the end and look backwards
They realize that kindness must be earn'd
Those who are kind will be thanked by others
So be kind and loving to everyone

Conor Tily, Grade 8
Grosse Pointe Academy, MI

Day Break, Nature Awake

Day break, nature awake
Dew has covered the grass and flowers
As a doe and her fawn
Wake at dawn
The quiet uncovers
The birds start chirping
The noise isn't alerting
The morning sun rises
Full of surprises
As the doe leads her fawn
To the lawn
Of a nature lover
There are carrots and apples that were bought
The rabbits' and deer's sight has been caught
There are birdhouses all around
Hanging from trees near the ground
Corn for squirrels are nailed to trees
And flowers all around for the butterflies and bees
Day break, nature awake
This yard is full of treasures

Michelle Froman, Grade 8
Centreville Jr High School, MI

When Tears Run Away

When tears run away, they fall like toddlers
They hit like boxers
And on the black Friday they run like shoppers
No one knows when they come out
It shocks and burns like hot dogs on the fire
They can be like fireworks and funeral tears
It can feel like army gun's steel
But we'll never heal
From pain no matter what we gain
It's like people doing drugs, it's just so lame.

Aaliyah Beal, Grade 8
Washington Middle School, WI

My Cat

My cat named Tubby was one of the best cats, she always kept me company whenever I was alone, someone to talk to all day long. Always spent time with her, listening to her purr. One of my best friends, always there for me, petting her and taking care of her, seeing her every day kept me going. But one day she would be gone, thinking about that made me cry, I wouldn't know what to do, but that day had come.

Joshua Maenke, Grade 7
Valley View Middle School, MN

Race Day

They line up to the starting line like racers from the darkness their eyes glowing, and their hearts pumping. The engine's roaring and fans are screaming. When the green flag drops they speed off wanting, wishing, and hoping they win. They line up wanting, wishing, and hoping that they can pass one another.

Jacob Kasinger, Grade 8
Bloomingdale Middle School, MI

Sports

Sports are not for everyone;
but once you get into them, they are like a good book.
Once you're hooked on them, you can't put them down.
You have to have the determination and the heart to want to keep going.
If you are motivated to keep getting better, you can go as far as you want.
You have to be as tough as leather so when you get knocked down you get right back up.
You have to be as brave as a lion so when you go up against a person
a foot taller than you and 100 pounds heavier, you won't back down.
You have to be as strong as an ox.
Not necessarily physically strong, but mentally too,
so that people don't get inside your head.
You also need to be as cool as a cucumber so that you're not nervous
to face the opponent you know you're better than.
Every minute that you take off is a minute your opponent moves closer to you.
You need to be as hard as nails and as solid as a rock.
If you do these things, you will be flying as high as a kite in the sport you love.

Alexander Copa, Grade 7
Roosevelt Middle School, MN

Crouching Tiger, Hidden Dragon

I am a tiger. I am fast and powerful and as lithe as a trickling fire. I am as sly as a fox, and I creep like an Arabian venom cobra. I charge the night of Costa Rica. What I do or where I go no one knows, because I blend in with the night as perfectly as a Bengal does with the tall grass of the Indian Plain. I pounce on my prey as secretly as a stealth fighter plane. I pinpoint my target and produce my own perfect market. I kill with ease. I could kill a man with my smile. When my teeth glow my enemies cringe and spring back to the hole they came from, if they can make it. In this world I was made a man, but in the animal kingdom I am a tiger.

I have no mercy, I have no contempt. I like what I eat. I know what I do and I do what I want. The lions of this wilderness think they rule this realm, but they see with their pride and not their eyes. They think they can hurt me, but they've never seen me, because I don't let them. They feed on their ignorance while I feed on them. They don't know who I am, but I will show them if they do dare come.

My life as a tiger, I do like fun. I do love the sun. This is where I live and settle down and run. I am free and I plea that no one shall escape me. In the night is where I fight, but in the day is where I sway. I watch over what is mine and am careful with what I sow. I have a passion for what I do. I love my work and how I chew. My hidden dragon is my heart. I have a family and a start. In my business, I am smart. I leave no traces to show. I burn with fury in my dreams; sometimes they will make me scream.

I am a night watch tiger.

Kahyil Humbach, Grade 8
Abundant Life Christian School, WI

The End

Waves crashing
Volcanoes erupting
Earthquakes shaking
Buildings falling
People screaming,
World coming to its death
Silent and motionless

Lucas Pritzl, Grade 7
Elkhart Lake Elementary-Middle School, WI

Black

When you look to the sky, on a cold fall night
The clouds are dark, and have no life
And sometimes can be a fright

The pain you feel can be quite a lot
Even when it should not
Agonizing and cruel
Are double the pain, and make you feel so insane

Trying to swallow shattered glass
The pieces are like a car crash
Everywhere things are broken, and people are freaking out
The chaos continues without-a-doubt

The screaming and yelling are all so loud
It sounds like a million people in a crowd
Yelling and screaming at you for all the mistakes you have made

It's screaming at you with all of its rage
Not caring how you feel
All the disgrace is being revealed

That's the color black without a shield.

Abby Mermuys, Grade 8
Lake Fenton Middle School, MI

Up Above

The sun shining brightly down
Making everything look like it's glowing
Children running barefoot dressed all in white
On the grassy hills
And through the shallow rivers
They are laughing and playing
Meeting with friends
They used to know
Finding pets they seem to remember
Basking in the sun
Bright, healthy, happy
They seem to have found themselves
In
Heaven

Emily Wusthoff, Grade 7
Elkhart Lake Elementary-Middle School, WI

The First Snowfall

Small crystals fall from the sky
Blanketing the earth in endless supply.
Children look out excited from their beds
Hoping for a day of playing ahead.
The small pond waits
To be cleared and carved by skates
As the cold of winter transforms
It in the December storm.
The snow quiets the charming town,
Glistening on every surface around.
The magic leaves its effect
With no one to object.
The thickening snow cloaks
Roofs, cars, and great oaks.
Hot cocoa brews out of the cold
To warm the souls of young and old,
And as the wonderful day comes to an end,
The people silently wish for a snowfall again.

Kirsten Thompson, Grade 8
Boulan Park Middle School, MI

The Missing Thing

Inside I felt somewhat confused,
About why I am so frustrated,
I examine all the evidence and ran over it again.
Beside me was my former friend,
from my elementary school,
I began to realize that I was mistaken.
After seeing the answer I knew I was defeated,
Next to noticing that I am wrong,
I welcome her into my life because I knew she belonged.

Taylor Hall, Grade 7
Beer Middle School, MI

Siblings

I have three siblings, two sisters and one brother,
"I knew I could handle you all," said my mother.
"But I can't," I reply. "Because...well, they poke my eyes!
Hit my arm,
Push me in the mud when I'm at the farm.
They kick my legs,
Hide my shoes,
(If you have siblings this isn't big news.)
They hit me in the head,
Steal my candy,
Steal my friends! Isn't that just dandy!
Pull my hair,
Stomp on my feet,
Steal my spot,
My favorite bus seat.
I get one fourth they get all,
I get one used thing; they get twenty new from the mall!"
And just one more thing, this is the worst one...
MY MOM'S HAVING ANOTHER ONE!!!

Cierrah Stampfli, Grade 7
Core Knowledge Charter School, WI

Yellow

Yellow is sour
It is tart
Yellow is cautionary
It is fruity
Yellow is new
It is a fashion statement
Yellow is cute
It is funky
Yellow is bright
It is an unripe apple
Yellow is a post-it saying I love you
It glows with light
Yellow is a sunset in the mountains
It is a life saver in the sea
Yellow is an M&M
It is a highlighter to mark the spot
Yellow is an autumn leaf yellow is unique
It is a smiley face
Yellow marks the way on the map
It has pucker power
Yellow is the sunshine's rays

Elysia Nix, Grade 8
Washtenaw Christian Academy, MI

Searching

Searching, searching, searching…
For something even Google can't find.
I wait for you, but you cannot find you.
You elude me like a mouse does a cat.
Slipping through my fingers,
Like light through a mist.
Never to share a warm embrace again.

Rachel Solberg, Grade 9
John F Kennedy High School, MN

Puppies to Dogs

Dogs are someone to
Clean up after.
From the slobber
To the food on the floor.
Dogs are someone you can love.
Take them home with you
From the Humane Society.
Playing fetch with them
Is what I like to do.
With their strong teeth
Grasping the chew toy
As they growl so loud.
Taking them for walks
As I strangle the leash
When he tries to pull away.
But, dogs are
A man's best friend and
That is their greatest quality.

Maria Fisher, Grade 7
Luxemburg-Casco Middle School, WI

Finger to Finger

Gracefully gliding, finger to finger,
a harmonious noise comes from the instrument planted in front of me.
White and black does not describe the melodies it makes,
but it does describe the shape this beautiful vibration comes from.
Key to key, finger to finger
creating chords that make even the most pleasant of things
sound like absolutely nothing.
The clamor and commotion behind my back is drowned out
and I sink into the sheet music placed in front of me.
My right foot moving up and down
helping the tone blend together ever so perfectly
and my left foot keeping in time to the rhythm.
Finger to finger I create a masterpiece.
Finger to finger I free myself to a different world.

Brianne Stephens, Grade 8
Walker Charter Academy, MI

Change in a Year

A lot can happen in a year whether it's love, happiness or fear,
But when it comes to change, nothing stays the same
Affecting the ones you know, something that you can't control
You might not want it to be, but it could be something you can't see
It might last a lifetime you won't get a sign,
It won't be that clear but you'll know when it's here,
Some things just seem to happen something that could be sent to happen
But change is so difficult, never ending with the same result
Never will happen again, just be glad that it will end
Change will always be there, appearing out of thin air,
A year can change anything in my case never ending.

Brennan Thundercloud, Grade 8
Spring Hill School, WI

Precious Moments

Have you ever seen

The look on a little girl's face when her daddy comes home from war,
how about when a puppy sits at his bowl of food begging for a little bit more

And when a baby laughs, or when a baby cries
then the mother wipes the tears that fall from her eyes

Yes, these moments are precious and priceless indeed,
and when having a bad day they are just what you need

Just think of these moments and you'll instantly cheer up
and maybe they will even bring you some good luck

Just remember one thing; precious moments are like love,
there is no limit that you can go above

These moments are what you adore,
and no matter what, you can always make more

Elle Coon, Grade 7
St Roman School, WI

Life Is a Highway

Life is a Highway
With bumps and turns
The long neverendingness
The yellow lines keeping me on track
Signs telling me what's ahead or what to do
Other cars honking or getting in my way
No stop lights for the more comforting feeling
All alone in the car
Stepping on the break to slow down and take a break
Realizing your surroundings
It's a never ending thing
Until you reach your exit

Ashley Krenzer, Grade 7
Royal Oak Middle School, MI

Beamer

Beamer.
Probably the stupidest dog the world has ever seen.
He perches on the edge of my brother's bed.
He looks up at me.
He's on Max's blankets.
He knows
Those blankets are equally forbidden territory.
His eyes are those of a convicted killer
Swimming with the knowledge he has done wrong.
He rises from the bed like a skyscraper.
Moments later the doorbell rings.
He rockets to the door
Sounding the alarm that someone is here.
The hair on the back of his neck
Standing higher than the ceiling
Though he's barely two feet tall.
I walk up behind him and give him a good smack.
He cowers away,
But in his eyes he can tell that I love him.
And he knows deep down that he deserved it.

Katy Downard, Grade 8
Paw Paw Middle School, MI

Nature

What is *nature*?
Nature is a world outside the city
A little known vacation spot full of wonders

Nature is not just forests and jungles
It's the landscape yet to be broken

Nature is calming, beautiful and plentiful
Made of trees and grasses and soils and skies

Nature is forever wondrous and serene
A place that is peace-filled

Nature is perfect in every way

Paul Young, Grade 7
Roosevelt Middle School, MN

Inside

I go through the motions of life, ignoring my inside.
Like bubbles on a clear stream, covering the dirt underneath.
My life is like a masquerade, which mask will I wear today?
If only I could stop and look inside.

I am like the big road, not the narrow twisted path.
I look inviting to the eye, unlike the other.
But once you go deeper, you see the troubles.
The holes and the broken bridge.

Nathan Ross, Grade 9
Clarkston Jr High School, MI

Time

Time is a strange thing
Then, now, when?
Minutes fly away
New ones come our way
What will we do with our time?
I want to do something important
I want to be remembered
And make a difference
In the lives of all that I meet
And even some that I won't
Time should not be wasted
Dwelling on the past
When we have the future to look forward to
We need to make our time last

Korina Hendricks, Grade 8
St Roman School, WI

It Is Night

It is night,
I look up at the calm,
Cool, velvet black sky and it soothes me.
It's like a lullaby,
The nighttime sky.
The stars sparkle and
Shimmer brilliantly,
Pulling me a million miles away
From the empty and
Lonely space I stand.
I wonder what's out there,
The stars seem to hold
So many questions unanswered,
So many dreams yet to be lived.
I stand gazing at the stars, amazed by their beauty
And I wish to answer those questions.
Live those dreams.
And it is night,
I look up at the calm,
Cool, velvet black of the sky,
And I hear the star's soft, sweet lullaby.

Tyler Rumbold, Grade 9
Clarkston Jr High School, MI

Here with Me
Wishing you were here
Here is next to me
Held warmly in my arms
That's where you should be

Wishing you could hear
Hear things within my mind
Searched constantly for thoughts
You're all that I could find

Wishing you would come
Come and be with me
I know that you'd be happy
That I guarantee

Wishing you could fall
Fall into my heart
Drown inside my love
We'd never be apart

Wishing you were here
But you want to go there
I wish that you could see
That there is here with me
Jason Gong, Grade 9
Troy High School, MI

Chocolate/Vanilla
Chocolate
Flavorous, milky
Flowing, drooling, melting
Dark, tasty, light, scrumptious
Dissolving, thawing, filling
White, creamy
Vanilla
Joe Boucher, Grade 7
Edison Middle School, WI

Rain
The rain falls hard and long
Then soft and short

It never stops, never ends
Keeps going

Making puddles both big
And small

Little kids running and laughing
Splashing through the puddles

The rain falls hard and long
Then soft and short
Nicole Peronto, Grade 7
Luxemburg-Casco Middle School, WI

Night to Day
Night to day
Is all we know.
Black to white
Again and again
Moon to sun
An everlasting show
Dark to light
Without end
Stars to clouds
Incessantly so
Twinkle to shine
Repetitively periodic
Rest to play
A never ending flow
Quiet to loud
Yes, these are all changes
Stop to go
Fascinatingly, though
Slow to fast
These changes happen the same way
Over and over from night to day.
Jacqueline Burke, Grade 8
Boulan Park Middle School, MI

Stars
Stars.
Bright, fiery.
Falling, watching, catching.
Brightest thing between land and heaven.
Amusing.
Lindsey Clements, Grade 7
Washtenaw Christian Academy, MI

Aloneness
What happened to our friendship?
And where has it gone?
I excessively miss you
Though you haven't been away long

Have you made new friends?
Do you even remember me?
Don't you realize I need you?
Can't you see?

There's not 1 person around here
That could ever take your place
I still remember when you told me
That you needed some space

Now you're gone forever
I know you will not come back for me
For I am aloneness
And you're letting me be
Maria Dechant, Grade 7
St Joseph Catholic Middle School, MI

All That Glitters
All that glitters
Ever illuminating my mind
Wanting, waiting, needing
All that glitters
Tell me, the lengths I will not go
To watch my dear possessions glow
Look at all my things!
Garnished with jewels and rings
All that glitters
I can possess them all
Wait and see
I shall only see what's in front of me
Out the window the sun draws me near
Wanting, waiting, needing
I need all that glitters!
Tell me, the lengths I would not go
To watch my dear possessions glow
The sun calls to me as it shines
Leaving all my friends behind
Hungry is the heart filled with greed
All that glitters is what I need
Terah Yoeckel, Grade 8
St Roman School, WI

Titanic
It was one of the greatest ships,
So elegant and charming.
Everyone so happy and cheery,
Sailing through the seas.

The ocean so cold and clear,
Yet not clear enough,
To see the giant iceberg,
That they hit that night.

There was panic,
Everyone so scared,
With not enough boats,
For everyone to share.

And when it was all over,
The tears still never dry.
They cannot help but think,
About that scary night.
Kara Pompeo, Grade 8
Our Lady Star of the Sea School, MI

My Bike
My bike
Takes me around town
When I want it to
On the burning hot black road
For a gentle ride in the summer air
Joseph Ribbens, Grade 7
Edison Middle School, WI

Math Class

I had a dream that I went back in time
I dreamed that I was among dinosaurs
The stink of dead animals in the air
I looked around to see a terrifying tyrannosaurus
It was running right towards me
I looked around to see what I thought was a giant hollow rock
I jumped inside it
But I noticed it wasn't a rock
It was an egg shell
And there were baby dinosaurs surrounding me
But for some reason they turned and ran away
I turned around to my displeasure
To see the tyrannosaurus was right behind me
I tried running, but it was too fast
And then I tripped over a rock
All of a sudden when all looked lost
I woke up from my dream
Realizing that math class was over.

Joseph Berggren, Grade 8
Abundant Life Christian School, WI

Love Is Like

Love is like a mother so tender and sweet,
Love is like a girl cute and petite,
Love is like space so full, and open,
Love is like Dr. King strong and outspoken,
Love is like Rosa Parks so brave and mighty,
Love is like a mountain sharp and pointy,
Love is like a bed warm and cozy,
Love is like a dog small and fuzzy,
Love is like a book so full of information,
Love is like school where you get your education,
But most of all love is like friendship long-lasting
And flabbergasting.

Mixon Golson, Grade 7
Hally Magnet Middle School, MI

Dreaming Cheesy

If everything were cheese curds I could…
Eat everyone everywhere, everything.
I could eat every bit of cheese to be seen.
I could eat all of China, Brazil, and Japan,
Every cup, every fork, every egg, every ham.
If everything were that glorious snack,
I'd probably die of a heart attack.
That melty cheese rolled in scrumptious brown crumbs;
It's no wonder they're gone after I've only begun.
I doubt there is anything ever come from a cow,
More delicious than that which is spoken of now.
If the world were all cheese curds,
Everywhere to be seen,
My tongue might be happy but my build quite obese.

Daniel Tarté, Grade 8
Abundant Life Christian School, WI

The View from the Top of a Tree

If there ever was a *monkey*
Precariously perching atop a tree
This ever was the *monkey*
Precariously perching.
For the *malevolent monkey*
Crookedly climbed atop the *tree*
To see what he could see,
From the view from the top of the *tree*.

But alas, as all the events eventually end,
The *malevolent monkey's* precarious perch ended,
F
a
l
l
i
n
g
Into various vines and
Particularly prickly *bushes*,
Teaching the *monkey*
Never to precariously perch again.

Zack Sorenson, Grade 7
Roosevelt Middle School, MN

Summer Ice

The summer mornings
Waking up to the chirping of birds
As I walk into the kitchen
A bright light shines on the floor
Making the floor so warm
I walk outside to breathe the fresh air
I hear the clanking of the ice in my glass
A drip of water drops from my glass to the ground
The sun shines down on my glass
Like the sun shining on the snow in winter
How it sparkled every morning
I hear a crack where the chipmunk cracks the walnuts
So glad the long winter days are over
No more short mornings and
No more long winter nights
Finally no more waiting
Summer is here and the long days
Are over
Finally summer is here!

Olivia Carril, Grade 7
Abundant Life Christian School, WI

I Just Don't Think

When I think, I don't just think,
I imagine, I hope, I dream,
about goals written down on ink.
When I think I can be anyone, anywhere, even any time.
When I think, I just don't think.

Andy Kieckhefer, Grade 7
Washington School, WI

all alone

i cry alone
wising you were home
i'm sorry i had you cry
but you're making me die

i need you by my side
because i hurt inside
i'm leaving tonight
remember me when i was bright

Taylor Feltson, Grade 8
Jerstad Agerholm Middle School, WI

Safe

I am safe, I am here.
Hope is now becoming clearer.
Bring me light;
Brighten this night.
I will be okay.
I will live another day.
Once again, I will smile.
I will be able to breathe in a while.
I try my hardest to hold my head high;
But I still won't allow myself to cry.
This life isn't over yet.
I won't give in to this regret.
This isn't where my story ends.
I will hold on until my hope mends.

Stevie Lee Weston, Grade 9
Sauk Rapids-Rice Sr High School, MN

Tie

Tight around
your neck
An extra
piece of clothing
making you look fancier

Stripy, straight
so many styles
Sometimes stupid
Can also be
Funny

Black, blue,
red or green
dressy and nice
or really
bad looking

Can come with
instructions
written on the
front so you can
actually tie it.

John Kutschke, Grade 7
Manistee Middle School, MI

His Name Is Kyle

12:02 in the hospital room, you are quietly adoring;
"He has your eyes," you say to the groom, in the first few minutes of morning.

Ten years gone, at a little league game, you watch him running the base.
Safe! He's home! He gets his fame, a smile all over his face.

Sixteen now, he gets the keys, nearly killing himself in the process.
Brings home his first girl, named Annabel Lee, sparkling in her bright prom dress.

Cap and gown, you try not to cry, he's going to spread his wings
To start his own life, my oh my, a song of sadness you sing.

A few years later, a nervous smile plays across his face,
Across a beautiful Annabel Lee, in a white dress of lace.

A loving husband, caring father, making the most of life.
How would you feel if he never existed? Tell me, does it cause you strife?

This is the case with many a child, who was considered an "issue"
Who could have had a meaningful life, tell me, was he *only* a blob of tissue?

Alexa Chiu, Grade 9
Lakeview Christian Academy, MN

The Cheetah Shell

With ferocious brown spots like a cheetah.
Vivid tan, brown lines like a piece of wood.
A bottom the color of New York Vanilla ice cream.
There's a tiny, jagged crack down the bottom like the Grand Canyon.

It's the size of a quarter.
Smooth like a fingernail.

It's a hill lying at the bottom of the ocean,
Or a snail just below the surface waiting to be found.

It begs to be looked at.
It pleads for your attention.
If you dare a glance…
You there is no doubt will see it's unmistakable beauty.

But then it's gone in a flash.
Like a cheetah.
Never to be seen again.

Sarah O'Driscoll, Grade 8
Chippewa Falls Middle School, WI

The Ocean

A most beautiful place.
Its gentle breeze and soothing scent that you just want to eat.
Gentle waves falling into the shore, the kind of things that make you want to live there.
But it has a darker side too.
Tsunamis and tidal waves crashing into the cold, sandy earth.
Hurricanes taking down cities at its expense, tropical storms flooding the coast
Like it were a clogged sink.

Dalton Hilbert, Grade 7
Elkhart Lake Elementary-Middle School, WI

Every Time

Every time I hear your voice
I can no longer pay attention to any other noise,
Every time I kiss your lips
a tingly sensation overcomes my fingertips.
Every time I hold your hand
my legs become so weak I can barely stand.
You and me seem to be like a bird in a tree
or like salt in the sea.
Your smile is my Earth, your eyes are my Sun,
and your love is my entire universe.

Unlike these flowers that will sadly wilt
nothing can compare to the love in which we have built.
I love you more than words can tell, emotions can express
to have you in my life I am truly blessed.

Kaitlyn Shawn, Grade 9
Petoskey High School, MI

The Forest

Where's a place where you can think clearly and be yourself,
You see everything come to life where the spring is dancing,
The leaves are flowing, the sun gives new life.
Where everything has a meaning and a purpose to exist,
The tree's big branches are like arms reaching for the sun.
You can hear the whistling of the wind in the trees,
And the trickle of the streams.
You hear the leaves crackle under your feet.
At night the crickets are chirping like violins
It's peaceful and calm,
Everything is quiet hush.

Kurt Bennett, Grade 8
J C McKenna Middle School, WI

Flying Solo

Have you ever dove from a one meter board?
As you swim to the top you hope the crowd roared.
Repeating the dive over and over in your mind,
Hoping today the judges scores will be kind.
Yes, I know this because I'm a lone diver,
Every difficult tuck and turn to be the best striver.
I will never give up on this nerve racking feat,
Because I do it at almost every swim meet.
My swimsuit goes on snug behind a closed door,
I start to pace back and forth on the cold wet floor.
The announcer then calls out each divers name,
I walk past my teammates and we all look the same.
But I am different from them and do you know why,
I am the only one who soars through the sky.
You see it takes all I have to get nerves of steel,
When hitting the board or slapping could be so real.
So I do my approach then dive, putting myself to the test,
As I splash into the water knowing that I've done my best.
Pulling myself up onto the deck I listen for my score,
Yep, it was all worth walking through that pool room door!

Keanna Carlson, Grade 7
Falls High School, MN

Fifteen Years Forgotten

You still try to convince us
that you were always there.
From when I was born until now,
seeing you has always been rare.
You've missed a lot of birthdays,
another one from this year.
I never saw you at my softball games
or supporting Mom's new career.
I've always wished for a real dad,
I guess you never heard my plea.
I'm not your little girl anymore,
but can't you see it's still me?
Sometimes I sit and wonder
if you love your car more than us.
You put a lot of other things first
and it creates more than a little fuss.
You work because you love us,
always making our wants come true.
But, Dad, you must understand
I'd give all the money in the world for you.

Beth Mader, Grade 9
Montgomery-Lonsdale High School, MN

The Power of Hunger

As I ride on my way home from the prison we call school
I sit there thinking,
What did I have for lunch?
Oh wait, Nothing!
So there I am, my stomach tearing at my insides
And then I see them
Those big golden arches
It was honestly the best sight I've ever seen
And as we pull in the drive in
I know we're pulling into heaven

Thomas Larson, Grade 8
Washington Middle School, WI

Jealousy

I wish I was her
I wish I'm the one that didn't have to suffer
I wish to have her confidence,
Her grace,
Her face
I wish I'm the one he would talk about
"Why am I not like her?" I wanted to shout
I wish I'm the one that people wants to be near
I wish to have no fear
I wish things were my way
I wish my time would come someday
I wish I'm always busy
I wish life was easy
I wish I'm not the one who's writing this poem.

Lee Long, Grade 7
Valley View Middle School, MN

Monster Patrol

Roaring through the noisy crowd
In the stadium
During the jamboree
To show off their massive madness
Of destruction.

Donald Angrabright, Grade 7
Edison Middle School, WI

Snow

Snow is a wonderful thing
tickling you as it falls on your face
making you squeal with delight
for it's comforting presence

Snow is a beautiful thing
a beautiful piece of mother nature
each one, unique to the eye
a priceless work of art

Snow is a curious thing
each one special, never the same
soft, and smooth, yet steady and firm
always asking to come over
never taking "no" for an answer

But wherever it goes
and whatever it does
it will always be there, to play with you,
snow,
snow,
snow.

Alejandro Loza, Grade 7
Ramsey Jr High School, MN

My Street Music

Robins sing
Telling me
Spring
Is here
Cats chasing
The lovely
Robins
Dogs barking
Winds are
Forcing
The trees
To sway
Woof
Wsh
Meow
Tweet
This is
My
Street Music

Tapanga Settler, Grade 7
Whitehall Jr High School, MI

Stars, Stars, Stars

Through the darkness, what could you see?
A happy life. Joyful. Feeling.
When then could you realize you're getting older and closer to the stars,
Like a shooting comet in reverse.
It's gonna make a big impact, but it will be forgotten.
You'll shoot into the everlasting life of the moon.
The stars are your audience.
Arouse them.
Make them yours.
Hone the moment when you're the most important thing out there.
Soon you'll just shoot up.

Nathan Stevens, Grade 9
Hill McCloy High School, MI

Dreams

Why can't life be a dream?
A place where your craziest and wildest fantasy can come true
A dream is somewhere to escape to
A place where no lawyer can sue just to get more money
A place where no one is mean
And you don't have to worry if you're fit or lean
You can live on a cloud, even have a pet dragon. You never feel bad or sad
Just because someone else is mad
A dream is a place that is yours and no one can take it
Only if reality was as good as a dream
Reality is harsh, cold and mean
But luckily, we will always have our dreams
To escape to when reality gets mean

Beth Rasmussen, Grade 8
St Roman School, WI

Down to You

One look is all it takes from you to make my heart beat ten times faster.
Those eyes are what's keeping me from loving anyone but you.
I feel so controlled, taken over, by a man I, never thought I'd love.
You're poisoning me from my soul.
I'm crawling into, another world I, never knew before.
Yet, I need strength, to believe. I need faith, to stay in love.
Give me something to hold on to. I'm falling down to you.
How do I know that you're different from the rest?
You're face, it tells me you're not the same.
My past, is what's giving me doubts, but my heart says, you're my future.
Yet still, I need strength, to believe. I need faith, to stay in love.
Give me something to hold on to. I'm falling down to you.
Take my hand and tell me lies.
I'll still love you in my heart.
Tell me what I do is wrong.
Show me what is right.
Just don't leave me alone, in the evanescent of the night.
I don't want to see the light just yet.
I need strength, to believe. I need faith, to stay in love.
Give me something to hold on to, because I'm falling down to you.

Jessica Gavrilovski, Grade 8
L'anse Creuse Middle School East, MI

Family

My family is the sun when the sky is gray
They take the fear away when I'm feeling unsafe
They turn my frown upside down
They are the reason why I live

Wendy Alonso Razo, Grade 7
Valley View Middle School, MN

O River

O river of eternal flowing
From where do you begin
What are all the things that lie below you
Some I step on with my feet
Some are smooth and round
Others are hard and sharp
What's that gooey slimy stuff I'm stepping on?
Through the crystal clear water
I see the cray fish scouring
The minnows grouping on your edge
As you pass under the covered bridge
What lies in your shadows there?
I see the sun reflect off your surface
The leaves slowly passing by
The lonely island
Where tubers swerve around
Where do you end,
A lake, a river, an ocean?
What's even around that bend
O river of eternal flowing

Alleck Heinzen, Grade 7
St Katharine Drexel School, WI

The Journey

If you feel you don't belong
And you want to find that place
Where you do belong, you will need to go on a journey.
Not saying it will be easy, it may be difficult,
It may be tough to accomplish.
If you want to go on this journey
You must have faith, believe, and imagine what
You've never thought of before.
For think like an adventurous child
And you will live forever and for always.
When you do this, you can fly through the clouds and sky.
You can glide through a wondrous rainbow
And wander up glorious and great mountains.
Along the white, sandy beach, you can walk beside
The gentle, silent, sleepy, blue ocean.
After the sun is down and the day over,
You can see the white, shiny moon.
While lying on the grassy hills as you watch the night go by,
You start to realize in the tranquil night,
This is what you were looking for, this is where you belong.

Brian Ore, Grade 8
West Suburban Christian Academy, WI

Alone

I am set alone
Silent…
All have vanished,
There is not a soul in sight.
I long for a companion.

As I rest alone in this cold stone room,
As I gaze at the barriers that surround me,
I note the temperature drop.
As I become lost within myself,
As I stare at the cage that surrounds me.

I notice an artificial glow,
And my soul begins to crave that essential brilliance.
My heart slowly pounds
And my breaths bottomless and distant.
As I start to marvel at what is beyond.

Michael Hart, Grade 9
Clarkston Jr High School, MI

A Miracle

A miracle of life, streaked with tears and ink.
Painted by your dreams,
Slowly sinking past the twilight.

Heavenly lighted, the snowflakes drift downward,
Sleepily toward the earth.
Lightly kissing our eyelashes.

Blues and purples blotched
Greens spiraled, in the sky,
Singing so silently, made by an invisible mind.

It is a new dream, see the padded footprints.
Hear the bellowing moose,
Whistling wind, rustling trees.

A walking picture, see the moving mural,
As silent as the hunt,
The snap of a creaking tree branch.

Fear how calm it is, creatures never knowing.
Beauty frozen in time,
A mirror image forever there.

Jessica Knapp, Grade 8
Chippewa Falls Middle School, WI

My Friend

She carried me away on her back like a bird.
She took me to a place far away.
Somewhere where that no one could find me.
An island full of wild animals and trees.
I like it here, but what she doesn't know is,
I want to go home to my family.

Tiffany Flannigan, Grade 8
Bloomingdale Middle School, MI

My Life

I know where I am now,
Not certain where I'll go.
I will create my own path,
For it's a one man show.

I hope to leave a footprint
On the Earth before I go.
My way of life is simple,
This is what I know:
I'll always work my hardest,
Because that's the way I roll.

The two rules that will guide me
On how to live my life:
Make myself the hero,
Do not live with strife.

Anna Simmons, Grade 8
St Roman School, WI

Katina Smith

Katina Smith
Beautiful, smart
Caring, praying, determining
Katina is a hardworking woman
Kaytee

Dondre Green, Grade 8
Langston Hughes Academy, MI

Music Is Me

My words,
My thoughts,
My senses,
Loud sound, hullabaloo,
It's more than that,
It's life.

My feelings,
My way of expressing,
Words with meaning,
Rhythm with joy or it's depressing.
Boom, boom, boom

My heart,
My head,
My soul,
Bubble gum pop to the sad jazz blues,
Day and night it's all around you,
Following like your shadow

I grew up with it,
It's my friend,
Don't try to pretend you can't hear it,
Music is me.

Alyssa Fricke, Grade 7
Ramsey Jr High School, MN

Peace

All that is
heard
Is the chirp of
The birds
and the wisp
of the wind
the sun rains
down on your hair
and shimmers in the waves
of the water.
You close your eyes
and all you can think of
is peace,
peace that is God given
Peace

Kaitlyn Schleif, Grade 7
Abundant Life Christian School, WI

Love

Love is like a story.
It's got a beginning,
it's got a middle,
and it's got an end.
What happens in between
is for your heart to decide.

Dana Kidrowski, Grade 7
Valley View Middle School, MN

Thunderstorm

Boom! Crackle! Boom!
Running, panting
Stalking closer
Oncoming freight train
Industrial dancing
Like metal striking sun
Rushing, headlong clouds
Tracks of trembling torrents
Angrily screaming
Stop!
Grinding to a halt
Like a commuter train: it passed
Sightless
Sweet, soft raindrops,
Slowly softening,
Boom! Crackle! Boom!
Fading

Stormy Gerndt, Grade 8
Suring Elementary/Middle School, WI

winter

winter is peaceful
winter is icy and dry
winter is snowy

Cody Chambasian, Grade 8
Jerstad Agerholm Middle School, WI

When Money Was Green

When money was green,
It was something that was seen.
Not red, nor yellow, but green.

Riches galore,
Even on your door.
Oh yes, when money was green.

As it grows up soon,
Just after noon,
Gray, old, silent, and cold.
No more would money be green.

For money will never lead,
It will do nothing but give you greed.
People are worth a whole lot more,
Money's not what you need.

Emily Michielutti, Grade 8
Our Lady Star of the Sea School, MI

Pandy

I miss you
you were my
favorite dog
and you were even
my first dog and
older than me.
Then one day
my mom just took
you away to the hospital
but she didn't
think that you
would have
to go to sleep.
I was very sad that day
because…
I didn't even
get to say
goodbye.

Lindsey Eberle, Grade 7
St Katharine Drexel School, WI

Dolphins

Graceful, peaceful
Lively dance
Jump high to the sky twirl and spin
Like on nature's stage
Ballet of the sea
Pirouette over sky high swells
Performing on blue vastness
Sadly coming to a stop
Dolphins' curtain call
Maybe another day of play

Sanorraine Vanderhoff, Grade 8
Suring Elementary/Middle School, WI

Two Ladies in the Park

Two old ladies meet in the park,
To see the kids play, to hear the dogs bark.
They sit on a bench,
Two coffees; they clench.
They sip and they talk,
They gaze as they walk,
Till their feet are so sore
They can't do it anymore.
They shake hands and ask names,
Then they leave as they came.

Nicholas Wagner, Grade 8
St Margaret Mary School, WI

People Are All Different

People are all different no matter what they say
People are all different in every single way
People are all different in a million ways!

People are all the same no matter what the name
People are all the same no matter how they look
People are all the same in one crash!

People are all family no matter where they are from
People are all family no matter how they are
People are all family!

People are all kids with all that they do
People are all kids no matter what the age
People are all kids!

Humanity is like a cloud!

Tori Osweiler, Grade 7
Ramsey Jr High School, MN

Bliss and Tranquility of Life

An eagle soars above a meadow,
Reflecting a life without any mellow
The slow sun rises above the cloud.
There is only silence, nothing loud.
Ripples form on the water's surface;
Nothing will ever detest,
With the peace and tranquility of the meadow.
Each species in harmony with its fellow,
But all life must end, sooner or later.
No other justice could ever seem fairer.
The rhythm of life: everything comes and goes.
But why, only God knows.
But out of the Old, New revives;
Coming forth, full of life.
And again the sequence continues to rotate;
Life has no other need to motivate.
The New learns, perfects, and advances.
The sun sets, overflowing with enhance.
Promising tomorrow, with endless possibilities.

Mark Kenney, Grade 9
St Thomas More Academy, MI

How I Feel

Ever since I met you
You have opened my eyes to all of these wonderful things
I look to the both of you for guidance
Sometimes we don't see eye to eye but I still love y'all
I appreciate both of you guys
I can't even explain how you do
Our friendship will last a long time
You're always in my heart and my mind

Ayla Hughes, Grade 8
Messmer Preparatory Catholic School, WI

The Farm

The farm is a very pretty place.
With a river
that's sort of wide and semi deep.
With really thick swamps and long grass.
There are also cornfields
that range from 6-11 acres.
The people who own it are the Remingtons.
The farm has dense
and not so dense woods.
In the forest and swamps
are trees
and trees
and trees.
Then there's the two farm houses which my
grandpa and my grandpa's brother own.
The farm house my grandpa owns has
a stable which holds three horses and a cow.
A two floor barn with hay on the second floor and
three lofts.

Theo Ambrosius, Grade 7
St Katharine Drexel School, WI

Fishing

Shamono, Shakespeare and ugly Stick
Some of the best years you can have
Crappie, Walleye and Bass
Some of the best fish you can catch

Setting the hook is like riding a bull
You're on for a wild ride,
Your rod sounds like a thousand people
Screaming at once
As the fish is pulling out more line and more line
And more line,
You fear that your line's going to break

Then the stress is over the fish is in the net
The fish of a lifetime,
From a 6 inch Perch to a 60 inch Muskie
Any fish is a good fish.

Charles Minea Jr., Grade 7
Ramsey Jr High School, MN

If I Could Fly

If I could fly, I would soar over the deep blue waters
If I could fly, I would never be afraid to sky dive
If I could fly, I would never need to pay bills for a car
If I could fly, there would never be any traffic to and from work
If I could fly, birds would not be so great
If I could fly, I would make millions performing at air shows
If I could fly, I could deliver pizza to anywhere on the planet in under thirty minutes
If I could fly, I would never burn a hole in the heel of my shoes
If I could fly, I wish I would have the power to control myself from becoming an air head
and forgetting the great friends I once knew

Matthew Grossholz, Grade 7
Abundant Life Christian School, WI

I Am Somebody

I am somebody that will have a life, I am somebody that will live until the end of time, I am somebody that will not play around, because if I play around my dreams could hit the ground, I am somebody that will have a dream, I am somebody that will someday be like Dr. Martin Luther King.

Terrance Adams, Grade 7
Sherman Multicultural Arts School, WI

Live, Laugh, Love Away

There is a bird on my window sill and I wonder if he's ever known the big green monster you have become.
You've made mistakes in the past and, yes, you did silently ask me to forgive. But it would help to know you care, you need to let me know you care, you have to give to get.
You and I have to grow up now somehow far apart. I need to make my own mistakes and you need to grow up not just old. Life is calling, "Live, laugh, love, cry, and learn from your mistakes now dear." I won't forget you, what not to do. Just let me live and do my school work, without you there I'll be ok.

Alexandria Lemmen, Grade 9
Unity Christian High School, MI

Baseball

You dig your feet in the batter's box,
You give the pitcher the death stare like you guys are long time enemies
Knock, knock, knock, you knock the bat against the plate as you are getting ready for the pitch.
You can smell the hot dogs in the stands behind you.

Your bat is a weapon.
That you will use to strike the ball as hard as possible.
As the pitcher winds up,
You get butterflies in your stomach like if you were dropping from 1000 feet off the ground.
You feel the tension between you and the pitcher.

The pitch comes, you swing as hard as you can, whoof! You completely miss.
You step out of the box and look at your third base coach,
He tells you the same thing that you have heard a billion times in your life,
Keep your eye on the ball.
Now you start to get angry because it's like your bat goes to sleep whenever you try to swing it.
You can see everyone is praying that you get a hit this time.

The next pitch comes faster, you swing and hear a sudden DING!
The ball went back back back, and gone!
Your coach comes over and says "see what happens when you keep your eye on it?"
You hear someone say "you hit that ball a mile!"
Yes I did you say, yes I did.

Michael Hannon, Grade 7
Ramsey Jr High School, MN

Credo

I believe in the pursuit of happiness
The idea of living your own life,
And not being fake.
The idea of having no fears in life,
And living your life to the fullest.
Courage, Bravery, Perseverance.

But the idea of not being yourself, and trying to be
someone else, is just plain absurd.

I believe that cheaters never prosper in the long run,
I believe that people need to be self-dependent,
I believe that all you need to be is yourself.
Respect, Honor, Trust.

I believe that people are not always as they appear on
the outside, they could be completely different inside.

Matthew Langreder, Grade 8
West Suburban Christian Academy, WI

I Am the Deer

I am the deer; I am mighty and strong,
I know what's right and I know what's wrong.
As I hear a bang off in the distance,
I know for a deer that could be a bad coincidence.
But not for me because I'm mighty and strong,
I know what's right and I know what's wrong.

As the leaves crunch under my feet,
I know that winter is coming to meet.
When winter is coming I know what begins,
The season where some lose, and some of us win.
But I will win because I'm mighty and strong,
I know what's right and I know what's wrong.

Connor Klavekoske, Grade 7
St Katharine Drexel School, WI

Me and Halia

I love my niece,
She loves me too.

She is the one who bumps her head and cries,
I am the one who picks her up and gets her to stop.

She is the one who giggles,
I make the silly face.

She cries to not sleep,
I comfort her.

She slowly calms down,
I watch her drift away to dreamland.

Laura Stegeman, Grade 7
Shakopee Area Catholic School, MN

Under the Water

Under the icy cool water,
the sand shimmers,
and rainbow coral glitters.
Here, tiny seahorses come to hide
from big, bad sharks,
looking for something to munch on.
Hidden beneath the water,
under the sand and
far, far away.

Under the icy cool water,
Magical mermaids come out to play,
swimming with their fishy friends
along the coral reef.
While others sit on the bay,
combing their long wavy hair,
with sparkly crab claws.

Above the icy cool water,
On the land,
I am there.
Soaking up the warm summer sun,
wishing I could just fly away.

Janice Finley, Grade 7
Shakopee Area Catholic School, MN

Daybreak

Water flowing rapidly
Sweet scent of the wilderness
Water hitting against rocks
Chilly breezes
Water droplets splashing everywhere
What a beautiful morning

Jenna Schanke, Grade 7
Elkhart Lake Elementary-Middle School, WI

Roller Coaster

I'm in line waiting,
My sister is nervous shaking.

In front and behind they wait,
We can't turn back it's too late.

My heart is quickly beating,
People are finally seating.

Our seatbelts we now fasten,
Other coasters are passing.

5, now we wait,
4, we know it's time,
3, we hold on tight,
2, our stomachs drop,
1, it has begun.

Kayla Igo, Grade 8
Saint Thomas More Catholic School, MN

Love, Hate, Black History

I am African American
I am intelligent
I float like a butterfly
and sting like a bee
I am me

I think about my people
and where they came from
I think about black history
and what black Americans have done

I care about school
I care about friends
I love God and my family
to the very end

I see the blood
I feel the pain
I wish there was love
instead of hate

love, hate, black history
truly four strong words

Kalu Abosi, Grade 7
Ramsey Jr High School, MN

Skateboarding

Skateboarding
Sponsors, Tournaments
Jumping, grinding, falling
Sometimes you land tricks
Tony Hawk

Devin Gray, Grade 7
Langston Hughes Academy, MI

Yellow Light

Every day and every night
The road becomes your home
Where you race round and round
And cars veer in and out
On the bumpy surface
The road rooted out for us
From the garage others come
Big yellow squares
Sprinting up and down the road
Which controls them
To the place they need to go
Pulled to the stops
The kids anticipate for them to come
And heed for the squeak of the breaks
When the yellow blurs come to a halt
And releases the doors
That lets the students on to
Go to the next stop

Kathleen Blust, Grade 9
Clarkston Jr High School, MI

Why?

I don't understand…
Why people think that it is ok to break someone else's heart
Why people think that love does not matter
Why people think friendships are no big deal
Why people say "Whatever" to really important situations
Why they chose to lie to your face

But most of all I don't understand…
Why a person can make you think differently about yourself
Why a song can be the guidelines of a relationship
Why hearing the words "I love you" makes you shiver
Why talking out a problem is so hard
Why a relationship can be wonderful and horrible at the same time

I do understand…
Why people care only about themselves
Why people think they know what it means to care
Why a hug can make you feel better in a split moment
Why a smile can give you a warm feeling inside
Why a little bit of love in your life can help you live it to your fullest

Alesha Marie Gorectke, Grade 8
West Suburban Christian Academy, WI

The Love That You Give

The love that you show her is not so true,
She didn't tell you but she told me the way she feels about you,
The love that you give to her doesn't show much caring at all,
You never ever picked her up from any of her falls,
The love that you had for her was dishonest and poor,
I bet you would've been sad if she walked out that door,
But "No" she stayed she thought it would get true,
She thought the love would come someday between her and you,
The love that you gave has not really vanished,
I don't know how but she stuck through it and managed,
The love that you say you have for her makes people say "he's a good man,"
Walking through the mall you don't hold her hand,
Your love is the wrong love to give her or to anyone,
You have two daughters and you have one son,
The love that you show is such a demeanor,
I bet you didn't act like this when you put the ring on her finger,
The love you showed her is not so true,
And this is my poem from me to you.

Andrea Bozeman, Grade 7
Hally Magnet Middle School, MI

Understanding a Teenager

Moms and dads don't really understand
We teenagers just want to be in demand
We ask for money to go to the mall
And the parents ask: "who's going to pay for it all"
All we want is to be understood
But people often say stop with that attitude
Understanding a teenager is very complicated
In order for us to remain sane we sometimes need to be isolated

Jamila Hightower, Grade 8
Messmer Preparatory Catholic School, WI

Storm at the Cabin

White caps crash in the dancing wind,
They peak and smash, but are born again.
They flow across darkness and wailing rain,
They won't cease coming till the light of day.

White waves dash the sand from the shore,
Bright lightning flashes throughout all the storm.
Wind gusts and howls till the glowing morn,
But at last the world's silent and the waves are no more.

There's rain in the gutter and dew on the sill,
Wind still whips the shutters in the morning's chill.
Black clouds linger in uncertain defeat,
But the morning brings new light to make darkness deplete.

Kaitlin Hackett, Grade 8
Wayzata Central Middle School, MN

Drum Set

Drum sets are very cool
And we have a nice one here at school
The bass drum sounds just like a bomb
And if I play it loud it annoys my mom
The snare drum sounds like loud clapping
And the ride cymbal sounds like smooth snapping
For dinner when my mom's cooking meat
I use the bass drum to keep a beat
On the cymbal I start jamming
And on the snare drum I start whamming
Then I hear a small tapping
I look up and see my mother clapping
Dinner!!!!

Nick Johnson, Grade 7
Luxemburg-Casco Middle School, WI

Not Ugly, Not Pretty

Against his tomato red face,
And his wild green hair,
His beautiful ocean blue eyes
Stick out like a sore thumb.

Screaming native warrior chants
Sounds angry yet sad
He's saying "Help me from this mess,
This problem that I've made!"

His tiny teeth like corn kernels
And his big baby cheeks
Matched up with his smooth-looking skin
Make for a weird-ish face.

Thick and pitch black, a unibrow
Tops off his face, followed
By a nose that looks like a pig's
Not ugly, not pretty.

Kayty Brick, Grade 8
Chippewa Falls Middle School, WI

Here Comes Spring!

Big, blooming, blossoming flowers.
Sun shining softly.
Tweet, tweet, tweet! The birds are singing.
Ha, ha, ha! The children are laughing.
Drip, drip, drip! The rain is falling.
Flowers are opening by the hour.
No more snow is what we need.
Spring is close to what we feel.
Summer will not be far behind.
We are counting down the days.
We cannot wait!

Olivia Puglie, Grade 8
St Stephen Elementary School, MI

A Dark Time

It was a dark time in our history
Hitler had the power
So many of innocence
Had their life come to an end
They took out frustration on Jewish families
All of their problems
Hitler had convinced
To blame it on the Jewish people
The Jewish people had no choice
They were overpowered
It was a dark time
Shall never repeat

Anthony Rajchel, Grade 8
St Roman School, WI

Tears: A Heart's View

Tears,
I see them all thc time,
A heart sees and hears everything,
Most tears I saw were sad,
But now the tears cry of happiness,
A heart must always jump for some joy,
Even when the master wretches with pain.

Tears and pain,
They are best friends,
Happiness is a thin sheet of glass,
Always breaking,
Always scurrying to safety,
Sorrow is always watching,
Always trying to find a way in.

Tears, pain, and sorrow,
Never leave them alone with each other,
Depression is sure to follow them,
But a glimpse of triumphant joy breaks through,
Bringing back smiling tears of happiness.

Kathryn Dickman, Grade 8
Washington Middle School, WI

Peace

Peace is love
peace is hope

Peace is when there
is no war raging
like an angry boar

Peace is when the
hungry are fed

Peace is when there
is no bomb

Peace is when no blood
is shed

Peace is when all
are loved

Peace is a dove
flying free over
trees, mountains, hills
and deserts and
over every head

Mariah Duncan, Grade 7
Ramsey Jr High School, MN

Spring

The big blue bird flies through the trees,
the kite soars high in the breeze,
and that little worm way down low,
digs and digs are far as it can go.
The frogs are hopping,
rocks are plopping,
the snow is drying up slow.
The birds retreat to their nest,
the children grab their vests,
the squirrels are snuggled sweetly,
and the ducks are lined up neatly.
The rain starts to pour,
so the children run to the door,
the animals run to their home,
then the mice start to roam.
The dogs start to bark,
because now the sky is dark.

Natalia Smart, Grade 7
Bristol Elementary School, WI

Soda

Fizzy, fizzy
Soda is like that
It gives you a sweet taste
Just be sure it doesn't get flat
Fizzy, fizzy

Andy Ratajczak, Grade 7
Luxemburg-Casco Middle School, WI

Me

I loved you, you made me.
So why would you do those things to me?
It must have been hard having me as a baby,
Or maybe you were just lazy.

All you had to do was try,
You didn't have to lie.
Every time you spoke I felt a piece of me die.
Just stay out of my life, bye.

You were there, too, my rescuer, my light in the darkness.
You helped me fight this, but then you left, too.
It must have been hard for you.
Go save yourself, isn't that what we all do?
I still loved you, I could never stop.
If anything ever happened to you my heart and soul would drop.

Now all I have is me, is it any different, I mean, really?
No one can get close or I'll flee, how much more hurt can there be?
There is nothing I can be to make you happy.
But I hold the key, the key to me.
So whoever I want to be, I will be.
I will cut through the barriers like a knife,
Because this is my life.

Sean Wiedel, Grade 8
J C McKenna Middle School, WI

Suddenly

I was alone and betrayed,
I had no light in my life,
There was nothing but
Deep,
Black,
Darkness.

All I needed was a friend,
But no one would hear me call out,
Nothing.
I had nothing.

Then you came along,
You were a friend to me,
A good friend,
You were the awakening of my life,
You were everything to me.
Suddenly, the most terrible, most horrible, tragic thing happened

It ended.
Ended into
Deep,
Black,
Darkness.

Quarteney Grinnell, Grade 8
Perry Middle School, MI

Earthquake

An earthquake rumbles in like a herd of elephants in the African Savannah.
They shake the earth until everything in sight is shook and crumbles.
It smushes earth plates together then sends massive plates around the globe.
They can vibrate the mighty oceans and continents of our earth occurring all over our coast and cities.
After the earth and the buildings are torn apart, it leaves humble with nothing left but rubble.

John Bettcher, Grade 7
Richmond Middle School, MI

Something Special

A tear runs down your cheek, glittering in the moonlight.
I catch the tear as it falls, on to the tip of my finger, and gently wipe it away.
I look into your beautiful eyes, glimmering with unshed tears, and I see an unspoken desire.
but mixed with that desire, I see something, that no-one has ever shown me before.
What I see is love, a love that can never be broken.
You and I, we have a bond, something special that we share.
And no matter what happens, between us, just know I'll always be there.
I care for you, I'd die for you, you're the love of my life.
If I ever, lost you, I would die of a lonely life.
I lean in and take your hand, kissing you softly on the lips.
I feel everything, that you feel, as your hands fall to my hips.
All your tears, all your fears, I've felt them all before.
Because every day, year after year, they show even more.
But now our lips touch, and our bodies are combined.
All those fears, all those tears, they all melt away.
All those tears, all those fears, now completely wiped away.
Side by side, as we fall into step, we walk together towards a new day.

Tyler Castillo, Grade 9
Forest Hills Northern High School, MI

My Favorite Room

My room is my favorite room.
It makes me feel calm.
When I am gloomy, I like to listen to music in my room.
My room to me is relaxing.
I love to be in there all the time when I have free time.
My room to me is peaceful.
My room to me sounds quiet, sometimes and full of music.
My room smells like my hair gel, my mom's perfume, my friend's perfume and my perfume.
My room also tastes like water because I like to drink water in there sometimes when I can.
It also feels cold sometimes when I have my fan on, and soothing too when it is.
I love my room a lot!
I would never ever leave it.
My room also looks bright green and a calm looking pink.
My room is where I can be myself, when I am not in a great mood.
I like to relax in my chair when school is over and when I am tired.
This is why I love my room so much!!!

Megan Lendvay, Grade 8
Jerstad Agerholm Middle School, WI

The Beach

When I go to the beach I like to hear the buzzing of the bees. The waves crashing against the shore. I like to hear the thunder roll in. I also like to hear the breeze rush through my hair. I also like to hear the camp fire crackle and burn I also like to hear the birds in the sky. I like to hear the splash of the water when I jump in. I like to just walk until I find that perfect spot. That's what I like about the beach.

Stormie Shands, Grade 7
Manistee Middle School, MI

Music

Music,
A sound that's so beautiful
Each beat has a rhythm to it
Music,
Lights up my day when I'm down
Music,
Bring me to a world of happiness
Music,
Each beat each word has meanings
Music, music, music,
Listening to the rhythm
Listening to the words
Music is a sound of beauty
Music is poetry.

Mariya Lay, Grade 7
Ramsey Jr High School, MN

My Life Is Boring/My Life Is Fun

My life is boring
It is not fun
like a soccer game
losing 2 to one
I hate to lose
It makes me mad
I want to win it's super rad
I know my team is not that bad
The game's not done
Yet when we've won
I change my mind
My life is fun

Jhony Blanco, Grade 7
Valley View Middle School, MN

Early Morning Ride

You get out of bed,
put on rough jeans, an old T-shirt,
pull some boots on.
The bridle jingles,
the saddle's leather creaks,
your horse whinnies,
the gate squeaks open,
the chain jingles.
Your horse's hooves hit the ground,
the sound seems to echo.
You're all tacked up, ready to go,
start down the side of the road,
the only sounds you hear
are gravel churning, and
your horse exhaling.
Such a peaceful place,
a peaceful time,
this is how I love to
spend my time.

Jessica Deaver, Grade 9
Montgomery-Lonsdale High School, MN

Alone

Wanting waiting,
So impatient,
Thinking missing,
Someone.

Me away from you,
Can't wait to see you next,
Why has it been so long?

From the first time I saw you,
Till now,
I can't wait to say hi,
Or see your smile.

You don't know,
What it means to me,
To see you,
To me you're a great friend,
And that will never change.

Angela Young, Grade 8
Lake Fenton Middle School, MI

School

School is your
Knowledge center
Its your pathway to success
School is your diploma
It's a pathway to jobs
But you need to have good grades
And it all starts when you're in school!

Jonah Tibbits, Grade 7
Valley View Middle School, MN

Mighty Warrior

Like a mountain standing tall
A hovering summer cloud.
No way he will ever fall
Whites and blues of his armor.

The warrior is weary
In triumph he raises his trunk.
The site of his tusks can be scary
He thrusts them into the air.

Like a rock he is strong
Even if he's wounded.
Like an elder he's never wrong
He knows what to do.

He howls to the night
Stomping his feet with huge pounds
He causes fright.
The mighty warrior wins once more.

Manny Meinen, Grade 8
Chippewa Falls Middle School, WI

The Thunderstorms' Song

Bing, bong, bing,
Metallic voices sing.

Blip, bloop, blip,
Watery creatures chorused.

Crash, clang, crash,
Thunder gods scream.

Drip, splish, drip,
Rain clouds swell.

Boing, ditty, boing,
Rusty metal speaks.

Shh, clack, shh,
In cold sneaks.

Pitter, patter, pitter,
Raindrops land.

Clomp, stomp, clomp,
The men ran.

Melanie Buskirk, Grade 8
Sandusky Middle School, MI

Popcorn

The corn is popping,
in the microwave oven,
until it is done.

Brett Strasser, Grade 8
Washington School, WI

Yellow Park

I miss the sound of children screaming,
cars honking,
friends laughing.

I miss seeing friends having fun,
eating McDonald's,
yellow rides.

I miss tasting that first bite of a burger,
McDonald's fries,
barf coming off the tire swing.

I miss the feel of the breeze,
rough grass
blistered hands

I miss the smell of freshly cut grass,
barf coming off the tire swing,
fresh food from McDonald's.

Natalie Garten, Grade 7
Valley View Middle School, MN

I Watched My Mother

I watched my mother make food for me.
I watched my mother clean the house.
I watched my mother's face when I gave stuff to her.
I watched my mother play games with me.
I watched my mother on the computer.
I watched my mother talk to my father.
I watched my mother leave us.
I watched my mother see me deal with it.
I watched my mother telling me she has a new husband.

I watched my mother show me Jeb.
I watched my mother packing our stuff.
I watched my mother show us the new house.
I watched my mother show me Colt.
I watched my mother's face when it is the end of the summer.

I watch my mother's name burn up on my phone every night.

Dakota Hubbard, Grade 8
Washington Middle School, WI

Pride

So along comes my Pride,
so fair.
All boys swoon for the thing they just can't have.
Now you see,
let me tell you a little about my lovely Pride.
You see despite all the looks and the stares that she gets,
there is one thing that will always remain out of bounds.
My wonderful Wrath,
is all she can see,
what a fool that girl is,
for she can't see.
All that staring and swooning at the mirror above.
With all her primming and preening,
it will all be put to an end.
That will leave without any meaning.
For one day while she stares at her mirror above.
Gluttony rushed in causing the house quite a tremble.
Sending Pride's loose mirror crashing down from above.
Poor poor Gluttony,
all stricken with sadness,
ran from the room to forget all the madness.

David Stauche, Grade 8
McKinley Middle School, WI

Shadows of the Night

Silent shadows in the dead of night.
The roar of a helicopter, taking off in flight.
There is a haze in the distance.
And the enemy is putting up great resistance.
There is no such thing as mercy.
This is a war.

Christopher Fawcett, Grade 8
Iowa-Grant Elementary-Middle School, WI

Spring Break

Exams are hard to do,
But we keep on pushing through.
We know spring break is around the bend.
We keep up hopes it will not end.
We love the warmth we get from sun.
The flowers blooming through the mud.
The snow keeps melting far away
Regardless that the clouds are gray.
When school stars up we will be blue.
Cause there'll be lots of work to do.
Our parents will say too,
"You keep on pushing through!"

Josiah Enrique, Grade 9
Maranatha Baptist Academy, WI

Rainy Night

The rain fell down very softly,
Weeping sorrow from the sky.
It was a magnificent waterfall,
Except much quieter!
I lay in bed trying to sleep.
I listened to the soft tiptoe steps of the drizzle.
It slowly got harder and louder.
The rain was a strong gorilla
That was pounding on my window.
Then, suddenly, it completely stopped.
There was no sound left to be heard,
The night was a quiet mouse,
Almost silently crawling across the floor.
And the calm darkness,
Soon put me into a deep, peaceful slumber.

Sarah Strand, Grade 7
Roosevelt Middle School, MN

The Succeeding Team

Baseball season is almost here
And the Detroit Tigers are getting ready.
They practice from morn to noon
And keep their long schedule steady.

The short preseason is finally here
And the long season is coming near.
After many games, the Tigers have all the fame
For their excellent record shows no shame

The playoffs should be the path for the great bunch
Because they never gave up with much fatigue.
The teams they're about to play are just a snack in their lunch.
After all, the Tigers are the best team in the league.

Detroit tried their hardest and had the best season.
Teamwork and perseverance was the main reason.
Their gloves are worn out and their cleats are now history
And next season is another great mystery.

Nathaniel Birt, Grade 7
St Thomas More Academy, MI

Drama

Why don't they get it?
They never understand,
they wish and wish,
and now they have,
they take advantage, of it all,
they say they're sorry, it can't be true,
otherwise, I'd be too.
It makes no sense,
it's only lies,
no more trust,
they're just like spies,
they cry, they wish,
they beg, they break,
all because one little thing,
it's evil, harmful,
hurtful too,
its name is simple,
never new,
it's drama, drama,
never true.

Abigail Adams, Grade 7
Marshall Academy, MI

Candy

Candy
Sugary, yummy
Sweetening, soothing, fattening
Kit-Kat, Hershey, Carrot, Celery
Helping, Blooming, Enjoying
Healthy, Benefit
Veggies

Brooke Hagenow, Grade 7
Edison Middle School, WI

Seasons

Snowflakes
Dancing in the night
Covering the quiet world
They slowly drift down

Summer
Swimming in the pool
Cold popsicles dripping down
Hot sticky summer

Signs of Fall
Colorful bright trees
Lovely leaves drift at my feet
Crunching under me

The Glistening Forest
Silver-lined birch tree
Quietly waiting for you
Blowing in the breeze

Jen Wagman, Grade 7
Core Knowledge Charter School, WI

Just Because

Just because I dress in so many colors
Doesn't mean I'm a rainbow
So don't try looking for a pot of gold under my feet
Don't be jealous if a leprechaun chases me and not you
Just because I dress in so many colors
Doesn't mean I'm a chameleon
Doesn't mean that I can't be hidden
Doesn't mean I can't go green
Just because I dress in so many colors
Doesn't mean I can't dress in black
Doesn't mean that everything I touch turns to Skittles
Just because I dress in so many colors — never judge a book by its color

Camille Cory, Grade 8
Central Middle School, MI

Relaxation

What happens when you relax?
Do you calm down and enjoy the quietness of the day?
What happens when you calm down?
Does everything go quiet or does it get noisy?
Do you take a hot bath, just to get out and answer the phone again
Who comes knocking when you're trying to take a break?
Is it the sandman?
Does he spray you with enough sleep to give you a nap?
What happens when you try to relax?
Does the phone ring? Does a baby cry?
Where do you usually relax?
Do you crash on the sofa? Or go to your bed?
What happens when you relax?

Madalynn Luedtke, Grade 8
Southwestern Wisconsin Elementary/Middle School, WI

the twilight zone

have you ever heard of the twilight zone
the one where only death controls
have you heard of death himself
he loves to eat the marrow in your bones
he haunts the shadows with feet like paddles
they say he was the first to die they say he came down from the sky
they say the devil brought him down but what they do not know now…
is that he was the devil himself and so on the rumors continued
every one with there own opinions and day by day a person died
until there was none but one alive
he was the dickenson's orphan boy who tended to wave and say ahoy
and that night he was awake playing with the ghost called jake
oh my! now you must be surprised for if you are i'm full of of pride
for the boy shall never be a man for he was none other than peter pan
and that night for death himself made his way through the town
he stopped at the graveyard gates and saw the boy and his mates
he slid through the bars and he looked up towards the star
and then came a sharp blast for the boy had attacked
he raised his sword high and looked up towards the skies and said:
look up towards the skies and you'll realize that love is mightier than hate
and death is none other than the start of a new adventure.

Imane Ait Daoud, Grade 7
Central Middle School, MN

The Colors of Me

Black is the color I feel when I'm depressed.
Red is the color I feel when I'm mad.
A sky blue when I'm very sad.
Pink when I'm happy.
A green when I need a nappy.
Yellow when I feel confused.
A dark orange when I'm hungry.
Gray when I'm bored.
Purple when I feel sick.
These are the colors of me.

Kierra McDonald, Grade 8
Messmer Preparatory Catholic School, WI

Glorious!

I don't know how I am so blessed,
To have a guy who is the best,
He is kind, loving, and caring,
Also curious, outgoing, and daring,
He looks like, no matter from what angle,
The very description of an arch angel,
His face glows brighter than the sun,
The first time I saw him, I knew he was the one.
Glorious!
He said: He loves me so much he'll never get mad,
Not lonely, or frightened, he'll always be glad,
And in dark, in hate, in jeopardy, and strife,
He'll love me as long as he has life,
His eyes are deeper than the sea,
And when I'm with him they're always fixed on me,
He looks at me like I'm his dinner,
Not the outrageously lucky winner,
Glorious!
His body is a pale white,
Now and forever he'll point me to the light.

Alicia Neuman, Grade 7
Albany Area Jr/Sr High School, MN

Nature

Nature is alive and moving.
Whether it be the towering trees swaying in the wind,
Or a bird soaring through the sky.
It never stops.

Nature is cruel and rewarding.
It can consist of bitter winters,
And dry droughts in the summer.
Even through the hardships,
There is always relief right around the corner.

Nature is wonderful.
It gives us the lakes and rivers that give us water.
It give us the plants that give us oxygen and food.
But most of all,
It give us a home in which we live, grow, and learn.

Faith Filipiak, Grade 8
Robert J Elkington Middle School, MN

My Elephant Daughter

A girl goes to the zoo and says
"I wish I was an elephant like you"
She leaves the zoo to go home to sleep
For a while, without thinking what might happen,
She wakes up in two hours to her mother's voice
"It's time to eat!"
She sleepily walks to the table, Ah!
She stares at her mother, what's the problem
Your nose…It's, it's long and rough
No it's not, you're joking
Look in the mirror, it's true it is
No, why did I say I wanted to be an elephant,
Pop, my ears!
From then on out she lived at the zoo with her
Hero named Dumbo.

Mercedes Schuchardt, Grade 7
Christ Child Academy, WI

Apocalypse

The day you hope will never come
The day you'll never see the sun
The day you'll all drop like flies
Until lit will be your turn to die
Before you do you'll scream and cry
Then you'll ask God to spare your life
Watching the people run like mice
Look at the building burst in flames
Feeling bad for the falling planes
Watching bombs fly in the air
Corpses lying everywhere
Good thing this day has not come yet
But it will I bet I bet
You'll know when it does
Because smoke will cover the sun
But until then remember one thing
This is the apocalypse

Hunter Cammack, Grade 8
Iowa-Grant Elementary-Middle School, WI

The Toy

A little girl is looking at cool new toys
But that is not what she wants for Christmas
She wants a little dog

She wants to play with that dog
Even though all of her friends will be playing with toys,
A dog is all she wants for Christmas

So here she stands on the morning of Christmas,
She hears a little whimper that sounds like a dog,
And she opens up the gift, and it is no toy
It is not a toy, but a Christmas dog.

Brittany Bindon, Grade 7
St Andrew's School, MI

Winter

Winter brings with it a gust of happiness, children near and far rejoice, families are eager for time together, of seasons it is surely the number one choice.

For the youth of the world it is a time of play, they run around merrily and laugh off their heads, hilltops everywhere are scribbled with snowmen, not one of them want to return to their beds.

Fathers sit happily gulping their eggnog, as mothers aggressively knit and knit, their children eat steaming soup by the fire, where they can rest and maybe just sit.

Christmas brings families closer together, from places like New York to the world's smallest town, little boys and girls are good for their parents, so they may get presents that won't make them frown.

Winter's a time for family and friends,
For youngsters and seniors and teens everywhere, for anyone who simply wants a good time, winter can surely be a blast anywhere.

Ali Hakim, Grade 7
Detroit Country Day Middle School, MI

The Middle School Doors

I thought it'd be simple like those years from before, I thought growing up was just nothing more.
Playing Barbie with friends and hopscotch outside, crying 'cause you're short for all of the rides.
Swimming with floaties and coloring at school while singing aloud, and not caring who's cool.
Scratch and sniff stickers and best friends at hello, the only thing broken was your big brother's toe.

It isn't like that, well not any more, it hasn't been the same since we walked through that door.
The middle school doors, now what have they done…we thought it'd be simple, we thought it'd be fun.
Look where we are and tell me we've changed…the classes, the look, it's all rearranged.
Barbie's not hip, and hopscotch is gone, so we earn extra cash by mowing the lawn.
We tan by the pool and do homework all night while we watch all the girls start stupid fights.
Striving for A's and looking for friends, it hasn't been easy to follow the trends.

Still we stand tall even though it's tough we have to learn even life gets rough.
If we walk with a smile and stay true to our heart, we'll end on high notes before we must part.

Kristina Kelly, Grade 8
Lake Shore Middle School, WI

The Glory Tree

The grass was airbrushed with a light coat of snow,
It crunched under our boots below,
As we scavenged for the ideal one that had to be perfect in height, width and color,
Each and everyone had their own slight imperfection just like every other,
We trudged our way deeper into the wilderness,
Hearing the chopping of wood a ways in the distance,
I lost my breath and gasped when I first laid my eyes on her beauty,
Knowing this was now my dad's duty,
I told him to bring the saw,
To chisel at the truck until his hands were raw,
And next we strapped it to our car,
Paid, and then argued who gets to place on top the star,
It shed pine needles all the way home even when we carried her inside,
It was like we took her from her home and she began to make sappy tears as she cried,
But once we dressed her up in lights, ornaments, popcorn strands and beads,
She beamed with life and glory, just like a perfect Christmas tree,
She was the greatest little tree we've ever had,
There she stood by the fireplace and waited for Santa, which we all know is dad.

Gabrielle Stark, Grade 8
Centennial Middle School, MI

After the Game

After the volleyball game I was exhausted,
Inside the school I wait for my parents,
I examine the clock that ticks while I wait.
I spot a car that pulls up in the parking lot,
behind the steering wheel my dad is waiting,
I begin to walk toward the truck.
I get into the car and fasten my seat belt,
We finally arrived home and stepped inside,
I welcomed the couch to my achy and tired body.

Autumn Kozlowski, Grade 7
Beer Middle School, MI

We

We met in first, at first it was great.
I thought I had it all —
for so it seemed I did.

Then we got serious in third,
the flirting went louder than ever before,
for I still thought I had it all.

Then in fifth he said those three lovely words,
"I love you."
Then a few months later he was flirting
with my best friend.

Now I wish that I could go back,
to put up a steel wall,
to protect my heart.

Mayce Bacon, Grade 8
Spring Hill School, WI

Reflections on the River

Stepping out of the bright, birch forest,
Finding flowers fit for the florist.
Sitting there, sprawled out a magnificent view,
A river of nothing but azure blue.

Swirling rapids, passing through rocks,
Trapping salmon, oh yum, Scandinavian lox.
Finches and sparrows come here to play,
Preferring here than down by the bay.

Lilly pads lay on top of the water,
Giving a perch to mother frog and her daughter.
Deer, bears, and porcupines with quills,
Come from all around to slop up their fill.

Something about the water seems to amaze,
Everyone who stops and gives it a gaze.
Winding through the countryside as far as the eye can see,
The river is a peaceful place to be!

Brandon Alexander, Grade 8
Bloomfield Hills Middle School, MI

The Changing of the Seasons

Winter is many things:
It is an ice cube, freezing the waters of the world.
It is a blanket that covers the land with never-ending white.
Winter is death. The trees go bare, the grass goes brown.
Winter is a burden, which is only lifted by the arrival of spring.
Spring is the paintbrush, bringing up colorful masterpieces
From a canvas of white.
Spring is the best joy, after a time of great sorrow.
As the weather grows hotter, spring evolves into summer.
Summer, the oven, baking the world into a sweet treat.
Summer is the wanted, the one sought after.
And summer is an emerald, the greenest emerald ever.
The emerald eventually becomes dirty, and fall takes over.
Fall is the warning. The warning that winter is near.
Fall is also the beauty of the year.
As fall freezes, winter begins.
And so the cycle continues…

Anna Van Berkom, Grade 7
Roosevelt Middle School, MN

Road No. 15

I miss the bells of rickshaws.
I miss the sound of cars honking,
drivers so impatient!!!
I miss the sight of long tall buildings
blocking the light of the sun.
I miss looking at the busy streets where I grew up in.
I miss the smell of kabas frying.
I miss the dry taste of the dust blowing in my face.
I miss walking on the rough and bumpy sidewalks.
I miss the old Raika, who is still lost in Road No. 15.

Raika Iftekhar, Grade 7
Valley View Middle School, MN

The Angel Not Forgotten

She was an angel sent down from the heavens,
With her trumpet of happiness
And hope to cleanse my soul.
For I have a sinned heart,
Trapped, in this world of pain and misery.
She set me free, but with a price.
A price which could not be paid,
But only with a heart of an angel, her own.
She stayed behind so I may have the second chance
To fix my sorrows and mistakes.
But who, who was this angel to come rescue me
From the depths of the abyss?
With a face of a glow of a lonely midnight candle.
Her hair as red as a basket of freshly picked roses
Glistening in the morning sun.
But now, now she is a lonely shadow.
Her beautiful red hair is now black
And for the midnight candle,
Extinguished by her tears, now left in darkness.

Cody Schwartz, Grade 8
Springfield School, MN

Dream Feather

Still and pressed inside a frame,
A hazel-eyed father dreams.
Of sailing on crystal flames,
A boat of cotton white flies.

Like an eagle soaring high,
Peeling away from the page.
Looping, swirling in the sky,
While like grass it stays rooted.

First to the left, then the right,
Waltzing along gracefully.
A whoosh; a scythe, claimed by night,
Is swept away by the wind.

Landing upon a crescent,
That cradles it with a splash.
Looking of true innocence
An echo of wishes thought.

Silence consumes the feather,
As it falls back into the frame.
Soon it thinks of another
Adventure to see next time.

Lauren Scobie, Grade 8
Chippewa Falls Middle School, WI

Funset Boulevard

Games
Laser tag, bumper cars
Soda
Pizza
Famous, fun filled, fun set
Not just a gaming place
Birthday friendly
Adults like it too
Funset Boulevard

Justin John Bertrand, Grade 7
Luxemburg-Casco Middle School, WI

Bathtubs

I'm shiny clean and new
I didn't know what I was in for
Dirty people sat in me
Water filled to my neck
They get me all dirty
Scummy all the time
Lime scale builds up on my side
Bubbles in the water pop
They are not from me
It's from the little boy right on top of me
The plug is pulled
The water rushes down my throat and
I'm all clean again

Lauren Brown, Grade 7
Manistee Middle School, MI

My Star

I'm sorry I must leave you now, but I think it's my time to go
Our lives together were so short, but I just want you to know
I have always loved you, and I know I always will
There's a place in my heart that no one else will ever be able to fill

I wish I could be with you and have just one more day
But fate must have a different plan, so I know that I can't stay
It's funny how just two kids could wind up so in love
I'll always watch over you when I'm looking down from up above

Do not cry for me, we'll be together soon
But I wish for just one more sunset, one crystal-clear full moon
I want to hold you in my arms and never ever let go
I love you more than you could ever know

I always promised that I'd never leave your side
I feel so awful now, because I know that I have lied
DO not blame God for his decision of making me leave you all alone
I would have done so much more if I had only known

It's funny how fate can deal us a very tricky hand
My time is running out fast, like an hourglass full of sand
So the next time you're lonely and gaze up at the starts in the night sky
I'll be the brightest one shining, just to tell you that I'll never say goodbye

Max Martin, Grade 8
Sandusky Middle School, MI

Along the Shore

While I walk along the beautiful golden shore,
I continuously long to come back every day for more.
Barefoot and feeling the sand between my toes,
I think good thoughts and forget all my woes.

Tidal waves washing up along the sand,
The sight is so wonderful, it is quite grand.
Sea shells all along the beach,
The pretty ones are just in reach.

Kites up in the beautiful sky,
Flying smoothly, up so very high.
The salty water's smell is all around you,
As you look at the water's dazzling shade of blue.

Relaxation is what you will see,
And also excitement, like a face full of glee.
Birds are drawing near,
For picnickers are here.

The day is almost done,
But you know that you've had fun.
The bright sun going down peacefully over the rushing tides,
So I let all the sights take me on a journey — take me on a ride.

Kelli Krueger, Grade 7
Core Knowledge Charter School, WI

Mr. Camaro

He sits in the driveway.
Waiting for a cool crisp night.
He smiles at us when we look at him.
He protects us when were riding in him.
He cools us off in the summer.
Rolling down his windows and taking his top off.
He always wants to please us.
Playing our music loud, and going fast when he is asked.
My father and I love him.
We wouldn't trade him for anything.
When we take him out, he gets so excited.
Adrenaline pumping through his body.
He likes to go fast. But only on a quiet country road.
Then he hits top speed at about 120.
His speed takes my breath away.
How he stays in shape amazes me.
He sits all winter long, under a warm blanket in the garage.
But once spring comes, he roars to life.
Driving perfectly after a long winters nap.
Mr. Camaro is part of out family.
He will be in our family until the day he dies.

Mackenzie Strampp, Grade 8
Washington Middle School, WI

What's Up There, High in the Sky?

What's up there?
High in the sky,
a bird and a plane
go flying by.
Up high, above the trees,
is a Frisbee floating through the breeze.
The clouds sit in the sky
changing shapes and sizes
always giving you different surprises.
Then at night, the stars come out
sparkle and shine
like a glass of wine.
There comes a shooting star
way up high
glowing through the midnight sky.
At dawn, the birds come out to play
and that is the beginning of a brand new day.

Danielle Pitrof, Grade 8
St Roman School, WI

What I Like About You?

I like it when you look me in the eyes,
It makes me melt.
I love that you make me feel,
so special when we're together.
I like it when you hug me,
I feel like you're never going to let go.
When we're together,
my heart will start to beat faster and faster.

Emily Gehling, Grade 8
Washington School, WI

March Madness

With the season of madness coming
No one knows what to expect
The players are on the court running
It will have a lasting effect.

Sixty-four teams come to the big dance
Only one will take home the gold
All of these teams have a good chance
Now it's time to watch it unfold.

There's Michigan and Akron there's UNC
Oklahoma and BYU
Ohio and Duke look good to me
But what about Purdue?

Out of all 64 I chose Pitt
But crazy upsets will come.
I'll never understand the gist of it
'Cause this game's for the smart, not the dumb.

So whatever happens on the court
Depends on the players' drive
They'll shoot, they'll score, and they'll play their sport
They'll do anything to survive.

Alan Blondin, Grade 8
St Thomas More Academy, MI

My Heart

My heart pounds in my chest every day
My heart tell me its breaking
My heart tries to fix itself
My heart tells me to find someone else
My hearts feelings are hurt
My heart tells me quick before I never love again
My heart heals itself
My heart fell for another man
My heart doesn't let him go
My heart whispers he's the one

Sarah Robertson, Grade 8
Jerstad Agerholm Middle School, WI

Nature

High in the sky
Dancing with the clouds
A death-defying screech
Brave as a fierce lion
Nurturing young at the sheer edge of a cliff
Dim brown body with a bleach white head and tail
Razor sharp retracting talons and sleek vision
An opposing foe
It lunges at its prey
Tonight, a guaranteed feast

Cody Christensen, Grade 8
Suring Elementary/Middle School, WI

Flying

I live on top of the world
Floating on the clouds
I can go where ever the wind goes
I could fly over the Grand Canyon
I could fly over Niagara Falls
I could fly over the Amazon

I am a bird

I can go where ever I want
Will I be caught
Sold to a pet store
Never
I will fly for miles
Over every country
Never to be found
Never to be caged

Graham Hervat, Grade 8
Washington Middle School, WI

Wailin' with VanHalen

Eddie VanHalen's
Guitar is wailin'.
His hair isn't level,
As he runs with the devil.
His riffs are mind-blowing.
It gets my stereo going.
He has his own band
And thousands of fans.
He rocks-out, with no doubt,
Making people scream and shout.
You know he's extreme,
When his guitar lets off steam.
Eddie VanHalen's
Guitar is wailin'.

John DeLeeuw, Grade 7
Cedar Springs Middle School, MI

The Shot

I hear the crowd roar
When I'm about to shoot and score

The game is tie
Down the lane I drive

Up I go
I hear a whistle blow

The clock is out of time
I go up to the line

Around the rim goes the ball
We all wonder will it fall

Blake Ravet, Grade 7
Luxemburg-Casco Middle School, WI

New Addition

nine months
waiting
pink or blue
nobody knew
Monday
October 13th
surprise
baby girl
open her eyes
hospital
nursery rhymes
lullaby's
big blue eyes
quiet cries
Katie

Kayla Carter, Grade 7
West Middle School, MI

Silver Is Silver

There is so much
That is silver
Yet so unnoticeable
That it's background
Such as when
Storm clouds hold
Onto the sun
Do we notice the silvery halo
That surrounds it

Or when dewdrops
In the dusk dwell
Delicately while dripping
And dropping in a
Deep fog
Almost always there
Yet not always seen
Silver lining in
The thick fog

Ian Addison, Grade 7
Luxemburg-Casco Middle School, WI

Achoo!

I think I've got a cold. *Achoo!*
For my nose keeps running bad.
I think my ears are plugged up,
For my forehead feels like lava.
I think I've got a cold. *Achoo!*

I think I've got a cold. *Achoo!*
For all the tissues in my house are gone.
I think my throat is going to burn,
And when I cough my dog runs away.
I think I've got a cold. *Achoo!*

Nikie Brand, Grade 7
Washington School, WI

The Best Place

I think the best place in the world
Is where you want to be
It has to be special
It has to be you

It has to be where you want to be
It has to be a place
Where your dreams can come true

It has to be a happy place
Where everything is better
Where you can feel happy

And you can be with
The people that you like
It has to have no drama
It has to be unique
It has to be the best place in the world.

Gabriela Negrete, Grade 8
Seymour Middle School, WI

Snow

Small, soft, white snowflakes
Dancing in the starry sky
Falling to the Earth

Grace Schwantes, Grade 7
Core Knowledge Charter School, WI

Retrospect

I climbed that wall and sailed through
the mist of uncertainty
the same thing again
growing but bigger

That wall knocked over
that mist cleared
the sun yelled out
and I yelled back
a hollow sound of greeting

A single thread
brought down a whole kingdom
the tug, rip, and snarl
as the whole thing fell

Millions of miles
trodden and tread
walked on again.
If I was gone by now
you'd be very much alone,
by now if I had stayed
we would've finally spoke
on the other side of time

Allison Stawara, Grade 9
Clarkston Jr High School, MI

Celebrate New Year

C elebrate the good times come on
E veryone likes it, mon
L isten to the ball drop
E veryone is at the top
B ombs explode in the air
R eally people eat pears
A nyone can have fun
T ipping on a hot bun
E ating so much on that day

N ew Year becomes a day of play
E veryone gathers together to celebrate
W hy are you sad on this day?

Y ou're celebrating the New Year day
E arly in the morning is when we all play
A fter is when we all go back to testing each other
R acing to top one another

Brandon Doxtator, Grade 8
Seymour Middle School, WI

Accomplishments

I have accomplished the impossible
I have accomplished the great
I have accomplished the unreasonable
At a very quick rate.
I have accomplished the caring
I have accomplished the heroic
I have accomplished the daring
With a face that is stoic.
I have accomplished these and many more
With many more to come to my door
I have accomplished these without a smirk
But I have not yet accomplished my homework.

Danielle Mijnsbergen, Grade 7
Central Middle School, MI

When Light Became Dark

As the sun faded
The moon started to wane
When darkness lurked
I became irked
I reached for anything
Yet I found nothing
Suddenly I found a cylinder
And it became less chillier
I found a switch
And I started to twitch
I flicked the switch
And my, the light was rich
Now whenever I go to an amusement park
I remember when light became dark

David Woo, Grade 7
Baker Middle School, MI

Softball

It's the 6th inning.
There are 2 outs,
and 2 strikes,
bases loaded.
I stand there sweating.
I bend my knees,
I lift my elbow,
I grip my hands,
and watch as the deadly sphere approaches.
I grit my teeth,
I watch the ball,
I swing my bat,
There it goes!
High in the sky!
Farther,
farther,
farther,
gone!
Grand Slam!!!
Crowd goes wild!

Sami Reis, Grade 7
Valley View Middle School, MN

Kite

I soar high in the sky.
My flamboyant colors are for everyone to see.
But as beautiful as I may be,
I am not free.
I am chained to my pilot.

Ettore Fantin-Yusta, Grade 9
International Academy, MI

Fear

I am Fear.
Keeping you on your toes.
I am the Shadow stalking you every night.
Filling you with fright.
I am Fear
You cannot shake me.
You cannot break me.
I am Doom and Pain.
That which makes you lame.
I am Fear.
Do not dare try to shake me.
I am a Wall built of ice.
Trapping your life.
I am Fear.
Killing your strife.
I am Death.
Ending your life.
I am Fear.
Your oldest friend.
I am Darkness.
With you in the end.

Dane Cole, Grade 7
Roosevelt Middle School, MN

My Proud Family

We are a proud family of Roffers.
I am proud of my family,
We are all proud of each other.

We keep each other optimistic,
We may play rough,
But, we make up.

I am proud of my family,
We are strong,
We are together,
And most of all we will love each other.

We stick to our name,
We stick together,
We stick to our homeland.

We stand tall,
And we stand together.
We are a proud family of Roffers.

Darcie Roffers, Grade 8
Seymour Middle School, WI

Football

F riendship
O pportunities
O utstanding hustle
T eamwork
B ecoming friends
A ccomplishments
L inking together
L iving your life

Taylor Krupa, Grade 7
Necedah Middle School, WI

Dead Lines

I wasn't aware, I couldn't see,
Bright yellow lights, in front of me.
I hit the brakes, I tried to stop.
My world went dark, I heard a pop.
He crossed the line, onto my side,
He saw me coming, he could have tried.
He was drunk and lost control,
But he survived, I paid the toll.
He shouldn't have been on the road.
He was drunk, it surely showed.
My lifeless body, lying still.
He walked to me with all his will.
"I'm so sorry," I heard him say,
"Hey there kid, are you Okay?"
I couldn't move, could not reply,
And with no hope I said goodbye.
He crossed the line and I crossed over,
Next time he drives he will be sober.

Maddi Poddig, Grade 8
Perry Middle School, MI

Freedom

It's the right to choose, to speak out and stand up
It's a chance to start over, to believe what we want

To speak out and stand up, things were never quite this easy
To believe what we want, the ability to voice our own opinion

Things were never quite this easy, many have died fighting for this right
The ability to voice our own opinion, it's the backbone of America

Many have died fighting for this right, it's what separates us from the rest
It's the backbone of America, not dependent on race

It's what separates us from the rest, it started with "I have a dream"
Not dependent on race, giving America a chance to shine

It started with "I have a dream," makes me proud to be a citizen
Gave America a chance to shine, to bear the flag where ever I go

Makes me proud to be a citizen, to keep my head high
To bear the flag where ever I go, it's the right to choose.

Shelby Penn, Grade 8
St John Lutheran School, MI

Mexico Visit

Oh the beauty how I loved it bright and sweet
The swoosh of the wind
And the push of the waves
The sand between my toes just jumping up to fall back down
The best part was the mixing of colors as the skin warming sun hides away
The light blue slowly turning pink, purple and yellow
I'd peacefully fall asleep here on my perfectly silent beach
I never had to hear about the drama or homework, no worries at hand
No one rushing about or in need of help like people back home do
The short week of a visit helped so much
The happiness in everyone's faces was the best to see
Oh the beauty was great to see

Brooke Coutier, Grade 7
Valley View Middle School, MN

Life and Death

It's sad to see a loved one go.
That's life.
Remembering all the good times that you share with that person.
Then they're gone.
One life passing by.
Emptiness.
No one can fill that part that was once there.
Can you ever fill that part that was once there?
Keeping memories that you both shared.
Remembering, those happy times.
That life was always part of you.
You will always have that special part of you that loves and misses her.
Here is how I go on.
Remembering that she is still with me.

Alejandra Villagran, Grade 7
St Roman School, WI

Who Am I

I am a very athletic person.
I wonder if I can be more helpful with my family.
I hear my friends calling.
I see somebody staring at me.
I want a peaceful family.
I am a Mexican person.

I pretend on Halloween as a vampire.
I feel happy on Christmas day.
I touch my parents when I am sad.
I worry that I am not funny.
I cry when my feelings are hurt.
I am a funny person.

I understand that people don't get what they want.
I say I don't love you when I am not happy.
I dream that I am with my family and everybody is happy.
I try to do better in school.
I hope I am caring enough.
I am an excellent person.

Carlos Escobar, Grade 7
St Andrew's School, MI

Shadows of a Shell

If you listen to it,
You won't hear the ocean.
The shell's colors,
Are like a rainbow,
In the way they change,
Except the colors of the sky on a rainy day.

It if a fish fin,
That glows like the moon,
With an underside that,
Has scars that show its bravery.

Its grooved top,
Is hard like a shield,
But,
Radiates with beauty.

Tyler Christensen, Grade 8
Chippewa Falls Middle School, WI

Stranger in the Night

Morning dew tiptoes into the night
As an owl swiftly glides to the ground
It blankets the grass with a thin coat of water
When the temperature drops
The morning dew drops too
In the mornings, you'll see it all around
Giving the ground a glossy shine and covering your shoes
With the mysterious liquidy substance
When you wake, you see nothing
But what it has left behind

Kari Gibson, Grade 7
West Suburban Christian Academy, WI

Beautiful

Grass on the ground with the sun above.
Shining and gleaning which glistens the earth.
So radiant that it warms your soul and so calm
that it makes you feel cold.
I thank God for the trees up high
with the birds in the sky.
With lovable animals and beautiful fish
it's like watching God smile upon the earth.

Neena Mathews, Grade 8
Messmer Preparatory Catholic School, WI

The Joy of Brothers

Sure my brothers can be a little wild,
But having them is better than being an only child.
I love my brothers and I'll tell you why.
If they weren't in my life, I surely would die.
Josh is the one who's always so nice.
All he wants is to enjoy life.
Caleb is the funniest of us all.
Whenever you're around him, you'll always have a ball.
At times, Jacob can be so careless,
But at the same time, really hilarious.
Now JJ, he's a totally different story,
But if you're around him, it'll never be boring.
You might wonder why I love my brothers so much,
I love them because they're such a hilarious bunch.
At times they may be different from others,
But they will always be my wonderful brothers!

Sarah Loschen, Grade 8
Iowa-Grant Elementary-Middle School, WI

Melty the Snowman

Melty the snowman was a jolly happy soul,
He was there one day,
Then he melted away,
Just as fast as he could go.

We built him with our love and care,
His mittens were a perfect pair,
He smiled at us,
And we danced around,
Until the sun went down.

We laughed and played every day,
Until it started getting hot.
Our greatest friend started melting away,
Then his hat went plop.

With his eyes floating everywhere,
Melty was a puddle,
His last words to us were,
I think I am in trouble.

Lizzie Tesch, Grade 8
Seymour Middle School, WI

Tears Are Crystals

Tears are crystals,
clear and numerous
when they fall.
Tears are crystals,
piercing like an awl.
Tears are crystals,
beautifully admired.
Tears are crystals,
until they retire.
Although remember,
like a fiery ember,
it soon dies out.

Destiny Densmore, Grade 8
Middle School at Parkside, MI

Remaining Strength

When your best effort is defeated,
And you feel that you have lost,
It may seem that all is depleted
But not completely ended.
At the very end of it all
Lies one remaining force.
Though it may be small,
It can keep anyone determined.

But in order for it to thrive,
There is just one factor:
You must still desire to strive,
And you must still believe.
When everybody still believes
That there is a way to succeed,
They have a will to achieve
And will never give up.

When all feels lost,
But you have not given up,
No matter the cost,
All will be accomplished.
Never give up.

Alex Wang, Grade 8
Boulan Park Middle School, MI

Papa!

Some people say Grandpa.
but I say Papa.
And that is just who I am.
He always starts the four wheelers,
but I'm the one to ride it.
He always drives us around,
but I'm the only one to get out.
He always sits by me and we talk
forever, and I can tell he enjoys it.
And for that one I just stay there
because I enjoy it so much.

Abby Fernholz, Grade 7
Shakopee Area Catholic School, MN

My Game

When I play my game, I have a sensation,
it is a feeling of joy, not of irritation;
see when I play this game, all disappears,
it's just me and the ball, not even the crowd's cheers;
the time ticks down, and I shoot the ball up,
It swooshes right through, and the crowd erupts;
But I don't play this game for the crowd or the girls,
I play this game for the feeling of me and the ball in our own separate world.

Jacob Baker, Grade 7
Lenawee Christian School, MI

Existence

Life.
Oh so simple, yet can be taken so fast.
Our time in existence seems short,
In reality our time measures, for most, to be in excess.
Life, as most know it is thrilling, challenging and free.
But in our afterward will we agree?
Death could be concealing, desolate or even open.
So, is death not the end?
Not just the end for you, but all your friends too?
Death may end up being that time for us to reflect and ponder,
On all of what could have been if you chose to live your existence differently.
Great friendships, loved ones and time
May all be so distant when our time arrives,
But then might we be able to serve them in our afterlife?
Possibly by showing them different ways from our remorseful errors.
May we be able to stop them from feeling overwhelming terrors?
Such an abundant amount of questions which will only be answered later on.
So, let none of us feel done when death is close in view.
But delighted for all that it may do.

Ashley Hester, Grade 8
St Roman School, WI

A Snowflake's Dream

On one dark snowy evening, a flake begins descent.
Its days and weeks inside the cloud were oh so badly spent.
It drifts toward Earth with other flakes, all hoping for some fun.
To laugh and play and whirl and dance under the midnight sun.

It settles to the frozen ground, one among so many.
It smiles to hear tiny boots of some small company.
Slowly, slowly strong wind picks up and lifts flakes off the Earth.
They swirl as if to melodies and prance as if they're worth.

It happens to stray near to me; I watch it gently land.
I roll it into a snowball and pack it in my hand.
The little snowflake laughs with glee: I've tossed it at a friend.
Gently, the flake lands on their tongue; it's met its joyful end.
Snowflakes can lead contented lives, why not we people too?
We are like snowflakes, swirling 'round; prancing in winter's hue.

Sandra Kinzer, Grade 8
Washington School, WI

Piano Hands

They say my hands are such a gift to me.
I only see them worked and oh so worn.
In every crease are hours, toiling times.
My joints are crushed by pressure that you gave.

I count the minutes rather than the beat,
And passion fades as time is melting on.
Still I endure the words and ruler so sharp;
I'm searching for the melody of life.

My Heart and Head and Life are on the line.
The reader sees my future full of pain,
I work to make it change, I know life will.
I'll bet my heart can win against my head.

I wait, I wish for someone meant for me,
To fill the valleys, take my hand and fly.
I look, but I can't find that kind of love.
I pray, The Spirit fills my hands, my heart.

Each strike of sound empowers me to live.
Each day I hold His hope in carefulness.
Each time I see my hands, I see a past
And future, just beginning to unfold.

Alice Liang, Grade 9
Troy High School, MI

Electronic Brands

A pple
B ravia
C ompact
D ell
E Machines
F ender
G eneral Electric
H aier
I nsignia
J .V.C.
K odak
L exmark
M icrosoft
N ikon
O lympus
P anasonic
Q -Logic
R .C.A.
S ony
T oshiba
U niden
V izio
W ilson Electronics
X andrix
Y amaha
Z une

Brian Stout, Grade 7
Washtenaw Christian Academy, MI

It's Just a Feeling

The light shined on me,
and I finally felt special,
like somebody cared about me
I guess it was just a feeling,
that would never come true.
Just make sure that when I see you,
I never get the same feeling as I did last year.

Sara Terrian, Grade 8
Washington School, WI

Blessings

I am blessed,
Blessed to be here on Earth.
Blessed to be alive, truly alive,
Blessed to be filled with God,
Blessed to have family and friends,
And blessed to be ME.

Blessings come and go,
Stay and stray,
You can't always count on them.

Always hold those special blessings close,
Keep them dear and near to your heart,
Otherwise they will slip away.

Always give others blessings, too,
Then yours will seem even more special,
Life will seem richer.

Always be thankful,
Because you are BLESSED.

Emily Wilczynski, Grade 8
Saint Thomas More Catholic School, MN

Bass

The best time to fish is in the spring.
When crickets chirp and sparrows sing.
I cast my line afar from shore,
A big fat fish I can't ignore.
I cast my line, I hear a splash,
A tug, a pull, I have a bass.
I let him go and he swims with glee,
I hope I can catch another one or maybe two or three.

Dane Mudri, Grade 9
Petoskey High School, MI

Forgetfulness

It's so easy to forget,
Get caught up in our lives,
Our problems,
Our worries,
And forget.

What goes on outside our privileged lives.
The lives of the other people of the world,
Their grief,
Their misfortune,
And forget.

How good we have it
And we realize,
Our problems,
Our worries,
Don't compare.

Rachana Gudipudi, Grade 9
Troy High School, MI

Fairy's Night

There's stars all around me is it true or is it fairies playing peek a boo.
There's images of flowers right in front of my eyes they dance like little butterflies.
Some are shy, some are bold and some even have hair of gold.
They like to play, even a trick or two, not out of spite, but just to be close to you.
They watch very close to every move even get mesmerized by something as simple as a shoe.
Their dresses sparkle in the moonlit night, fairy dust glistens in the starlight.
Do you believe in fairies because I sure do and if you do the fairies may actually come to you.

Chelsea Kiesling, Grade 7
Necedah Middle School, WI

I Know Where I Stand

I know where I stand. Being with you is never bland.
You make me feel like I matter. It is fun when we chatter.
We should have a night out. It would be fun without a doubt.
Friday night? Sounds all right.
The fun we have never ends. Oh, more friends?
Hello? I'm still here, even though I don't feel good, you know.

I know where I stand. Was this planned?
You led me on. Was I your pawn?
Take your fake kindness. At the time I was mindless.
I don't know what I saw in you. I just wanted to be by you even though I had the flu.
It never seemed like you wanted to know me. I've learned from you that nothing has a guarantee.
Here I am disgusted with your ways, knowing; not to get caught up in the day.
I know where I stand. I know I can withstand.

Jessica Bergmann, Grade 7
Bristol Elementary School, WI

Gone

I remember it like yesterday and it brings tears to my eyes
The night when everything felt so right but quickly all I remember is the flashing of the bright lights
I remember the tears rolling down my face as I prayed to God that it all would be fake
It felt unreal knowing that you were gone forever
I remember walking in the ER with your Bible, and your glasses hoping that you were alive
And that's when I screamed and cried when the Doctors told us that you were gone forever
After you died everything changed life, the family, auntie, myself, and even going to church didn't feel right
After all this I'm glad I still have Good Memories of you because it's what gets me through most of my day

Yvonne Archie, Grade 8
Hally Magnet Middle School, MI

Life

Days will go by and so will the years
But if I hold on tight enough, maybe they won't go so fast.
The songs I sing in my heart aren't the same ones I hear.
I try to run away but there's nowhere to go.
If I could, I would live my dreams, the ones I dream of when I sleep.
I would fly away through the clouds and stop for a second to sit.
I would travel the world, bungee jump off a bridge, spring off a tall rock into the ocean,
Record my songs, publish a book, and sky dive off a roaring plane.
I wouldn't care what anyone thought of me; just live the life He gave me.
Days go by fast, the songs are passionate and meaningful,
The world we live in is crazy and confusing.
Sometimes I just stop to think, what life would be like in heaven,
If it is what it's supposed to be like.

Aryanna Klemme, Grade 7
Elkhart Lake Elementary-Middle School, WI

Our Dreams

Blue bees buzzing as they fly around making beds
Purple elephants playing ping pong, as they dance in teal tutus.
Yellow marshmallows going to sit by the fire.
Kangaroos slipping on ice.
All in my head as I lay dreaming in my bed.

Cocky crocodiles cracking jokes.
Cute cats cradling cows.
Pink unicorns dancing in the rain.
Slimy snakes slithering through the swamp.
Sparkling stars dance through the sky.
All run through your head as you lay dreaming.

Sarah Cooper, Grade 9
Hartland High School, MI

Grandma

Your green thumb
Lights the house
With a soft glow
As your plants
Develop
And strengthen.
Your tomatoes
Turn a bright red
The size of my hand
The red and green peppers
Get hot and spicy
Your flowers have
Many colors
White, green, red,
And yellow
Your flowers brighten the house

Kevin Nguyen, Grade 8
Cedar Riverside Community School, MN

Basketball

There are five seconds left,
Your team is down by two,
If you win you are in the playoffs,
You have the ball,
You are guarded tightly,
Do you shoot it?
Or do you pass it to someone wide open?
You decide you want to be the hero,
So you shoot it,
It goes in but then it rattles out,
You feel terrible,
You know you could have passed it,
You feel really bad because you missed the winning shot,
Now your whole team is mad at you,
They won't talk to you,
It is tearing you apart,
After a couple of days the team starts talking to you,
But you always knew you gave 110%.

Nathan Kosewski, Grade 7
St Roman School, WI

A Weakened Strength

All gone, shot down,
No emotions to show
Just a faceless figure,
A mask, a drone,

No crying for dying
Unaccepted by society
Why don't we stop trying to
Fix a broken family?

The schools don't teach and the students don't learn it,
All this talk about faith so how do we confirm it?
A real man doesn't cry, what type of lie is this?
Just 'cuz you're a rock doesn't mean you're emotionless

You don't want to seem weak,
You want to seem wrong
I think we've lost the definition
For far too long.

A lot of people don't understand
How the systems works
But I'm off the subject now,
Thinking just hurts.

Elijah Small, Grade 7
Gesu Catholic School, MI

I Need You

The trees love when
The wind is blowing
The sand loves when
The waves brush against it

So how can you tell me you don't care?
You don't care about anything that happened
Nothing goes better together
Than you and I
I need you here
I need your comfort
I need your encouraging support
I need you with me.

We always need our special someone
You're my special someone.
I have to have you
You have to care
Chocolate needs Vanilla
Days need nights
Paper needs pen
Left needs right
I need you

Yasmin Valdez, Grade 7
St Roman School, WI

Full Moon Rising

Full moon's rising
The dead are waking
Full moon's rising
The dead are walking
Full moon's here
Vampires are feeding
Werewolves change
Full moon's setting
Vampires are done
Werewolves relax
Full moon's gone
The Earth can sleep
Until the next full moon

Hunter Christensen, Grade 8
Spring Hill School, WI

First Crush

My palms get clammy
And my cheeks get red
Every time I see your head.

My heart keeps racing
And my hands start to shake
Hoping that I'm really awake.

My breathing shortens and
Whenever I look into your eyes
My tummy gives me butterflies.

You probably think that I'm a klutz
My hair's a total mess
And yet, you still think I look my best.

Megan Nagel, Grade 8
Seymour Middle School, WI

Orange

Orange is the blazing sun
Hot with anger
Furious with rage

Orange is the color of a carrot
Yummy with sweetness
Crunchy like crackers
Full of nutrients

Orange is a big pumpkin
Full of slime and seeds
Tastes great in a pie
Fun to carve on Halloween

Orange is an orange
Full of sweet and sour flavor
Full of juice and pulp

Steven Moon, Grade 8
Lake Fenton Middle School, MI

The Wolf

The mighty, powerful wolf
Standing on a thick wooden stump.
Its undersized but rugged paws
Appear both deadly and powerful.
The fact that it's untamed and fierce
Makes it look a little out of place.
Its thick, muscular frame
Seems nearly set in stone.
As if it would be in the same spot
When we came back later.
Its dark, mysterious eyes
Are staring right into us
Almost like a human.

Nick Dahl, Grade 9
Clarkston Jr High School, MI

Me

I used to nap
But now I sleep
I used to walk
But now I run
I used to mumble
But now I talk
I used to ask for help
But now I help
I used to be small
But now I am bigger
I used to go to daycare
But now…I go to school

Alex Heiden, Grade 7
St Joseph School, WI

Volume Power

You turn me on
so I may speak
you let my opinions
spring a leak
I'm full of volume
you move me around
one day I'm up
one day I'm down
I turn around
My words are gone
Next thing you know
I'm back on
I'm singing this time
my volume is low
happiness and joy are aglow
my memories play
I watch and listen
just to show you
I did
glisten

Brianna Zich, Grade 7
South Middle School, WI

Cats Can Be…

Cats can be loving.
Cats can be mean.
Cats can be caring,
But cats can't be green.

When they get lost, we're sad.
When they get lost, we're mad.
When they get lost, it's a scare.
I hope it's not a bear!

Cats can be bad.
Cats can have fleas.
But mine is very bad.
Trust me, he put me through all of these.

Marcos Barajas, Grade 7
North Rockford Middle School, MI

I Am

I Am Big and Tall,
I Play Basketball with Friends
I Am the Universe,
Big, and Unexplored
I Am the Swish,
Swift and Sharp
I Am the Night Sky,
Mighty and Wondrous
I Am HDTV,
Clear Sound and Vision
I Am School,
Long and Boring
I Am Life,
Scary and Unpredictable
I Am Legend,
Feared and Loved

Austin Miller, Grade 9
Northport Public School, MI

Weeping Willow

The old weeping willow sinks
Into the snow covered ground
Limbs breaking, falling
From the weight of the snow

I wait, sobbing, searching
For reasons why
The weeping willow comforts,
Tells me everything will be okay

I return to the place where I belong
Waiting for the pain to begin
As I sit and wait,
I remember the weeping willow
My one friend

Mariah Johnson, Grade 9
Clintonville High School, WI

He

He is just a small guy hoping for a big dream
He is from Cambridge Wisconsin
He drives the DeWalt Ford
It's his 10th try at the dream
Matt makes many marvelous moves
He takes the lead, and then comes the rain
NASCAR ends the race
He finally gets his dream
He is Matt Kenseth
He just won the 51st running of the Daytona 500
The rain falls from the sky and the tears flow from his eyes
He has completed his dream
To him the win is as big as the sky

Evan Deprey, Grade 7
Luxemburg-Casco Middle School, WI

Spring

When the season of spring is near,
We think of all the joy and cheer,
That accompanies spring on its way,
And brings happiness without dismay.

Birds chirp and children play,
As we so fervently pray,
For the many gifts God has blessed us with,
And the beauty of spring that is not a myth.

As spring comes and its beauty blossoms,
Like wildflowers springing in large sums,
We laugh and sometimes sing,
For the joy that spring may bring.

Now that we smile,
Knowing God is with us all the while,
The flower of our heart grows,
And that is where the beauty of spring shows.

Angelica Abbott, Grade 8
St Thomas More Academy, MI

Safiyo

Sleeping away in her darkened cave
Blanket wrapped around her
Like a cocoon
Boiling cup of tea beside her
Her cave-like bedroom smelling
Like Vick's Vapor Rub
She's softly snoring away
In the sun like temperature cave
The heat blasting from the vent
She's still softly snoring away
The perfect way to end a good day

Muna Ali, Grade 7
Cedar Riverside Community School, MN

My Pond

My pond is as bright as the sun
My pond has the fragrance of the country air
It can be as cold as the snow
It is as clear as a crystal

Mitchell Tlachac, Grade 7
Luxemburg-Casco Middle School, WI

Life

All our lives are plays and we are just the actors.
We come and we go, taking part in many scenes.
Scene One is the newborn baby,
a cherished treasure, loved by all.
Next scene is the young child,
her face like the shining sun,
on her way to the first day of school.
Scene Three, the teenager
the flower of love blossoming in her heart
and the world's a beautiful place
During the fourth scene of life, she's a young woman
amazed at the wonders of this land
and blazing her own path in this world.
Next scene, she's a grown woman with husband, kids, and job,
sometimes struggling to find her way
in this messed up, crazy world.
Scene Six, the woman is in her golden years
happily retired with her husband and grandkids,
spending her time enjoying life.
In her ending scene, she has become dependent on others.
Though her freedom's gone, her spirit will carry on forever.

Allison Fouks, Grade 9
Northwood School, WI

Sand Tornado

This shell is like the dime you find on the street,
Or in the hall,
One that stands out instead of blending in,
With the rest of the change on the sidewalk.
Its sandy color would camouflage it into a long beach
Rolling with the waves
Empty but still so complete.
Your eyes follow the swirls 'round, and 'round again
Like a bottomless pit, it looks like it ends when in reality
It's so deep you may never get out after falling in.
A tornado winding down from the sky,
Getting smaller until reaching the earth's surfaces
Anxious to devour the waiting contents of the small town ahead.
A girl's eyes so small yet deep with confusion
And a story waiting to be heard, to be told.
Or an old man's life,
Used to be so big, so full of excitement
Slowly dwindling downward nearing the end of his years.
A shell so small with a story so big.
It deceives the eye, puts you into a spiraling world of confusion.

Laurelanne Fasching, Grade 8
Chippewa Falls Middle School, WI

Wondrous

Wonder, wonder
Is what I feel whenever an animal is near
Not just any animal
A certain undermined animal
A worm to be exact
Think how it must feel
To know you're prey
To know your insignificance
To know how you disgust everyone
But then again
There are certain worms
Those are more fortunate
Than the rest
They are not prey,
But predators
They are Wonderful!!

Noah Rueckl, Grade 7
Luxemburg-Casco Middle School, WI

My Star

My star
Lives up there
In heaven
At night
And in the morning
Even though
You can't see him
I know that
He is still there

Cassie Massart, Grade 7
Luxemburg-Casco Middle School, WI

Coach K

Dear coach,
Thank you

Thanks for all you've done like…
Believing in me when I didn't
Because I was the worst
Not giving up
Encouraging me
Inspiring me
Teaching me the basics
Passing
Setting
Spiking
Serving
Underhand and
Overhand
Telling me what I do wrong
Making us winners
Doing your best
Being my coach
Thank you for all you've done

Sara Schliesman, Grade 7
St Katharine Drexel School, WI

Rainy Route

A cool *droplet* of rain slid down my face and dropped off my nose.
A fresh, *soothing* feeling rushed over my skin,
The pure, *tasteless* rain hit my tongue while holding my head to the sky.
I took in a deep breath of *moist* air and smiled.
My eyes gazed at the *bright* spring sun shining down upon us,
a *vibrant* moment that is held in our *hearts.*

Malena Maxwell, Grade 7
Valley View Middle School, MN

I Will Never Forget You…

There once was a man that cared for his family more than anyone else,
I will never forget you…
A man that loved to work, and worked until he couldn't work anymore,
I will never forget you…
He spent all his days in the fields of his family farm,
I will never forget you…
He was always there for his kids, and his whole family,
I will never forget you…
He always loved his canned peaches, and working at the orchards,
I will never forget you…
He always told the most interesting stories from his childhood,
I will never forget you…
He was very positive, and always saw the up side of every situation,
I will never forget you…
A man that was positive even after he got the sad news.
I will never forget you…
A man who wanted to finish his life in the house that he lived in for many years,
I will never forget you…
Memories of my great grandpa Reuben Kiehnau will be engraved in my heart forever,
I will never forget you…

Josh Hopkins, Grade 8
Seymour Middle School, WI

Katrina

People from Katrina suffered a lot.
The Katrina came through and just didn't stop.
Washed all the houses and buildings away.
Thousands of people had no place to stay.
Lots of people were killed.
Some had injuries that couldn't be healed.
People lost jobs and wealth.
The Government didn't pick up one finger to help.
Many hopes and dreams were lost.
People had to pay the cost.
Walked around with their heads held high.
Some refused to cry.
Others gave with open hearts.
And tried to care right from the start.
Water filled up to the brim.
People climbed up tree limbs
They traveled for miles with nothing on hand.
They tried to help each other stand.
The street turned muddy the sky turned blue.
It's not what you can do to help me, it's what I can do to help you.

Trelijah Miller, Grade 8
Fairview Charter School, WI

I Don't Understand

I don't understand why loving parents vote for murder
Why color separates society from society
Why people don't think before they act

But most of all
Why people enjoy fighting
Why people are easily angered
Why the wrong thing is always popular
And why fantasy can't exist

What I understand the most of all is
Why we have our rights
Why smiles spread like germs
Why friendship keeps us alive
Why the wind blows through your hair
And why summer makes us so happy

Marissa Fritz, Grade 7
West Suburban Christian Academy, WI

My First Circus Show

Peroo, go the elephants,
as they urge to start the show
Kerchink, groans the tiny car,
with all the clowns in tow

Shook, go the lights,
fading out of sight
Ayee, goes the crowd, some from joy,
some from fright

Scree, is heard,
after the ring master turns on the microphone
Woo, goes the music,
setting an ominous tone

Oooh, goes the impressed crowd,
as the magician vanishes without a sound
Aaah, goes the awestruck crowd,
soon after he is found

Aww, goes the crowd,
as the tamer plays with a ferocious lion
"Hey!" yells a costumer to the beast,
"Want some popcorn? I'm buyin'!"

Marques Dotson-Baird, Grade 8
Seymour Middle School, WI

Ghosts

G hostly ghouls in the night
H aunting you in plain sight
O WWWWW! They're coming to bite
S caring off all the victim's hair
T oo many sharp teeth, makes me scared
S o be very very prepared.

Cody-James Dobbs, Grade 8
Roseville Jr High School, MI

Pounding in the Night

The mysterious music chills me to the bone
It's powerful and majestic like thunder
Pounding in the night
The darkness of the music surrounds me
As if to suffocate me
It's cryptic and frightful
At times depressing
But shocking and astounding all the same
It's horrifying and fills me with terror
As it sends shivers down my spine
But yet it's amazing to hear

Katie Aleck, Grade 8
Sandusky Middle School, MI

Snow

It's beautifully clean and perfectly white,
And makes the winter an amazing sight.
Great for sledding and playing and all sorts of fun,
Until all of it melts under the red hot sun.
It fills children with joy when it first starts to fall,
And means Santa will soon bring some presents for all.
When caught on a tongue, it melts in a blink,
And always surrounds, the outdoor ice rink.
Compacted and shaped, it can form men,
That have names, such as Carl or Sven.
It is plowed off of streets and shoveled from drives
By the men, their young kids, and even their wives.
School is canceled, when it rises too high.
That never could make little children cry.
Each flake is it's own, and extremely unique,
Who wouldn't want to grab one, just for a peek.
Cushioning your fall when your foot slips on the ice,
Is one of the qualities that makes it so nice.
It's snow of course, and brings bundles of joy,
To every child, whether girl or boy.

Jeff Holmes, Grade 9
Troy High School, MI

Just Because

Just because I like playing sports
    Doesn't mean I'm a pro
    Doesn't mean I'm the best athlete
Just because I like playing sports
    It doesn't mean I don't need practice
    It doesn't mean I won't make a mistake while playing
    It doesn't mean I'm the best player on the team
Just because I like playing sports
    I will always be a team player
    I will give my teammates encouragement
    I will ask for God's help when I play
Just because I like playing sports...accept me for how I play!

Jonathan Hiddings, Grade 8
St John Lutheran School, MI

Star/Moon

Star
Bright, light
Spikey, sparkling, sterling
Lumpy, falling, rounding, glooming
Blooming, glowing, shining
Glamorous, luminous
Moon

Jenny Her, Grade 7
Edison Middle School, WI

Sadness in Vain

Dark and gloomy days,
Sunny summer rays.
We live nights and days,
But still nothing pays.
We are in vain,
They can feel the pain.
But still we must live on,
Just to see another dawn.
Many people hate their life,
They just can't see the nice.
Sadness and pain,
Life in vain
They think the future's gleam,
But they just can't dream.
They sit there in gloom,
They're waiting for their doom.
They've done wrong in the past,
They just can't last.
They love the color red,
They wish they were dead.

Brooke Schulstrom, Grade 8
Saline Middle School, MI

Wishing

Make a wish upon a star,
Hoping to see that open door,
The one that leads to dreams afar,
And past wishes galore.

You can be near or far,
There is still room to explore.
You can catch a falling star,
It will be forevermore.

There is a place so far,
Where wishes are hoped for,
That place is far from bizarre,
It would describe a metaphor.

Don't be afraid to wish upon your star,
It will be yours till there is no more,
A star can be your faithful friend,
It will be there till the end.

Mary Benson, Grade 7
St Thomas More Academy, MI

The Tissue

Tired of looking like sickness? Well, I've got something for you.
Instead of that hankie you're using, why don't you try my tissue?

It's only been used a few times, ten times max. Well, maybe more…
And while it may seem kind of dirty, it's clean — it's been on my floor.

The dog thought it was a chew toy, my brother thought it was maché.
I assure you the tissue's not dirty, though the maid nearly threw it away.

I used it to wipe off my shoe once, after I stepped in dog poo.
And I think it maybe is molding — it's looking fuzzy and blue.

It served as a smusher of insects, a wiper of mouths and feet.
A sweat remover when running…its history really is neat.

You say you don't want to use it? It's clean, I say, why not?
It's perfectly clean and you'd add to its story — so what if it's starting to rot?

My family really enjoys it. In fact, we named in Michael.
What I really love about the thing is how it is recycled!

It may look like trash to others, but to us it's a symbol of Earth.
So while we wait for it to be used, Michael just sits on the hearth.

Rebecca Kidder, Grade 9
South View Middle School, MN

Mr. Ant

On a clear summer day the sun shines on the cracked sidewalk
Dots march along the place where grass and stone meet; one by one
Hoses run like waterfalls quenching water deprived yellow-green lawns
Kids stamped on burning black tar while parents lounge in air conditioned porches

But a silent storm was approaching
First came the thunder
Then the earth began to quake
They scurried away from open space searching for cover

Because they knew what was coming
The shaking reached its peak as a hill fell from the sky
Brothers and sisters vanished
Gone forever

The shaking stopped
As a tiny girl stooped on the curb to see the bottom of her worn black Converse
Upon site she found ragged remains
Flattened into sheets as if they were rolled through a printing press

Turning her attention to the dotted lines she inspects them with a puzzled face
Until enlightenment leapt across her face
Leaning closer she whispers in a hushed voice
"I'm sorry Mr. Ant; I believe I walked on your friends"

Mary Pederson, Grade 9
South View Middle School, MN

Memories

On a cold, dreary campground night,
Frigid air brushing up last season's leaves,
I glanced into the firelight,
Where its flames danced, bright and free.

And there, as I sat in the falling snow,
Wind howling over the desolate ground,
As the fire started to burn low,
In the dying embers, I found…

The sun, in full glory, shining,
With its radiant display of light.
The soft, melodic whining,
Of a bumblebee in flight.

Warm, green meadows of summer,
Under my feet, soft loam.
The pattering footsteps of a runner;
My brother returning home.

But the world soon fell into evening,
Over the frozen and unfrequented ground.
In the ashes no longer meaning,
Ever to be found.

Allen Chen, Grade 9
Troy High School, MI

Earthly Angels

The blind will guide you to heaven's gate
The mute will be your key.
The deaf will ward
off those who'd harm you,
in hopes to set you free.

And all around the angels sing
though they be not seen nor heard
for their message breaks all boundaries
and speaks solely to the heart.
love, peace, oh gracious warmth
when in the heaven's hands.

The gate cannot be seen, but still it is there
The key cannot be held, but still it is there
And guarded they will be
by those who don't hear scorn.

And be whomever they may be
they all can still come forward
And they all can hear the song
And they'll all forever bask
in the heaven's warm glow.

Melissa Wright, Grade 9
Chelsea High School, MI

Rain

Drip, Drop, Drip,
I look outside my window as everything goes calm,
Drip, Drop, Drip,
I reach my hand out and catch a raindrop on my palm.
Drip, Drop, Drip,
I hear the soft *hush* of the trees,
Drip, Drop, Drip,
I hear the *whoosh* of the soothing breeze.
Drip, Drop, Drip,
nature is like a lullaby,
Drip, Drop, Drip,
I lay down and slowly shut my eyes.

Even in my dreams I hear the soft relaxing sound of,
Drip, Drop, Drip,
nature's beauty I have found.

Marissa Eggerichs, Grade 7
Roosevelt Middle School, MN

I Am Beautiful

I am beautiful
not only because of the curve of my hips
or the shape of my body
not only because of the fullness of my lips
or the curl of my eyelashes

I am beautiful because I have confidence
I am beautiful because I have my own styles
I am beautiful because I have a brain
and that's a beautiful thing
I am beautiful because I have goals and plan to reach them.
I am beautiful because I am always there to lend a helping hand
and that's a beautiful thing

I am beautiful because I want to be
I am beautiful because God made me that way
I am beautiful because in my eyes there's beauty
I am beautiful and that's just me

and no one could replace me!

Mary Xiong, Grade 7
Ramsey Jr High School, MN

Sadness

Sad can be:
Grey like thunder clouds
Hot like lying on the sun
Cold like being in weather below 50 degrees
Sounds like rain drops hitting the deck
Tastes like eating brussel sprouts
Smells like damp air on a wet day
Looks like round droplets of rain
Texture like smooth water from a river
Moves like the Nile River on a stormy day

Lexi Koschtial, Grade 7
Manistee Middle School, MI

Not So Perfect

She thinks she's perfect
but you don't see her imperfections
she is weaker than she looks
Ripped up, torn apart
Doesn't let it show
she covers up her imperfections
She makes others feel bad
feel small
Look through her
She's not so perfect after all
nobody is
That girl that everyone wants to be
isn't what she appears to be
You don't always see her imperfections
She sees them
She knows she isn't perfect
But she can't admit it
Her mistakes, her regrets
are covered in layers of makeup
When the makeup is washed away,
you will see the real person that she is

Abby Mikita, Grade 7
Kenowa Hills Middle School, MI

Nature Adores God

Trees sway to His voice,
Mountains fall down before Him,
Nature adores God.

James Pipe, Grade 7
Washtenaw Christian Academy, MI

Success

Her eyes,
Stay focused,
On what she wants,
Her body,
Fit for decisions,
Choosing,
From this,
And that,
Using opinion,
When finding,
Which door,
Will reward the future,
She keeps her task,
As her goal,
And makes that goal,
A key,
To unlock,
Another goal,
She is preparing,
For her key,
To success

Alyssa Dooley, Grade 7
South Middle School, WI

Dice

The roll of a dice
It could change your life
Even though it's pure luck
You could make a choice
That could sucks
Pressuring the dice
To roll the right way
And if it doesn't
You have a price to pay
As you lay the dice down
You wear the crown
Of perfect luck
But as you know
You cannot maintain
So you stop the game
People get mad
But it's all the same
You have lost your luck
To the roll of the dice.

Rita Kawak, Grade 7
South Middle School, WI

I Remember

I remember being little
I remember Parry Sound
I remember Seagull Island
I remember Tucker the hound
I remember catching catfish
I remember being happy
I remember the word "Bic"
I remember the ole' Chappy
But things are different now
I never go to Parry Sound anymore

Eric Poisson, Grade 9
Hartland High School, MI

Travis

Travis
torqued-up
NOS accelerated

street slicks

on a hot
summer day
cruising in
his Trans Am
down to his
torqued-up
3 V8 engines
with NOS
40 ft
of fun.

Nic Sutherlund, Grade 7
Valley View Middle School, MN

Graduation

Oh, how the time has flown
We are now all grown
We all must be moving on
Because the time has come and gone

Some of our visits have been cut short
And some are of the longer sort
Yet we still remain together
Like we will forever

I will truly miss you all
Because you're the best I can recall
We were there for each other
Like a sister and a brother

So let's have a ball
Until the curtain call
For when it does come
We might be mum

But we must say goodbye
And take a deep sigh
For we all may cry.

Jackie Berndtson, Grade 8
Our Lady Star of the Sea School, MI

Christmas

Christmas is coming
People filled with glee
I can't wait for Christmas
It's my time of year.

When people open presents
I love to see their faces
Cause there's no nicer thing to see
Than the smiles on their faces.

Christmas comes once a year
So enjoy it while you can
I know I look forward to it
And I love to see the man (Santa).

A.J. Mueller, Grade 8
St Roman School, WI

Tornado

Tornados spin in very sneaky
Like the slithering of a silent serpent
It rotates in during violent storms
And destroys everything
With its ferocious winds
Then it spins away as fast as it came
Leaving a path of destruction in it wake
All over the great plains

Sam Bohrer, Grade 8
West Suburban Christian Academy, WI

Point;

And when it comes down to it;
you're right and you're right,
you're wrong and you're wrong.
You do your own thing he does his;
you like to sing, he likes to write.
There's nothing wrong nor right; we see
through different eyes; just the fact of life.

Tania Carroll, Grade 8
Centennial Middle School, MI

The Journey of a Marble

I start the way down the hill,
Rolling, rolling, rolling,
To watch it bounce off all the little pebbles,
Still rolling, rolling, rolling,
To roll past Hultgren striking the ground,
To bounce off a bump,
And hit a car,
So big and hard to cause a dent,
Still rolling, rolling, rolling,
Still goes on its epic expedition
Starts to slow,
Rolling, rolling, rolling,
I think it will stop but it plops in the sewer,
Uh oh,
That's another journey for the marble.

Michael Jost, Grade 7
Valley View Middle School, MN

Summer

I can't wait until summer
summer is when kids play all day
you can hear the pitter patter of kids feet running
big bouncing balls people playing peacefully
it's like an everlasting day of fun

It's a day where you can be free
no need for rules no need for parents
no need for work no need for curfews
just fun fun fun
we can run we can jump we can do what we want to do

Summer is a fish swimming freely in the ocean
it's an amazing change between fall school starts
winter school is halfway spring almost there
then BAM summer is here and school is over

My favorite day is the last day of school
when we can break the chains off our wrists and ankles
waiting at the classroom door the last three seconds of the day
ready, set, GO.
Now at this point I can't stop thinking about
it it's on my mind 24/7
it's what I want it's what I love it's summer.

Mathew Bougie, Grade 7
Ramsey Jr High School, MN

Summer Things

In the summer
You don't have to use tools
You can just have fun and play in the pool.
Lay in the sun and just have fun
Lay on the beach
To feel the sand on your feet.
You can sleep in
No alarm clocks going beep, beep, beep.
No tests.
Just make a mess.
Staying up late.
Going on a date.

Brooke Oldenberg, Grade 7
Centreville Jr High School, MI

In the Ocean

I am the top predator of the deep,
with razor sharp teeth,
and a dorsal fin.
I am a great white shark.
I swim through the cool, blue sea.
As I swim deeper I see only darkness.
I sense movement above me.
I feel ripples on the surface of the water,
made from a wounded fish.
As I approach the fish
my electromagnetic sensors on my snout get more sensitive,
detecting every sense of movement.
After I had the fish as my dinner,
blood filled the water.
I headed into the water again.
Deeper,
deeper,
I'm gone.

Kirsta Lutes, Grade 7
St Katharine Drexel School, WI

Christmas Eve Magic

Christmas Eve magic fills the cool air
As birds soar above bringing a blanket of peace
Tall silver trees dance in praise in the quiet night

The snow glistens in pastel colors in the night
While the red bird's song fills the air
The whole forest is waiting for the morning in peace

The trees whisper to one another in peace
All of the forest is alive on this one special night
Joy and wonder glistens off the snow into the air

In the air is a feeling of peace, shining bright in the night

Allison Arnold, Grade 8
St Andrew's School, MI

Light to My Life

Alone as always I sit
The beautiful book lay open
Words flow freely from the pages
My happy heart eagerly listens

Songs from the Psalmist
Glorious life in the Garden
Unfair judgment on Jesus
Precautions from Proverbs

Each dawn of day
And exposure in the evening
Makes my soul sing
How grateful to God I am for these pages

I hope and persistently pray
That my prevalent passion will never fade
This radiant revelation is a gift
The Bible is a light to my life

Elizabeth Shirley, Grade 9
South View Middle School, MN

Tomorrow

Please just give us tonight,
Tomorrow I'll swim back to shore
The water feels perfectly right,
Tomorrow I will let go.
My heart doesn't do what it should,
For a moment let me hold you.
Tomorrow I'll completely forget,
And start everything new.
With the words that you had said,
So I'm not thinking about tomorrow.
You have my heart for the night,
Even if it is borrowed.
I'm going to lie here tonight,
And the words going through my head.
Fall asleep in your arms,
Until this is dead.
I'll take my heart back tomorrow,
When I swim back to shore.
Knowing what will happen,
Tomorrow will be more.

Makenzie McMahon, Grade 8
Riverview Middle School, WI

Canfield Lake

Wind streaming through my hair
Calm rippled water hitting the shore
Dull boats hitting the dock
Rain bouncing off the shimmering lake
Cattails swaying from side to side
Smell of fresh new lake water
The trees waving to me from across

Caitlan Edenburn, Grade 7
Manistee Middle School, MI

Friendship

I hit the bottom and was hurt
I wanted to lay there and die
You came along and I hated you right away
You stood there looking at me,
Not like all the others, not down on, not through me or past me, but into me
You saw my pain and tried to help,
But I pushed you away
Until you came down to my world to help
Your compassion to help was like a blazing flame
The smile on your face is the symbol of honesty
You grabbed me and pulled us up
You did what others wouldn't have done
You did what others believed couldn't be done
You did what others said shouldn't be done
You acted as a light and relit my world.
You are friendship.

Zachary Rabideau, Grade 9
Clarkston Jr High School, MI

Hazel

I'm really going to miss you!
My heart will never let me forget you.
You were there when I just needed someone to listen.
The feel of your soft brown fur is something that I can't help but miss.
Your incredible personality rubbed off on everyone that met you.
I miss those cold days when you would warm my feet at night.
And, when I was lonely you were always cuddled right there by my side.
I just wish I could have said goodbye.
I love you!

Kassidy Schaut, Grade 8
Central Middle School, MI

Trouble in the Sky

Passengers were filled with glee,
They stepped on the airplane and were able to travel for just a small fee.
The flight was going fine,
The service was divine.
The plane was only 6 miles away,
Suddenly it made a dramatic sway.
People were screaming and shouting too,
The fate of the plane, nobody knew.
Nose first it went,
The plane had been more than severely bent.
It had crashed into a house,
Killing a man on the ground and a mouse.
That was not all who died,
Every single passenger as well, their families cried.
A huge flame could be seen,
It was not the least bit serene.
This was Continental Airlines Flight 3407,
Where all the bodies flew up to heaven.
The pilot had flown on a number of missions,
But was troubled by the icy conditions.
This plane crash occurred and surely people will always remember it if they heard.

Sydney Freedman, Grade 8
West Hills Middle School, MI

The Field

An open field flat and green
A blank canvas waiting to be painted
The object of a perfect scene
Some settlers come to claim
The field's color is now tainted
With brown cottages all the same
Soon one cottage turns to fifteen
And the settlers increase their fame

The field is now a town
With roads built all around
Merchants come from far and wide
To trade their goods with pride
The town gains money and power
It's changing by the hour

The brown roads turn to gray
With skyscrapers blocking the sky
Constant lights turn night to day
The population reaches a new high
The town is now a city
And beneath its crowded shade
Lies the canvas on which a masterpiece was made

Isabelle Birt, Grade 9
St Thomas More Academy, MI

Lisa in Kindergarten

Kindergarten is hard when you're a little bit shy.
Lisa sat at her desk and stifled a quiet cry.
No one to talk to and no one she knew.
Other kids were happy, but Lisa was oh, so blue.

This was not like Preschool with naps and ABCs.
Kindergarten was way different, it was not a breeze.
New concepts to learn and homework to do.
When to play dress up, Lisa had not a clue.

There were kids laughing and playing funny games.
Lisa wanted to join, but she didn't know their names.
Too shy to speak and too shy to smile,
Lisa stayed in her chair and just sat for awhile.

Finally taking a sigh and sucking in air,
Lisa stood up, tugged at her skirt, and fixed her hair.
She walked to the girls in the corner and said "Hello,"
The girls grinned and said "Hello" in a quiet echo.

Soon little Lisa was feeling much better.
She took a leap and complimented a girl on her sweater.
Lisa had a great time and was sad when she had to go.
She was gleeful to find kids she'd soon get to know.

Courtney Chennault, Grade 7
Detroit Country Day Middle School, MI

I Don't Notice

It's there beyond that wall I see, hiding from me.
I look and look, but it never comes forth.
Colored with hints and prints,
something I once thought I saw, but never did.
I retrieve back searching for something right there,
it's what I didn't notice.

Samantha Jahnke, Grade 8
Washington School, WI

At Ease in the Morning Breeze

The morning breeze rustles my hair
I breathe in the salty air
It's just me
I feel deserted by the sea

The waves crash against the coral below
This is a sound I have come to know
But it's different when no one is around
Just you to hear the sound

The coconut trees slowly awake
Yet I have awakened at day break
The sun's sweet rays creep up to the beach
Pouring onto the water near reach

Here I stand
Toes tucked beneath the sand
Suddenly my face turns to a grin
I am done with the past, my life can finally begin

Lauren Roggenbuck, Grade 8
Sandusky Middle School, MI

Today's Economy

Today we live in interesting times
Each day we wait for the market to climb
And gasp for air as the numbers fall low

Low, much lower than we thought they could go,
Why do we live each day with such fright?
Who is to blame for this strange plight?

The big corporations are huge and in need
All causing this mess because of their greed

Now as a mere student, where might I go?
Looking at this from so far below
I think that small business is the way for me
To be in the place that I can be

I plan to begin my business of choice
With smart plans and good assets

With secondhand items restored with great care,
And marked-up, leaving profit to spare.

Zacary Keryluk, Grade 8
Core Knowledge Charter School, WI

Back Stabbers and Gossipers

Oh I see you, whispering to her as I walk by, staring at me as you talk.
Don't act like I can't hear you, talking about me all the time, spreading lies and telling rumors.
Before you spread one more rumor, I want you to know something, it might help in the future.
Get your facts straight! Before you go around telling people things, especially when they aren't true.
Gossip hurts, if you don't stop spreading lies, you aren't going to have any friends.
What is wrong with me? Thinking you were my friend? You're just a back stabbing gossiper!
All you do is talk to talk, you just need to knock it off! Stop spreading rumors!
Well I hope you take my advice, and good luck in the future, you may need it, because our friendship is through!

Alexis Rosario, Grade 8
Lake Fenton Middle School, MI

Max

Max was a dog who was smart and cunning,
Who had a bark that could send people running.
He was a mutt, whose favorite snacks were cheese and peanuts.
He was a mix of a terrier and a shepherd.
Whose eyes were bright and soared like a bird.
He was playful and smart and very nice,
He would sometimes nip but never bite.
When he was a puppy and saw himself in a mirror,
He would bark and bark and get nearer and nearer.
Then as he would run and jump away with his big floppy ears and big awkward paws,
That sight would just have us laughing and hearing "awes."
We had also many laughs whenever we would give him a squeaker toy.
He would almost always swallow the squeaker and when he would bark, he would make a funny noise.
As the years went by he got older and older until one day we found out that he had an ulcer.
Max was a good dog and I miss him greatly.
But God had said that it was his time and he is in a better place with others and my granny.

He passed away on Sunday, January 4, 2009.

Rachel Gabrich, Grade 8
St Margaret Mary School, WI

New York City

Streets are lined with shiny yellow cabs
The buildings are an array of flashing colors trying to grab my attention
An advertisement for a computer
And another for a show that is playing on Broadway
The Subway is a whole new experience for me
Underneath the city the trains squeak and rumble as they go from point to point
There are so many restaurants that I get a headache whenever it is time for a meal
The cheesecake is HUGE
In China town everyone speaks Chinese so we could barely understand what they wanted
When they were really trying to sell us pirated DVDs
People crowd the streets like a thick fog that makes it nearly impossible to walk through the city
Ground zero brings fear to some
Grief and disbelief to others
And in a way
A streak of confidence
That our great country can make it through anything that the rest of the world throws at us
The Statue of Liberty is another monument
She holds the flame towards the new world
A place where everyone is free to be what they want to be
A place like New York City

Miranda Jacobs, Grade 7
Whitehall Jr High School, MI

The Twin

He is extremely awesome and very loud;
If he wanted to, he could distract a crowd.
His voice was an overwhelming, high-pitched shriek,
As if it was coming out of a bird's beak.
This boy wasn't exactly real tall;
You could barely see him in the hall.
His best friend was six foot three;
He was filled with lots of glee.
He played cymbals in the Troy High drum line;
This boy crashed those cymbals from five till nine.
This kid had six different classes,
But could not find them without his glasses.
He was part of the Troy Colt Marching Band,
Aka The Best Band in the Land.
He played for the Troy High Tennis Team;
Winning brought out a delightful scream.
This boy loved to watch something called TV;
This unique small child was someone like me.

Shalin Shah, Grade 9
Troy High School, MI

Drive Safely

Driving can be really fun
But it can also be really dumb
If you drive with no caution
You might end up in a coffin
Hurt the people that you love
It doesn't matter how good you are
Don't just jump in and speed with your car
Don't get road rage
Don't get scared
It will all just end in tears
Don't go fast
Don't drive reckless
You might end up with no license
Drive with care drive with caution
Then you won't end up in that coffin
Be sincere
Don't drink beer
While driving it can be dear
Always remember that they gave you a chance
To be a good driver or…
End with a BANG!!!

Dylan Baum, Grade 9
Beaverton High School, MI

My Beautiful Boy

He is the beautiful boy
I met on that summer night
He is the beautiful boy
Who gave me my first kiss, which felt so right
He is the beautiful boy, my first love
He is the beautiful boy
That is my angel from the sky above

Ana Perales, Grade 8
Bloomingdale Middle School, MI

My Mother

My mother is a hero in my eyes,
When I tell people and they ask me why
I tell them,
She's the military fighting world war three,
She's my Statue of Liberty
She never cries in front of her kids,
She stays strong,
'Cause that's just who she is,
She is the sun in the sky that shines upon me
She's the rock in the ground that's beneath me
She's the hug we all give each other,
She's my mother.

Tonya Felton, Grade 8
Spring Hill School, WI

Ode to Florida

Give praises to Florida!
Thrilled are those who cook out on your grounds,
glad to have your great seafood,
having a ball with their folks.
Happy are the charmed people who eat your grapefruit,
which blooms abundantly.
With that fresh, delightful juice and fruit
that melts in someone's mouth.
Lively are the tourists who soak up your sun
that puts genuine heat
on someone trying to tan.
Jubilant are the bodies that splash into your waters,
laughing and having a blast,
in the warm, salty ocean.
Cheerful are those who jog around your cities,
working up a sweat, even in the morning.
Blessed are those who walk on your beaches,
their toes in your sand,
striding with loved ones on your ground.
You are guaranteed to have a good time,
in wonderful Florida.

Haley Fiegel, Grade 7
St Katharine Drexel School, WI

Yellow

I am the bright hot sun
The color of Chris Paul's jersey
I am the peel of a banana
The brightest of the iPod nano's
I am the inside of a pineapple
The strength of Pennfield's football helmet
I am November's birthstone
The pencil, I use
I am the mustard on a hotdog
The lemon in your water

Winston Stephenson, Grade 8
Pennfield Middle School, MI

Vacation

Vacation,
The anticipation.
What to do first.
Counting down the days,
Seems to take so long.
Packing, unpacking, repacking,
Getting in shape,
Tell everyone I see.
Reminiscing past vacation memories,
Thinking about new ones to come.
Checking off everything on my list,
Planning on a great time,
And leaving all the stress behind.
Vacation will go too fast.

Jonah Sibley, Grade 8
St Roman School, WI

Love Toes

My toes are like stars
they twinkle at night
and even at dawn
on the beach
and by the shore
my toe nail changes color
every time the water comes near
red, blue, pink, and even green
but my favorite is purple
and that only happens
when I am in love.

Angelika Tylka, Grade 8
Spring Hill School, WI

Sleep

I am tired.
I haven't slept
for years!
My eyes are
sagging out of
my head!

My arms are gone,
they've gone to bed.
My legs can't move
they've fallen off
to sleep.

My hair is like
rotten spaghetti.
But my favorite
show is on!

I can't go to sleep,
I can't go to sleep,
I can't…"zzzz."

Sia Xiong, Grade 7
Ramsey Jr High School, MN

Spring Is Becoming

I stand here in my black polka-dot rain boots
On the first day of so-called, "spring."
The wind is blowing in my hair,
Making it brush to my left.

The coldness at my frozen fingertips…and the numbness in my ears…
The stuffiness in my nose, that matches my rosy cheeks
But the sun is still bright,
Shining in my blue eyes.

Across the road, the fields are plowed to a checkerboard of
Black and faded yellow.
I close my eyes and feel
How the birds tweet, to the welcoming back home and
How the grass is popping up from its winter nap below…
All brown and muddy
The wind is howling its song…
Knowing that nothing has gone wrong

I take a step forward…
I breathe in the freshness of the air
Spring is becoming…
The sun will rise and the moon will fall
It's only the beginning of what else is to come in Mother Nature's call.

Taylor Kraemer, Grade 7
Osakis High School, MN

Smudges

The stark canvas on the easel alone
Frozen by the shadows of time
Without specks of color
Without its capture of light
Intensity with each stroke
More passionate and ferocious than the next
The colors not important
The bristles gliding, moving themselves
The contour's nothingness
The mind tainted with inspiration
Blocked by reality
The brush unreliable

Splotches of paint grow worn
Thoughts are interrupted
The unique luminosity fading away
Faster, quicker

Suddenly reality is setback
A star in the night, a glimpse of fate, a twinkle in your eye
The brush begins to stroke again with a mind free of obstructions
But this time more fervent
The colors very important

Abbey Hubregsen, Grade 9
Clarkston Jr High School, MI

Love

Hearts are the symbol to love
Hearts show the sweetness of a dove
Hearts dance around the beauty of one
Hearts explain the passion of two
Hearts open the key to happiness
Hearts are the colors of a sunset
Love plus hearts equals forever
Red, pink, purple once so ever
Hearts are the valentine to hugs and kisses
Hearts are also like chocolate candies
So soft so flexible hearts are special
Hearts are the symbol of love

Sierra Hamilton, Grade 8
Jerstad Agerholm Middle School, WI

The Meadow

I used to lie down in a meadow,
The sweet smelling grass between my toes.
I loved the wind blowing in my hair,
While I ran like I didn't care.
The swaying of the beautiful trees,
Made me feel even more free.
I loved to think and read,
While I watched the animals feed.
I watched the birds fly around,
Listening to their lovely sounds.
I wish I could go back to that special place,
To feel the sun shine in my face.

Anna Harrington, Grade 7
St Joseph Catholic Middle School, MI

The Secrets We Hide

The things we keep concealed,
Right beneath the surface.
The things we never show,
The things we fear for others to know.

The things that desecrate,
All our freedom and liberty.
The things that enslave the mind
And bewilder the tongue
A string of dishonesty from our voice is rung.

But eventually we are betrayed,
We give ourselves up as we turn ourselves in.
And it is always,
The little things that give us away.
The little things that leave us in pieces
For others to tread upon.
The things that leave us to reconstruct the image,
Of what once was.

Kevin Stiles, Grade 9
Clarkston Jr High School, MI

Why Cry?

It's useless
So suck it in
You need water
Water can't be wasted on Earth
So keep your precious water to yourself
The next time someone cries
It better be over something good
and NOT over the shoes that were sold out in your favorite store
Stop crying
It's useless
It's just a waste of time
Because through the end it will all be better
If anything you should enjoy your time on Earth and stop crying
Because you only live once

Kellie Lutz, Grade 8
Washington Middle School, WI

Gone for too Long

Gone one day,
Feels like a year.
Gone two weeks,
Feels like a century.
Think you're going to be back soon,
Find out you're going to be gone another two weeks.
Another long century gone by.
You miss the warm air in your face,
The beautiful flowers at the parks,
The scent of grass on your lawn,
But most of all you miss your friends.
The wanting to experience it once again,
Is agony to you.
Later, when you experience it all again,
You feel like you have won the world,
Like you've never felt that way before in your entire life.
People say that you've been gone,
For much too long

Isis Bucio, Grade 7
St Roman School, WI

Lily

It all happened in fifth grade
I entered a contest that led me to her
She was a beautiful husky hiding behind bars
Her name was Lily

My writing of words about helping animals
Rewarded me $75 to help the Humane Society
I made blankets, bought food, toys and leashes
I had no idea that she would be there in a cage

When I saw Lily's face, I wanted to take her home
But my life already consisted of two other dogs
My happiness came when I walked out the door
I met Lily's adoptive owner coming for her

Alyssa Urso, Grade 8
Core Knowledge Charter School, WI

Camping
We'll be going to the Big M
Camping in a tent
It'll be as cold as sleeping on ice cubes
Hope it don't snow

Camping in a tent
Throughout the dark night
Hope it don't snow
Because the woods will come to life

Throughout the dark night
It'll be dark for eternity
Because the woods will come to life
Until the morning sun comes to light
Seth McLaughlin, Grade 7
Manistee Middle School, MI

Summer
In summer when the sun shines bright
The world is an amazing sight

It is nice at night
It makes me want to yell with delight

The dew glistens in the sun
WOW! Summer is so much fun

In summer I like to swim and play
In the sun's basking rays

Oh, how summer is the very best
It is way better than all the rest
Braxton Phillips, Grade 8
Northwood School, WI

New Beginnings
Racing down,
like teardrops from my face.
I intently watch it fall from the sky.
Many flakes falling and
falling
like a never ending storm of rain
but this time prettier.

As it strikes the ground and piles up,
I watch the sun beam bright
like a smile on my face
the snow slowly drifts away.

As the snow stops,
my past feelings stop,
and a new beginning starts
today.
Brienne Peers, Grade 9
Clarkston Jr High School, MI

Manchester United
U-nit-ed they chant
Rooney scores a goal again
United prevails
Gabe Prieur, Grade 7
Centreville Jr High School, MI

The Neighborhood
I am going out to walk the
neighborhood
To breathe in the fresh morning air
And see what is new today
I shan't be gone long — you come too

I am going out to jog around
And let my mind soar
I'll see all that nature made
I shan't be gone long — you come too
Mitch Mox, Grade 7
Assumption BVM School, MI

The Sunset
I sit on the shore,
A quarter past dusk,
I see something radiant to me,
It's glory is bright,
The beams in my sight,
The orange and the pink,
In the height of the sky.
I watch the birds,
As they fly right by,
They look like they're glowing,
As they flutter past.
Through the orangish night sky,
Afar and vast.
The rays light the water,
All is aglow,
The beauty is amazing,
The Creator, my God, made it so.
KateLynn Gerry, Grade 8
Abundant Life Christian School, WI

Me
I'm the Eagle
Loyal and overlooks the land
You're like the pearl in an oyster
Mysterious and buried in the sand
I might give you a scare
But if you dare
You will be friends with me
And it will be in perfect harmony
Until that day
I will wait and pray
Hoping you come to stay.
Demetri Denny, Grade 8
Freedom Middle School, WI

Love
Love can be a dark night
When you're looking for a hand
It may be hard to find
But it's always sneaking around
Quiet as a mouse
You just have to look for it
Once you find the one
You were looking for
That's when love surrounds you
Like a warm blanket
But remember
Love is something you can't
Always hold on to
Melody Moua, Grade 7
Luxemburg-Casco Middle School, WI

Rainforest Music
I was walking through the forest
I hear the birds chirping in the air
The thunder cracks
It gives the birds a scare

I hear maracas getting shook
I listen to the piano go up and down
The thunder cracks again
The music stops and makes me frown

The birds chirp to one another
Then thunder cracks
It awakens all of the instruments
The sound never lacks

It keeps on going and going
The sun is going down now
The flute is dying out
The thunder ends with a pow
Andrew Particka, Grade 8
Sandusky Middle School, MI

Purple
Purple; shy and quiet,
Like a violet

Graceful and elegant,
As a ballerina

Royal and collected,
Like a queen

Cool and peaceful,
As a dove.

Purple, my favorite color.
Mackenzie Grieman, Grade 8
Grieman Home School, WI

Secrets

Whispers from one person to another
Turning heads make me wonder.
What is being said close by.
Seeing the secrets fly into the sky.

Is it about her, him, or me?
All these secrets keep me wondering.
Telling someone's secrets never lead to good things.
Bringing sorrow to someone's feelings

You always tell someone that you trust.
When they tell others it's so unjust.
But then there are people who don't tell a soul.
But then there are some who lose control.

The next day the whole school could know.
Everything I said would be exposed.
My darkest secrets would be disclosed.
My face I could never show.

If you tell their secrets
You will have a lot of regrets.
Because you never know what could happen
They might feel forsaken.

Prishtina Gjonaj, Grade 9
St Thomas More Academy, MI

Heaven

I wonder what Heaven will be like?
I suppose it is too magnificent for us to comprehend
No sorrow
No pain
There will always be happiness
Joyfulness
We will never hunger or thirst
That's what Heaven will be like
Friends and family surrounding us
Better than the annual family reunion
No fear of death or hurt
Just the relief that we will be there forever
No regrets
No doubt
Only our thankfulness of the choice to serve God
Surrounded by His glory
Praising the Lord every second of the day
It will be perfect
That's what Heaven will be like

Tory Hoffman, Grade 7
West Suburban Christian Academy, WI

Fiery Red

Her hair is red like it is on fire
and so beautiful as if God sent her to be admired,
and only her love can take me higher.

Patrick O'Leary, Grade 7
Marshall Middle School, MI

Christmas

All the children make their list,
And hope that Santa brings their wish.
Santa Claus is not so skinny,
But still somehow manages to fit down the chimney.

When the children wake up
They look on the plate and cup.
When it is empty and they see the gifts,
They know that Christmas is not a myth.

John Maxey, Grade 7
Our Lady Star of the Sea School, MI

Pain

Pain hurts like crazy
Not just physical or emotional,
but to be encompassed by both.
Some people cry, while others yell!
Some are heartbroken,
while others are broken completely.
We may be on our knees or up on our feet,
it won't change pain.

Najalie Stroud, Grade 7
Sister Academy/Harvest Prep School, MN

Dreams

As big as they seem, I have them.
My escape from reality
And my good night showcase.
My dreams are what make life worth living.
Each day I wake I have a new one in mind;
Inspiring me to take the next step.
I don't just dream when I'm sleeping
But also when I'm awake.
My dreams help me anticipate;
My dreams help me decide my goals;
My goals help me decide my dreams.
Dreams are what make me —
They take me to a new high.
I don't know about you, but you can't live without mine.

Tareya McCright, Grade 8
West Hills Middle School, MI

Memories

What do memories mean to me?
  Retaining the past
  Remembering at long last
  Not forgetting but keeping sacred of long ago
  Holding together happiness or sorrow
  Memories are very special to me
  Each time I think about them, I smile with glee
That is what memories mean to me!

Jordyn Dunlap, Grade 7
St John Lutheran School, MI

My Best Friend

My breath is held
My heart is pounding
And I'm terrified
Of the water that I'm surrounding
I take a deep breath
Almost as deep as the water
I turn around
And I saw her
With her arms out
And an evil look
I ran
And snatched the things she took
So much for forever
I guess that's the end
Forever from now
You will never be
My best friend

Payshence Kettlewell, Grade 7
South Park Middle School, WI

My Story

Your hands are like a furnace
That warms my body,
Your eyes are like a Pearl,
That I value,
Your face is like a Globe
That lets me see right though you,
Your house is like an animal
That I never want to leave,
But your Heart is like the world,
That I carry in my pocket.

Na'chelle Smith, Grade 8
Bloomingdale Middle School, MI

Lazy Me

I like to laze around all day,
Cuddling in my warm pjs,
Doing nothing is what I do best,
Taking it easy and getting lots of rest,
Lying on the couch I watch TV.
And think of nothing except for me,
It drives my mom a little crazy,
She says I am a tad bit lazy,
Maybe I will surprise her soon,
And get up early and clean my room.

Leah Stoner, Grade 9
Petoskey High School, MI

Rose

Rose
Red, eye-catching
Loving, growing, spreading
Charming at all times
Dazzling

Stephanie Topci, Grade 7
Edison Middle School, WI

The One

The one who is there the one who cares
The one who washed my back the one who has my back
The one who feeds me the one who has glee
The one who worries the one who hurries
The one who has many friends the one who never ends
The one who I can trust the one who I can talk to
The one who understands the issue the one who I look up to
The one who I know is always true
The one who teaches me the one who inspires me
The one who comforts the one who gives effort
The one who is never wrong the one who is very strong
The one who rarely gives up the one who always stands up
The one who protects me the one who I respect
The one who makes me healthy the one who wants to eat healthy
The one who gave me life the one who is a wife
The one who will always love me
The one who I will always love
Mom, you are the one and only one for me

Alex Menke, Grade 8
Sartell Middle School, MN

Beauty

What makes something beautiful?
Is it the appearance?
The way something appeals to one's eye?
Like a periwinkle flower in full bloom, bursting with color
Or the spectacular view out the back window of a cabin overlooking a clear lake.
Or is beauty in the sound of something?
A long and graceful note held by a flute, making music to all ears
The calm rushing sound of a stream rolling over tiny stones
Is beauty the touch or scent of something?
The fluffy hair of a pet dog
The sweet smell of spring's first rose.
Beauty is all around us, and it is what we love.
It's as simple as a baby's teddy bear and as intricate as a view of the Grand Canyon.
Beauty can be ignored when we rush through our lives
And don't stop to notice each unique little thing in our universe.
We realize beauty when we stop to ponder.
Smelling.
Seeing.
Tasting.
Hearing.
Feeling.

Frannie Schirber, Grade 8
Saint Thomas More Catholic School, MN

Fishing with Dad

When I am out fishing with dad on the lake,
I feel there are no worries in the world.
The lake is like glass and we are catching fish left and right.
Some of the fish are big and some are small.
Our fishing poles are getting worn out from all the fish we have been catching.
We go back to the cabin, roast s'mores, and tell fish stories.
Fishing with dad.

Clinton Gumieny, Grade 7
Elkhart Lake Elementary-Middle School, WI

An Injured Soul

The pain left behind
Never to be forgotten
The pain born of loathing and disgust
How am I to start again?

Sorrow of the mind
Moments of respite every now and then
Sorrow deterring love and trust
Waiting for the fog to lift; for the sky to brighten

Allison Barton, Grade 7
Core Knowledge Charter School, WI

Rounding Third

You hit far into the outfield
Hoping the runners in front of you don't yield
Your runners keep running
And you know you hit that ball right on the money
Your heart starts to beat
And you can feel the heat
The fielder throws
And the ball begins to flow
The catcher gets the ball
And you accidentally fall
He gets you out
And you begin to pout
Even though you won the game
You won't get the fame
And you wonder if only
A little farther

Jarid Reikowski, Grade 8
St Roman School, WI

Bunny!!

Since I wanted a pet bunny,
Together With my family,
Outside we went,
Up the steep hill,
Away From the skunk family.
Considering the great danger of coming,
Upon a black and white striped creature.

Underneath a pile of brush,
Since a bunny family lived,
My brother scared them Out,
By shouting and pounding, roaring like a lion.
The wood cracked and
A cute black and white creature hopped Out and said hello,
Scaring the living daylights out of us Because Of,
It's incredible likeness to a baby skunk.
We took my bunny with us and placed her,
Inside Of our large home.

Megan Hovell, Grade 8
Seymour Middle School, WI

Freedom I Seek

Mother got sick and could not work anymore.
So the white man killed her as she fell to the floor.
To him she was a possession, something to be kept.
I bound out the door, I ran, I leapt.
Heart pumping franticly, lungs gasping for air.
My goal was to make it far away from there.
I leave behind the beating, the yelling, the pain.
My freedom I wish and plan to regain.
My mother spoke of a haven not too far from here,
Where colors could blend without an ounce of fear.
To this haven I will, I can, I must go.
For she would have wanted me to do so.
My feet are cut by the thorns across my path.
The wind chilling, showing me its worst wrath.
Moonlight guiding me, not looking back.
The "Master" one slave he is going to lack.
...one month later...
I reach the haven, given shelter and clothes,
Through the clouds my bravery will always show.
I made it to a place that I can be free,
But if only my mother could be here with me.

Emily Carter, Grade 8
Perry Middle School, MI

Trilogy
Jaycie

Strong but so broken
Too much hatred toward her life
Friends that care for her

Life

So unfair sometimes
There's bad and pure, what are you?
So many choices...

Love

It can be insane
It can break you or make you.
It has broken me...

Bree Litz, Grade 8
Wheatland Center Elementary School, WI

Bacon!

Bacon,
The aroma of hickory arouses my nose
The crackle, the sizzle excites my ears
The brown long strips of crunchy delight are a sight to see
The warm greasy strips feel rubbery and crunchy
The salty hickory flavor dances in my mouth
Mmm...how I love,
Bacon!

Jordan Loudermilk, Grade 7
Whitehall Jr High School, MI

His Love

Cloudy white eyes
Shaggy brown hair
Sweetest guy ever
And I know he cares

Won't let me go
Holds me tight
I won't even try
To put up a fight

Butterflies in my stomach
Goosebumps down my arms
I cannot control this feeling
For he leaves me no harm

Why does he love me so much
I can't seem to understand
Words can't even explain it
Forget it, I'll just take his hand

Sydney Ertman, Grade 7
Centreville Jr High School, MI

As the Summer Night Drifts On…

As the golden honey sun
embraced me
with one last radiant departure
In a blink of the naked eye
It vanished from the skies
Velvety blanket of warmth
All that was left was a sliver
of silky ribbon
dancing on the line of my
dreams and non-existing hope
The night air filled my lungs
with hot passion
the stars smiled down on me
introducing me to the perfect
summer night

Danielle McClenton, Grade 8
Achieve Language Academy, MN

changing

changing
a new one comes when one goes out
each different each the same
one is raging
one is timid
one is bashful
one is splendid
winter
spring
summer
fall
changing

Madeline Wilkinson, Grade 7
Chippewa Middle School, MI

Summer

I walk along the sidewalk barefooted
The warm pavement rough against my soles
All around children play together
Running and swinging, jumping and laughing

My eyes close and I raise my head up to the sun
Its gentle rays kissing my skin and hair
I see the sun's orange glow under my eyelids
It's warmth caressing my cheeks

A pool comes into the view and I sigh
Oh! How I ache to lie on the surface of the cool fresh water!
How I yearn to have the glass waves break against my skin
To feel the cool water flow through my hair, making it long and straight

I glance around and without hesitation dive into the pool
Finally I come up to the surface of the water, completely content
I flip my hair back, now heavy with water
Laughing as cool droplets splatter all over

I can hear the birds chirping
Singing their little song of happiness
I smile to myself as the notes ring into the moist air
What a perfect summer day it is!

Pooja Singhi, Grade 7
Detroit Country Day Middle School, MI

Untitled

Sitting inside on a sunny day, saddened and burdened by doubt,
Was a girl about to pull the trigger, but then she heard a shout.

She was next to a window, and it offered a glimpse
Of happy, laughing children and of the life she'd miss.

And then she looked outside again, she caught a fleeting glance
Of what her life could really be if she gave it a chance.

A chance to be unselfish, a chance to make a friend.
A chance to live a life once lost, and for it not to end.

Out of that chance came a spark, a spark of hope and a will.
A will to live, a will not to die, to live a life fulfilled.

Out of that spark came a flame, that knocked that gun to the side.
A flame that decided to live, to live her life with pride.

And out of that flame came a fire. A fiery passion to live.
To live a life not taken, but to life a life that gives.

She finally realized with tears in her eyes, that this life won't be taken away
That this girl could be happy, and live another day.

Emily Harman, Grade 7
Field Community School, MN

Hockey

Shall I compare thee to a hockey game?
It is a very beautiful, magical game.
You don't want to get cocky.
Toward the goal he came.
One team wears purple.
There are a lot of pads.
The puck is a circle.
The coaches are sometimes dads.
A wrist shot, a snap shot and a slap shot.
You must learn many things.
There are 5 different dots.
My favorite team is the Detroit Red Wings.
Fights break out a lot.
The goalie takes a lot of shots.

Nick Ormsby, Grade 8
Pilgrim Park Middle School, WI

Mommy

I treasure each memory we have
When we make each other sad
When we make each other laugh
Yes, we do sometimes make each other mad
But at the end of the day you're
Still the best mom I could ever have
You know that I love you
So I'm never letting you lose
You have the sweetest voice
The softest touch too
No one lives forever
So, I'm holding on tight
I pray that you will always be here
Through the day and through the night
I feel that you hold our family together
Without you we wouldn't even last through
The toughest of weather
This bond is true
The strongest it could be
So never let go
And it's always going to be mommy and me

Amber Peoples, Grade 8
Hally Magnet Middle School, MI

Life

Our life is like an unending story,
Chapters unfold, then come to a close.
But every time a chapter ends
A new one begins.

As we grow older,
Our story grows larger,
And even when we leave this world,
Our story continues to expand.
As we begin our new life in heaven,
We can now look back on the precious chapters of our life.

Ashley Rahi, Grade 8
Our Lady Star of the Sea School, MI

Old Leather Shoes

My oh my
These shoes are old.
When you wear them
Your feet get cold.

They leak.
They squeak when you run.
These shoes are so brittle,
They're not fun.

Most people used to say
Those shoes are famous in the day.
They are ripped and shattered.
They used to be worn by the baseball batter.

David Harenda, Grade 8
Washington School, WI

The Midnight Rose

Upon the horizon, the sun is descending
The heavens are dark
It is desolate
As if in a mirage, an image of beauty appears
A simple rose of midnight
Encompassed by a field of crimson petals
That seemed to deject it
But only the midnight rose summons me
It is flawless
More beautiful and luminous than any star
A symbol of elegance, yet simplicity
As I leave the garden, there is something I take with me
It is knowledge
It is appreciation
Appreciation of differences as well as similarities
An understanding of…
Being myself

Quilon Patterson, Grade 8
Langston Hughes Academy, MI

I Like…

I love poetry,
The warm sunshine June brings
I like the way a bubble bath feels
Or the sound a bird makes when it sings.
I like chocolate and smoothies —
The fragrant fruit
The salty spritz the ocean makes
Dolphins splashing in the distance.
I like the mall, loud and busy
The sight of the green stuff makes me jump.
I like to chew gum, the burst of flavor
When you pop it in your mouth.

Amanda Chappie, Grade 8
Fairview Charter School, WI

Ashes

Within this pulsating heart there is only desire hate and unforgiving rage. But it too is unforgiven for what it is. Where it lives, flaming snowflakes are always falling to the ground. All the butterflies are black and lifeless. The phoenix's flame has been put out forever. Never to be born again because for him there are no ashes. But we all still fall down. This is a land where no man can live, but yet we all still live in ashes.

Suzannah Weiss, Grade 7
Saint Thomas More Catholic School, MN

Beneath the Surface

Can you see it? I'm in a total pit. Help me out, or I'll always pout.
I see glowing friends, the pain suspends. Fake smiles for them, or else it's all mayhem. Friends are wondering, is she just acting?
Happiness seems so natural, mine is missing its angel. All my friends are worried, my life's not hurried.
Books are another reality, 'cause they have no boundary. Friends are all around, so I never hit the ground.
They're one of those things that keep me going. They make sure my life is never boring.
My sorrow is sometimes, inescapable rhymes. They're so strong, how can they belong?
They come unexpected, never are they splendid. Reasons behind them, are hidden behind the poem.
I take time to myself, by the beautiful bookshelf. The stories are all different. Without any judgment.
Always in the end, they never offend. The books stay true, and they never rue.
The endings in one book never get changed, they have too much power to be rearranged.
They don't have changing personalities. They each have their own beauties.
My train of thought is distracted, it's about to be bounded. There's so much expected, not everything is connected.
I'm hoping for an answer, music is forever changing. I love the originals, even with the same label.
They can fit any mood, not only ones that are rude. Books are written, songs to be sudden, BING! BAM! BANG! No time to hang.
Back to the surface, wish it was cloudless. With clear directions, to go with my actions.
It's all a complicated mess, that I can never completely access. Hope to never have a need for it. Time for a new series.
New beginning every time, those don't cost a dime. Just don't try to rhyme, might as well become a mime.
The sorrow takes over, with a lot of power. It overwhelms all things, this really stings. The reasons rush up next, it's now in text.
The tears start to fall, who am I to call? The walls are pushing down on me, into a deep valley.
I let go into this emotion, all without any caution. What's left to fight for? The feeling is deep to the core.
I'll never submit to the deep, empty, darkness. All that I've done has never been aimless. Sorrow is a rife, in my awful, awful life.

Rhema Dapaah, Grade 8
Roseville Area Middle School, MN

Same Old Love Story

The first time I laid my eyes on you
I thought I'd discovered true love
In my eyes, you were perfect;
Your flaws only made you more real.
Every time you spoke to me, your words would form a poem
Every time our eyes met, I felt like I was star gazing
In my eyes, you were perfect in every way;
So much that it blinded me to the darkness in your heart.
So hear me out when I say that what we had was the opposite of love;
You were the big, hairy spider and I was the helpless little bug caught in your web of lies.
So hear me out when I say that your poetry was nothing but cheap pick-up lines from HOTTIES-R-US.COM;
You were the eerie, tempting gates and I was the innocent little girl lured into your haunted house of debauchery
So hear me out when I say that your eyes were flat and empty, like champagne without the bubbles;
You were the masked stranger behind every corner and I was your willing victim,
stolen away like the moon passing behind a cloud
So lie to me once again — give me a little more salt for my self-inflicted wounds;
After all, that's all you're really good for, right?
The first time I laid my eyes on you
I *thought* I'd found "*true love*"
In my eyes, you were perfect in every way;
It's just the same old love story.

Courtney Farrier, Grade 8
New Richmond Middle School, WI

Reasons to Love

It's never enough
Just to say
"I love you."

You have to tell them why.
Is it their eyes as round as moons?
Hair as hot as the sun?
Smile?

Are they smart?
Funny enough to make milk come out your nose at lunch?
Sweet like candy?

Or is it their clothes?
Friends?
The money they spend left and right?

That's not love.
That's power.

Take your time
Walk up to them
And say "I love you."

Claire Weyrauch, Grade 7
Jackson Middle School, MN

Shattered

Thump, thump-thump, thump, goes my heart
faster and faster as he squeaks out the words.
I glance down and see tears
as they start to drip from my face.
Heaves and grumbles escape from my throat
when I try to steady my breath.

The world beneath my feet shudders,
it crumbles as if an earthquake is beginning to form
but, when I look again the world is still.
And then I fall,

the universe whooshes past me
and I land in a groaning sea of black.
I float there, aloof of anything but the waves
crashing around me.

Suddenly a crunch escapes my chest,
the pieces of my shattered heart plop into the sea.

Along with the memories that me and him once shared,
a part of me fades away,
as the pieces plop, one by one
never to be seen again.

Hannah Timm, Grade 7
Roosevelt Middle School, MN

George Washington

He was our first president
He helped us get a government away from England
Some people told him he would be king
He said no
He would be a president
He is as old as dirt
Washington lived an exciting life
In exciting times
Washington went to school
When he was only
14 to 15-years-old
Washington helped shape the beginning of U.S.
He was a general of great skill

Hamdi Mohamed, Grade 7
Cedar Riverside Community School, MN

I Give Thanks

I am thankful for the things I eat,
For they are nice and sweet.
I'm thankful my family,
For they are caring and neat.
I am thankful for all the love I have
And all the love I give
I am thankful for my dog,
For he keeps me company.
I cannot forget my awesome friends,
Cause they care for me for who I am.
I'm also thankful for the holidays,
Cause I can reunite with my family.
I am thankful for our family business,
For it teaches me responsibility.
Most of all,
I am thankful for God,
For He opens His heart to anybody and everybody!

Nicole Bablitch, Grade 7
Pulaski Community Middle School, WI

Ode to Sunday

Sunday, Sunday, Sunday…
The lazy afternoons,
The times together in Mass,
The times alone on the couch.

The smell of bread baking,
The sun so bright, the grass so green,
The rays of God warming us,
The cares of the world gone for one last day.

The day is over, gone and through.
As I wander up to bed,
My mind starts to think,
Of the dread that will await me tomorrow.

Monday.

Luca Grieman, Grade 8
Grieman Home School, WI

Puppies

Puppies
Nice, friendly
Playing, barking, running
They make me feel fantastic
Rusty

Armond McMurtry, Grade 7
Langston Hughes Academy, MI

Something Went Awry

Something went awry
in the plans that God had made.
That is why we die,
and that is why He bade
adieu to me and you.
Something went awry
in the plans that God had made.
He messed up
in the line of evolution,
because we rose up
out of the darkness and confusion.
Something went awry
in the plans that God had made.
That is why we die,
and thus is why He bade adieu.
To me. To you.

Anna Lunak, Grade 8
Shakopee Jr High School, MN

Yellow

Yellow like a buzzing bee,
In the heavy summer air.
Yellow like a relaxing summer beach,
Or a very ripe pear.

Yellow is a dry, dehydrated desert,
Sand, nothing more.
Yellow like a rain coat,
Hanging by the door.

This color may be a dandelion,
Which are the sparks of a dull field.
Or the color of wheat,
With a bountiful yield.

Yellow is the sign,
Of a bright new day.
Even a small, hyper chickadee
Finding a song, for us, to play.

A light, relaxed mood
Reminds me of yellow.
A happy, friendly smile
On a carefree fellow.

Nicole Stock, Grade 7
Luxemburg-Casco Middle School, WI

The Wild Child

I am the strong,
the spirited and the powerful,
I abide in the wilderness,
alone, and untouched.

I fear no one person,
nor animal, nor creature,
they flee from my presence,
for I am their conqueror.

I climb all the mountains,
I sleep in their caves,
I wander about,
seeking,
but not finding.

I sleep with the wolf,
I eat with the lion,
for I am their master,
I am the Wild Child.

Rachel Lee, Grade 8
Derby Middle School, MI

One Hot Day

The ocean's cool breeze
The sand in between my toes
Oh no, I'm sun burnt

Megumi Bower, Grade 7
Centreville Jr High School, MI

Time

Time goes on
never speeds up
never slows down
never stops

But my time
feels like it's
going at an unusually
slow pace

Since that day
that changed
my very existence

That day that
started as any other
day and ended badly

But time goes on
never speeds up
never slows down
never stops

Anna Hughes, Grade 7
Shakopee Area Catholic School, MN

War Call

Rhythm like a beating drum fills
The soul with colors like the rainbow

Excitement fills the still air like
When the first crack of thunder

Is heard in the still, dark night
As the brooms danced across the floor

Soon the loud applause could be heard
Finally the work was done

Taylor Bemis, Grade 8
Sandusky Middle School, MI

What Is a Friend?

What is a friend?
You might ask.
It's the person with you,
Through a difficult task.

What is a friend?
You might want to know.
It's the person by your side,
Whether rain or snow.

What is a friend?
Some can't tell.
It's the person by you,
Whether you're sick or well.

What is a friend?
Some can't see.
It can be the person,
Right next to you and me.

Emily Backes, Grade 7
Osakis High School, MN

Relaxed

Under the blazing sun,
Floating with the water.

Listening to the hum of dragonflies,
The croak of frogs,
And the coo of loons.

Being content with the person I am,
And the simplicity of life.

It is as if the worries of the world,
Have been erased allowing all to breathe.

Relaxed is freely swimming,
In a quiet lake.

Kealie Gransee, Grade 8
J C McKenna Middle School, WI

Fear

Stop being scared. Fear is the city bus rolling by.
Fear is the darkness creeping up behind you.
Stop being scared. Fear is a bomb going off.
Fear is a roller coaster going up and down.
Fear is spiders waiting to attack.
Fear is heights high in the air.

Jalen Pompura, Grade 7
St Andrew's School, MI

Tennis Tournament

A twelve year old boy ready for the tennis tournament,
The training, hard work, and conditioning.
The ball flies as he hits it through,
Racing around the court,
Screeching at every step.
Long rallies a strong feeling in his swing,
Chasing the ball around the court like a lion chasing his dinner.

Quickly, racing to the net,
He volleys the ball back.
Waiting, ready to return the ball.
It bounces off his racket,
Out of reach for his frustrated opponent
His opponent without any hope.

The net is lowest in the middle
The court is longest corner to corner
A crosscourt stroke is safe,
And that is his plan for winning.
He takes his time to serve,
When his turn comes.
Throughout the match, he plays competitively
And ends with victory.

Rishi Patel, Grade 7
Detroit Country Day Middle School, MI

His Presence

The night wind blows my hair,
The back of my neck stands up to its very end.
No one is with me but I can feel him next to me,
I turn around but no one is physically there.

I call out his name and the wind blows against me again,
I can feel his presence in the air.
How I wish we could talk,
How I wish I could tell him of the past two years.

But I know I cannot,
For I cannot even see him.
I call his name once more,
To tell him I must be going.

He wails against my neck once more,
And I know that the presence of my grandfather is gone.

Madeline Brey, Grade 7
Jackson Middle School, MN

Free Time

Getting home from school today
Is like being freed from jail.
You don't have to do homework and projects.
All you do is nothing.
You get to spend time with your family,
Your body smiles with satisfaction,
You stay up late with no intimidation,
You sleep like a bear in the midst of hibernation.

As the sun peeks through the window
Birds chirping as your peaceful alarm clock
You learn you overslept school's second session.
But you discover it's Saturday!

Doing whatever you want.
Playing outside in the fresh fresh air.
Time flies like a New York minute.
Time flies like a New York minute.

Go to bed Sunday night.
Wake up next morning
To an early beginning
Ah man, it's miserable Monday!

Ben Slattery, Grade 7
Ramsey Jr High School, MN

Martin Luther King Jr.

"I had a dream" that is what he said
Before he died and went to bed
He is as important as Charles Darwin
At least he didn't marry his own cousin
Martin Luther King was our greatest civil rights leader
He had a speech that will live on forever
Martin Luther broke the gate between blacks and white
He never gave up without a fight
"I had a dream" that is what he said
Before he died and went to bed

Sahaam Ali, Grade 8
Cedar Riverside Community School, MN

Fall

The leaves *crinkle* under my feet.
I watch as they leave their tree branch home
to fall onto the ground with a slight *rustle.*
My friend and I make a pile of *crackling,*
and *crunching* leaves.
As we jump into the pile
leaves *scream* under our weight
as they *crumble* into dust.
The sun is *sliding* down the darkening sky
as we ride our bikes home in the *crisp* evening air.

Nellie Buttweiler, Grade 7
Roosevelt Middle School, MN

Snow

Snow on the ground sticks
Footprints of many sizes
Of wild animals.

Maurice Matthews-Peace, Grade 8
Langston Hughes Academy, MI

Gone Away

As I lay in my bed
Thinking my thought
I think to myself
I should probably not
I know I should sleep
As I was told to before
I wish I could sleep
It would help me so much more
As I close my eyes
I am certain to see
Myself sitting there
staring at me
I say my prayers
I wish I would go
To a wonderful world
Which no one knows
As I drift off to sleep
I'm sure you can see
God looking here
Watching over me

Sadie Rinehard, Grade 7
Pilgrim Lutheran School, WI

Sherra

My big sister, Sherra,
is a super nice gal,
fun to be with,
and quite a pal.

She's pretty and witty,
and funny as well,
that sweet sis of mine
is really swell.

She's always been there,
through good times and bad;
Reader be warned though,
DON'T MAKE HER MAD!!!

With a heart of compassion,
overflowing with love,
Sherra will surely be
blessed from above.

I, for one, love her so much…
can't wait to see her
and get back in touch!!!

Merra Milender, Grade 7
Abundant Life Christian School, WI

The Cry of the Poor

I am the weak and the hungry
I wonder what new challenge I will have to face each day
I hear the cry of my starving village
I see the hurting deep down inside
I want to feel a sensation of peace
I am the weak and the hungry

I pretend to live my life like there is no tomorrow
I feel my stomach turn and ache as I haven't eaten for days
I touch the bleeding wounds of my dying family
I worry about where I will have to travel for survival
I cry for food as an only desire
I am the weak and the hungry

I understand that life isn't fair but has reasons for everything
I comfort my siblings and assure them that everything will turn out
I dream of having a life with no stress or worries
I try to hold back the tears bursting within my soul
I hope to persevere through this hardship of poverty
I am the weak and the hungry

Alyse K. Nierzwicki, Grade 8
West Suburban Christian Academy, WI

My Love

School, school, how cruel,
Every day I have to put up with another incompetent fool.
The endless hallways, the excruciating classes, the abysmal number of books,
Each day my treacherous teachers give me dreadful looks.
However, one day, my world was uprooted upside down,
When this beautiful girl with endless love for me came from out of town.
She entered my useless school, which was so dreadful to me,
And she herself filled my school days with complete glee.
She is magnificent, and to this no one could disagree,
I just knew God had answered my prolonged plea.
She is gorgeous beyond measure, she is kind, and she is always on my mind,
She is a girl that is one of a kind.
She is compassionate, she is intelligent, no other girl would I prefer,
She knows just how to get me to love her.
Often I spend nights laying in bed thinking about my love,
I can just tell she has been sent from above.
I have fallen head over heels for this chick,
But every time I look at her I have to kick myself until I become sick.
For I know I cannot have her, for she is my very own flesh and kin,
My dear cousin always stares at me with a "you're a creeper" grin!

Macauley Rybar, Grade 9
Powers Catholic High School, MI

War

The color of war is the camo like the jungles of Vietnam.
It looks like an amputated arm of a POW [prisoner of war] of the Korean war 1959.
It smells like Iraq's dusty dunes during desert storm 1991.
It sounds like zipping bullets and the screaming of D-Day 1942.
It tastes like moldy clam soup for the British naval men 1812.
It feels the hate we had felt toward the enemy's awful deeds toward humanity.

Trevor Waggoner, Grade 7
Northwood School, WI

Family

Family is wonderful,
Unless something goes wrong.
It may be a bumpy road,
But if you have a Mom and a Dad,
To say it will be ok,
Then you know that is family,
Family is what you need when something goes wrong,
If your family sticks together,
All you can do is pray to God,
To make it all better.
In the end,
It will be all better,
Because the family sticks together!

Mallory Kleczka, Grade 7
St Roman School, WI

The Broken Promise

What happened to you and I?
Our friendship has died.
Conversations turn awkward with your halfhearted replies,
and each hour we grow further apart.

You said you'd be here in a hurry,
if I was ever to worry.
Those days are so far away that the memory is blurry,
and each hour, still, we grow further apart.

So we leave our past tattered and torn,
no chance of being sewn.
Into what once was so well known,
because far apart we have grown,
and to where we started we can never return.

Thea Jorgensen, Grade 8
Iowa-Grant Elementary-Middle School, WI

Strong

A bird sings, a child laughs.
Her quiet sobs, his whispered secrets.
Why did he do this?
She never did anything to deserve it.
This is unfair and not right.
Her tears won't stop running down her cheeks.
All of this was part of her fears.
So now he's gone, and she's broken in two.
She thought this was the end of her.
Then she stopped and noticed something.
She noticed that she could do better.
She won't let this heart break hold her back from life.
Now she's going to show him who she really is.
That she is a girl who is stronger than she looks
That she is going to live through this.

Bethany Johnson, Grade 7
Pilgrim Lutheran School, WI

The Storm

The rain came down with a splash,
the wind howled in my ear.
The lightning tore through the sky with a bright flash.
I was suddenly filled with a horrible fear.
The twister spun, like a blender set on high.
It ripped right through my own house,
And took it UP into the sky.
I ran away. From the rain I was doused.
I had reached a large field, and fell to the ground.
My legs were numb; I had no feeling in my hands.
I felt lost, but not yet found,
I was stuck in a no-man's land,
But at that very moment I didn't care,
As long as my home was taken by Mother Nature,
It seemed pretty fair…

Natalie Aguzzi, Grade 7
Scranton Middle School, MI

My Face

I have my glasses on, there is a glare.
No one can see, where I stare.
I wear a face mask, showing no expression.
In this game, there is obsession.
No one can see, what I got.
So I can win, the same thing my friend bought.
Nothing can beat, my big mush.
Because I have, a royal flush.
Click, clank, I am thinking.
While the clock on the wall, keeps tinking.
All in. For the win
This is my poker face

Jen Keohen, Grade 7
Shakopee Area Catholic School, MN

I Am

I am a farmer
I wonder what it would be like to be a millionaire
I hear birds chirp
I see that the sky is so beautiful
I am a farmer

I pretend to cook
I feel scared
I touch weird things like a shark
I worry when I am home alone
I cry when a cow steps on my foot
I am a farmer

I understand why people can't have certain pets
I say funny things
I dream about my future
I try not to get bad grades
I hope my family never splits apart
I am a farmer

Megdalena Walz, Grade 7
St Mary's School, WI

Nature

Ground thawing
Awakening like a newborn
A shooting rocket
As proud as a peacock showering colors
Blossoms reach and grasp
Bee buzzing, passing
A pollen magnet
Darting and dashing
Stuffed as a teddy bear
Content

Jessica Gauthier, Grade 8
Suring Elementary/Middle School, WI

Are You Ready?

The evil tornados are coming!
They are on the way.
Everyone get ready.
It will be a dreadful day.

You feel the wind stop.
It all becomes still.
The calm before the storm.
These winds intend to kill.

The sky surrenders to dark
Then fades to pale.
Overtaken by green.
While you are pelted by hail.

You witness its destruction,
As it rips through the town.
You try to bolt away but get hit,
As trees and dirt rain all around.

The tornado has passed.
The damage is done.
But you will be ready
For the next one.

Brandon Eason, Grade 8
Sandusky Middle School, MI

Fighting Soldiers

What do you do?
While you sit there…
Waiting.
What do you eat?
While standing on…
Guard.
What do you think?
While you are out there…
Fighting.
What do you wear?
While fighting and running in the…
Heat.

Harleigh Lewis, Grade 7
St Charles Catholic School, MI

My First Vacation

Getting up at four o'clock in the morning
Thinking of the plane I'll be in, that'll soon be soaring
Finally on the airplane looking down
With a smile on my face, not a frown

Patiently waiting to arrive at my destination
We're finally there, stepping out with no hesitation
Now on our way to the hotel called, Flamingo
Wondering where we will soon explore and go

We walked in the burning sun to the Hard Rock Café
We all got so hot and tired; we only made it half way
So we headed back to the hotel for a swim so nice
The water was so cold it was like ice

We also rode an elevator in the Stratosphere
Ding! The doors opened and I showed fear
I glanced down out of the slanted windows so high above the ground
There was a roller coaster on top and it even spun around

After five days of so much fun
I didn't want to go home and leave the hot sun
What fun-filled city is this?
The one and only, Las Vegas!

Mariah Metoxen, Grade 8
Seymour Middle School, WI

Time

Do you remember when you were younger and you couldn't wait to grow up?
All those nap times you hated?
The bed times drove you nuts.
You wanted to get out of school, you thought you were so cool.
You wanted to be just like the "big kids."

And then you became a teenager.
You couldn't wait to drive, or graduate school.
You talked back to your parents and broke the rules.
You went to parties and past your curfew.
You wanted to live on your own.

And then you became an adult.
Then you got kicked out of your house to "live on your own" and had to get a job.
You had to work over time to pay back loans.
You have to watch what you spend the money is tight.
You have a job but it's not very good and you want to go back to school.
But, that's too bad because you can't afford school.
Now all you want is to be young again.
To go to school, to live with your parents.
And to be taken care of by mom and dad.
Now your parents are old and sick and can't take you in.
You want to be young again but you can't go back time. And you can't gain years.

Stephanie Stevens, Grade 8
Washington Middle School, WI

Winter

Sparkling crystals drift down from above,
Twirling and swirling, landing on my glove.

Up high on the roof icicles begin to form,
People huddle together and try to stay warm.

Children bundled up in layers of clothes,
Make snowmen with coal eyes and a carrot nose.

Ice skating, sledding, and snowball fights,
Decorating the yard with bright shining lights.

The rich smell of hot chocolate fills the air,
Icy cold weather perfect for a polar bear.

Winter is one of the most magical seasons,
It's my favorite time of year for many reasons.

Laura Robertson, Grade 9
Troy High School, MI

Prison

Crash! Boom! Bang!
The sound of broken souls, spirits, and lives

The sound of desolate people in desolate places
Lives shattered never to put the pieces back together

Sentenced to life or death
It doesn't matter your life is dead

That is prison

Kyle Paulson, Grade 8
Adams Friendship Middle School, WI

Seasons

A delicate, lace of snowflakes swirl from the heavens
Cascading down and forming a blanket of glitter
Elegant icicles twinkle in the light
In the hollow emptiness, not a single soul stirs.

Droplets of rain quench moisten leaves
A glorious rainbow paints a mural in the sky
Adolescent bulbs bloom into luscious petals
And majestic trees bear juicy, tender fruit.

A blazing wave of heat hovers the air
It caresses my skin and kisses my cheeks
Sidewalks sizzle and scorch beneath bare feet
Nearby, I inhale traces of a salty, ocean mist.

Leaves twitter and twirl with the breeze
Like ballerinas, full of grace and magical beauty
A kaleidoscope of colors gently embraces the Earth
As they fall in place and form a snug patchwork quilt.

Alice Shang, Grade 9
Troy High School, MI

My Favorite Flowers

My favorite flowers are tulips and morning glories.
The tulip is as pretty as a star.
The morning glories are as pretty as a pink laced dress.

My least favorite flower is the dandelion.
It is very rough and it is a weed.
It makes the ground look like a landfill.

Morning glories come up all year round.
The tulip stays up for a few weeks.
The dandelion makes me sick.

Courtney Berns, Grade 7
Our Lady Star of the Sea School, MI

Darling Child

My dear darling child, it's time for bed.
Come and rest your weary head.
Have dreams that are meek and mild.
No they are real my silly child
You shouldn't have a fear, I'm right here.
Get wrapped up tight in your quilt.
And get in the bed your dad built.
It's late, time for bed Kate.

Wake up sleep head,
Get out of bed.
It's not too early,
Go and brush your teeth so they are pearly.
Morning isn't bad.
There's no reason to be sad.
It's sweet and sunny today.
Why don't you go out and play.
Come on Kate it will be great.

Abbey Chappell, Grade 7
Bristol Elementary School, WI

World War II

WWII is my favorite subject
It all started in 1939
And for the destruction, all would object
The Germans tried to enslave all mankind
America was attacked by Japan
There was no mistake to enter the war
Support came from each kid, woman, and man
Every family's lifestyle was torn
From the dry deserts of North Africa
To the battlefields of Central Europe
They were Britain, France, and America
Allies fighting for truth, justice, and hope
After the scare of the atomic bombs
Our troops finally came home to their moms

Dominic Egizi, Grade 8
Core Knowledge Charter School, WI

I Am Happy

I am happy for Henry hen,
Henry's happy for his yen.
I am happy for my father,
but he tells me not to bother.
I am happy to draw dresses,
Darcy's happy to wear dresses.
I am happy for the world,
even though it makes me hurl.
I am happy when I'm with you,
or better yet when you have the flu!
I am happy to be happy few.

Amanda Salawater, Grade 8
Jerstad Agerholm Middle School, WI

Orange

Orange is bright.
It looks like the rising sun.
It represents medium sauce.

Orange is loud.
It screams "Caution!" at you.
It sounds like a caged tiger.

Orange is friendly.
It smells like brand new crayons.
It tickles your nose like tiger lilies.

Orange is bumpy.
It feels like squishy Mac 'n' cheese.
It's rough as a basketball.

Orange is tangy.
It tastes like fresh orange peppers.
It's yummy as baked sweet-potatoes.

Orange is orange!!

Becca Hughes, Grade 8
Washtenaw Christian Academy, MI

I Don't Understand…

I don't understand
Why people make fun of others
Why there are fights
Why we only see the bad in things
But most of all
Why people leave
Why people stop loving
Why there is death
What I do understand is
Why there is nature
Why we need love
Why we have friends
Why we need help

Madeline Klomp, Grade 8
St John Lutheran School, MI

Time Goes On

Times comes time goes
Pain leaves so slow
It hurts it leaves
It leaves you with grief
So bitter not sweet
Don't let it stay
Because when the time comes
It will tear you away
I once let it do that to me
I cried I grieved
Once I was free
I felt so relieved
The pain was gone finally
So take this advice
And you will let the pain go
Go go go go
And tell someone
About how you feel
And the pain will go
As time goes on

Zhané Hall, Grade 8
Hally Magnet Middle School, MI

Summer

I take a dip in my pool.
The water is very cool.
The day is almost done.
But it was very fun.
I really don't want to go away.
I want to stay and play.
It is very bright with the sun.
I never want this day to be done.
I get out and sit on my chair.
As people walk by I sit and stare.
It's the end of summer.
I think to myself what a BUMMER.

Reba VanBeek, Grade 8
Adams Friendship Middle School, WI

Choose

Every night I seem to be somewhere
I'm not always home
Though I should be
Because I'm getting behind
In chores and schoolwork
It's getting harder and harder
To try and catch up
Because I fall farther behind every night
That I see my friends
So I may have to choose
Between friends or school
And no matter what I choose
I'm going to fail one way or another

Adam Walczak, Grade 8
Bloomingdale Middle School, MI

New York City Night

New York City Night.
Moonlight shining on the wet sidewalk.
Steam rising from the ground.
Fog slowly settling.
Couples walking the streets.
Broadway shows just letting out.
Quiet alleys with old parked cars.
Bright high-rises coming to life.
Neon lights lighting up.
Restaurants filling up.
New York City Night.

Anna McCambridge, Grade 7
Assumption BVM School, MI

Ode to Duct Tape

O, duct tape
Your plastic skin
Is indestructible
You stick like screws
To whatever I stick you to
O, duct tape
You are the easiest seal
You don't let air
In, or out
O, duct tape
There are so many uses for you
Like fixing a car
In a pit stop
At the racing track
Or even pulling a
Truck out of a ditch
O, duct tape you
Overpower any
Adhesive

Joey White, Grade 7
Japhet School, MI

Bird Nest

Birds flutter around the yard
Protective
And move further away
Nervously flying
Bearing twigs, branches, leaves,
And more.
They strive to build the best nest possible
For it is their duty
The life of the baby depends on
The structure of the nest
They sing while working
As they scramble in and out
Only birds understand
A hidden world
They spread their wings and take off.

Rachel Pytel, Grade 9
Clarkston Jr High School, MI

Green Skies — White Grass

The sky turns green and the grass turns white
I turn in and you turn right
The birds stop chirping, dogs whimper out of sight
My eyes are burning as I run away with fright.

Run after me and chase me down
Kiss my tears don't let me drown
Save me from you or save yourself
Help me over and hold me tight.

My heart beats cold, but my skin turns warm
I lose you in a bitter hold, we both fight the storm
Will you forget me? How could this end?
I want you to stay with me — with me until the end.

The sky turns green the grass turns white
Something's wrong...but you're out of sight
I cannot fix what we both repair
Save my heart, catch my fear.

Hannah Stoloff, Grade 8
James R Geisler Middle School, MI

Halloween

Halloween is coming near,
Tell me friends, can you hear?
Children racing through the street,
The pit-pat noise of running feet,
Kids dress up and join with friends,
Having fun that never ends,
Door to door they race with glee,
Hoping to get the "good" candy,
Scrambling to doors from the dark street,
When they get there, they yell, "Trick-or-Treat!"

Nicole Smith, Grade 8
Trinity Lutheran School, MI

Nuregami

It is a snake, slippery and smooth.
A butterfly, beautiful and free.
It is a torrent, reckless and strong.
Nuregami, God of Water, is the sea itself.
She is the rush, the quiet hum of the ocean.
She is the crash, the raging of the sea.
Nuregami is the water,
Beautiful, strong yet thoughtful.
Nuregami is the waterfall,
Reckless, unforgiving, but meaningful as well.
She is the life-giver,
And she is the life-taker.
Nuregami is the beautiful,
Reckless waters.

Erin Mazur, Grade 7
Roosevelt Middle School, MN

The Kingdom

It's a kingdom for the ice princess
The stronghold walls reach up
Towards the open air
They are dusted with ice crystals
And they glimmer in the sun's rays
As if each has been placed by hand
There is a tower with watchful guards
And a strong, mighty base
And each limb is yearning more and more
For the openness of the heavens
There is a dungeon
Big, white, and chilling enough
To enclose the wrongdoers within
There are vast fields for the children to play in
With plenty of white, fluffy toys
And an imagination
It's decorated with
Long crystals suspended from the walls
And blankets of white have been draped all around
And the only way to go to this magical place
Is through a child's eyes

Chelsea Chase, Grade 9
Clarkston Jr High School, MI

Flower Cart

She lies upon the flower cart
Careless about anything around her
As the city runs, still at fast pace
She smells the sweet fragrance of the bed beneath her

Careless about anything around her
Melody slipping from her lips fills her mother's heart
She smells the sweet fragrance of the bed beneath her
She takes a deep breath in letting time go by

Melody slipping from her lips fills her mother's heart
As the city runs still at fast pace
She takes a deep breath in letting time go by
She lies upon the flower cart

Cecelia Nemetz, Grade 7
West Suburban Christian Academy, WI

Freedom

Freedom.
Being free to be me.
Boundless.
No locks, no need of a key.
It started with putting slavery to rest.
Ignorance and violence, another reason to call us useless.
Martin Luther King Jr. led our people to a new generation.
One where not color, but character matters.
It's the choices we make,
The lifestyles we choose,
That determine the type of person we are to become.

Kianna Greene, Grade 8
Messmer Preparatory Catholic School, WI

Trapped

I am a reckless elephant stumping through the zoo
I am a slave trying to escape to freedom
I am a song waiting to be heard
I am a bird wondering what the sky is like
I am stuck in the rain on a sunny day
I am a deer running through the fields as a hunter chases
I am a bee going BUZZ, BUZZ, searching for pollen
I am like the Great Wall of China as a little girl watches the day go by
I am trapped in my teenage body as my mind follows a little girl with naps and Cheerios
I am TRAPPED

Mikayla Anderson, Grade 7
Jackson Middle School, MN

Admiration

Why I admire you, because you have quick legs like you are always four steps ahead of life!
That's why I admire you!

I admire you, because you talk like you have wisdom running through your blood!
That's why I admire you!

I admire you, because you walk proud like you have gold stones on your shoes.
Like our ancestors who were kings and queens before they were taken as slaves.
That's why I admire you!

So why do I admire all the Black women in my family?
Because they are wise, strong and persevere and are always four steps ahead in life.
That's why I admire you!

Safiyyah Washington, Grade 7
Sister Academy/Harvest Prep School, MN

Something New

The big door barricading me from you.
The damp air smelling of earth and barns as I think to myself this is the start of something new.
Running through the door that breaks.
Seeing your small poodle-eyed face.
Stumbling up to take in your surroundings.
As a shiver of cold air came through, you sat back down near the ground.
Sadly looking up at me as if you had something to say.
Though that doesn't surprise me for the brown poodle eyes seemed to be chanting "I'm homesick though I love you anyway."

Karri Perion, Grade 8
Centennial Middle School, MI

Blueberry Muffins

I remember the hot breakfast, and the blueberry muffins. The memories of Thanksgiving, and the good old stuffin'.
I remember the games that we would always play, the memories that were made on those beautiful days.
I remember the times of Hide the Key, the memories of the days that I wish I could once again see.
I remember the times of when we would think, of what kind of "Soda Pop" that we wanted to drink.
I remember the Freezies and the faces made, the memories that will never fade.
I remember the garden and what it held, the memories of getting stung which made us yell.
I remember the times of the old wooden swing, the memories of songs that we would always sing.
I remember the records of Peter Pan and Mickey Mouse, the memories that were shared within that house.
I remember the day when he was brought in, the memories that were not ones to win.
I remember that day, July 3rd to be exact, the memories of the days that I will never get back.
I remember the man, he was always happy and jolly. And I will never forget the memories that I shared with my Grandpa Wally.

Makenzie Walker, Grade 8
Washington Middle School, WI

Forever Love…

Three words are all I have to say
The only words I can think today
'Cause when I saw you standing there
All broken apart, and full of despair
These feelings were too much to sway,
And just let you get up and walk away
So I asked you, to be my own
And to this day our love has grown
From the time the sun rises, to the time it sets
In this past year I have no regrets.
With the world against us, and no one to lean
The pain we felt, our tears made a stream
But through all this, I won't dismay,
My love for you grows, each and every day
And though we've slowly, slipped apart
You will always be, my true sweetheart
My feelings for you will never change
Our lives have been forever stained
So like I said before, every day my love grows
Three words to say, "I love you"…Rose

William McMurray, Grade 9
Prairie Lakes School, MN

Love

Friends, family
Feeling, dreaming, holding
Butterflies, hearts, dark, evil
Yelling, fighting, hurting
Enemies, cold
Hate

Miranda Sippel, Grade 7
Elkhart Lake Elementary-Middle School, WI

If You Mark Mc Tardy Today…

If you mark me tardy today
It will go on my permanent record to stay
I will always be known as the boy who was late
But if you do, this will be my fate…
I will drop out of school at the age of fourteen
And take a job on the Burger King team
Lose that job for being late every day
Convince my parents to still give me pay
I will live in their cold and gloomy basement
Explaining every day why I can't pay the rent
I will never get married have kids or a house
I will scamper around just like a mouse
I will finally get kicked out and live on my own
The sky as my blanket, the ground as my home
I would die at the age of twenty-eight
Sad and alone and full of hate
No one would be there for me when I die
No one would even care to say "Goodbye"
And on my gravestone it would sadly say:
Here lies the ungrateful boy who was late

Kian Robinson, Grade 7
Core Knowledge Charter School, WI

The Moon

Staring at the moon,
a girl cries, wishing that she
could be there, but she knows
that it's impossible.
And it disappoints her, knowing that she'll
never get off of the Earth.
But still, she stares at the moon,
yearning for another world.
Now she's 23 and an astronaut,
and as she floats in a weightless world,
she still dreams of a new world,
one that no one has ever been to, and smiles.
All of those planets out there were calling out her name,
so she dreamed and there she was.

Destini Sneath, Grade 9
Hartland High School, MI

Easy Come and Easy Go

They always say easy come
And easy go
But you want to know what I think so
When you meet the one that you let in easy
Sometimes you feel a little better
Knowing they've got your back forever
But when it comes the day that they have to go
You think about what you said long ago
"Easy come and easy go"
When they go it's not really all that easy
And sometimes you will feel a bit queasy
Knowing that they have to go
They'll say "I will miss you now and forever!"
But remember
They got your back forever

Sarah Law, Grade 8
Saline Middle School, MI

An Eerie Night

The creepy music jumps into my ears,
I can hear the scurrying of feet,
As if a murder has occurred,
The black night, creaking boards, and the bare street

Alarming sights of people in eerie masks,
Like they were trying to scare the past,
Then the demonic music went calm,
As if the monster was drowned out by the cast

But, yet it was sad in a way
In the dark scene it was hard to be swell,
The thick dusty air becomes thicker,
Then it cleared away and all was well.

Lizzie Frisbey, Grade 8
Sandusky Middle School, MI

River

River is flowing
So gracefully passing by
Carefree and lazy

Keith Cline, Grade 7
Centreville Jr High School, MI

Chameleon

What if we were all chameleons?
Maybe then the color of our skin
wouldn't matter.

Maybe then we'd all be treated
like equals, and no wars and
genocides would occur no longer.

Maybe then no race would think
they're superior, and think of the
color of your skin, hair,
and eyes mattered.

Maybe then no religion would be
thought of a lower, and there'd
be not one person who would care.

Maybe then the world would be
a better place.

Rachel Bork, Grade 8
Spring Hill School, WI

Is It True?

You say you love me
Is it really true?
When we are together
You seem so blue

Your smile brightens my day
I just want you to say
I love you baby,
And just maybe…

But when you're with your friends
Everything ends
You don't even notice me
But you're all that I can see

Today you told me
How you truly feel
Friends is all you want to be
I knew this wasn't for real

You said you loved me
It wasn't really true
We're no longer together
So you don't seem so blue

Jenna Golliher, Grade 8
Seymour Middle School, WI

That Dog

When that dog runs, she is as beautiful as Lassie
Her fur goes flat against her body, like human hair when wet
When that dog runs across the field, she looks as graceful as a bird

When she chases another dog across that field, she seems to run as fast as a cheetah
When that dog stops running, she starts panting like a locomotive
When I whistle for that dog, she obediently comes, without hesitation
When I am sleeping, that dog is faithfully by my side

Katelyn Jakubowski, Grade 8
Washington Middle School, WI

Merry Way

Small elves in green gowns laid his red sack in his sleigh
And with a happy "Ho Ho" he was ready to start his day.
With a mumble of his low voice and a shudder of his sleigh,
The reindeer hoisted him into the sky and on his merry way.

The strong wind blew hard as they flew through the air,
Nearly snatching his hat swiftly off of his white hair.
He stopped at the first house, then a second and a third.
After leaving the gifts, he took off like a bird.

He would slide down ash blackened chimneys with the quickest of ease,
Then leave great gifts for kids to see under their beautiful green Christmas trees.
Up the chimney he would slide into his sleigh
And with another "Ho Ho" he again flew onto his very merry way.

Finally the last house, the last stop on his list,
He lays down the last gifts in the sack clenched tight in his fist.
With all the houses past, no more shining gifts to deliver
Santa heads back to the North Pole in the golden morning's first sliver.

Hugh Day-Williams, Grade 7
Detroit Country Day Middle School, MI

If You Haven't

If you haven't been to Ohio,
You don't know the hills,
You can't know the hills.

Like mountains that crowd in Montana,
Huge bluffs and cliffs all warm and steep.

If you haven't been to Ohio,
You don't know the hills.

If you haven't been to Ohio,
You don't the floods,
You can't know the floods.

Like oceans waves washing up shells and small stones,
Mud, dead fish left on the roads — Nothing to do except stay home.

If you haven't been to Ohio,
You don't know the floods.

Sammy Glaser, Grade 7
South Middle School, WI

Yum!

S o juicy
T ender on the inside, and crispy on the outside
E atable all the time
A lways a joy to have
K eep it coming

Preston Arndt, Grade 7
Abundant Life Christian School, WI

The Stormy Night

The magnifying sound of the thunder brings the forest alive,
The gray clouds up above as dark as the night,
The sound of the rain hitting the trees,
While the stormy night allows no light,

The animals calling out making strange noises,
The sound of the distant man talking,
You call back and there's nothing,
But the sound of the man walking,

You fall back hitting the hammock,
The rain speeding down with all its might,
You can feel the cold water trickling off your face,
The booming voice rumbles into the blurry night,

The thunder rumbles like a train on the train tracks,
The lightning brightens up the sky like a thousand lights,
The train stops to a screeching halt,
With nothing in sight but the sunlight.

Stacie Pupi, Grade 8
Sandusky Middle School, MI

Day of the Crying Sky

As the rain trickles down
Giving a bath to nature's frown
Clouds ruled the sky in the gloomy morning
This can make day boring

The thunder booms with a vengeance
Making even the bravest jump in a prance
The cracks sound like a battle
Thunder makes houses shake and rattle

Children are not fazed
No rain or thunder can ruin their craze
They play and roll in puddles
While others would rather cuddle

Relaxing on my porch
As the rain covers the ground like fire on a torch
While the rain flows
Out comes a beautiful rainbow

Chase Baysdell, Grade 8
Sandusky Middle School, MI

TV

It's a painting that never ceases to amaze
It emits a soft hiss, like a stream on a waterfall
Soft and subtle

Great artists fill the page with many shapes and colors
Almost everyone gazes upon it,
But nobody sees the whole picture

Some look for hours either laughing or crying
It is a painting that is always changing
Each brushstroke tells a new story.

Kevin Bowles, Grade 9
South View Middle School, MN

Family

Connected together but still separate parts,
Different people and different hearts.

A history shared, started with love,
Tied together with help from above.

Joy and laughter, and sadness and tears.
Understanding calming all fears.

Each piece important in making up a whole,
Wrapped together, sharing the same soul.

Unconditionally loving each different part,
With an accepting, hopeful, and strong family heart.

Anne Lesha, Grade 8
Our Lady Star of the Sea School, MI

Drowning

The water, trickling onto the grand football field,
Slivering over the green grass,
Drowning the Y in the center of the field,
Flooding, slowly, from yard line to yard line,
Circling the bottom of the shiny yellow goal post,
Running, dancing along in little streams and tributaries,
The water, so mighty and cool, flowing everywhere,
Conquering everything it touches.
Snickers escape the lips,
The flow of the water, trickling,
The wind, whipping on our faces,
The icy sting of the water as they devour our shoes,
The splash as the teens creep away, stepping over puddles,
The moon shining bright, illuminating the ebony sky,
The next morning, as the teens pass by,
They spot workers and coaches,
Staring horrified at the drowned field,
The water spilling into the parking lot,
The worried tones of the staff,
Flashbacks appear, of the adrenaline powered night,
Never forgotten, this hilarious sight.

Kelsey Schwarzkopf, Grade 8
Centennial Middle School, MI

Finders Keepers Losers Weepers

Finders keepers losers weepers
The worst line of them all
I found a dollar
Just sitting there
No one beside it
No one to claim it
Or claiming to dropping one
It was just sitting there
I picked it up
Looked around
No one
Slip!!
Right into my pocket
Then I did it
I used it
I bought chocolate milk

Trevor Veeser, Grade 7
Luxemburg-Casco Middle School, WI

Stormy Nights

Trees are quiet
So are we as
We sit here calmly in a tree,
All we hear are humming of bees.
Was that lightning?
The trees are swaying
Back and forth.
The sky clears up
But we lie here
With grins on our faces.

Grace Thelen, Grade 7
Luxemburg-Casco Middle School, WI

Light vs Dark

Light
Bright, comforting
Guiding, showing, revealing
Sun, lamp — night, moon
Hiding, concealing, protecting
Overwhelming, black
Night

Aidan White, Grade 8
Fairview Charter School, WI

Mountain Dew

Mountain dew, mountain dew
O how I love you —
you're a rainbow in a bottle
waiting for me to swallow.

You're cold and kept in plastic
and you taste so fantastic —
you help me flee and give me energy
which makes my mom very angry.

Trevor Fettig, Grade 9
Petoskey High School, MI

Unwanted

Unwanted by the trees, we tumble all around,
Dancing with the wind, as we fall to the ground
We land without a sound, but the wind causes a rustle,
We are thrown into the air, with a hustle and a bustle

We land on the ground again, waiting our immanent doom,
To be raked into a pile or swept up by a broom
We lie still on the ground, all in the yard through,
But with the sound of a crunch, we are stepped on by a shoe

Like a gentle feather, we can be soft or rough,
But we cannot hang onto the trees, proving that we are not so tough
We can be a brilliant brown, or a ruby red,
But the beauty is lost, knowing that we are dead

Thin as a sheet of paper, we can bend and tear,
So you can neglect us, but that wouldn't be fair
We are mini trees, that grow every year,
But we do not live long, we will die right here
We are people, that grow old each day,
Our lives will end sometime, in many different ways

Charles Jorstad, Grade 8
Chippewa Falls Middle School, WI

It's Never too Late

When the person you trust the most lets you down,
Don't give up.
When the world has seemed to close you out and not let you back in,
Don't give up.
If you lose someone you love and you miss them terribly,
Don't give up.
You always have another day and there's always tomorrow, so
Don't give up.

Haley Hansen, Grade 8
Wheatland Center Elementary School, WI

Live, Love, Laugh!

Today is beautiful; the sun shining bright,
I went to the park, oh what a sight!
The raspberries on the bushes are more luscious than ever,
This vista is quite a lovely place, captured in my mind forever.

The fountains nearby have a glistening flow,
I've watched the goldfish merrily glow.
Tomorrow is the future, but look no further;
Today is today so capture the memories and remember.

Life is short, so make it last;
Be prepared for the future, but reminisce the past.
Be happy and enjoy the life that's all around you,
Life is special so just relish the moments and let the good times ensue!

Samantha Huebler, Grade 7
Whitehall Jr High School, MI

Snow

A blanket of snow comes silent like a snake
About to strike
It falls gently onto the ground
Falling gracefully with no sound
It happens during winter
And it leaves the sun in return.

Alaijah Bashi, Grade 7
Richmond Middle School, MI

Just the Way I Am

I am glad I'm myself.
If I were not, everything would be different.
If I had one wish,
I would not know what to do with it.
I have all I would ever need.
If I wished for superpowers or money,
People would not see me the same.
If I could be superman then that would be great.
I could fly across the ocean blue,
I could lift buildings and bring world peace.
I could fly and shoot laser beams out of my eyes
That would be so fun and heroic.
I would be known worldwide.
I would be admired and respected.
But the one thing I wouldn't have,
Are my friends and family.
People would never see me the same.
I am already satisfied and thankful
For the things I already have.
And that is why I am glad I'm myself.

Steven Ebert, Grade 7
Abundant Life Christian School, WI

Lost Friends

Funny how friends say forever,
people never seem to stay together.

You told me not to worry, told me not to cry,
you said we were best friends, it was a lie.

I'm here still pretending not to care,
pretending I don't notice you're never there.

To have a bond like we did was amazing,
but you picked a boy over that, over me, just replacing.

You hurt me so bad you will never know,
and the pain I keep inside I will never show.

You'd probably see it if you just tried,
and know how many nights I have cried.

But don't worry I'll be fine,
I'm not the one who left all my friends behind.

Briana Metcalfe, Grade 8
Spring Hill School, WI

Desire

Desire is a purple fire
See the dancing flames
Smell the smoke
Hear the crackling wood
Feel the heat on your skin
Taste the melted chocolate on your tongue

Sarah Wallace, Grade 9
Hartland High School, MI

Sunrise

The brilliant sun peeks over the proud mountains
The light of a new day
It rises slowly and majestically
A new hope

Ascending higher in to the growing dawn
Lighting the path for all to see
From red to orange to a lavishing yellow
Coming with a new sense of purpose

Each day the sun rises
Promising a brighter future
Each evening the sun sets
On a job well done

Look at the little things in life
Happening so often you take them for granted
What if they were to suddenly stop?
What then?

Think of the little things in life
And live life to its fullest.

Savannah Herman, Grade 7
South Middle School, WI

Leaves

The bud on a tree
could drive a mother crazy.
Slowly transforming into a leaf.
With time you develop
while sitting on that branch.
Spreading out to capture all that sunlight.
As you grow the seasons pass,
and before you know it autumn hits you.
Your colors finally mature.
Then the days get shorter as the nights get longer.
Soon you know that it's time.
You slowly let go, so that it's not too fast.
Drifting down, until you hit the ground.
Leaving behind all the things you once knew so clearly.

Angela Niezgoda, Grade 9
Clarkston Jr High School, MI

Who I Am

I am happy and curious
Always waiting for things to happen
I am the universe
Mysterious and misunderstood
I am the swish of a hoop
Nice and successful
I am a lightning strike
Bright and fast
I am an Alaskan island
Cool and interesting
I am a fudgy
Annoying sometimes and a traveler
I am our area
Liked and quiet sometimes
I am excited
Wanting more of a challenge
And looking forward to things

Nicolas Dickinson, Grade 9
Northport Public School, MI

Winning Game

The game is on the line
I have the ball,

The score is 100 to 100
They have the ball.

I fouled the guy who has the ball
It's 1 and 1,

They missed the basket
I got the rebound.

I'm dribbling down the court
30 seconds left in the game

Timeout us
The play was really complicated,

So, I had the ball and I shot it
Swish, the game is over.

Jordan Vogel, Grade 7
Springfield School, MN

Life Is a School

Life is a school
You are the student
The world is your teacher
You are learning every day
Learning how to live
Your parents are the principals
And you are just the student
Learning.

Robert Hasenbank, Grade 7
Manistee Middle School, MI

Untitled

When you are lost
I know how to find you
When you are worried
I will give you light
To shine the way
And make you feel comforted
When you are alone
And want someone to listen
Reach out for me
I am always there
I am ready
To laugh and cry and sing
To dance and jump and smile
I will be your friend
Always your friend

Franclyn L. Emerson, Grade 8
Gesu Catholic School, MI

Soft Shell

This shell is as soft as a feather.
If you look at it from the side,
It's a cinnamon swirl.
The inside is a screw,
Twisting in a spiral.
The hole is a disfigurement of a shell.
It's almost the size of a small rock.
It's more circular than others.
The top is like a crown.

Brooke Amdahl, Grade 8
Chippewa Falls Middle School, WI

Summer in the Lands

As I clasp the railing,
And look out over the sandy hills,
The wind whispers to me,
And tells me of summer.
Of how the ever-present rain clouds,
Give life to the grass.
Of how the sun
Dries the ground,
And it waits for the rain.
And of how the wind itself,
Made the beautiful sight,
I look at now,
And call
The colorful hills
Of the Badlands.
And I wish one thing,
For this special place.
Take care,
For I will come again,
And listen to your story,
Of summer.

Yvonne Tessman, Grade 8
J C McKenna Middle School, WI

An Unexpected Explosion

The volcano was silent
A chimney
Smoking while the villagers slept
More smoke poured out
A science experiment
And unexpectedly exploded
The sky was black
Doom's day
Red hot lava poured out
Overflowing coffee
Toxic gas filled the air
Pool chemicals
Pompeii was death
A battlefield
Gone forever
Until now

Megan Kallestad, Grade 7
Roosevelt Middle School, MN

Fear

Fear
Is when you are
Scared
But being a coward
Means that
You don't think
You can do it
Or you're too lazy
To get up
And do it
Fear can be useful
To overcome it
Is to gain courage
Fear can be
Discouraging
Due to the lack of
Success

Taylor Tenor, Grade 7
Luxemburg-Casco Middle School, WI

Right Now

Right now I could use some fresh air
Right now I just need some peace
Right now I want to go somewhere
Right now I know no one cares
Right now I can barely stand
Right now I can barely talk
Right now I am ready to just go
Right now I can barely walk
Right now I know I have to stay strong
Right now I am going to pull through
Right now I am walking out this door
Right now my life starts new

Kevin Illes, Grade 8
Washington Middle School, WI

Sailing

Sailing is a sight to see.
The whooshing sound of water hitting the boat.
Hearing the birds chirp in the air.
Chirp, chirp, chirp.
Waving high to the workers on the freighters,
waving low to the speed boaters.
Traveling to East Tawas for an eight hour trip.
Sailing nonstop for three whole, cold, windy days
to Mackinac Island.
Dangling feet over the edge.
Sailing on a 30 degree angle and trying not to fall.
Finally getting back to the dock,
ready for delicious chocolate fudge.

John Wojewoda, Grade 8
St Stephen Elementary School, MI

Four Seasons

Winter is the coldest season of all,
It seems to never end,
Next comes spring, when the birds begin to happily call,
Gardeners head out to their gardens to tend,
Summer follows bringing its heat,
And people take flip-flops to put on their feet,
Last but not least, here comes fall,
Where leaves begin to drop and change color,
It's a season like no other,
These are the four seasons, each and every one,
In each, there is something to do that is fun,
So go out and experience the beauty,
Because nature has four seasons and only one is on duty!

Hannah Maurer, Grade 8
Adams Friendship Middle School, WI

Blind

You can't see the hurt,
The pain in her eyes
But you can judge her and make her cry.
Your cruel words make you feel good about yourself,
But they put a dent in her soul.

She respects you,
cherishes you
But you turn her down
She is too nice to say a thing,
But it breaks her heart to know how hated she is.

You are Blind,
You can't see her hurt and pain.
But when she is gone
You are to blame.

Margeaux Moore, Grade 8
Gesu Catholic School, MI

The Holocaust

The Holocaust was a time…
When many innocent men, women, and children died.
The Holocaust was a time…
When concentration camps were all over Europe.
The Holocaust was a time…
When people were forced out of their homes.
The Holocaust was a time…
When Adolf Hitler committed mass murder.
The Holocaust was a time…
When Jewish people were persecuted for being Jewish.
The Holocaust was a time…
When death and terror ran through Europe, Asia, and Africa.
The Holocaust is a time…
That should never happen again.

Alex Nogalski, Grade 7
St Roman School, WI

Boarding

Snowboarding
Feeling the snow fly under my board.
The air in your face as you ride down.
Intensity and motion beyond description.
Going flying through the air like a bird.
A place where I feel true joy and no worries.
The place where I don't worry about teachers,
Or school,
Or parents yelling.
Snowboarding

Bryce Barrone, Grade 7
Luxemburg-Casco Middle School, WI

A Yellow Summer

Yellow is the sun, shining in the sky
Yellow is the bumble bee, buzzing quickly by
Yellow is a smiley face balloon at the fair
Yellow is the color of the tint in my hair

Yellow is the flowers, blooming bright and pretty
Yellow is so beautiful, it simply makes me giddy
Yellow is the beach towel, lying in the sand
Yellow is a seashell, glistening in my hand

Yellow is a butterfly, landing on a branch
Yellow is a horse, galloping on a ranch
Yellow is a ticket you buy to get on a ride
Yellow is the lifeguard, warning you of the incoming tide

Yellow is the sand, soft beneath my feet
Yellow is a popsicle, it simply can't be beat
Yellow is a duckling, swimming in a pond
Yellow is a cheetah, of which I'm very fond

Yellow is the beach ball, winter is just a bummer
Yellow, yes yellow, is definitely summer.

Janice Christensen, Grade 8
Seymour Middle School, WI

What Is a Friend?

A friend is someone who is there,
Or is someone that does care,
To pick you up when you're down,
That releases you from your frown,
Happy or sad that they see,
He or she is always there for me,
Someone to trust,
So they can trust you,
Also they will be there for you.

Cole Kirchman, Grade 7
Luxemburg-Casco Middle School, WI

I Don't Understand

I don't understand…
How lockers stay organized
How card tricks are done
How pencils are made
Why people like coffee.

What I don't understand most is…
Why people get drunk
How God wasn't born
Why there are criminals
How our brain works.

What I do understand is…
Why people blink
How to operate a computer
Why teachers are mean
How to play chess.

Isaiah Gorski, Grade 8
West Suburban Christian Academy, WI

How to Make a Sandwich

A sandwich is something
Easy to make
Don't get your mom
You don't have to bake
Go to your fridge
Get out some meat
A delicious sandwich
Can be quite a treat
Gather some bread
Two slices is good
Put it together
I knew that you could
Lettuce and pickles
Cheese and tomatoes
Get a big can
And scoop out some mayo
PB and J
Turkey and ham
Make a big sandwich
And give it to Sam

Luke Lana, Grade 7
Pilgrim Lutheran School, WI

Girls Under Pressure

Tell me I'm beautiful, tell me I'm smart.
Help me through times when boys break my heart.
Tell me I don't need makeup, and be there in the morning when I wake up.
Talk about my dreams, tell me they'll soon come true.
Tell me "Good job" on the drawings that I just drew.
Take me somewhere my siblings can't go.
Take me shopping and buy me ribbons and bows.
When I am in the right crowd,
Give me a pat on the back and say "I'm proud."
At the end of the day, when the night is new, *always* remember to say, I love you!!!

Victoria Forner, Grade 7
Allendale Middle School, MI

Street Music*

S e p a r a t i o n
The world outside I do not wander that far
I wander out to the road every morning
The only thing I hear is the *rickety* old bus
No other cars may go by it is just me, myself, and I
I may hear the sound of the neighbor's goat singing the sightful songs
I wander through the woods with my pup
And we listen to the sad bird's song
The song of a loner; his friends all left, but it's still here alone
Alone as one could be
When we wander kcab towards my house
I think of S e p a r a t i o n
A long way to go to the road
A long way to go to hear the
Soft *Swishing* of the occasional cars
I hear the quiet road music
I am a long way from the Orchestra of the town's road
I hear a little child playing the kazoo
But I am content with MY road music; the soft essence of MY life
The S e p a r a t i o n of me living nowhere
The population small where I am a road with peaceful street music

Sarah Schmiedeknecht, Grade 7
Whitehall Jr High School, MI
**Inspired by Arnold Adoff*

A Caring Person

All I want is someone to be there for me.
Someone to be there when I am sad.
All I want is someone to be there for me.
Someone to be there for me through thick
Someone to be there through thin
All I want is someone to be there for me
Someone to be there when I am happy
Someone to be there when I am alone
Someone to be there when I am mad
All I want is someone to be there for me
Someone to go to at all times
Someone to help me when I have a problem to help me through anything
Someone to be there when I have a problem
Someone to be there for me always

Jordan Denton, Grade 8
Pennfield Middle School, MI

Tae Kwon Do

A kick and a punch,
Oooo, I knew I shouldn't have had a big lunch.
The punches are like sticks hitting a drum,
"Bam boom, boom bam!!!"

I try to catch my breath but my opponent keeps kicking me.
Yes, he's slowing down!
I kick my opponent a few times.
My opponent does a back hook kick;

I barely dodge it.
I bent back so far I thought I was Neo from *The Matrix*.
I trip my opponent making him land on the mat.
I'm thinking his back is screaming in pain.

He's getting angry.
He throws a few punches,
But I'm too fast,
I dodge the flying fists easily.

Tyler Skone, Grade 7
Ramsey Jr High School, MN

The Little Mermaid

The Little Mermaid comes to mind,
As Ariel glides through the water with glee,
Her tail happily swishing,
Of the thought of being free.

Flounder starts to sing,
As he leaps into the warm drizzling rain,
That is draining from the sky,
With no sign of bane.

Sebastian is playing clam drums,
He plays with a smile on his face,
His music is unique,
You can hear it even in space.

The music is like honey
Soft and sweet
As Sebastian hits the last note
The curtain falls to their feet.

Logan O'Mara, Grade 8
Sandusky Middle School, MI

Emotions

Calm, quiet, and hard to hear
Ringing and ringing
Like a phone that didn't get answered
Pounding like someone banging on the door
People are heated and frustrated
As if something miserable accrued
Laughter
Like you were laughing at a joke

Kara Blank, Grade 8
Sandusky Middle School, MI

Come on In!

Come with me,
on a magical journey.
Let's glide over
a radiant rainbow,
like a shooting star
racing through space.

We'll encounter politicians such as
spirited Hilary Clinton
and inspirational Barack Obama.

Leap back into history
and travel to
Italy and Poland.
Chow on delectable dishes,
savoring every bite.

As we adventure through amethyst waterfalls,
I hope my wondrous whirling self
shines through to you,
like the morning sun
glimmering behind the haze,
in each and every one of my poems.

Hannah Drozdowski, Grade 8
Holmes Middle School, MI

If Only You Were Here

If only you were here a lot of things
Could have been prevented

If only you were here my heart wouldn't
Feel so empty

If you were here I would feel better
Every day that I wake up

If only you were here I wouldn't feel that
I'm not loved the same as when you were here

If only you were here I wouldn't feel so alone and
Down at times

If only you were here you would witness me
Graduate sitting in a chair

If only you were here I wouldn't have to cry
Wishing that you were here

If only you were here I would still
Feel like your little sweetie pie

Rayshell Green, Grade 8
Hally Magnet Middle School, MI

My Education

While kids want a long vacation
I'll work for my fine education
It needs my hard work
And all the effort
It may take some modification

Amishade Ashe, Grade 7
Langston Hughes Academy, MI

Soccer

I feel the wind whip past my face
While to the goal I race
I must rush back to help defend
Their team must not win in the end

I hear the calls for the ball
I try to look and not to stall
Everyone wants to win the game
But only our team must get the fame

Now it's tied 5-5
Something's made up in my mind
There will be but one more goal
I will play with heart and soul

The closer I come to the net
The more and more nervous I get
I blast the ball
And we win it all!

The crowds are cheering
And my eyes are tearing
Win or lose we love the game
Through and through it stays the same

Patricia Houbeck, Grade 7
St Thomas More Academy, MI

My Life

My life is perfect
My life great
My life is fun
My life is straight
Every single day

My life is neat
My life is sweet
I play my video games
And call my friends
I go outside
It never ends

But the night has come
The day has end
But the next day
I will start over again

Tré Hawkins, Grade 8
Gesu Catholic School, MI

Mother, Daughter Day

The sticky bright colored yoga mats greet us,
The lilac sauna air swirls around mixed with soothing music,
Calm breathing of relaxation from everyone in the room,
A hazel dimmed light setting on the hard floor,
The crunch of leaves as we walk up to the wood fence,
Hard helmets and rough saddles,
Big brown eyes with thick black eye lashes,
A horse trotting as their hair rubs against your legs,
Your hands sweating as you grip the leather reins,
They neigh as you encourage them,
Fresh country air mixed with dry grass and hay,
Rows of unpainted pieces and every color of glass imaginable,
Music flowing in with summer's night breeze from the open door,
Smells of heavy duty glue and grit take over,
A once in a lifetime bond.

Alexis Fryatt, Grade 8
Centennial Middle School, MI

Just Because He's Black

People stare and people gap, just because the guy is black
he isn't bad, but he is sad because people think he's crap

Just because he drives past, people duck in fear
He turns around and keeps on driving, as the people rise and sneer

He is no different than you or I
But people look away as he passes by

Put yourself in his shoes, just for one short day
See how well you feel, when people run away

The next time you see him, you won't give him crap
He's no different than you or I, just because he's black

David Lamar, Grade 8
Saugatuck Middle/High School, MI

Black Women

Black women are our African Queens.
As black men, we must do anything to fulfill their dreams.
Let her know that she's cream, the cream of your cake.
Without her mix, you won't be able to bake.
Let her know that without her, you're made out of plastic, something fake!
Let her know that she's the food on your plate.
That she was the healer and without her, your body starts to ache.
That when she leaves, you won't eat.
When days go by and she comes home, you smile and stand on your own feet.
Let her know that you will take her country-to-country, state-to-state, and city-to-city.
On a nice night, when the moon is bright.
Let her know that she's pretty. That she's your light.
Let her know that she's your star and she shines bright.
Let her know that you will be willing to be wrong when she is right.

Rio Jones, Grade 7
Sister Academy/Harvest Prep School, MN

My House

Where family is friends
Where pets are good company
Where love is so sweet
Where I sleep
Where noise is really annoying
Where the food for my tummy is
Where entertainment is when I'm bored
Where memories are
Where good times and bad times are spent
A loving house
Filled with a loving family

Jessica Liebeck, Grade 7
Luxemburg-Casco Middle School, WI

Hiding Away

The ugly caterpillar frantically crawled on the harsh ground
Desperate to find a safe haven
She struggled through this mortifying routine each day
Wanting badly to forever hide herself from reality
The hideous creature burrowed herself into a hard shell
Blocking out the surrounding world of hell
Just when she thought all hope was lost
The cocoon cracked open

She could see the outside world again
But this time through new eyes
A robin swooped towards her suddenly
Ready to bully her like the others always had
She panicked and ducked out of its grasp
Before noticing she was soaring away
Out of the robin's aggressive reach
And to heights previously unknown to her
She flitted past a newly cleaned window
Catching a glimpse of the being she'd become
She was a beautiful butterfly
Full of grace and newfound freedom

Alyssa Setting, Grade 9
Clarkston Jr High School, MI

Untitled

Hear a bird sing,
A sad, mourning song.
Smell the rain,
The sky crying.
Feel the cold wind,
Whipping the leaves into a tornado.
Taste the words,
All of them unspoken.
See the pictures,
Of what is forever lost.

Bridget Walde, Grade 8
Saint Thomas More Catholic School, MN

My Life

My life has been an uphill climb
up a very steep, very cold, mountain.
I've sometimes sidetracked,
and strayed too far.
But I've gotten back on track.
There have been avalanches
where I am completely buried.
But I dig my way out and slide down a ways
but I always manage to find my way up.
And when I finally make it to the top,
I plan on staying there.

Trevor Lafavre, Grade 8
Northwood School, WI

The Magic Hour:

They call it the 'magic hour'
between 4 and 5:30 am
the time when everything seems still
I wonder if the sun will rise
or if this glow will last forever
peace is on this land and hope makes the leaves turn green
It seems as if angels have descended upon this field
So full of light and mysteries
It's the time when the devil's work is done
And everything can only get better from here
I wonder if the birds will rise
Or if this happiness will last forever
faith is on this land and love makes the leaves turn green
spring time, so much movement summer time, so much heat
fall time, so much changing winter time, so still
Now I wonder if the stars will rise tomorrow
Or if this magic will come again
joy is on this land and smiles make the leaves turn green
Now I wonder if trees will rise to the sun
Or if my mind will be as clear
I live on this land and care makes the leaves turn green

Victoria McGowan, Grade 7
South Park Middle School, WI

Pink

Pink, the best color.
We see it every day,
Maybe by the bay,
Or maybe I dare not say.

It is a red and white blend.
It is the color of my room.
It makes me want to go boom,
Because the flowers are all in bloom.

Several shades like hot pink and light pink,
Those happen to be my favorite of all.
When you see pink you're bound to have a ball.
Watch out! Pink might make you fall.

Kimberly Langolf, Grade 7
Central Middle School, MI

A Snowflake Falls

White blankets everywhere carpeting every surface
More white more white more white.
Play, laugh, run into the once green, green field.
A quartz clear dawn awakens.
Inch by bright inch does it accumulate to what a white wonder it is.
Fall, fall, fall from the white sky
Each an individual; all different
Run out to catch them on our tongues, white lace that dissolves before you taste.
Inside, inside, inside mother yells.
Our bodies cling to the glass in which is our barrier that fogs from our breath,
only emphasizing our wish to stay outside.
The only color here is white. White peace, white milky twilight,
white love spilling out and into our hearts that beat, beat, beat white hot blood.
Which stain when broken.
Leak, leak, leak out of our eyes as if the trails of salt water were to be embroidered into our skin,
like flowing satin across our bodies as we dream, dream, dream
of the bright naked moon shining on us and of what will come tomorrow.

Alexandra Sedano, Grade 9
Clarkston Jr High School, MI

What Has the World Come To???

The world is not how it used to be, I feel the only ones that are affecting it are the others around me, the population is decreased because people are shot and killed each day, it seems as if all the speeches Dr. King and Obama have said are just faded away, never have I seen such a monstrous tragedy. From I have a dream to yes we can believe, I want to live for a long time but as of right now it's all in my mind, I hope this poetry was important to you because if you wanna live right we got to do the opposite of what we do! But answer this question what has the world come to???

Diamond Russell, Grade 7
Sherman Multicultural Arts School, WI

Love

Let's see your smile, your laugh, your frown. Your face just makes my world go round.
In the morning when I arise, I think about your sweet blue eyes.
Just the thought of you makes me smile. I hope you'll stay around awhile.
When I'm with you, I can be myself. I don't have to act like anyone else.
I can count on you to make me laugh. You give me your whole, not just a half.
You're always fun to be around. That voice of yours, an amazing sound.
"Love," they say, is a very strong word, but there are sometimes it must be heard.
Maybe love is not here yet, but it will come, that's my bet.
Those three words, "I love you," Are an ancient three words,
But they feel so new. What I'm trying to say is…I love you!

Julie Welch, Grade 8
Boulan Park Middle School, MI

White, a Color

White is the feel of soft, squishy cotton swabs in between your giggling toes!
White feels like a soft warm bunny resting upon your lap.
White is the smell of vanilla candles lit in your soundless bathroom.
White smells like mint gum being chewed by the shy little boy beside you.
White is the sight of sparkly snowflakes gracefully falling to the ground.
White looks like harmless clouds drifting every which way through the sky.
White is the sound of peaceful waves of the ocean crashing against the shore.
White sounds like a dove soaring through the clear blue sky!
White is the taste of sweet powdered sugar dissolving in your mouth!
White tastes like the sweetest and gooiest marshmallow melting on your excited taste buds!

Callie Osborne, Grade 8
Washtenaw Christian Academy, MI

Uncle Brian

The little tricks you did when we played Monopoly,
That helped you win.
You didn't think we saw,
We did.

The raptor noises you made while hiding in trees.
I miss wrestling with you
I miss the "snug as a bug in a rug"
That you did so well.

I miss the animals over our heads,
That you did right before we went to bed.
I miss not having you there almost every night
I miss trying to steal your hat and sunglasses

I miss everything about you,
Your craziness,
Your solidness,
Your smile
I miss you Uncle B.

Sarah Johnson, Grade 8
Springfield School, MN

TV

I love to watch TV.
Just like any other kid.
It's fun and relaxing,
Just to kick back and watch your favorite channel.

Sometimes there's nothing good on.
Sometimes it's too many good things on.
And sometimes you decide to just play the 360.
But you always end up watching TV.

Plasmas and HiDef TVs are not worth it.
Just watching a regular sized TV,
Is fine with me.
But sometimes watching TV can be addictive.

So I just do other activities.
But I always come back to it.
I've watched all my life.
And it hasn't been a day in my life that I can remember,
When I haven't watched TV at all.

Antonio Fillmore, Grade 8
Gesu Catholic School, MI

Life

Life is like the blood that keeps your heart pumping
Without the blood it is like a body with no soul.
The heart is the key to the gates of Heaven.
Your blood is the spirit that lives inside you.
Your heart is the piece of God that's with you at all times,
Only in your heart you hold the power to be an angel.

Amani Bass, Grade 8
Middle School at Parkside, MI

Last Chance

I was walking through the hall today,
I heard you call my name,
But it must have been a joke, I guess,
Is this really just a game?

I know you see it in my eyes,
You know the way I feel,
I really wish you could just understand,
To me this is so real.

I know those things you said about me,
I know the things you did,
And when I tried to talk to you,
You just stood there and hid.

I heard you call my name again,
But this time I didn't even glance,
I walked right pass with my head held high,
You blew your last chance.

Allison Hanek, Grade 9
Montgomery-Lonsdale High School, MN

The Tortoise Won

The tortoise may be slow
The hare may be fast
The tortoise knows quick isn't always good
The hair thinks he's ahead
But he didn't study the course
And the tortoise did
He takes the shortcut on the map
The hare is astonished
That the tortoise won

Kevin VanSchoyck, Grade 8
Spring Hill School, WI

Just Because I Live in Wisconsin...

Just because I live in Wisconsin...
Doesn't mean I love snow
Doesn't mean I like the cold
Doesn't mean I don't like the beach.
Just because I live in Wisconsin...
Doesn't make me obsessed with cheese
Doesn't make me German
Doesn't make a me a Green Bay Packer's fan.
Just because I live in Wisconsin...
Doesn't mean I have an odd accent
Doesn't mean I live on a farm
Doesn't mean I call the drinking fountain a "bubbler."
Just because I live in Wisconsin — Come see our happy cows
and have a bratwurst and cream puff.

Sara Van Weelden, Grade 8
West Suburban Christian Academy, WI

Day and Night

For the sun that sparkles in the day
For the horizon that spills on the bay
For the everlasting heat it always gives
For all the things that make it live
God has left this all to us

For stars that shine through the night
For the moon glowing oh so bright
For the whispers flying in the air
For all the people that really care
God has left this all to us

Eric Chavez, Grade 8
St Andrew's School, MI

Fearful

Lying in my bed
can't help but wonder what will happen
anxiety rushing through me
my stomach turns
I tremble
my soft tears fall
I'm alone
I'm fearful

Kaylynn Brown, Grade 8
Pennfield Middle School, MI

Dark/Light

Dark
Scary, black
Shading, frightening, shadowing
Nightfall, hazy, warm, yellow
Inflaming, sparkling, burning
Bright, sunny
Light

Adrian Trinidad, Grade 7
Edison Middle School, WI

I Miss You

I see you in the hallway
I see you at the game
But you don't see me
We were friends
But not anymore
I lost you
When you moved on
I will be here
When you come back
I know you will come back
We will be friends again
I miss
Talking to you
Laughing with you
I miss you

Rachel Havens, Grade 7
Centreville Jr High School, MI

Pumpkin of Death

It's dark, depressing, lonely
Surrounded by death
No one around and no one to care

It looks lazy and relaxed.
Sharp teeth like a vampire
It sits in the shadows, in the dark night
Where there's no moon
To brighten the night

So it sits and waits
For a person to notice
The quiet and shy
Pumpkin of death

Dakota Ellithorpe, Grade 8
Chippewa Falls Middle School, WI

A Path

A path leads you,
it leads you through things,
it just leads you,
it leads you through the woods,
leads you through mountains,
leads you through happiness,
leads you through success,
and it leads you through life,
you can follow it or,
you can break it.
It's your choice.

Ahkeel Carter, Grade 7
Valley View Middle School, MN

My Dog

My dog is the best
He is black
And loves food
My dog is playful
He loves to play

Though he is old
He seems to never
Lose any pep
My dog is always hungry
He will eat anything
From broccoli to peanut butter
He is always waiting
Waiting for the next "plop"
The sound of food on the floor
My dog is lovable
He is loyal
And is always there for you
My dog is the best
The best in the world

Alex Politowicz, Grade 7
Abundant Life Christian School, WI

Rufus the Dog

Beyond my reach
Within my bed
Under my head
Around my shed
With his toy
By my side
During my sports
Throughout my house
Down the street
Down the stairs
Rufus

Austin Kolbeck, Grade 7
St Joseph School, WI

Wisdom

I am used by people
Filling the mind.

I am nourishment
Bringing well-being to the body.

I am understanding
He set the heavens in place.

I am the jewel
Seeking righteousness.

I am the righteous man's
Thinking.

I am the key of
Knowledge.

I am wisdom.

Samson Sturm, Grade 7
Washtenaw Christian Academy, MI

Love Is

Love is life
Love is nice
Love is sweet
Love is something that you can't deny
Love is like a sunrise
It is high up in the sky
Love is like an ocean's breeze
Love is a disease
But it can surely please
Love is something we can't feel
But love is something that can heal
Love is me
Love is true
So what are you waiting for
Write your love is poem too!!!

Brittany Walker, Grade 7
Gesu Catholic School, MI

Why?

You say, "We need to talk,"
then take my hand
and pull me along.
You say, "I love you babe,
but this thing isn't going to work."
I hold my tears from drowning my face,
and try to keep a steady pace.
I try to say, "It's okay" or "I understand,"
but you can see it in my face, that there is no other man.
My pace stops,
my breathing slows,
and I take a moment to realize,
why I lost you so.
I say "Goodbye," then take my things,
before I let you go,
I pull you in,
and ready my lips,
for this final blow.

Amanda Elliott, Grade 8
L'anse Creuse Middle School East, MI

Chocolaty Brownies

I live in a land of brownies.
A second doesn't go by that I don't covet
a morsel of chocolaty goodness.
Gentle, rich, bathed in melted love.
A heated, silken coverlet of crust covering its mass.
Brownies adore singing in harmony
with the rest of their ingredients.
They enjoy going solo in their melodies.
Standing at attention, in rows,
upholding their high reputations.
Taunting me with their delicious bodies,
Laughing at my humility with their big heads of chocolate.
I hoist one up with my fingers, then shove it in my mouth.
Its punishing stickiness cakes to my fingers.
Brownies are havens of warmth, but will chastise you
if you eat too many of their friends.

Seth Foust, Grade 7
Triumph Academy, MI

Love

Love is like a fire pit being lit.
You enjoy it. It's all warm and cozy.
But then all of a sudden, it's gone.
Love is like a true story.
You remember the events and then it's over.
Love is like the Lord and the devil.
A wonderful thing and then it goes bad.
Love, you like it. Then you hate it.

Gabrielle Banks, Grade 8
Middle School at Parkside, MI

Layers of an Old

The years have gone by,
Like the tide of ocean waves,
lapping up against the rough sand
that tames their hectic rage.

The years have gone by,
Along with the memories that are dwindling from my mind,
All once having able to disperse in a glorious hue,
For once I was able to feel my daughter's hug,
For once I could taste my husband's kiss
For once I could picture my star-sparkling family;
Who now fly with the clouds.

The years have gone by,
and each year is now presented on this cake,
Of another year…

The years have gone by,
and with each year, a layer has been added,
and my wish for this birthday
Like all the ones before this,
Is to have the layers cut off
One,
By one…

Caroline Roers, Grade 9
Discovery Middle School, MN

The Flag

To some people,
The flag is just a piece of cloth.
But to others it is a symbol of freedom,
A symbol of life, love, and unity.

To some people,
The Pledge of Allegiance is just something you say.
And though we say it every day,
Some people don't know what it means.

To some people,
The flag means nothing.
But to others it stands for those who died defending it.
For those who couldn't stand to see our country fall.
Yet, to those who made the ultimate sacrifice,
The flag means hope, love, and opportunity most of all.

Anna Lang, Grade 7
Springfield School, MN

Anger

Anger is a wave crashing into the shore.
Swirling, raging, absorbing everything in its path.
It is rage, building until it erupts.
It takes no sides only prisoners.
Anger is a refuge for those without patience.
It is like a bubble, growing and growing until it bursts.

Morgan Katzenmeyer, Grade 8
J C McKenna Middle School, WI

Ode to Turkey

Ode to turkey not just the food
But the bird so delicate when it
Walks yet so delicate
In my mouth
So many things to do with turkey
Like hunt it, eat it, and maybe
Even deep-fry it

The turkey brings joy to kids
And adults it sits on your
Table or in your yard
Oh turkey you're like M&Ms
You melt in my mouth
Not in my hand

Matt Hendrix, Grade 8
Washington School, WI

Heart Surgery

10 years gone by
Another heart surgery
Emerges for my aunt

My aunt scared as can be
This had all started
In her early 20's

We know she is tough
But we all still worry

Of the heart failure
Like an engine dying

But now she's back
Healthy and good

Until the next 10 years later
Her heart may not make it

Kaitlin Vanden Avond, Grade 7
Luxemburg-Casco Middle School, WI

Courage

Courage
Is a tiny, frightened fish
Swimming upstream, conquering fear
In the fast pace river of life,
Dodging the proud, fearless bear,
Known to be brave.

If courage is the mastery of fear,
Not the absence of it,
The proud, fearless bear is a coward,
With no fears to master,
The tiny, frightened fish is
Courage.

Sarah Michalak, Grade 8
Anderson Middle School, MI

Like Christ

I walk behind everyone else
They stop and look at her
I don't stop and just look I stop and help her up
She can't get up she is too weak, because of the lack of food
I help her
She is homeless, she sleeps on the street
I am not I was here shopping
She is sitting there begging
Begging for food and money
But most of all for love
I help her up and give her a dollar or two for some food
As I helped her up everyone that is walking by stops and stares
I turn around they wrinkle their noses at the sight of me helping the homeless
I was nice to her
I choose to help her, to act like Christ
Everyone else that walked by was not
She thanks me once she is on her feet
I tell her "you're welcome"
As I walk away she yells after me to stop.
I stop turn around, look at her
And she yells after me that she will never forget ME!!

Alexis O'Loughlin, Grade 7
Shakopee Area Catholic School, MN

Calling Me Home

Open the gate. Step through.
Feel the rush of air. Sprint up the stairs,
Bouncing to avoid shattered glass. Hear the roar. Hear the crash.
Close my eyes. Take a step. Breathe in. Open my eyes.
Try to get used to the brilliance. Fail.
Look out in awe, hear the cry of the gulls.
Touch the tall, green dune grass.
Feel the soft sand filling the gaps
Between your eager toes.
Taste the salty breeze on the tip of your tongue.
See the different shades of blue clash together as earth and sky.
Heal as the essence flows into your veins, through your body,
Exhilarating, satisfying, healing.
Like a drug to an addict.
Look out again. Hear it whisper stories.
It tells you not to be afraid, but to respect.
It is angry. It is happy. It is sad.
It is calm. It is playful. It is loud.
It is quiet.
It is the ocean, calling me home.

Christiana Eisenhut, Grade 7
Scranton Middle School, MI

A Spring Foggy Rain

When rain pitter patters on the roof, it sounds like crickets on a spring day.
It brings out all the worms for the fishermen to collect.
The rain drenches the soil to the point where it is too wet for worms.
This all happens between the drenched ground and the rain clouds.
It leaves by running into a ditch into a river that leads to the ocean.

Matthew Holden, Grade 7
Richmond Middle School, MI

Inkblot Clown

Your nose is big like a ripe tomato.
You make me explode with laughter like a volcano.
I always see you at fairs, dancing all around.
I would like to be like you Mr. Silly Clown.

Joshua Gossett, Grade 8
St Margaret Mary School, WI

Deeper

Calm and peaceful. Looks so great.
The slight tug at your feet
Tells you to go deeper, farther and
Let yourself be free.
You listen and walk forward
Feeling the light crash on your legs
And the sun beating on your neck.
All just a trick to go in deeper.
You fall for it. Up to your knees,
Your waist, and then your chest.
Floating around, being moved from side to side.
Close your eyes and relax.
You open your eyes, startled.
You've drifted far away.
Being sucked under and tossed around.
Holding your breath trying to come up for air.
Trying so hard to stay alive.
Fighting against it but
It just isn't working.
You give up.
Everything goes black.

Rachel Prastitis, Grade 9
Clarkston Jr High School, MI

Summer's Rain

The welcoming sound of a faint rumble
Ripples through the heavens like a shock wave.
I lean my head back
As the sprouts of the smoky clouds
Trickle a single drop of rain
Upon my cheek.
Tear by tear, the rain continues.
Dripping like a leaky faucet,
Until my windswept hair is soaked.
It takes but one glance at your face
To know we're thinking the same thing.
"Let's dance" I say.
And we skip to the street;
A river produced from the crying clouds.
I spin in circles, relishing the time
Like a childhood.
Glancing up thoughtfully,
I allow the warm plummeting water
To give me one last summer memory,
Like a single breath,
Before the clouds break and the water dries.

Kelsey Stevenson, Grade 9
Clarkston Jr High School, MI

I Wish…

I wish I could be with you all the time.
I wish I could stay in your arms forever.
I wish I could keep that kiss and lock it away.
I wish our hands would always be intertwined.
I wish our eyes would lock forever.
I wish I could hug you ever second.
I wish I could talk to you all through the night.

But more important then that is what I hope;
I hope we can stay together,
You and me, always and forever.

Alexis Blackford, Grade 8
Spring Hill School, WI

I Am a Mysterious Person

I wonder if I will see myself in college
I hear many comments about high school
I see all my friends with me
I want to be a writer or lawyer
I am proud of myself for setting a high goal

I pretend to actually have a career in my life
I feel that my dreams will come true
I touch many difficulties in my life
I worry what will happen to my life
I cry when I think of my future
I am someone who wants a good future

I understand that my parents want the best of me
I say that I can conquer my goals
I dream for my dreams to come true
I try to be the best me possible
I hope that I could get to be a writer like I want to
I am proud of myself

Nohemi Toledo, Grade 7
St Andrew's School, MI

Sports Out the Wazzo

Softball, football, soccer, basketball, luge
Way too many sports to choose
Just want to pick one so I have something to do
Hockey's too rough, lacrosse is too
Bowling takes skill, dance you can't slack
Cross country and track I'm never going back
Airsoft, paintball, and laser tag
Would someone please fetch me a barf bag
Pool, billiards, and cribbage aren't they the same
Either way it's not a fun game
Baseball and cricket have dangerous bats
I think I'll just stick to petting cats

Molly Hanson, Grade 8
Seymour Middle School, WI

Family

F orever
A lways
M om and Dad
I
L ove
Y ou

Jordan Officer, Grade 7
Gesu Catholic School, MI

Spring

Spring
A time to sit on the grass and
watch the sunset.
Spring
When you sit outside with the nice cool
breeze blowing on your face.
Spring
When you hear the morning birds
sing aloud when you wake up.
Spring
When you listen and see the rain
crash on your window.
Spring
When you walk on the beach with
the moist sand between your toes.
Spring.
An amazing time of year.
Spring
You gotta love it.

Alyssa Rodriguez, Grade 7
Shakopee Area Catholic School, MN

Music

Music is me.
I am music.
Twenty-four hours a day,
Seven days a week,
365 days of the year.
I love music.
It affects the way I feel
Or do I just
Listen to songs
That reflect
my mood…
I don't know but
Music is the key
to my heart
It's the love
of my life
And as long
as I'm here
On this Earth
I'll always say…
I LOVE MUSIC

Najah Johnson, Grade 8
Gesu Catholic School, MI

Rain

Pitter-patter on the earth like the sound of a mouse scurrying across the ground.
Coming from the clouds gracefully giving the Earth water for all its living
Falling Falling Falling
Starting in the sky because God decides to cry
Evaporating away leaving only a trace of wetness eventually becoming dry.

Kaitlin Niebauer, Grade 7
Richmond Middle School, MI

Ice Cream

I had this big fat ice cream cone,
With caramel, fudge, and sprinkles.
Surely it had to have shown,
It went from my mouth to my ankles.
There was vanilla, strawberry, grape, and even cherry too,
Any flavor good enough for you.
Since I'm adventurous
I tried a new flavor today,
It was sweet, and delicious if I do say,
Neutromatic was its name.
I just had to tell everyone,
Everyone I know must try it,
"What makes it so good? Do you fry it?"
"No you don't fry it, you just have to try it!"
"Is it good? Will I like it?"
"I promise you'll like it, come on try it, don't throw a fit."
"Oh! It's scrumptious, I love it, delicious. Where did you get it? I want it for myself!"
"By the little blue elf on the corner on the shelf."

Olivia Stapleton, Grade 8
Adams Friendship Middle School, WI

Dancers Say

A silent pose facing the crowd
the music comes and the music is loud

While the audience displays their adoring stare
we display our hours work of graceful dance and well done hair

A graceful leap, a neat pirouettes
each step hit perfect with each eight count set

The wooded stage makes not even the slightest sound
because we dance as if we weigh the mass of a feather and not a hundred pounds

We live to dance, we love to dance
we are often in a fifth position stance

Music slow or music fast
we can always make the dance last

Tap, jazz, lyrical, and ballet
we love to dance and that's what any dancer would say

Paige Kusmierz, Grade 8
Ionia Middle School, MI

The End

It is almost the end
Goodbye to the best of friends

Almost time to decide what to do
Soon everything will be new

How did nine years go so fast
Making memories that will always last

Memories of soccer, football, and basketball
Good times were had by all

Who knows what will happen when
Always remember how much fun it's been

Soon it will be time to find a new space
But my roots will always be in this place

Colton Stanislawski, Grade 8
St Roman School, WI

Laurie Lauren

Loves to watch *Laguna Beach*
Eating her luscious Lemonheads
While her brother Lucas plays with his locomotive
Saying she's a loser from loserville
That she's too lazy to do the laundry
Laurie Lauren doesn't care
Just shakes her long hair
And walks away with her lemonheads

Laura Vo, Grade 7
Cedar Riverside Community School, MN

The Courtyard

On a calm spring morning
A slight breeze makes the bush's leaves sway
Birds fly from tree to tree
Chirping to each other
A duck sits on top of a rock
Another one swims around in the pond
Looking for food as it dips their head in the water
The trees are starting to bud
A bird flies into a small birdhouse
Made of wood
Leaves on the ground move with the wind
Flipping back and forth
The sun,
Peaks through the clouds
On a cloudy day,
Filling the small area
With light.

Jordan Henney, Grade 9
Clarkston Jr High School, MI

Just Me

Full of pure excitement and wrongful doings,
Full of anxiety and fear of myself,
Times fly by and I reflect to see;
The person I'm showing is not really me.
Full of lies and silence, I try to know
The feelings and thoughts, how I've sunk so low.
I smile, I frown, I try to care
But all in all, my heart's not there.
My head aches of sorrow; all the bad things
I've let myself amount to, it so loudly sings.
I look into my past, and try to see
Innocence and modesty when not drinking tea.
I'm telling you now
I'm ready to let go
This person this thing
I've come to know.
So, let go of this hurtful past
Forget the daunting future
Right here, right now
Just plain me.

Taylor Hefty, Grade 9
Clarkston Jr High School, MI

Song of My Life

This life I lead…It is a lie.
You may see me…so strong and bright.
But you will never ever know…
That every day. I die. Even more on the inside.
I wish that the world.
Would just let me be.
Because I can't take this imperfect melody…

Olivia Gallenberger, Grade 8
Oostburg Middle School, WI

Streets of Heaven

Floating above many skyscrapers so high,
reach out my hand and skim the milky blue sky.
Gazing down upon a playful child, or two,
and maybe take a peek above an overcrowded zoo.

Dreaming of lands where no one would cry,
and butterflies hummed sickly-sweet lullabies.
Laughter rings out like Beethoven's chimes,
while children, so mellow, sit and read rhymes.
Surrounded by people of every size, every shape, every age.
Are you sure this isn't a fairy tales torn-out page?

Is this a dream?
Is this for real?

Is this really how Heaven's supposed to feel?
And if this is a dream — dare do I say,
I still play like Peter Pan, forever eleven,
and dance and sing along the streets of Heaven.

Brieana Darwin, Grade 7
Valley View Middle School, MN

Spring Fever

Springtime is here once more.
Through the air the chirping birds soar.
They sing their musical call
As springtime fever infects all.

While spring is in the air,
The flowers bloom everywhere.
Tulips and daffodils both short and tall;
As springtime fever infects all.

The apple trees grow tall and sure.
While their blossoms are white and pure
Soon from their branches they will fall
As springtime fever infects all

When the ice on the stream thaws;
The water will flow by without a flaw
Everything grows both big and small
As springtime fever infects all.

June Redman, Grade 9
St Thomas More Academy, MI

Work

Work work work
I want it to be done
work work work
I want to see the sun
Work work work
I want it to be it
Work work work
I want to call it quits

Truth Otto, Grade 7
West Middle School, MI

Soldier

S trongly built to
O nly protect the
L ess trained in
D efending their
I ndividual selves or their
E ndearing country for the
R ight reasons

Taylor Godsey, Grade 8
Fairview Charter School, WI

Fess Up, Mess Up

It's time to fess up
Because I messed up
All the lies, all the pain
Sometimes it flies, sometimes it rains,
But most of all I want to say,
I pray some nights that you will say,
Hey it's okay I'll forgive you on this day.

Trinity Weldy, Grade 8
Spring Hill School, WI

Honey

There once was a boy named Bunny
but everyone thought it was funny
so he changed his name
to a name called Jame
but his mommy still calls him Honey.

Emily Ploeckelman, Grade 7
Christ Child Academy, WI

A World of Black and White

Black things are beautiful.
The notes that you sing,
The crow's angered cry.
Black holes pick up everything,
Darkness in the sky.
Stripes on a zebra,
Spots on a cow,
Chocolate's sweetness,
The magician takes a bow.

White things are beautiful.
The sparkling snow,
The wedding bells ring,
A marshmallows puff,
The swan's flowing wing.
The steaming hot milk
On a cold winter's day.
Outside stands a snowman
After the children's long play.

Dani D'Alessio, Grade 8
Pilgrim Park Middle School, WI

One Way Street

The thrill of learning a new trick
Mingled with the loss of the sun.
We made repetitions,
In a circle, synchronized.
Pedal to pedal,
We pumped and we pushed,
Pulling us closer
Like a gravitational force.
The feel of freedom
Running through our veins
And the taste of the present
On our tongue.
Seven, eight, eleven, the number
Did not matter,
Our pattern was for once
The same
Riding the street
On that warm felt night.
Our figures,
Throwing shadows
As we rode on that one way street.

Alyssa Currao, Grade 9
Clarkston Jr High School, MI

Football

F ans
O verwhelms with excitement as
O vertime means a
T ie game
B alls must pass the end-zone
A s players
L eap through the air and
L evel the other players

Nicholas Cerniglia, Grade 8
Fairview Charter School, WI

Ocean

Water so peaceful
Sounds of the waves crashing
Against the shoreline

Jake Kellen, Grade 7
Core Knowledge Charter School, WI

Breaking the Seal

A frozen puddle
Stands alone amongst the frosted grass
It's protective layer breaking
Weakened
Beginning to break its seal
Water below emerging
Not yet flowing
Peaking out
Waiting
Tips of surrounding grass are damp
Drip of dew
Onto the matted grass
It's weathered
Faded
The remaining snow melts
Wet
Landscape awaken
Escaping the captivity of winter
Welcoming the freedom of spring
Ready

Madison Lightfoot, Grade 9
Clarkston Jr High School, MI

A Perfect Day

I wake up and my heart beats
I walk out in my bare feet
The sun rises and the birds sing
As I see the calm water and start running
Father in Heaven we thank thee
I watch the fish in their schools
As I stand there I get calm and cool
I am relaxed in the spring time
At that moment I was very fine
Father in Heaven we thank thee

Connor Saukas, Grade 8
St Andrew's School, MI

Together Again

It was winter on the streets, icy and cold
A man in his box shivered, cold and alone
Days and days passed without one piece of gold
Every day he went to his wife's gravestone

"I miss you," he told it, knowing she would hear
He sat down, the ground feeling cold and dead
Then leaned against he gravestone, forming a tear
He felt depressed and alone, sick and unwed

"Come join me then," said a voice from the sky
And the man rose, soaring away from the gloom
He wondered where he was and what was awry
'Twas the voice of his wife in full volume

Knowing he was dead, he hugged his wife tightly
And the man was smiling, happy, clean. Finally.

Megan Rousso, Grade 8
St John Lutheran School, MI

Unreadable

Her face is stained with washed out memories
and no one seems to notice.
She walks alone at her worst,
but no one even seems to care.
Her eyes scream the words she cannot speak;
No one has ever understood.
All she really wanted was someone,
someone to be there
but no one ever came.

Taylor Lovelace, Grade 9
Hartland High School, MI

The Longest Fifty Yards

I had been training
With all of my might
So that I could compete
In the Plymouth swim meet
And now was the time
That my training would finally pay off
As I stepped up to the block
My heart started to beat
Faster and faster thump, thump, thump
I was watching the other swimmers
To see what I was supposed to do
I curled my hands around the block
My heart sounded like a clock counting down
Then all of a sudden, splat
I had fallen off the block before the bell rang,
But I kept going
And that fifty yard race
Felt like I was swimming a mile
But still I kept going and I may not have won,
But I finished that race.

Kristin Kmecheck, Grade 8
Seymour Middle School, WI

Forever

When everything is just too much
and life seems frightening
turn to me and I'll help you through.

When your mind won't sleep
yet your body's exhausted
come, and I'll be with you.

When you want to give up and cry,
so you can drown in your own tears
I'll build you a boat 'cause you must go on.

When you have no friends
'cause you pushed them all away
There I'll be, by your side standing strong

When you want to die
I will help you

If you want to live,
together we'll be
forever.

Angeles Baez, Grade 8
Achieve Language Academy, MN

Click Click Click

Click click click
A picture of a bird
Click click click
Worth a thousand words
Click click click
So unique, so preferred
With every picture,
A wink is heard

A chink, chunk, chu
Pictures of
Leaves
Bunks
Shoes

No matter where I go
No matter what I do
I'll always find a billion ways
To picture something new

My camera giggles like
A tickled kid
Opportunities should strike, like lightning might,
And then they did

Sara Baranczyk, Grade 7
Ramsey Jr High School, MN

Feeling Safe

Feeling safe is when you don't have to worry about what's going to happen next.
Feeling safe is when you have good friends around to help you out.
Feeling safe is when you know that you have people who care enough about you that you don't need to worry.
Feeling safe is when you have your own little place where no one is around.
Feeling safe is always a good feeling, especially when your friends and family are there with you.

Chelsie Wack, Grade 9
Northport Public School, MI

Remembrance of Childhood

It felt as though ice blanketed me when I ran into the chilled air.
Thump after thump, my bare feet squished the tall, green grass below.
"Stop!" she cried while I chased her, pink chalk in one hand, sea foam in the other.
I swiped the colors onto Stacy's cobalt Detroit Lions jacket.
My laughter was impossible to bear when I drew on more rose stripes as she dashed in circles across the hill.
The emerald leaves bustled together atop the monstrous oak tree, rapidly dancing in the cyan sky.
I raced back up to her with all the energy I had left inside.
Swipe! Ha-ha-ha-ha!
The ends of her dark chocolate ringlets brushed my fingertips.
Stacy flew down the yard and onto a black driveway coated in Crayola sidewalk chalk masterpieces.
She finally dragged her feet back to her house, with tears traveling south of her granny smith eyes.

Sarah Taylor, Grade 8
Centennial Middle School, MI

Depress Over Time

The 20's, were great times in people's lives, all felt good, all felt right.
Among those days, although all felt good, then came the great blight.
Endless, some thought, the day that crashed, without jobs, without pay, without will to continue.
With broken spirits, and the nation in crisis, all remain in doubt.
Until the day, when the great light will save us all, and hope and happiness, will prevail.
Such past is like the future today.
Things are more modern.
The Problem is just the same
Jobs are lost, cuts on pay
We will all wait until that day,
When the nation's only help will come about
The Great Barack Obama.

Andrew Placzek, Grade 8
St Roman School, WI

Losing What We Love

Loss brings us sorrow, it brings us no joy.
As we search for a better tomorrow, it sucks us into the void.
Loss leaves us empty, hollow and dark inside.
It leaves us with memories, of wondrous things in our lives.
Be it a person or a place, a best friend or a pet,
Loss makes us remember, what we want to forget.
We remember all of our love, and all of those great feelings of joy,
When we saw the one we loved and cared for, and that we once enjoyed.
After time, loss lets up a little, it lets us forget,
Bit by bit, a little of our sadness and regret.
We will always remember, in a tiny part at least,
Whatever we have lost, as memories cannot totally be thrown out or released.
But the pain will then subside, and it will fade to just a shadow,
As the tide of pride we have, for whatever we have lost, comes back in a true form, not in the least bit shallow.

Patrick Mullen, Grade 8
Resurrection School, MI

Doggy Dearest

Lady is an Angel!
I say that now 'cause she is dead.
She died of a dreadful disease.
She was the best dog anybody could ever have.
She was smart,
Clever,
Brave,
Lovable,
And of course she was protective.
Now that she is gone I have to live on.
Now I only have her in my pictures and memories.
Lady is an Angel!

Angelic Thompson, Grade 8
Washington Middle School, WI

Fault

The bubble of security surrounding me,
Shot past me in a blinding light of red.
Remembering the happiness and warmth clench my soul.
Nothing left but the cold feeling of despair stabbing at my heart.
My tears of Joy now tainted with blood.
Knowing the dark truth,
I will never say out loud.
Too scared to say those words,
Lost in darkness,
Forever.

Alexandra Berg, Grade 8
White Pine Middle School, MI

Through the Window

Someone's climbing through the window
Breaking their way through
So I run out the door
Into the other room
Someone's climbing through the window
I can't let them through
I try to leave the room
I see them climbing through the window
I try to run away
But all of a sudden I cannot move
From the place that I must stay
So I climb through the window and look in front of me
And I see a full length mirror
With a reflection of hostility
Behind me is the window
Right where it shall stay
And facing me is the future
So I'll start to make my way
But I won't think about that now
I'll save it for another day

Shelby Sawyer, Grade 8
St Stephen Elementary School, MI

A High School Story

High school is a story,
You have to write yourself.
The front cover says, "High School,"
The main character is you.
Chapter one is freshman year,
You touch your pen to paper.
You could be shy, you could be outgoing,
You could even have a date.

You either try hard in your classes,
Or you could care less and fail.
You might be on an athletic squad,
Or maybe you're the class president.
You turn the pages in the story,
"Sophomore, Junior, Senior."
It's now the final chapter,
Your pen is running out of ink.

It is now graduation day,
There are mixed feelings…laughing and crying.
Then you take time to flip back through your book,
You look at the past and write on the very last page…
"The End."

Tyler Skluzacek, Grade 9
Montgomery-Lonsdale High School, MN

My Report Card

During Language Arts, I was happy,
Upon my report card were all A's,
I examined the room, seeing sad faces.
Inside my head were happy thoughts,
Behind me, were my friends congratulating me,
I begin to smile widely, filled with excitement.
At home, my parents were proud,
Inside my house we hung my report card on the refrigerator,
I welcome the praise my parents gave me.

Amanda Estacio, Grade 7
Beer Middle School, MI

Rock-N-Roll

When you listen it has to be loud
When you jam you know to be proud

It's the best kind of music ever
If you listen to it you are clever

When you listen to it you get pumped
If you listen to rap you sit there like a stump

It goes back to the old days
You can be a rocker like Brandon Hayes

In Rock-N-Roll you can head bang
When your listening to it be prepared for some pain

Cody Koukal, Grade 8
Washington Middle School, WI

The Way People Work

In many ways people are like clocks.
They keep working from the time you
put the batteries in until about the time
the batteries die. Just waiting for their
time to stop ticking.

Matt Wyckoff, Grade 7
Centreville Jr High School, MI

I Am

I am trustworthy and determined,
People can count on me,

I am the future,
Full of opportunity,

I am laughing and smiling,
It's the best cover-up,

I am Chicago lit up at night,
Beautiful and bright,

I am trouble,
Lurking around the corner,

I am education,
It's all up to me how it will be,

I am a young girl,
Trying to understand.

Megan Elaine Henderson, Grade 9
Northport Public School, MI

Alone

Someone everyone dislikes
it's what I look like
that throws them off
from who I really am
a part of me the world
will never know
I am all alone in the world
in my own world
where people don't judge
on what you wear on the outside
but judge on what's on the inside
a part of me I feel is hurt and alone
never knowing what they think
about who I really am
set aside in the world
to be my own friend
respectful but not respected
I feel left out from the world
just another person
to be mended to when I'm old
it's just another day of my life

Steph Tesnow, Grade 9
Park Falls High School, WI

Little House by the Sea

I wish, I wish that I could be
In a little house by the sea
But only if my friends were there
So the joy I had, I could share
I would also have a little cat
That kept away the tiny fruit bat
My friends and I would laugh and fight
But then make-up before saying goodnight
In the morning the sun so bright
Would silhouette the clouds in flight
Later our parents would come and say
That they would take us home today
I'd say "No way! We want to stay"
So we would not leave that day!
Our moms and dads would decide to wait to leave until tomorrow
But we were still all filled with sorrow
These things I say I must regret
Have not happened to me yet
But I bet if I bought a little cat
I would teach it to keep away the tiny fruit bat

Drew Agnew, Grade 8
Abundant Life Christian School, WI

Love

Love is a feeling my heart cannot explain
When I feel love my heart feels very vain
But when I see him I get this pain a funny feeling in my heart I cannot explain
Love it makes your heart sing like a bell going ring-a-ling
He is a song in my head the beating drum of my heart
Love is a feeling my heart cannot explain
Love is a feeling my heart cannot explain

Gabrielle Dixon, Grade 8
Jerstad Agerholm Middle School, WI

Fairy Tale Endings

I want to run.
I want to run and never come back.
I'm stuck in this messed up town that has no fun
where happily ever afters are what we lack.

I want to live in a fairy tale wonderland.
A world where the rules are able to bend
Where there is a prince and a maiden who takes his hand,
They fall in love, and that's the end.

Can't that happen in reality, maybe just one fairy tale chapter?
Is it all just one vague lie?
Where's the happily ever after?
Has there ever been one, or is it that people are just too shy?

We can run, run far away
Maybe then, there can be a happily ever after
But for now together we will stay
That's ok with me, as long as we can live just one fairy tale chapter

Hannah Tubbs, Grade 8
Sandusky Middle School, MI

Turning 14

The whole idea of it makes me feel
Like the little old woman on 42nd street
The idea of 14 creeping up on me is slow but consistent
Week by week, day by day
Hour by hour, minute by minute
It's like the lioness about to pounce on her prey
It is like an ocean full of "Happy 13th Birthday"'s
Swarming around me
Trying to drown me
You might wonder why?
Why are you afraid?
But, they expect so much more
They expect you to be great
You see, turning 14 isn't all that bad
But it's the door to independence
The door to freedom, college
Being me of course,
I would never want to think of all this
So right now I'll just sit back and relax
Concentrate on, not being 14,
But being 13

Christine Leong, Grade 7
Baker Middle School, MI

Springtime

Springtime is a wonderful time.
The snow is melting and the sky is greener.
Best time to play basketball and a game of soccer.
Take a very fresh and joyous walk on the beach,
While eating a very, very sweet peach.

The air is hot and the birds are flying.
The flowers have bloomed and I'm going swimming.
Springtime is the best time and everyone knows it.
It's right when you go fishing and have fun doing it.

Springtime is an exciting time,
When school is about to let out…
When kids play in the rain,
Then run back in the house.

Springtime is the best time,
And everyone knows it.
But, springtime is up
And it's time for summer.

Patrick H., Grade 9
Thomas More School, MI

Downpour

A tingling shiver runs down my spine,
A subtle rumble picking up pace in time.
The clouds come together as if to enclose me in,
A raindrop hits my nose and rolls down my chin.
The spring downpour is about to begin.

Grace Hersey, Grade 8
Saint Thomas More Catholic School, MN

Spring

It always smells like rain
And everything is wet
All of the snow melted away
You can hear the birds jump in the puddles
The sun comes out eventually
You start feeling more relaxed
Summer is coming fast

That's when you know it's spring

Alexis Shong, Grade 8
Winter Middle School, WI

My Loss

It broke my heart the day I found out,
I never imagined her not by my side,
Her collar ringing where ever I go,

Why did this have to happen to me?
How come I'm crying myself to sleep?
What do I do now that she's not here?

It broke my heart the day I found out,
Her big brown eyes that were full of love,
The way she knew when I was very sad,

I cried for a day when I found out,
She's the one I want to comfort me…but now she can't,
Her soft black fur to soak up my tears,

It broke my heart the day I found out,
She died in my hands on a Sunday morning,
Now she's gone forever and I don't know why.

Bryanna Woldt, Grade 8
Seymour Middle School, WI

Chocolate Swirl

It looks to perfect
Sitting there doing nothing
It was not created to do anything
Just sit there on the beach
I think it's possible that someone molded it themselves
Perfectly
It's perfectly smooth
No flaws in it at all
It looks just like chocolate and vanilla swirl ice cream
On the top
If you were to flip it over it looks just like a bowl
It looks like a Korean worker's hat
But so much smaller
Like an ant could wear it

Kailee Gunderson, Grade 8
Chippewa Falls Middle School, WI

The Ocean

The ocean flows from side to side
The deep blue ocean shiny and bright
It covers the sand like a big blue blanket
Then it quickly moves away

Kasia Lee, Grade 7
Valley View Middle School, MN

Life

Life is a valley,
so bumpy yet smooth.
Life is a roller coaster,
that never ends.
Life is a maze,
full of surprises.
Life is your life,
that is always priceless.

Danielle Petruska, Grade 8
Oak Grove Middle School, MN

Leaves

Out in the forest
Many leaves fall to the ground
On the crisp fall day

On top of the trees
The branches and twigs are bare
In the winter chill

Out in the backyard
Little green leaves start to sprout
As snow starts to melt

In the shady woods
The leaves are growing bigger
In the summer heat

Back in the forest
Birds are chirping on the leaves
Not long after dawn

Out in the meadow
Leaves in the wind are dancers
On a windy day

Trisha Wilquet, Grade 8
Seymour Middle School, WI

Spring

As I sit here,
I can hear,
The roar of the river,
The sound of the
Wind-chimes.
Everything I hear
Tells me spring is here.

Joanna Hargas, Grade 7
Winter Middle School, WI

Voices in a New World

I hear voices in the wind
Voices of the hungry
Voices of the weak
They call me in closer; pleading for help
To provide for them their daily needs
I do what I can to help them
But I am not all powerful

I feel another burst flow by
This time, voices in deep pain
Voices with sorrow on their tongue
It's a bittersweet taste, something I do not want
But they lure me in
Like human blood to a thirsting vampire
The sound and smell enticing
They question me then drag me away to a world I've never known

This world is full of life and everyone full of love and laughter
People help you along, and don't tear you down
They give second chances and show undeserved love
I dream of our world being like this
No voices with sorrow that call my name
And everyone understands with love all around

Kylie Pratte, Grade 8
West Suburban Christian Academy, WI

Sound Waves

When I first touch the cool, cold metal
I think.
I think about what I will listen to next,
how fast, how slow, how calm, how rough.

Music.
It calls to me, screaming my name.
My head becomes as calm as a deep sleep,
or as hurt as a million sound waves hit my ears.
I think of the colors the sounds make up:
red, blue, black, purple.
The familiar "Boom da boom boom" continues the steady beats.

I am a safe haven, to become one with the guitar and percussion.
The white earphones never disappoint,
and as the song ends, I click around for
just one more, and my heart craves.

I am like my friend's old jukebox.
I take the fast beats, slow beats, long beats,
short beats to a whole new level.

The days when I have died,
I trust myself to let sound waves overcome me.

Minette Saulog, Grade 7
Ramsey Jr High School, MN

Navajo Bridge

It was a warm and sunny day.
The sun beat down on my shoulders.
I saw the bridges in the distance, the condors overhead.
The distant sound of voices
And the rush of the wind.
I ran to the view point and stood in awe.
The giant and magnificent
Bird had just flew passed.
Her eyes met mine.
I heard the whistle of
The wind between her fingers.
I walked onto the bridge
And my dad followed behind.
I had a smile on my face and joy in my voice.
I had seen the California Condors.
With the baldness of their heads,
Reflecting off the sun.
Then the glow as the sun set,
As the air grew colder.
The day was coming to an end.
A day I will never forget.

Sierra Reece, Grade 7
North Rockford Middle School, MI

Life

From little girls and boys
Laughing and screaming making noise
To running, falling and crying
Just awful timing

When you have your first crush
And your heart turns to mush
Being heartbroken
Then just mopin

From being a preteen
Girls need to make a scene
While boys fist fight
Oh they just might
From As to Fs in a second
Your parents saying they've had it

To slamming doors in rage
To turning a page
A new chapter in life
Where there's even more strife

From a child to an adult
You didn't want your childhood to halt
All grown up nowhere to go won't forget playing in the snow

Sydni Bull, Grade 7
Core Knowledge Charter School, WI

Grandma's Pearls

I lock the golden bracelet on my left wrist.
My stomach twists at the thought of being close to you.
It was a cheerful feeling though,
like being reunited with a long-lost friend.
I have often dreamed of being with you,
even if it is only through a piece of your past jewelry.
A dozen lustrous white pearls shimmer at me,
gleaming into my eyes to say, "Hello."
I imagine — only for a second —
that you were saying your greetings to me,
instead of your pearls.
Why?
Why could that not be you,
wrapped around me, hugging tight,
instead of your dinky bracelet?
No bracelet can show love like you could have.
I lock the golden bracelet on my left wrist.
My stomach twists at the thought
of never being in your arms.

Jacqueline Colvett, Grade 8
Oakview Middle School, MI

Mom

Mom who is there for me
Asks me if I need help
Who is loving
Who is caring
Whose hair is as silky as sheets
Who tells me she loves me
Who used to call me Rue
Is helpful and joyful
Doesn't care what people think
Whose eyes sparkle like the stars
Who is thankful
Who will never be mean
Who will always be there for me no matter what
Who is my loving mom

Marissa Cevigney, Grade 8
Central Middle School, MI

Winter Night

The waves of a sea green sky
blue and light purple, paint the night sky.
The moon is like a ball of snow,
illuminating the whole world.
The white, fluffy snow floats to Earth
like humans in a parachute.

You can hear the loud sound of
the rustle of the leaves in the wind.
The crunch of snow of the soft snow
under the hooves of the moose is also present.
The tree sways in the wind like
a human would in a raging storm.

Hunter Gaber, Grade 8
Chippewa Falls Middle School, WI

Just Maybe

Maybe I should talk
Maybe I should cry
Maybe I should sing a song
and never let it die.
Maybe I should cuddle up
And never let you go…
But before you push away from me
I want to let you know…
But maybe just maybe
We can sit and think,
about us staying together
And let the water sink.

Bre'Ana Lynn, Grade 7
Valley View Middle School, MN

The Sound of the Wind

A songbird caught and taught to fly
A breath of air pulled from the sky
Expelled with force the puff of air
Then split in two by embouchure

Tornado loosed inside the flute
Forced into a narrow route
Contained and formed by silver keys
Transformed from gust to gentle breeze

With notes as soft as children's prayers
A fresh spring breeze in winter air

Laura Reimann, Grade 7
Prairie River Middle School, WI

Fourth of July

Boom! Snap! Crackle!
Fireworks soaring
through the sky
as audiences
laugh with joy
as the fireworks
roar in the sky
the audiences
dance with happiness
as others sit and
watch and let out
oohss aahss and
great cheers as
the final show
begins everyone
sits in amazement
with the final
Booms! Snaps! Crackles!
echo throughout the sky
everyone leaves in disappointment
as the show ends.

Andrew Fjerstad, Grade 7
Ramsey Jr High School, MN

Regrets

I gave into my stupidity
I became naive
you said you would change for me,
and I believed.

My love was too great for you
to see the damage you had done.
I didn't want to see,
I couldn't see.

Everything I loved was an illusion
everything I want is out of reach
everything works against me
everything is dead to me

What's the point of living
when you are all on your own?
Why should I show love
if none for me is shown?

You were not the one for me…
I won't make that mistake again.

Julian Dahlberg, Grade 9
South View Middle School, MN

The Hat

Bumps like a rocky mountain
Half dug hole on my bottom
Shaped like a Chinese hat

A stingray without a tail
A color of a mountain
Looks like 3,000,000 foot mountain

A person with a very pointy head
Like spikes coming out of the ground
Watches the world go by

People come and go
All the while watching with amazement
Curiosity
Wonder
Breathtaking eyes
Then it's all gone
It sits all alone
In the midnight sky

April Martinez, Grade 8
Chippewa Falls Middle School, WI

The Big Dog

I am a mastiff
So majestic and loyal
My owner loves me

Morgan Bullock, Grade 7
Centreville Jr High School, MI

Let Me Never Become…

Let me never become a thistle.
Poking up when no one wants you.
Causing pain and misery.

Let me never become a thistle.
Choking life from living plants.
Being killed time and time again.

Let me never become a thistle.
Making people mad.
Being the cause for problems.

Sabrina White, Grade 7
St Mary's School, WI

You Still Remember Me

Heart to heart,
Beat to beat,
I never let him,
Ever get the best of me,
Now he can finally see,
He's not really good enough for me,
It's best that he can see.
I never loved anyone,
As much as he loved me.

Rachel Goodell, Grade 9
Melvindale High School, MI

A Summer Canoe

Splash, kaploosh
the paddle goes under,
it comes back up,
then under again.

The waves crash into the shore,
and dampen the sand,
like the breeze cooling the air.

The birds sing their high beautiful notes,
chirp, chip, chirp.
The breeze runs through your hair,
taking long deep breaths.

You smell the peppermint trees,
you taste the fresh summer air,
you see the constantly growing forest.

The long boat is a rocket,
moving you on.
Your paddle is a kid,
splashing the water,
and laughing with delight.
Canoeing!

Kira Church, Grade 7
Ramsey Jr High School, MN

Snake Story

Silently, swimming
The stars dancing overhead
Like the wind.
You feel it's there
Nothing can be seen
In the dark mysterious depths.

The snake cuts through the water
Like a jet in the sky.
Leaving only a faint trail behind
It searches for its next victim.
A lone frog splashes in the waves.
The noise can be heard from miles away.

A ribbet, and a failed escape.
The snake devours it whole.
The only thing that the snake leaves behind
Are the stars overhead
And the water below.

Courtney Congdon, Grade 8
Paw Paw Middle School, MI

Briana

B is for beloved, priceless and dear
R is for refreshing, a heart that's sincere
I is for innocent, Beauty so rare
A is for appealing, without compare
N is for nice, a beautiful soul made from gold
A is for angel, a gift from above
Briana, so precious and loved

Briana Osterman, Grade 8
Fairview Charter School, WI

The Path

It begins outside the cherry stained wood
The doors that seal a flying magic
The cage, to a raging life on a path.
The tight vestibule
Where colored chaos meets a dull silence.
Center stage
Captures the eyes of the interested artists
This is the path
Of the theater impact
The path that gives way toward gifts
And brings forth emotion,
All through performing
Back behind the curtains
Shields the secrets
Of talents forming
This land grasps the work of human beings,
And unlocks a path
I surrender a second to reflect
On the footprints created on this path
Not long do I linger, for the theater only restrains limited life.

Kendall Kotcher, Grade 9
Clarkston Jr High School, MI

Pantomime-in-a-Box

I tightly clutch onto lace curtain,
Refuse to end up 6-feet below,
Patch of Kentucky bluegrass,
Keeping me safe from rain that seeps,
Into earthen cracks above my cardboard box.
My smile eroded with the compost,
Made the grass green, the days short and sweet.
The air has evaporated as I gasp for oxygen.
Asphyxiated by reality and comforted by illusions.
Ears cannot hear my cries for help as I scratch on the box,
My name, I cannot remember.
I remain homeless, nonexistent,
Guilty, till I finally decompose.
Forever exiled and confined to this place,
Not even God can save my soul,
He mocks my attempts to break the latch.

Mariah Neuhauser, Grade 9
Detroit Lakes High School, MN

Triangular Zebra

Looks like a triangle from above,
It is highest at the tip,
Gently slopes downward
Toward broken boarders,
You can scoop up water in its hand.

Its color is sandy,
The outside is striped like a zebra
While inside is a pane of glass,
A smooth sand dune,
Hold it up to see rain streaming down a window
Or tears down its face

McKenna Heintz, Grade 8
Chippewa Falls Middle School, WI

Wrestling

Wrestling is a hard sport
Wrestling takes passion
Wrestling takes and gives pride
Wrestling can make a person famous or not

Walking out on the mat
Crouching down
The referee blows the whistle
You win in ten seconds

You watch your match
See what you can improve on
Work harder on
Never give up

Tim Krueger, Grade 7
Springfield School, MN

Unwanted Information

The deserted room's walls
Bulged out at me.
I shouldn't have entered.

A journal's treasures lay open,
Giggles could be heard,
And then a wet smudge glints.
I shouldn't have entered.

My mind grew blank,
The fish ceased all movement,
The ticking clock fell silent.
My skeleton comprehends no emotions,
No aggressive pain.

Reluctantly I returned to find it waiting.
The sturdy door-frame helped me up,
And the door slowly closed behind me.
I shouldn't have entered.
I had no grasp of the right way to feel,
The right way to act.
I simply walked on,
With a fake grin plastered,
Hiding my knowledge.

Erin Gray, Grade 9
Clarkston Jr High School, MI

The 1960s

When I took the first leap on the moon,
The world watched in awe,
The TVs all in tune,
The history that they saw.

The world watched in awe,
The war in Vietnam raged on,
The dreams that wished to reach,
The peace yet to be drawn.

The war in Vietnam raged on,
The TVs all in tune,
The peace yet to be drawn,
When I took the first leap on the moon.

Jessica Chan, Grade 8
West Suburban Christian Academy, WI

Wonderful Noises

Up north is what I love
Snap, crackle, pop
Goes the fire
Waves wash wonderful
Memories into my mind
The trees swish in the back of our cabin
Birds singing
Wonderful songs

Becca Ronsman, Grade 7
Luxemburg-Casco Middle School, WI

Ode to My Hockey Stick

This is my hockey stick
Not much right
It is war-torn from past hockey games
Yet it still helps me, and is the best
The weight of it is as light as a feather
The length is as perfect as the writing on a typewriter
The chipped paint
The worn-out hockey tape
The curved blade that makes slap-shots with the flick of the wrist

Jon Watkins, Grade 7
Assumption BVM School, MI

Trust

Trust is something we all want or contain
Although sometimes it can drive us all insane
You don't know who to trust when someone broke the trust once
And that person must face such pain
When the trust gets rough and there's nobody there
Things around you give you a scare
You want to dream a better dream but you still scream
And you want to find trust but where?
Trust is when someone listens and stays
Not someone who counts the days
When they want your voice to end but then they pretend
That they are there always
Trust is when someone makes you feel fine
Not when someone would sit there and lie
Not when you feel your worst or when it really hurts
To have someone that's really close by
You'll feel trust when the moment is right
So don't feel bad and hold on tight
You can close your eyes but to your surprise
Trust won't go down without a fight

Ariel Jackson, Grade 7
Manistee Middle School, MI

Washington DC

The first sight — magnificent Washington monument, so tall and lean
The buildings were 10 times the size of Whitehall's, such a scene

Lincoln and Roosevelt's monuments lined with cherry blossom trees
National Cathedral's huge structure just as far as the eye can see

Memorials of Vietnam Veterans and the World War 2
By the Kennedy Center is the Potomac River; it was a shimmering blue

The Arlington Cemetery's sign said: careful, the ground is hollow
I was so tired, the voices and footsteps were hard to follow

We saw the National Zoo and the Eternal Flame
DC definitely put any other city to shame

I loved the shiny baby hippo, and at Mount Vernon the soft paled-white sheep
When we finally got back I was grateful for the well-earned, pleasant dreamless sleep

Amber Kelley, Grade 7
Whitehall Jr High School, MI

CeCe

CeCe stands in the grooming stall,
Waiting patiently.
Looking for a treat in my hand
Like a spy on a mission.
Her eyes transfixed on me,
Asking me for a tasty treat.

Time to work
The lunge line is clipped snug
Under her chin.
She starts to walk out,
Slowly like a turtle crossing the road.
The crack of the whip sends her into motion,
Cantering as fast as lightning.
She throws herself into her work,
As if trying to please me.

As the day ends,
I tell her what a good girl she is.
She gives me a last look,
Telling me she loves me,
Before going into her stall for the night.

Samantha Flory, Grade 8
Paw Paw Middle School, MI

Chevy

I needed a truck, wanting it to be heavy,
I searched high and low and decided on a Chevy.
As I left the dealership and drove down the street,
I was so proud I sat high in the seat.

As I drove along I smelled a burnt odor,
so I lifted the hood and checked the motor.
It wasn't the motor it was the tranny,
"Oh great!" I thought it will shift like a granny.

As I drove to the garage I started to lose oil,
I started to panic; I was in a great toil.
I found out it was the motor and started to cry,
I was so sad; would my new truck soon die?

Then the next week the bed started to rust,
that's when I knew I had lost all trust.
It started in the fenders and ate through the door,
I even noticed there were holes in the floor.

Bumper to bumper rust continued to spread,
Even the tires had lost all their tread.
Then one day I got mad and kicked that V8 head;
I kicked it so hard my toe turned red.

Colton Havey, Grade 7
Abundant Life Christian School, WI

Forbidden Worlds

It's just that some things that cannot occur at most
Yes, I know, I was in love with a ghost
The two worlds of living and dead
Were sewn together like needle and thread
You see it's the choices that make us who we are
Choose the wrong path, and you will stray far
But with this choice, there was another
How about you, my innocent lover?
I listen carefully, to your sweet voice
I cry sadly as *you* make my *choice*
I knew this was the right selection, this was fate
Still I knew that, you, I could never hate
I open my hand for you to hold
You back away, the air filling, cold
You open your arms and give me your smile
As you already know, it's off by a mile
This eternity wasn't meant for us
We hold on tighter, and then, part as we must
You take my hand, flying away, and you pull
While doing that, you haul away —
My soul

Ka Vue, Grade 8
South Middle School, WI

Clouds

Clouds come in soft
Like the sound of a bird gliding through the air
Sitting there quietly just waiting
Sometimes even crying
Throwing its tear drops at the earth
Up in the sky the clouds quietly scamper away

Jake Hoskins, Grade 7
West Suburban Christian Academy, WI

Bashful Blue

Blue is the color of the ocean,
so peaceful and stress-free.
When I swim in it, it relaxes me.

Blue is the color of the sky,
so big and wide.
It would be really hard to hide.

Blue is the color of beads,
so hard and hollow.
It will hurt if you should swallow.

Blue is the color of a Popsicle,
so sweet and sticky.
When you drop them in the sand they taste so icky.

Blue is the color of blueberries,
so squishy and sweet.
They are my favorite treat.

Shannon Dawley, Grade 8
Wheatland Center Elementary School, WI

I Do Not Understand…

I do not understand…
Why people are made fun of for their race and qualities.
Why there is violence.
Why children are abused.

I really don't understand…
How some people don't believe in God.
Why mothers-to-be have abortions.
Why some prayers aren't answered.

What I understand most is…
That Jesus was sent to this Earth to save us because God loves everyone.
God wants you to be in Heaven with him, but it is up to YOU to do what is right and get there.

Andrea Patterson, Grade 8
St Mary's School, WI

Friendship

Our day of meeting was interesting enough,
Learning likes and dislikes and all our other stuff
Days of us laughing and joking around
Figuring out which one of us was the biggest clown
Meeting up to do fun things around town,
Supporting each other, when we are feeling down,
Best friends I've gained throughout the years of my life
Taylor, Kristen and Cindy…BFF's for our lives
Going here and there, riding bikes everywhere
Always knowing, no matter what, we all really care
Sometimes we have our problems, not getting along
So we get together, and sing some happy songs
Having fun jumping around on the trampoline
Our smiling faces…so far to be seen
Getting on the computer on Facebook and G-mail talking that way, keeping in touch so our friendship will stay
These friends I've met at this age that I am, I will cherish to keep for as long as I can.
My friends are important to me, that I know
And I hope throughout the years it will continue to grow.
Everyone needs friendship to survive day by day
I feel very blessed that my friends came my way.
Thanks for all the help friends, you really are true friends.

Kelsie Street, Grade 7
Cedar Springs Middle School, MI

Summer Days

Those summer days, where everyone plays.
There is no school, no! That would be cruel.
Where my friend Thomas and I would do things, until summer was over and it was the spring
Some days I look back then, I wish that I could do it again
I would be playing basketball at night, he would be playing his guitar all right
Waking up late would be just fine, staying up late would be divine
That is what makes summer, without the fun it would just be a bummer
The best thing to do during those hot days, is to jump in the pool and give out praise
But no matter how much you wish, school will be back in a swish
And you will be thinking back about that time, when the days went as smooth as chimes
Those days will never be the same, and that is a very deep shame
But all you need to remember, is that school does not last forever.

Ethan Lawler, Grade 9
Lakeview Christian Academy, MN

Emotion

Love feelings
Love is red like a garden of roses.
It tastes like the sweetest candy,
It smells as lovely as the sweetest perfume,
It looks like a colorful rainbow,
It sounds like birds whistling with the wind,
It feels like you're never alone.

Cara Barnes, Grade 9
Hartland High School, MI

Just Say No

A secret lies beneath my feet,
something I can't tell anyone.

Sometime so horrible,
that if I tell,
a friend will be lost.

I want him to stop,
say, "No."

If I tell,
I'm scared it will jeopardize our friendship.

I'm scared for him,
I know he will make the right choice,

sooner or later...

Paige Geis, Grade 7
Shakopee Area Catholic School, MN

When I Play Tennis

Like a bird, free, fast I run
I feel like a child learning
Exploring the green, white court
Once in a while

My racket rings with force when it counters the ball
Swish, tok, swish, tok — I feel the steady swings of my racket
My head clears
My body is at ease
When my side is clear
I feel glad, cool, confident

No matter how I swing or how much force,
When I deflect it
I always feel, glad, happy, proud

Through hot and cold days
Through sticky, salty, sweaty boring days

The time I felt good to play tennis
I couldn't feel my feet
I run, I hit, I run.

Xinxy Xiong, Grade 7
Ramsey Jr High School, MN

Prayer's Gifts

Prayer gives you wisdom and strength
Prayer gives me forgiveness
Prayer gives me thanks
Prayer gives me courage to push
Prayer gives love and care
Prayer stops violence
Prayer creates love in the Gesu community and help shine
And lets us grow as a community

Eric Brown, Grade 7
Gesu Catholic School, MI

Softball

Softball is my life
Passion and soul
It allows me to be myself
I'm very competitive
So watch out I play second
I pitch like you can't believe
Without it I wouldn't be me
Softball is the best it really gets me pumped
When people come to the games
They all holler and shout
When my team is up to bat
Everyone holds their breath
But deep down they know we won't be defeated
We score runs one by one
Until we're far in the lead
When it gets to be the final inning
We can all feel the tension
As the clock runs down to the last second
We know we got it, yes we won
Softball is the greatest
It's my number one

Kayla Vandermuse, Grade 7
Luxemburg-Casco Middle School, WI

Time

I control everything,
People call me a man,
They say that I am old.

The young watch me intently,
The old plea that I stay,
I am tracked by sands and gears,
I am the fastest thing alive.

No one can stop me,
Not one can interfere with my plans,
I prevent chaos and determine when we will end,
I am the father of all.

Dustin L. Klaas, Grade 8
Iowa-Grant Elementary-Middle School, WI

Bear

He was beautiful inside and out
With his big golden heart
And sunshiny soul
With his thick dark fur
And big brown eyes
He loved you no matter what
With all his heart
And all his soul
He didn't care what you looked like
How much you were paid
All you had to give him was love
And he was happy
Bear remember me and Jennifer?
We love you
Bear remember Mom and Dad?
They love you
Especially mom — you were hers
Bear I will remember you forever
Now I hope you're happy
Playing with Buddy

Justine Barnes, Grade 7
West Middle School, MI

The Dark Side

Black is a pit with the unknown in it,
Black is a mystery,
Black is a predator's friend,
Black sleeps in low areas,
Black is a damp prison,
Black is a night with no moon,
Black is nothing,
Black is space and evil,
Black is the end of time,
Black is fear

Sean Becher, Grade 7
St Joseph School, WI

Here and There

Neither here nor there,
I wish I could be everywhere.
Either place I choose,
I lose.

The choice was made for me.
I'll make the best out of it.
There is green everywhere I look,
Inside me too.
Green are the grass, the trees, the plants
That grow without much care.
Green are my dreams, my plans
And all I want to share.

Here and there.
Green grass grows everywhere.

Enzo Fantin-Yusta, Grade 8
West Hills Middle School, MI

Two Surfing Penguins

There once was a penguin named Will,
Who had a friend named Bill.
They liked to swim and surf,
Rather than walk on the cold, tundra turf.

One day they went out to swim,
And saw that the sky looked dim,
But they said, "Hey,"
"We can go swim and surf anyway!"

So they went out,
And swam about.
As the wind started to blow,
Bill said "We should really go."

"Let's keep surfing!" Will said,
But he was not thinking ahead.
When it started to thunder,
The penguins realized their blunder.

The waves became very rough
And the penguins found reaching land to be very tough.
Once they reached shore,
They knew that they would not make a mistake like that anymore.

Rachel Welch, Grade 7
St Roman School, WI

911

There was much bravery in 911
It was America's worst sight
There was a reign of terror
Over the heart of New York

The Twin Towers were blazing with smoke and fire
The brave firemen and police officers went in the towering inferno
I felt bad for the victims
The families that lost loved ones

The reckless terrorist act killed thousands
They did the unexpected
Early in the morning the break of day
People falling to their death was a sad sight

People running and screaming in shock
No one will forget the brave souls that risked their lives for others
Who saved many people out of the fiery trap
All the victims and loved ones will not be forgotten

Those brave men and women inspired me to save lives
They did their job and did it well
911 was America's worst day

Austin Liddell, Grade 8
Fairview Charter School, WI

So Is Life

Today, I feel like ocean blue —
free and unstoppable,
happy and welcoming,
beautiful and sparkling.
There is nothing I can't do.
Other days, I'm prison gray —
trapped and overworked,
gloomy and lifeless,
haggard and stressed.
I feel like a caged animal!
Sometimes I'm blue, and sometimes I'm gray.
It just depends on the kind of day.

Laura Paulson, Grade 9
Kettle Moraine High School, WI

The Ride

Life is just a roller coaster ride, riding on wheels
Rolling and rolling for a minute or two
Yet the man gets sick, and feels an empty feeling inside
Who gets dizzy and sorrowful
And steps away from the wheels.

Yet when the man hasn't fulfilled his dream
He looks around and sees one little particular scheme
He asks himself why he likes it so much
But saw a little gold heart inside
He thinks of his wife and stares down
He sees his big frown and pulls out his wallet

Winning it with all the money he has
He walks to the cemetery in pride.
Putting it on her grave,
As he wipes the tear away
And wishes he was with her now!

Kelsey Platz, Grade 7
Springfield School, MN

Football

Tiring practice,
All leads up for that special moment.
The feeling to gear up in uniform for a game,
Brings an adrenaline rush.
Then to step on the field,
Makes me anxious.
When that whistle blows,
I am in my own world.
All I can think about,
Is getting a sack.
And after that my mentality,
Is to Win, Win, Win!

Leonardo Gomez, Grade 8
Washington Middle School, WI

When I Look at You

When I look at u I c pain that I want 2 take away.
When I c u cry I want 2 cry 2.
When ur happy I'm happy.
Don't u c we r meant 2 b,
mind body and soul.
U mite not feel the same way.
But I don't care.
I'll wait 4 u thru night and day,
cloud and rain, until u come.
But if not I hope u find ur true luv.
Because I already have.

Jordan Lyons, Grade 8
Great Oaks Academy, MI

The Single Cry

The man saw the town
It was demolished to the ground
Not a thing was left in sight
Not a living thing to be found

He walked around the town
Burned down buildings surrounded him
Shivers went crawling down his spine
As he continued to search around the town

Then he came across an orphanage
He heard a small cry coming from inside
He walked inside and to his surprise
Was a small little boy crying in the corner

He talked to the boy and asked him what happened
His story was sad and brought a tear to his eye
And by the time the boy finished he started to bawl
The answer my friends is simple, just war

If people cannot unite in peace
Then what hope is there for a brighter tomorrow
If only we could come together as one
Then we could truly live a life worth living

Cody Baldry, Grade 8
New Auburn High School, WI

What If?

What if we are always in a war?
What if we run out of gas and oil?
What if our world gets over heated?
What if polar bears soon go extinct?
What if there are soon to be no more forests?
What if we use too much water?
What if we lose our house?
What if our grandchildren never see a panda bear?
What if we get overwhelmed with technology?
What if our world gets overpopulated?
What if we can't stop all this from happening?

Monica Miley, Grade 7
Saint Thomas More Catholic School, MN

Baseball

Baseball is a game of mind
The mound I stand behind
I wait for the pitch
My arms I quick switch
I stand ready for the ball
Swing, hit over the wall
My team cheers loud
I round the bases so proud
It's the last inning
We are winning
The pressure is on
We knew we already won
1, 2, 3 smack last hit
The ball lands in the mitt
In the end their butts were whipped
We had won the championship

Tricia Glinski, Grade 7
Luxemburg-Casco Middle School, WI

My Bowling

I rolled the big, black, bowling ball
Down the long narrow lane,
I am amazed all the pins fall.
I jump for joy and my ankle does sprain.

I find myself on the sideline,
My feelings furiously, flinging out.
I can only sit and whine.
While my team declines, I pout.

Harlan Ellsworth, Grade 7
Bristol Elementary School, WI

Snorkeling

As I float about in the waves
And the sun shines on my back,
I see coral in lots of caves
As for the fish there was no lack,

And the sun shines on my back
The humid air makes me sweat,
As for the fish there was no lack
Millions of them I would bet,

The humid air makes me sweat
Through my mask it's hard to breathe,
Millions of them I would bet
Back and forth the critters weave,

Through my mask it's hard to breathe
I see coral in many little caves
Back and forth the critters weave,
As I float about in the waves.

Caleb Lovell, Grade 8
West Suburban Christian Academy, WI

Old River

Old River tell me of your past.
Speak only the truth.
Who really was the first,
To see your magnificent beauty?
Have you ever seen a crime,
So horrible it caused you misery?
Old River tell me please,
Have things ever been this bad?
Have people ever been so desperate?
Old River tell me will things be
Okay once again?
Old River thank you for your time
But before I bid you a farewell
I have one more question.
Do we still have a chance to
Change the damage we have done
To our beautiful planet?

Stephanie Krus, Grade 7
Northland Pines Middle School, WI

Games

Sometimes the world is
just a game and we are all
just the game pieces.

Austin Schroeder, Grade 8
Washington School, WI

Chicago

Southside neighborhoods packed
tighter than a pack of meat
People sitting on their porches
enjoying the hot as fire July heat.

Cars flying down the street
fast as jets.
Kids running through sprinklers
ice cold water, clothes dripping wet.

Smiles large as the city itself
friendly and inviting.
Neighborhoods at night still bright
as day from all the city lighting.

Drive-bys happening at every corner
faster than you can blink.
Pollution heavy as smoke
choking, strangling really stinks.

People higher than the
Sears Tower from drugs.
Break-ins, robberies, shootings
from dangerous thugs.

Jonathan Rader, Grade 8
Washington Middle School, WI

Calvary

C hrist died for me
A mazing grace
L ove demonstrated
V ictory from Satan
A gift from God
R esurrected
Y our free gift.

Alissa Turner, Grade 7
Washtenaw Christian Academy, MI

Daylight Sleep

A place of wonder
Is revealed in minds
Of daytime slumber.
Changing images
Of letters and numbers
To amazing adventures.

Free from society
In another dimension
Waiting for the moment
Of an exciting conclusion,
But only to discover
That it's all just an illusion.

Dylan Goitz, Grade 7
Our Lady Star of the Sea School, MI

Darkness

You are alone
No one there
No one that loves you
No one that cares

You're sitting in the dark
Can't see anything
You yell out
No one hears

You're lost
No one can save you
No one is there
No one is coming

You start to cry
No one hears you
No one is with you
You're alone in the dark

You wish you had someone
To love, to care
But you're all alone
In the DARKNESS!!

Rachelle Wiard, Grade 7
Centreville Jr High School, MI

Life Is Full of Dreams

Life is full of dreams,
But dreams come and go,
Life stays for a long long time,
But dreams fade away,
Life is full of surprises,
But dreams just dissolve,
So don't hold onto just one dream,
Live life now, in the present, but not too fast.

Breanna Vanderhoof, Grade 9
Petoskey High School, MI

Washington

School is like a prison cell,
You can't get out of it.

It's really boring and there's
Too much snoring, which is too annoying.
The teachers are like police guards,

They're always looking over you
Waiting for what you do
They think you'll do something bad.
They are like your underwear
They're always on your tail.

Except for my teacher she's really cool
If I get an A.

Anthony Posada, Grade 8
Washington Middle School, WI

The Storm

Fluffy, floating swirl
Before the world, floating by
I'm the open sky.

Dark, gray clouds
A soft pit-pat upon the withered plain
I'm the gentle rain.

Icy, chilling breeze
To the eternal blackness forever pinned
I'm the bitter wind.

Brilliant white flash
Glare illuminating the blackest night
I'm the lightning strike.

Sharp, quick crash
Wave of booming thunder in its mightiest form
I'm the roaring storm.

A light in the heavens
After all's been said and done
I'm the morning sun.

Walker Lee, Grade 7
Saint Thomas More Catholic School, MN

The Day

Sun is rising on a newborn babe.
Wondrous light shining upon miracle of life.
Time eternal stretches ahead and
Opportunity abounds.

Bright noon-light grinding on working man.
Strength of light bright on the prime of humanity.
Time eternal stretches ahead and
Opportunity abounds.

Evening's dying light falling on withered woman.
Failing sun twines with failing life.
Time is short and
Opportunity is fading.

Ellen Abolt, Grade 8
Pilgrim Park Middle School, WI

Basketball

Basketball is my favorite sport.
I have the most fun when I am on the court.

The fun includes catching a pass, dribbling the ball.
Using my talents, playing hard, standing tall.

My team and I are always on the run.
Trying so hard to score points before the game is done.

The game goes on, as the fans can see.
Scrimmaging, scrambling, bumping a knee.

We hear a loud cheer, then an exciting sigh.
As my teammate scores a basket, jumping so high.

Another two points, we sure have a chance.
To win the game, and finish the dance.

Wow! What an amazing game!
I sure can't wait to have more of the same.

Eric Malecki, Grade 8
St Roman School, WI

School

People say school is lame.
But would they rather be a vegetable?
People take school for granted.
School can make options for later life.
Such as…
Jobs, money, houses, shiny cars.
I say "school is the gateway to the good life"
School is cool.

Carlos Peynetsa, Grade 7
Luxemburg-Casco Middle School, WI

Friend to Friend

All the times we've been together
All the times I spent with you
All the things we shared together
listening to me is the least you can do.
All the people you hurt in your life
me, your mom, your dad, and uncle,
aunt, cousin even your little sister
has a fright of you.
Why don't you stop?
What you're doing isn't cool.
Now since I have told you,
maybe now you'll get the clue.

Rakiya Veal, Grade 8
St Margaret Mary School, WI

God

Joy be to God,
Glory be to God,
Praise be to God.

We bow down to you,
And we praise Your name.

Come and rejoice over Him;
He rules forever;
He watches over us;
He has preserved our lives;
He has kept our feet from slipping;
He has tested us;
We will fulfill our vows to Him.
Now, let me tell you what He has done.
For many great things you will
Hear!

Revised Psalm 66
Katherine Ferge, Grade 7
Abundant Life Christian School, WI

Conflicting

Earth's way to argue
Rain, tornados, thunderstorms
Clear, when she is calm.

Kendall Dumas, Grade 8
Langston Hughes Academy, MI

Life Is Powerful

P ower
Is full **O** f
W inning
E xtreme
R oughness
F ull
U ntil
L ife is over.

Matthew Kowalis, Grade 7
Christ Child Academy, WI

Sorry Is as Sorry Does

It's a cool summer night.
Clink, clink go the pebbles as they hit my window.
I open my seaside window and see him standing there, at my window's edge.
He whispers in my ear, "Come down. I have something to tell you."
I tiptoe downstairs and out the back door.
He is there to meet me.
He murmurs, "First, can I have a dance, under this beautiful, starlit night?"
He takes my hand, in his and we dance the night away.
We lay in the dew-covered grass, silently looking up at the spectacular stars.
Life is so precious when I am with him.
He makes me feel like I am the only girl in the universe for him.
He whispers in my ear, "I love you so much but…
I have to leave you and this small town.
I'm sorry! I wish I could stay, but I can't."
Tears of pain run down my face as if I was a baby who lost its toy.
As he kisses me on the forehead…for the last time and walks away.
Never will I see my prince charming again.
I guess in this world, we are not meant to be.

Ashley Crowe, Grade 7
Cedar Springs Middle School, MI

Evening Cruise

The motor of the pontoon purrs like a hungry kitten across the water
The water is as smooth as glass
The trees surround the lake like a powerful army
The sky is like something out of a painting with all its beautiful colors
The loons are out singing their song in harmony like a grand opera
The sun slowly sets like a lantern running out of light
The sun disappears under the trees as if playing hide-and-go-seek
The campfires light up around the lake like many large candles
We return to the cabin like a pack of wolves returning to their cave

Dylan Jansen, Grade 7
Roosevelt Middle School, MN

The Old and the New

Youthful things are beautiful:
A tadpole in the water,
A newborn baby with his father,
A puppy and a kitten,
And the tiny places you can fit in.
Like a brand new song will make you fall to your knees,
The fresh fallen snow on the ground begs, "Santa, come please!"
A crush on a boy makes a girl feel smitten.
The warmth of the child's hand in a mitten.

And elderly things are beautiful:
The coliseum is a showplace.
Mona Lisa with her smiling face,
A granny sitting in her rocker,
And to be over 100 years old is quite a shocker.
The planets plunging around in space,
A hardy horse and carriage race,
Cooking with old Betty Crocker,
And an antique door with a wooden knocker.

Vanessa Fritsch, Grade 8
Pilgrim Park Middle School, WI

Showing Cattle

They're fancy all blown out and dry
Even better when they're fluffed up and not dyed
They're tame and ready to go
Even if the temp is 20 below

They may deceive you all full of hair
You never know, they may not make it to the fair.
They are spoiled, pampered and all
They just love to have a clean stall

They all are in a line
Their hair just shines
Watching is what we do
And sit and say "thank you"

We are strong and tough
Even though we may be small
I might look weak I might appear
That I can't handle, a big show steer

That is the life of showing cattle
And don't worry we all are still gentle

Allison VanDerWal, Grade 8
Springfield School, MN

Considerable Questions

Want to be good at a sport?
Leave it on the court.

Do you want to go to Stanford?
Control the Academic Standard.

Want to be the one who made it change?
Never limit your range.

Want to start a new revolution?
Find the next defying solution.

See the thing is you want to do it all,
But you never ever want to fall.

You want to be the very best?
But never allow any rest.

Want to construct every chapter?
But allow no laughter.

Want to reach the top shelf?
I'm, here to tell you…you can't do it by yourself.

Aaron DeWeerd, Grade 7
Allendale Middle School, MI

Tootsie

Tootsie is my cat,
She likes lying on our welcome mat.
My cat, she brings lots of cheer,
All day, she runs and acts like she cannot steer.
She is really fuzzy and also she's very cuddly,
And I will tell you what, she is my best buddy.
Tootsie zooms around chasing,
My other cat that's hissing.
She is a calico,
And likes to play with yo-yos.
I love my cat,
She is part of my habitat.
Tootsie is also sweet,
When she walks around my feet.
She is so loving,
And she likes to play with string.
When she finds a Polly Pocket shoe,
She grabs it and looks like she's playing Kung Fu!
Every night, Tootsie climbs in,
She purrs, purrs, purrs as I sleep with a grin.

Sheyanne Eliason, Grade 7
Northstar Middle School, WI

Sports

Sports are fun to play,
especially on a sunny day.
Don't be afraid if you hit it the wrong way,
golf is a game not everyone can play.
Golf can be frustrating if you don't hit the ball,
so then go play baseball.
Baseball is all about hitting homeruns,
hit the ball and you are sure to have fun!
If baseball isn't the sport for you maybe soccer is right!
All you have to do it kick the ball with all your might.
If you don't want to kick maybe you want to serve.
In volleyball you don't want the ball to curve.
Volley the ball and keep it off the ground.
Keep the ball going round and round!
Football is a very rough game,
the pros that play have a lot of fame.
I hope that there is a game here that is right for you,
pick a sport and grab a friend or two!

Danielle Strelecki, Grade 7
Kenosha School of Technology Enhanced Curriculum, WI

An Ode to My Nanna

Nanna.
A five-letter word that means the world to me
She is my hero, my inspiration.
She's my best friend and I love her with all my heart.
I love the way she laughs.
I love the way she cries.
If she were the moon, I'd be the stars.
No matter what I'll always love my Nanna.

Katie LaBarge, Grade 7
Assumption BVM School, MI

Bald Eagle

So wondrous and flying
without the slightest of ease
was the beautiful bald eagle
doing just as he pleased

With his bald, white, feathered head
and his illustrious, red, orange beak
he wore it so brilliantly
and he DID NOT look like a geek

It is our national symbol
and rightfully so
could another bird do it?
I would have to say NO.

Nathan Toenjes, Grade 7
Pilgrim Lutheran School, WI

Saturday's Storm

The clouds are strong
The wind is woefully weak
The rain pours
As the storm crashes in

The wind is fierce
Cold and harsh
As the storm crashes in
Outside my frightened window

Cold and harsh
Thunder roars
Outside my frightened window
Which now makes a creak

Ashley Tomaszewski, Grade 7
Manistee Middle School, MI

My First Trick

So there I was sitting on the lift
Thanking God for this gift
Thinking if I can land the trick
So here we go off the lift
My board touching the snow SLISSH
The snow slowly, silently, straight falling
Then brushing by my face
Zooming down the hill
Hearing the wind pass in my ears
Approaching the jump
Feeling like I'm going 100 mph
I'm going up the jump
My board leaves the jump
Now I'm airborne, I twist my body
See everything around me
Then the board hits the ground SWACK!
I am the gladdest person on Earth
I landed my 360!

Cody Mauthe, Grade 8
Seymour Middle School, WI

I Notice America Crying

There are some things no one knows
Some people conceal, so nothing shows
I notice the tears of the people without jobs
No way of supporting their family, yes, I hear the sobs
I pass the children with wetness sliding down their suffering cheeks
They wonder why Daddy's not here, I know what they seek
I have seen the violence and rape
I notice tears wishing for a new slate
I observe these discriminating by race
I hope they see my disappointed face
I watch the people struggle to get by
Taking it step by step, little by little, they die
I notice crime "going down"
Murder, stealing, I wish they could see my teary frown
I have felt the harsh sting of a cheater
I have witnessed the wrath of a beater
I take in the pregnant teen shed tears
No way of supporting their baby, so many fears
I detect the loss of trust
I listen to the wishes that someone must
Looks deceive, there is lying, dying, and America crying

Hattie Rhode, Grade 9
Clintonville High School, WI

There Is a Reason

I wake up every morning
I look out my window and I wonder why we have snow
I ponder about this season
Every time there is a snow storm I get more and more depressed
The snow just keeps on coming down
I dream of what it is like in the summer
How the beauty of the grass and the bright sun bringing warmth
Then I think of the beauty of the white snow that lies upon the ground
Why does God have Snow?
Is it because He wants to show us His creativity?
Whatever the reason is thank God
Thank God for everything that He has given you
Even though something looks bad there is always a purpose for that something

Jamie Seidel, Grade 9
Lakeview Christian Academy, MN

I Am

I am just another fish, in a tank, waiting to be fed.
I am just another book, in its binding, waiting to be read.
I am just another stone, on the ground, waiting to be thrown.
I am just another seed, from a flower, waiting to be grown.
I am just another voice, in the dark, waiting to be heard.
I am just another question, in the night, waiting to be answered.
I am just another teddy bear, sitting on a shelf, waiting to be hugged.
I am just another girl, all alone in the world, waiting to be loved.

Rachel Morgenstern, Grade 8
Oakview Middle School, MI

Nature

The trees spread their arms
They stretch out to touch the blue of the sky
They let themselves sway in the breeze
And bathe in the sun's golden rays.

When the sky goes to sleep
It folds a blanket of dark over the land
The trees stop swaying for the day
And all is peaceful throughout the night.

When the sun appears again
The rain clouds come
And they cleanse the land.

Logan Micek, Grade 7
Roosevelt Middle School, MN

My Pocket Watch

From a time in the past
You have been forgotten
You were used so much
But now you're no longer in anyone's pocket

Now it is so complicated
Stop watches and digital time
All those buttons, so hard to set
Attached to the wrist

Now you are so unique
You're great because you are simple

Adam Stember, Grade 7
Robert Kupper Learning Center, WI

Roses of a Valentine

Love is a red rose.
Let it grow.
Nurture it,
feed it,
give it sunlight that is your heart.
Leave it in the soil that is your bond.
When it blooms,
it's red,
breathtaking,
beautiful.
The roots will only tie you together,
never to be harmed.
For when you cut a rose,
it will slowly wither,
left to rot at the bottom of the trash can,
on the rainy day after Valentine's.
The rain pounds against the window,
while the roses lay helpless listening to the tears fall.
They fall limply, and say one simple wish.
We wish it was the 14th,
or a day just as joyous as that.

Tracy Pham, Grade 7
Valley View Middle School, MN

Civil War

In every school across the land,
There is one group who stands above.
With the coolest friends,
The "in"-ist clothes.
Everybody wants to be them.
But there, on the sidelines,
Watching, waiting,
Are the others, displaced by the elite few.
The ones who always ace the tests,
Who always stand below the rest.
Society has separated them under one flag:
Red, white, and blue.
A silent struggle,
A Civil War
Between those high, and hip, and cool
And those below just trying to make it through
These tough and difficult times,
When the brains and beauty collide,
And everyone must choose
A side.

Amanda Roberts, Grade 9
Montgomery-Lonsdale High School, MN

My Nightmare

I sit alone in this dark, cold room,
when all of a sudden I hear a loud
BOOM!

I went to the window so close and so near,
I glanced outside it was crystal and clear.

"What was that?" I said in my mind.
When I felt a tap from behind.

I turned around no one was there.
"What's going on?!" I said in a scare.

I went to my bed to rest my head,
when I heard a knock on my door.
How could it be, and what was it for?

I walked to my entrance, as the floorboards creak.
I heard my blood, it went leak, leak, leak.

I twisted the knob as quiet as a mouse,
I felt my room was a haunted house.

When I opened my door…
Boo!!!!!

Madeline Herbold, Grade 7
Valley View Middle School, MN

Nature

What a sight what a view
The sky is so blue
The river has a gentle flow
The sun gives off a perfect glow
The animals go passing by
The trees look so big in the sky
Fish swim through the stream
In this nothing is mean
I see the grass nice and tall
There can't be a wolf there at all
The light has gone and went away
I will come back another day
I say goodbye to all the things
I say goodbye to all the things

Alex Suprise, Grade 7
St Roman School, WI

The Cat

Once there's no one around,
Nobody to implore,
Slowly peeks a small head,
From the east corridor.

Finally, feeling full of power,
Like the noon sun in the day,
She gains enough courage,
And enters the hallway.

Into the main room,
Running stealthy and vein.
She slickly glides
Like a small airplane.

She's reached her destination.
Though there's no toy to tug.
No yarn or ball to play with,
Just her and a patterned rug.

Rolling on the carpet,
Creating friction with her fur,
A tiny kitten smile,
And she lets out a prrr.

Chloe Olson, Grade 8
Pilgrim Park Middle School, WI

Guardian Angel

When you lose someone close to you
You know it hurts inside.
You have that big gap inside
That is waiting to be filled,
But nothing anyone says or does
Will fill the gap of someone you love!

Heather Schulner, Grade 7
Northstar Middle School, WI

A Gift

The storm subsides.
Left is a blanket,
Fresh, white, pure,
Diamonds, glittering, shining,
A new morning, a new day,
A first step,
An imprint left,
Step, step, step
Right, left, right,
Treading in a shallow sea.

A hand,
A mass of jewels,
Flying, soaring,
Drifting, falling,
Down, down,
Into Wonderland.
Wide eyes,
A smile bright,
At the shower of love,
From the sky above.

Lily Chen, Grade 9
Troy High School, MI

Winter

Winter is chilly.
It is also very cold.
I love this season.

Zack Kujawa, Grade 7
Washington School, WI

School (Drama)

Do you see that girl?
She thinks she's cool
She walks around
Like she owns the school

I do good and I read books
I don't know why people don't look
I want to be fun
I want to be the "one"
Can't other people shine?
Not her group, but mine
She has lots of friends
But watch who is there in the end
Best friends for life
Stay true and tight

Do you see that girl?
She is super cool
She walks around
And she owns the school

Haley Melby, Grade 8
Adams Friendship Middle School, WI

I Am Me

Today I'm who I want to be
Just me, a girl so strong and free
Don't judge me by my skin or sound
I'm only a normal human being
The words I say are from the heart
For I mean what I say
It may not turn out right sometimes
But people make mistakes
I've got my life ahead of me
I have so much to do
I'm hanging on tightly
With a positive attitude.

Casey Wing, Grade 7
Central Middle School, MI

July

July, July, July
sweet July
you are uncle Sam's birthday
how I like your fireworks in the air, and
the beating sun on my back
how I like the color of your illuminated
sky of red, white, and blue on a special
4th of July day
Sweet July.

Aaron Wilson, Grade 7
Shakopee Area Catholic School, MN

Dog/Cat

Dog
Big, hairy
Cuddling, caring, barking
Strong, helpful, dumb, furry
Clawing, killing, cuddling
Evil, dangerous
Cat

Jose Acosta, Grade 7
Edison Middle School, WI

Candy Man

Popcorn on my nose
Sprinkles on my toes
I'm a yummy snack
I got chocolate on my back
I've got licorice for my hair
Lollipops are what I wear
I've got marshmallow shoes
I work for that Willy Wonka dude
This isn't what I choose
It's just who I am
I'm thinking you have guessed
I'm the candy man

Paige Matteson, Grade 8
Spring Hill School, WI

Achieve

Today's your day! Thank God for it.
You have awakened to do something in the world
To help someone get through their day
You are an amazing human being
A wonderful lively young lady
Ready to take on the world
Nothing can stop you now. You're on a roll.
You are an amazing human being
A wonderful lively young lady
Your life comes from you
What you choose, choose wisely
Make good great decisions
The world is yours!
Who you will be,
What you will do,
How you will feel,
Depends on this day.
This hour. Minute. Second.
This moment right now!
Start off strong and you will succeed
One step at a time, you will achieve!

Kristen Crain, Grade 9
West Bloomfield High School, MI

Night Time Symphony

Notes rise up from the pond below,
Falling sweetly on your ears.
The night takes on a life of its own;
Sweeping away all of your fears.

The soft breeze falls on your face,
Peeling off the sorrows and cares.
The fragrant wind leaves a trace,
In the heavy, dark night air.

The moon peers through the clouds below,
Turning the grass an eerie white.
Listening to what we do not know,
The creatures sing out in the night.

Whispering, the leaves do lend,
Their rustling throughout the trees.
Never bound by man nor pen,
But by the evening breeze.

This masterpiece is the night;
Put together it may be,
Beautiful, your escape,
A night time symphony.

Becky Meylor, Grade 9
Maranatha Baptist Academy, WI

Unfaithful

Away from each other, no talking at all,
They could hardly stand an order so tall.
For when apart, the girl was not true.
I think this is terrible, don't you?

Guilt gripped her as she walked through the door,
She thought of all the unfaithful things she had done before.
She looked in the mirror, thought how she hadn't been true,
I think she deserves this guilt, don't you?

You see, she had thrown his love away,
And replaced it with another's love each day.
She knew that she must turn away from this sin,
This adulterous life she had been living in.

She talked to him, confessed what she had done,
But when she told him, he started to run.
They both felt awful and mad at the other,
Then they tried to find one another.

Oh yes, they met. He met her on the altar.
She was being married to a man named Walter.
His eyes filled with tears as she said "I do."
I think this is extremely tragic, don't you?

Rae Lynn Niles, Grade 7
Bristol Elementary School, WI

Don't You Just Hate It When…

people wear their pants really high
when people wear really small clothes
when someone bumps you when you were writing
when you sit next to a right handed eater at lunch
when people say weird comebacks
when class seems to take forever
when people brag
when people eat in front of your face
when people get in your face
when someone argues till they get proven wrong
when your pen goes dead
when your marker bleeds through
when you get in trouble for something you didn't do
when you are so mad you just go to bed
Don't you just hate it when…

Kellen Bornbach, Grade 7
St Joseph School, WI

Night and Right

When dawn hits it's a new world
the moon sets a light tickle around my face
the silence makes my legs feel unusable
I look to my right nothing
I look to my left nothing
is right left or is left right
is my pink your red no one knows.

Jay Robinson, Grade 7
Valley View Middle School, MN

Blessed

To be blessed is to be loved
The world is a blessed place but it can be hard to find the love
Buried beneath the ruins of crime, famine, economic corruption, and war
We can see the affection, contentment, and peace in the life around us.

I am blessed
With everything I have
The good and the bad, the chances I take
The surprises I wait for, the life I live
The life I anticipate, and the dreams I live for

I am blessed
With the universe, with nature,
With life, with everything around me

Here in the world, the fire goes down and the sun rises
With the hope of shining and healing a universe filled with war, but overflowing with love.

Maddie Scanlan, Grade 8
Saint Thomas More Catholic School, MN

Randy Moss

Born on February 13, 1977 was Randy Moss. One day in football he would be the boss.
He attended Marshall University. Played football and did not earn a degree.
In 1998 Moss left Marshall for the NFL draft. The Minnesota Vikings were not getting the shaft.
Moss has a temper and hit a referee, with a bottle it showed his hostility.
Randy Moss is a father. He has four kids, a sister and a brother.
The rookie record is held by Randy Moss. He is the receiver boss.
Moss has the most receiving touchdowns as an NFL rookie at the age of 17. He is the best I have ever seen.
The 1000 yard receiving mark has been met. But a degree he did not get.
1998 Randy Moss was drafted to the Vikings. Here he would take a liking.
Likes to make touchdowns a lot. In 2007 Moss set a record with sixteen touchdowns in the first 10 games.
He is a great touchdown receiver. In football he is an achiever.
Went to the super bowl and lost at the last minute. Famous for Playing on the patriots.
Randy Moss is 31 years old and is still alive today. And will be at the first game on a Sunday.

Jordan Geister, Grade 7
Lakeview Middle School, MI

Family Is...

Family is as strong as steel, unbreakable.
Family is as sturdy as the walls of a well built house.
Family is always there like the sun and the moon; you might not see them but they're always there.
Family is as memorable as a photo album.
Family is as loving as a brand new puppy.
Family is as trusting as your closest friend you tell everything to.
Family is as wonderful as your first bite of chocolate.
Family is as caring as a nurse taking care of a sick patient.
Family is like a puzzle, it's made of many different pieces but they all fit together perfectly.
Family is like teddy-bears; they come in all shapes, sizes, and colors, but are all the same in some way.
Family is like a child's blanket, always making you feel safe and secure.
Family is like a rainbow, made up of many different colors.
Family is like a basketball team, you win some, you lose some but you always have each other.
Family is like a band, you need more than just one person to make great music.
Family is like the seams of a shirt, holding each other together.
Family is like dominos, if one falls they all fall.

Emily Leisgang, Grade 8
Seymour Middle School, WI

When You Look at Me

When you look at me, I'm not who you think.
When you look at me, you can't see I'm real.
When you look at me, you don't know how I feel.
When you look at me, you just see a face.
When you look at me, you say I'm a disgrace.
When you look at me, you don't see inside.
When you look at me, I'm not going to hide.
When you look at me, you just can't see.
When you look at me, I don't care.
Cause I know who I am and I will always be there.

Sabrina Mary Marie Schlichting, Grade 7
Lincoln High School, MN

Beyond Space

The sky is a wonderful thing
It is the king
There are birds that will fly
Dreams that cannot die
Cannot become deceased
A place where imagination will increase

Space is the slate black place beyond the sky
The place were humans can die
It is a dark abyss
With an evil kiss
To any one that dare to challenge it
Although it grasps beauty beyond imagination
But what is beyond space

Beyond space no one knows
Is it a place that is great or a place to hate
Should we care or just not dare
What is beyond final frontier

Bradley Barnes, Grade 8
Washington Middle School, WI

Rain, Rain

I can hear the rain falling down from the sky,
watering the town.

The rain brings everything to life,
while people stop and listen to the sounds.

Little children out at recess giggle while they splash,
because to them, life is about learning to dance in the rain.

The blue birds in the street
bathe in the bubbling puddles in the road.

While the golden flowers gleam and glisten,
the town all stops to listen.

I can hear the rain falling down,
splish, splash.

Savannah Kuehn, Grade 7
Lombardi Middle School, WI

A Tree

I am strong and tall.
I give shade to all.
When children climb up me,
I will not let them fall.

I bring homes to many creatures,
Birds in my branches and,
Squirrels in my trunk.

In the fall my leaves are shed,
Children dance among them.

In the winter my branches turn to ice.
People smile when they see.

In the spring my blossoms bloom.
Ladies remember years ago.

In the summer it starts over.
Children play,
Animals rest,
And it goes on forever.

Tricia Boeve, Grade 7
Hudsonville Christian Middle School, MI

Footprints

Without conscious knowledge
You leave me behind
Stranded on the ground
Waiting for when you need me

I, your footprints, will always be here
Though I pray you look back
I know that you won't

You focus on the future
And those that are not
Get left behind without a single glance
Like me, your footprints

In a land of tomorrows
What good do I, your footprints, do
If I only remind you of hardships

But if you ever lose your way
Just remember I am here
Not to guide your way
But to remind you of where you've been
And to warn you of who you could become

Shannon Brisse, Grade 9
Clarkston Jr High School, MI

The Future

Will we be ruled
By little green men
Or live in space
On giant stations

The future is scary
No one knows
If we'll be around
For as long as we hope

Giant robots
Flying saucers
Bio suits
High speed racing

Artificial forests
No ozone layer
People dead
Evil rise

No matter what
The future may bring
Know that every new day
Is yesterday's future

Andrew Harder, Grade 7
South Middle School, WI

My Mom

My mom is good at art
She is also very smart
And has a big heart.

My mom is cooler than everyone
She also is a lot of fun
I would take her over anyone!

Jacquelyn Schwark, Grade 7
St John Lutheran School, MI

The Thunder Storm

A flash of lightning
A roll of thunder
A gust of wind
The pitter patter of rain
The sky is dark
No sun
No moon
No stars
A flash
A roll
A gust
The pitter patter of rain
The terrifying noises of a storm,
Yet so quiet
And I am safe

Mariah Kromanaker, Grade 7
Abundant Life Christian School, WI

Spring

You feel the wind blow on your face
Birds have come back from their winter vacation
You can see little specks of green bursting through the hard soil
The trees are springing to life with the many colors of the rainbow
Kids are awaking from their physical hibernation
You hear shouts and laughter outside
You hear splashing and buzzing from the bees hard at work
You can see the enjoyment and happiness on every creature's face
Like the start of creation everything is lit up with life
You see a whole different world that you haven't seen in the last few months
God created the world to see what you are seeing now
Coldness turns to warmness
Love and care replacing the grumpy and lazy
You know that spring is here

Cris Avila-Lopez, Grade 8
St Roman School, WI

I Am

I am proud to be Mexican
I wonder what will happen when God will get really mad at the world
I hear night and day, children laughing and playing with each other
I see my future as a great veterinarian
I want to improve my work and grades in school
I am going to stay organized with my homework

I pretend that I'm a princess in a magical kingdom
I feel that God is always with me, in my heart
I touch all kinds of stuff when I am curious
I worry about my and my family's bad habits
I cry when I see things that scare me or romantic movies
I am a girl who loves animals and cares about the earth

I understand people that are upset about things that happened in their future
I say good stuff to make others feel better
I dream that the war will end and there will be peace everywhere
I try to cheer people up when their down in the dumps
I hope for a better world that there will be no global warming
I am the oldest in my family and will do whatever it tacks to provide for my family

Nina Hernandez, Grade 7
St Andrew's School, MI

Stop Before It's too Late*

Why, why are we doing this?
For what is happening, we should begin to dig graves as deep as oceans,
We fight, and fight back with guns, and explosives,
No one will ever grin of this horrifying horror,
People think, and say this is an untrue matter,
Innocents from Iraq and America are dying in inexplicable ways,
They will never get the chance to live their lives,
Complete their dreams,
And reach for the stars,
Also, remember what we lost and who we lost in the world wars; the Holocaust,
If we don't learn from our mistakes we are in danger of repeating them!

Taylor Wallis, Grade 8
West Middle School, MI
**Dedicated to my father.*

The Flowers

The flowers grow in the middle of
The field where only grass would grow,
Although it might take room where grass
Could grow, it brings many other things.

The flowers bring more color to the field
The orange makes them stand out,
But shows their pride and confidence,
In themselves, to the greater majority.

Eventually the seeds from these first flowers,
Will become two then four and eight.
The grass will then have a new neighbor
That will make both their home
Beautiful and colorful.

The grass and the flowers will then
Share the water and soil.
This cooperation is the only choice
For both or they will both not thrive.

To the other fields of grass,
It could show that the other fields could thrive
And be ready for their eventual change.

Zachary Angel, Grade 9
Clarkston Jr High School, MI

One Last Time

The warm air envelops me
In the smell of summer
Its gentle arms hugging me
The light of the sun becomes dimmer and
Out in the distance, a light far across the green fields
With their neat little plaited rows
The fence could extend until forever
The light is suddenly coexisting with another
And then, in an instant, as the last flickering light of the sun
Dissolves into the rolling hills
The fields blossom with pinpoints of light,
Dancing, shimmering, flickering,
Sparkling as if glitter was poured on
Settling in the velvety grass,
As the breeze toys with my hair,
The sights and sounds of the night begin to materialize
The crickets with their symphonies,
From someplace, a cat meows,
And the fireflies, twinkling dazzlingly
In the warm summer sky,
One last time.

Jessica Moreno, Grade 9
Clarkston Jr High School, MI

Deepest Abyss

Fear is the deepest abyss
Fear is the shadow that's not yours
Fear is the scary person breaking down your door
Fear is the boogeyman under the bed
Fear is the person shooting over your head
Fear is the deepest abyss

Gabriel Arradondo, Grade 7
Valley View Middle School, MN

Snowy Night

Screech, screech, screech
The skis of the snowmobile
Like fingernails to the chalkboard
Sprinkling dust of gold

The trees around us shake and shiver
In the cold and bitter winter air
Of Two Harbors

My uncle tells me it's my turn
He hands me the reins
We take off at the speed of light

The snow falls out of the dark, deceiving sky
With no helmet
I have no worries I'm in control
And at that moment it hits me
I've found the place that I belong
Surrounded by life, love, and laughter.

Samantha Etienne, Grade 7
Ramsey Jr High School, MN

Morning

At early morning as day breaks
the sun greets the dew tipped trees
where birds sit and chirp
perched merrily upon the leaves.
The green covered tree bark
dried by the light's insistent gaze
plays home to many grateful creatures,
appreciating this everyday sight
they too join the bird's chorus,
determined to rouse the life covered land.
And as they sing a morning tune,
the rest of the world stirs.
They flutter and drift through
the chilly March breeze
to shake the sleep from their eyes.
The enormous green monsters that serve as a home
stretch to the yellow and bright sky.
And when the treetops touch the clouds,
to kiss the morning mist,
the birds they wish and hope and pray
every day was like this.

Jenna Herkness, Grade 9
Clarkston Jr High School, MI

Freedom

What is Freedom?
The Statue of Liberty
Liberty of doing what you want
Independence Day
Emancipation of the slaves
Power of acting without force
Quality of being free
Liberation from slavery
That is freedom

Alyssa Carnagie, Grade 7
St John Lutheran School, MI

The End of the Road

My journey has come to an end
I have no family or friends
So I have no one to ease my pain
My life is full of sinful stains
So my pain cannot gain
I have no memories
Of my family
So here I sit
Getting ready to quit
My life is like a road
That is not finished
But has been diminished
I have come to the end of the road.

Stephen Johnson, Grade 8
Spring Hill School, WI

Little Johnny Ned

Perched atop a lonely twelve stair
Stood an intrepid Johnny Ned
He dreamt to dream and dared to dare
That one step didn't like his head

Johnny jumped as high as he could
And landed in a crashing heap
His caring parents said he should
Look before he would take a leap

Little Ned started skating by
The time he left his mother's womb
By the time he was standing high
He had dug his very own tomb

He learned the back flip and front flip
Whatever others could not do
Every now and then take a trip
A skate park and some snicker-doos

Now has to be on life support
With a tube going down his neck
His train of thought was too short
Too bad his life is now a wreck

Luke McCloskey, Grade 9
Troy High School, MI

The Most Special Blanket

A friendship is like a blanket
It comforts you when you are sad, and no one else seems to understand.
There are stains from memories, to make you laugh or cry.
Rips and holes from those awful fights, which you wish never happened.
Sometimes we forget about old friends, or move on to new ones.
These friends are stored in boxes of memories.
And hopefully will come back out someday.
When the holes and rips outnumber the stains, the friendship struggles.
This friendship can't last, it's falling apart; like a loved blanket that is lost or forgotten.
Sometimes you wish you could find the stains underneath all the rips,
but it's impossible.
Maybe you've outgrown the friendship.
You've both changed too much and grown apart.
Even though there are no rips, it's lost.
Maybe your friend lives far away and you've lost touch,
like a never used blanket that you forget about.
Losing a friendship is hard; be thankful for the friends you have.

Megan Baker, Grade 7
Washington School, WI

Dead Like You

Light into dark,
Pride into vain,
optimism into negativity,
kisses turn into tears,
We never worried about what the better hearts had to say and,
when the world turned its back on you I was always there.
I swallowed your fears and promised you bliss
Memories of you will always be alive inside my heart,
even though you are now dead to me.
You tied my soul into a knot and got me to remit those memories
Though I can't change you I have to say,
even heaven will be hell without you.

Desirae Contreras, Grade 8
St Roman School, WI

A State of Bliss

A place where there are no troubles
A place where there is no war
A place where there is peace and unity
A place where everybody is accepted
And not divided by the boundaries society makes
By splitting certain individuals into social classes
Such as race, beliefs, wealth, and other things
That are judged by the prejudice and racist
A place where even the most immoral of souls can enter
And be purged by the holy aura around them
Where even animals can come in contact with humans without distrust
A place that is known as a state of bliss
But it is said, ignorance is bliss.

Charles Johnson, Grade 7
Gesu Catholic School, MI

Surroundings

On cool spring mornings,
The outdoors becomes my quiet place,
Where puffs of clouds are
Surrounded,
Surrounded by the powerful beams of sunlight,
Just peeking out,
The barren, tall trees reach up into the sky,
Knowing it can never be reached,
As the trunk continues downward into the soil
Surrounded
Surrounded by the limp yellow grass,
Covered with beads of dew that weights them down,
This is the place where I feel
Surrounded
By nothing.

Lea Tanton, Grade 9
Clarkston Jr High School, MI

Why?

I don't know what to do with you anymore.
I watched you walk out the door.

Sad as I was I didn't try to stop you.
And what do you repay me with?

You went back to your old ways.
But yet something changed.

Why?

I hate that question, but I'll have to hear you out.
Even if you shout.

Or perhaps I've been lied to again.
By one particular friend.

Truth or lie,
Can I let my faith die?

Ashlynn Cameron, Grade 7
Valley View Middle School, MN

Madison Madison Why Did You Have to Go?

Madison Madison why did you have to go
We didn't get a chance to play in the snow
Or say goodbye

Madison Madison now you're in the sky
I will always remember you the way you died
Madison Madison now you are free,
To live you life peacefully,
To not feel the pain and suffer every day

Madison Madison I will always remember you
The way you were

Morgen Koronka, Grade 8
Spring Hill School, WI

Basketball and the Beach

I start running,
I can feel the basketball rubbing on my hand,
The crowd is cheering,
The sound of the basketball beating on the ground,

The sweat rolls off my face,
I blink my eyes for only a second,

I'm standing on a beach,
I can feel the warm sand on my feet,
The sound of the ocean,
Everything is so calm for a moment,

I open my eyes,
I'm back in the game.

Megan Hammond, Grade 8
Adams Friendship Middle School, WI

Trudging

Trudging up the mountain towards the clear, blue sky
Gasping for fresh air, as the trees wave goodbye
These hiking packs are aching.
Our sore bodies are shaking.
But we keep on trudging like Mountain Demons.

We reach another bluff, more disappointment
Another thunderstorm comes, down the valley we went
Hail pelts our bodies, but we remain tough girls.
Some of the hair on our heads turns to puffy curls.
But we keep on trudging like Mountain Demons.

Finally, we spot the peak, glimmering in the sun's rays.
Patches of thick white snow that has blanketed for days.
We stumble past loose rocks, tripping along the way.
Our muscles tremble and strain, and our bodies will pay.
But we reach the top, trudging like Mountain Demons.

Chandler Warren, Grade 8
Grosse Pointe Academy, MI

Essay

Click, clack, smack,
I'm typing really fast.
Buzz, whirr, beep
Computer's working hard.
Copy, click, paste
Check out that pic!
File, save as …
Shoot, dang, rats!
I forgot to print my essay.

A.J. Lallensack, Grade 7
Elkhart Lake Elementary-Middle School, WI

War

This is it,
Don't get scared,
It will all be over soon…
I ducked behind a tree,
I squatted on one knee,
I took one eensy weensy peek.
The coast was clear,
I wiped away a tear,
Then moved to the next bunker.
I dove real quick,
Gave my reloader a click,
And aimed around to see.
No one…
I got up, quite clueless,
And looked around.
In a blink of an eye,
I was down.
I was hit in the chest,
But I did my best.
After all, it was only paint.

Charlie Erickson, Grade 8
Oak Grove Middle School, MN

My Brother

While skiing down a hill,
With an unseen ramp ahead,
Matthew went along,
Singing in his head.

He came upon the rise,
But was looking the other way,
Over it he went,
Wishing to see next day.

In a pile he landed,
Then slowly rose and grinned:
"That was really fun!
Let's do it again!"

Ellen Lively, Grade 8
Home School, MI

Hypocrisy

In a world full of hypocrisy,
The preachers are the sinners
And the doctors are diseased.
Your lies are my denial.
Your thoughts are my belief.
Your idea is my envy.
My heartbreak is betrayal.
Don't count on me if you're alone.
Don't count on me to be that shoulder.
Hypocrisy is my bloodshed.

Kimberly Martinez, Grade 8
West Middle School, MI

God's Creation

Outside.
usually green,
not yet…
snow melting,
almost gone…
birds chirping
I wish…
sun is out,
half of the time…
trees growing,
a little bit…
animals coming out of hibernation,
almost out…
God's creation,
Outside…

Mariah Lattery, Grade 7
Shakopee Area Catholic School, MN

Before the Bell

The sun tests the sky
Like a child in a cool lake
It sends cautious rays
Painting the clouds
As if a painter's brush
Messily blotted the sky
With red stripes
The miraculous pinks and cyan
Greeting the cool air
With a warm smile

It takes a dive

In mere moments
A resounding splash
And the world around
Is filled with color
And the warmth
Of the cautious sun

Conor Foley, Grade 9
Clarkston Jr High School, MI

Brother to Brother

In need of help every day
might never know what's coming
we always push away
never ever parting
the true bond between us
Is truly unbelievable
The help we share between us
May get us in trouble
but no matter what the problem
We always push on through

Ryan Hmielewski, Grade 8
Fairview Charter School, WI

Track

Running is very fun —
Especially in the sun.
Running keeps you fit —
And it doesn't take any wit.
When you get sore —
It's hard to run more.
But it will pay off in the end —
When you round the final bend.

Ethan Broman, Grade 9
Petoskey High School, MI

Life

You live for a reason.
You love for a reason.
You die for a reason.
Life is good sometimes.
It will have it's ups and
Downs, but oh well!
You can do a lot in a
Lifetime, but
You have to work for it.
You live for a reason.
You love for a reason.
You die for a reason.

Cheyanne Charpenter, Grade 7
Ramsey Jr High School, MN

Baseball

Baseball
Gives kids something to do
All summer long
At the ball park
America's pastime

Jesse Brown, Grade 7
Edison Middle School, WI

I Don't Understand

I don't understand
Why people fight
Why people call each other names
Why my friends fight over stupid things

But most of all
Why people are racists
Why people commit crimes
Why people start wars
Why people would want to go to war

What I understand most is
Why my family loves me
Why my friends like me
And why I pray to Jesus

Justin Paton, Grade 8
St John Lutheran School, MI

My Day

Beginning at six in the morning,
when I start the day with an alarm-clock warning.
I go to school when it's still dark,
where it is no walk in the park.
My first class is a French lesson,
where my English habits lessen.
Next is my government and civics class,
where learning about our government is a fast pass.
Following is my biology labs,
and everything is organized by tabs.
After biology comes math,
where it will affect my future path.
Soon after would be English and literature period,
there are many terms and meanings to learn like a myriad.
Ending with personal communication,
my favorite class of education.
Leaving to go home from school,
just to do more homework which is the rule.
Finishing the day at eleven at night,
sleeping until it's light.
My days are like this and forever I will be bliss.

Kelly Feng, Grade 9
Troy High School, MI

Mysteries of Life

My brother is a pickle, the pickle is my cat.
My cat's on top of Sister, who is, it seems, a hat.
The hat is filled with jelly, the jelly's really coats
The coats aren't coats at all, you see, but really, tiny boats.

The boats are really butter, floating in a flip-flop sea.
The waves keep getting bigger,'til they reach half-up a tree.
The tree is made of applesauce, the leaves are teddy bears.
The teddy bears aren't bears at all, they're really silverware.

The silverware ain't silver, I think it's made of rope.
Each strand of it is ten feet long, and some of it is soap.
The soap ain't nuthin but a cow, the cow's a giant mouse,
The mouse is stepping in the pond, the pond's really a house.

The house is made of bubble gum, the gum ain't gum it's trash,
The trash is just a soccer ball, the ball's a purple sash.
The purple sash is but a snake, the snake's a chocolate bar,
The chocolate bar is really birds, the birds are in a car.

The car is driving down a road, that really is a fiddle,
And now my friend, I'm asking you to figure out this riddle.
The answer is quite easy, just come and visit me.
It's my little brother's drawings. Just so you know, he's three!

Megan Mulder, Grade 9
Maranatha Baptist Academy, WI

Courageousness

Courageousness can be:
Gold like a lion's mane, rippling in the wind,
Hot as lava, bubbling furiously beneath my feet
Cold as Lake Michigan, in the middle of February,
Sounds like a trumpet — bold and strong
Tastes like a rich cup of dark, hot coffee,
Smells as sweet as icing
Looks as big as the Killer Whale,
Feels like a feather, smooth but strong
Moves like an eagle, gracefully,
Flying and soaring across the endless blue sky

Elizabeth Selbee, Grade 7
Manistee Middle School, MI

Stars

S hining, brightly up above watching our every move
T winkling, flashing, catching my eye
A ll around the only light in the moon lit sky
R adiantly glowing showing the midnight sky's every blemish
S parkling, like a glistening lake

Allison Chorey, Grade 7
Perry Middle School, MI

Shadow

There's this thing that's been following me
I don't know what it is
It always has one shape
But it doesn't have one size

It seems to hate cloudy days
And I never see it at night
But when the sun shines bright
It pops right into sight

My friends just point and laugh at me
My family thinks I'm strange
Everyone's calling me crazy
But I know I'm not insane

Elizabeth Groebner, Grade 7
Springfield School, MN

Life

Life has its ups and Downs
Life can make you Frown
Life is unexpected
Life is a Mystery
Life can be Misery
Life is Short
Life must be lived to the Fullest
Because
Tomorrow is a mystery
Yesterday is history
And today Is
Whatever you want it to be

Lucian Coutier, Grade 7
Valley View Middle School, MN

Two Eyes in the Back of Your Head

In the back of your head,
Two eyes are long from dead.
Though they don't look behind,
They see all from inside.

The two back eyes can speak,
Telling us what to seek.
Right shows us what we should,
While left shows us no good.

The two always dispute;
Dispute, but do not shoot
Right from wrong is a fight.
Champ isn't always right.

So, it is you to choose.
Who will win, who will lose?
And now you can know why
Conscience is double eyed.

Danny Paglia, Grade 8
Our Lady Star of the Sea School, MI

Into the Blue

The sky is like the sea
building and swelling over me
making everything fade to dark
but for me there's no ark
nothing to save me
and my only hope is
for the sky to see
me struggling through the night
in my long lasting fight
to find the strength
to make it to the light.

Keagan Potts, Grade 9
South View Middle School, MN

Speechless

Living through this tragedy
all because of you
understanding what you've done to me
is almost impossible
crushing my dreams
a joke
and I trusted you…

Lindsey McCarty, Grade 7
Richmond Middle School, MI

Poems

P eople telling you what to do
O ut of ideas
E veryone is yelling
M y mind is running low
S arah is confused

Sarah Olson, Grade 7
Northwood School, WI

Summer

The sun rises early in the morning,
Greeted by the chatter of the birds.
Days are filled with laughter and good times.
The sun radiates its warmth to children playing
And spending time with their families,
Awaiting the pleasure of eating ice-cream.
Summer is a chance for you to spend time with your friends and family,
Whether you are outside doing yard work,
Or taking a walk on the trail.
Summer is enjoyed by most.
Though the mosquitoes annoy,
And the early sunrise wakes you up,
It's all worth it.
Because summer is the best season of them all.

Jenn Bell, Grade 7
North Rockford Middle School, MI

Last Fall

Last fall on a cold September;
I was in the woods and this is what I remember.

I was waiting in my deer stand when I heard the breaking of a twig;
I knew it was a deer, I just hoped it was big.

When I saw it on my bait pile;
I couldn't help but smile.

My body went tense;
The feeling of joy became immense.

My heart raced like a hummingbird's wings;
I drew back slowly to silence the strings.

I put the deer in my sight;
I hoped my shot would be just right.

When I let go of my arrow aiming at the doe;
I knew my shot was a little bit low.

Crap! I was disappointed that I missed the deer;
But at least I would have a story for people to hear.

Hunter Effa, Grade 8
Seymour Middle School, WI

Sun Kisses

Trickling water over rocks makes my heart flutter.
Warm spring air calms me.
Green grass, chirping birds, ravishing fish.
I know everyone is escaping the winter jail to enchanting spring air.
Laying in the dancing grass, the sun reaches down and kisses my soft skin.
Nothing seems to matter when the snow flows into spring rivers.
The thoughts, actions, and silent words of nature infuse me.
With grass as a bed and blooming flowers as a pillow.
I lay in a springtime dream.

Dayna Seymour, Grade 9
Clintonville High School, WI

That Girl I See

That girl I see in my eyes, she is not like others.
She is lovable in every way.
She loves everything with all her heart.
That girl I see in my eyes is fighting the disease she can't get rid of.
That disease is taking her very, very, very slowly.
She knows somebody is watching her every passing minute.
She knows not to try to be normal because everybody's different in one way or another.
That disease that can hurt her is not like others.
It can take her away.
That disease is hard to keep control of.
It's called Cystic Fibrosis.
I know that girl I see in my eyes, because that girl is me.

Kendra Smith, Grade 8
Bloomingdale Middle School, MI

Hold On

When my days are dark and are headed the wrong direction,
I should always know that I have someone there with me each step of the way.
They provide me a shoulder to shed tears on when my emotions are down.
They offer their own time to listen to my dilemma.
They embrace my head up high even though I feel like I have approached the end of the road.
Even though I have fallen numerous times they have told me to get right back up and try as many times as needed to succeed.
Yet, there is this presence of a voice inside my head telling me that I can't do it,
They are right by my side, like a guardian angel to chase away those voices I hear.
When I take one step backward they don't give it the name of failure,
They look at it like an opportunity to fix my mistakes.
When I feel like I am on my own and have no faith in anyone,
They are there to uplift my spirit.
When I feel like all the pressure is on my shoulders,
They offer to take it away from me.
When I fall, they are like a safety net waiting to catch me.
Even though there are mountains, they make me believe in myself.
They tell me to wonder of what it's like on the other side.
It may feel like you have lost it but "HOLD ON!"

Daisy Kabaka, Grade 7
Jackson Middle School, MN

Baseball

I wait all year long for baseball
When baseball comes I practice as hard as I can
I practice all through the fall, sometimes in the winter and I go to baseball camps in Minneapolis.

During games I feel like I'm in the right place
When games end I never want to leave the baseball diamond
When I get home from games I play baseball with my dad or my friends.

When I bat I pretend I'm taking all my anger out on the ball
When I am playing the infield I hope they hit the ball to me every time
When I pitch I feel as if I am the strongest player on the field.

I listen to everything my coaches say
If my coach tells me to work on something I practice until I get it right
During practices I play as hard as I can, but when games come I try to play even harder.

Dylan Wersal, Grade 7
Springfield School, MN

The Beach

The air was salty with a slight breeze.
The wind blowing across my face.
It felt good.
The joy of children laughing and playing in the sand.
The nonalcoholic pina colada with the little umbrella on the side sitting right in my hand.
The coldness felt good from the glass.
The sun hitting against my shoulders like a big bowl of fire.
The beach was beautiful.
It had shells and crabs with big claws bigger than their heads.
The ocean was cold when you first step in.
But it gets warmer after a while.
The ocean was very salty.
When a wave hit your face, you made sure you closed your mouth.
The beach was beautiful and that's all I asked for.

Michelle Szymusiak, Grade 8
Spring Hill School, WI

The Future Is Bleak

I walk through my bedroom door slamming it on my way, glancing around my room I attempt to put the horrific day behind me, I examine my life through tear-filled eyes and stare at my reflection wondering why.

Beside my mirror are pictures of smiling faces that only anger me more, after I tear down the pictures of my family and friends, I start to become depressed, I begin to realize the future that awaits me is bleak and uninviting.

Eventually, I walk down the stairs and out the back door where the freezing rain hits me, I sprint to behind the shed letting the darkness surround me, I welcome the silence as peace finally fills me.

Emily Laws, Grade 7
Beer Middle School, MI

Midnight

I grow as the midnight grows darker, and the stars come out to play,
Only if I knew why the midnight slides and a new light comes out to shine and play.
I whine and I cry for the blue sky to fade away and the midnight comes to darken my day.
I may sound weird to only like the midnight days but until I die I will come out every midnight
To sing and play.

Raymond Lee Lanning III, Grade 7
Manistee Middle School, MI

Never Again

You were once mine but then you turned away.
We were once close but now so far away.
I don't know what I did or what I said to make you feel that way.
Now you have moved away and I say "I miss you" I miss you in so many ways.
In the end I realized that my life's not a fairy tale and you were mine but now you're gone.
I have moved on and you should too!

Darian Smith, Grade 8
Adams Friendship Middle School, WI

Love

Love is not just caring deeply about someone,
Love is a cry for help from a lonely person letting their heart guide and not their brains,
Love is the emotional pull that helps you find your other half.
Love is a broken heart waiting to be healed and lifted from its sorrow.
Love is a gift from God that we deny,
Love, the fire that never stops burning.

Aisha Silvers, Grade 7
Valley View Middle School, MN

To My Mommy

Mommy you used to do bad things,
And every day and night I would pray to God
To make you better like an angel with wings,
Then the day came when you made up your mind
And you put all the drugs and drinks behind,
Mommy I love you so much,
I wish I could hug you a bunch,
Sometimes when I cry I wish you were there,
So that way you could wipe away my tears,
Today is your birthday Mom,
And so today you are the bomb,
I wrote this poem that came from my heart,
And I just hate that we live far apart,
You are my mother so sweet so true,
And I am your daughter who truly loves you!!!

Maria Reyes, Grade 9
Fennville High School, MI

Wishes

I wish I had an Escalade
I wish I had a sister
I wish I had a best friend
I wish I had a pair of green eyes
I wish I had a mansion
I wish I had a nice brother
I wish I had a smarter brain
I wish I had straight A's
I wish I had a toy store
I wish I had a special talent
I wish I had a fairy godmother
  to just poof down
  from the sky
I just wish all my wishes would come true.

Alicia Carter, Grade 8
Anderson Middle School, MI

Let Me Never Become...

Let me never become someone who hates.
Never to love.
Never to smile.
Never to sing.
And it's all because of hurt.

Let me never become someone who doesn't care.
Never to listen.
Never to know.
Never to share.
And it's all because of conceitedness.

Let me never become someone who shuts out the world.
Never to learn.
Never to laugh.
Never to live.
And it's all because of fear.

Alexandria Gates, Grade 8
St Mary's School, WI

Key to Love

I say to you
Love is so true
Thru love, you can find anything
Maybe even a song you can sing
But love can't be found without one thing
Friendship is where it starts
You could probably find that with your smarts
But you can't go on without love
But to find love
You mustn't be lonely
You can already see
What you must not be
You need love in your life
But without saying a word
To the one whom you want to speak
You will never find what you want to seek
You see,
The key to love is friendship
No matter how many times you say you don't have anybody
I can assure to you,
That you've always got me

Rebecca Nguyen, Grade 7
St. John the Baptist School, MN

Here Is Where...

Here is where...
I can be free
Sing a sweet melody
Yell my barbaric "YAWP!"
Hide from the truth

Here is where...
I can live
Paint the wind
Piece the clouds together
Run with my shadow

Here is where...
I can be me
Learn to breathe
Fly through the trees
Dream of Heaven

Here in reality...
You scream over my melody
Stomp on my shadow
Suffocate my throat
Bring me to Hell
And remind me of why I TRIED leaving...

Alexandria Grimme, Grade 9
New Auburn High School, WI

The Lighthouse

Through the mist I saw the light,
bright and eerie in the night.
Guiding boats from the rocks
safe and sound to the docks.

Standing as a sturdy wall,
towering over trees and all.
Cutting through the misty blanket
so the sailors would safely make it.

Sitting on a lonely bay,
Waiting for night to fold over day.
The keeper sees dusk coming,
so he climbs the tower humming.

He strikes a match on his finger,
watching as the flame does linger.
He puts the match to the wick,
his movements he must carefully pick.

Now the light is shining,
a sailor's silver lining.
The lighthouse memoirs here will stand,
always and for every man.

Quinn Colvin, Grade 7
St Thomas More Academy, MI

Intense Ride

The ATV is extreme.
The ride is amusing.
The dirt flying.
Cool air blowing in your face.
The tires spinning.
The bumpy trail.
Going so fast.
It's such a blast.
The goggles fogging up.
The shifting of the gears.
The dust you leave behind.
It's an intense ride!

Cody Wendt, Grade 7
Springfield School, MN

A Summer Night

A sweet summer weekend,
Lying on and smelling freshly cut grass
While staring at the glistening stars.
As the fire cracks beside me,
My friends and I laugh and talk
As the night rolls on.
And soon,
As the fire dies,
We go inside,
And say "Goodnight."

Josh Balcom, Grade 7
Assumption BVM School, MI

All We Remember

Flowers that smell tickle your nose
Sand that sticks between your toes
Being with your friends and pals
And shopping around with the gals

But the things you really remember are the ones that you want to forget
Like the death of a loved one and the pain of a heart break
Like the cruelties of divorce and the stress of growing older
Things that follow you through life are not always sugar, but spice

Still you hold your head up high
You say hello and goodbye
You put on a happy face
And smile toward the human race

And when it's time for you to part
You pledge an allegiance with your hand on your heart
You take your leave without a doubt
And salute to the ones that shut you out

You never forget what you had
Even though it may be bad
Though life is full of many things
Your journey to come is one fit for kings.

Sarah Stigall, Grade 8
Ionia Middle School, MI

Kids

People say that children play, from dawn to dusk, and day to day.
Not a care in the world, not today, and surrounded by friends they begin to say:
"That kid in the corner is all alone,
Why does he try to talk to us, while we roam?"
"Stay away, don't say a word,"
Says the leader of our pack to its herd.
"He doesn't fit with us, he's not our brother,
He'll be grouped, by others.
While even we, will play a part,
In the opposite of his start."

You paint me black, without my say
Not another hue, or even grey.
You pretend to know me, by my color
While you group me, with another.
So please stay and listen, what I say
From dawn to dusk, and day to day
While first impressions, shed away.
As time has told, beauty has seen
In nature's first gold, green.
So let time be taken for you to see
The green that shines bright, inside of me.

Troy Hughes, Grade 9
Clarkston Jr High School, MI

All Good Things Must Come to an End

Life is like a flower;
beautiful and bright.

Flowers are like glass;
delicate and light.

Glass is like guns;
can bring pain or joy.

Guns are like the truth;
can provide, and destroy.

Truth is like rules;
often and easily bend.

Rules are like promises;
exist to be broken.

Promises are like secrets;
shouldn't be spoken.

And life, like all good things, must come to an end.

Alex Van Hoof, Grade 8
Washington Middle School, WI

Fred the Frog

There once was a boy named Achoo
He would sneeze until his face would turn blue

One day while out walking his dog
He came upon an odd looking frog

It was blue, pink, purple and red
And said to him, "Hi, I am Fred!"

The boy was so scared that he ran
He ran right into an old man

The old man said, "Don't fear!
Fred the frog has a cure.

Touch his head, close your eyes,
You will be pleasantly surprised!"

The boy touched his head
And said, "Thank you, Fred!"

You made my sneezes go away
Now I will have a great day!

Alexis Huiras, Grade 7
Springfield School, MN

The Family Bullet

My family to a bullet.
I am the lead as fast as can be.
My dad is the casing subtle and clean.
My mom is the powder that sends us in the right direction.
My sister is the brass shiny but dumb.
My dog is the primer fast and quick-witted.

Taylor Yoder, Grade 7
Manistee Middle School, MI

Watching the Dancers

1, 2, 3, 4,
The dancers leaped on stage,
Erupting with energy.
The thundering beat from above,
Like a pulse running through their veins.
Jump, jump, higher, higher,
Just a little further,
A spectacular sight
Girls flying, soaring, floating
As if they were frozen in the air.
With the final counts of the music,
The dancers were growing weary but they continued on,
Showing nothing but pizzazz on their faces.
Spin, spin, faster, faster…
The last move of the routine — like a tornado;
The girls all turning as one.
The music stops — silence
1, 2, boom!
A thundering response from the crowd.
All of the hard work, stretching, lifting, repeating,
Was worth it for this moment.

Grace Scorpio, Grade 8
Saint Thomas More Catholic School, MN

The Writing of a Poem

A boy, about thirteen
Was trying to write a poem
He thought perhaps he would write
Of places far away from home.

He couldn't decide of what to write
Maybe of cities great and tall
Or of a forest filled with life
Even an insect so very small.

Thoughts were flying through his head
Whirling just outside the grip
Of his mind's invisible hand
For between his fingers they did slip.

Then "Aha! I've got one!"
The jubilant boy cried out
And the writing of a poem
Was what he wrote about.

Solomon Poulose, Grade 8
Saint Thomas More Catholic School, MN

The Darkness
Each day I wake up
I look at the sky
I think of all those who live
And who die

I can see their faces
But do not know who they are
They're from many different races
From near and from far

They try to talk
but I do not understand
They try to walk
I see their demand

They want to live
that's what they said
They want their family
But they're still dead
David Frailey, Grade 7
St Roman School, WI

My Kitty
My kitty lies
On the front
Porch daydreaming
About being in the middle
Of the desert.

When he is around
He acts as if he
Is in charge of the whole world.

He lies in my lap purring
Like a clarinet player.
The air swishes as he plays.

Even though he is gone
He still lies in my heart
With all of the wonderful memories
He has given me.
Heaven Marshall, Grade 8
Paw Paw Middle School, MI

Marine
M any cannot survive
A re you ready for a physical challenge?
R ecruits are…
I nsane
N ormal people become more
E veryone like family
S urefire way…something better
Luke Elbe, Grade 8
Suring Elementary/Middle School, WI

Best Friend
Standing, looking at him,
While he was looking at me.
He yelled,
And I listened.
What did I do wrong?
I wiped under my eyes
Checking for tears
Why him?
Why now?
They all made fun of me,
But I didn't stick up for myself
My eyes looked around,
They started to water.
I told myself no because I was strong.
I looked at him one last time,
Then I turned around and walked.
Walked away, down the hill,
My head held high
And thought,
I don't need them anyway.
Abbey Hall, Grade 9
Clarkston Jr High School, MI

Wildfire
The fire burned wild
Started in an instant
Raged out of control
Consumed everything in its path
Nothing stood a chance

One moment things were calm
The flames devoured the peace
Blinded by the smoke
Not noticing until too late
The destruction left behind

When the flames finally burnt out
And all the heat had gone
And in its comparison
Everything seems colder
And ruin is all that's left behind
Paige Miller, Grade 9
Clarkston Jr High School, MI

Rainbows
Red, orange, yellow,
Green, blue, purple.
Full of joy and happiness.
A big pot of gold at the end.
After the rain,
An arch of color,
Across the sky.
Jennifer Mohle, Grade 8
Adams Friendship Middle School, WI

Overtime
My heart is beating faster
faster
faster than ever.

The championship game in
overtime.

You either win
or
you lose.

Overtime!
Kyle Walker, Grade 7
Shakopee Area Catholic School, MN

Snowflakes
Each one different, drifting
Down, down, down
Snowflakes silently
Sit on the ground.
They whisper,
Whirl,
And whiten the world.
The blizzards
Blanket and bleach
Flakes fall,
And freshen,
Cover and clean
All around.
Leah Dauterman, Grade 7
Roosevelt Middle School, MN

A Melody
From the sky, to the ground
Rain is falling all around
Thunder, rain, and wind
A song of storms begins

Play a song, a melody
Then everybody will see
The Hero of Time
Has come

If you play, the melody
It will travel 'cross the sea
Thunder, rain, and wind
A song of storms begins

A light will shine, from the sky
Bringing harmony all around
The Hero of Time
Has come
Brooke Thill, Grade 7
Altoona Middle School, WI

All I Want

All I want is someone to care
Someone to look at me
All I want is someone to try
Someone to not make fun of me
Someone to not judge me by my size
All I want is someone to not yell at me
Someone to think of me
Someone to get to me
Someone to understand me
All I want is someone to help me
Someone to give that extra push
Some one to give me a shove and say good luck
Someone to give me a chance
Someone say he's short, but who cares
All I want is some true friends

Taylor Brown, Grade 8
Pennfield Middle School, MI

Hidden in the Trees

In the morning the trees awake.
Wind starts to blow and branches start to shake.
The forest starts to sing its chirping bird songs.
When the song stops you know something is wrong.
The sky turns black and thunder starts to roar.
The forest's nap has begun and he is beginning to snore.
A breeze flows through the leaves and makes the forest cold.
Then a rainbow starts to shine, which leads me to a pot of gold.
Hidden in the trees is a quiet and relaxing place to be.
The forest is a great place and will always be a part of me.

Bryan Rutkowski, Grade 8
J C McKenna Middle School, WI

The Dream

I dream of being a football player
juking, driving, and jumping in the air
Flashing lights, nice new cars
my fans, they greet me with open arms.
Be better than better, quicker than quick
when you get that right, it's all legit.
Get that ball don't stop till you're gone,
dive into the end-zone and get the freak show on.
Give 100% day in, day out,
show the enemy what is all about
I dream of being that football player
Quick as lightning, solid as a rock,
these dreams of mine can never be blocked.
Show the world you have got what it takes,
no matter the pain or what's at stake.
And once you become that football player
juking, driving and jumping in the air,
be the best you can be,
Forever strong until you die and are forever gone.
It's the legacy which for all care,
that all started with a dream of a football player.

Eagen Keeley, Grade 8
Abundant Life Christian School, WI

Meandering Mind

As I paddle my small canoe,
Paddle through the water blue,
I think of thoughts that I once knew,
Forgotten thoughts remembered anew.

As I row through the water cold,
I think, "How much water could one river hold,
How many thoughts could one mind behold?"
Many, but not all remembered or told.

The river seems to have no end;
Our minds infinitely comprehend.
Who knows how far our minds will extend?
Who knows what's around the river bend?

The water seems to twist and wind,
Flowing through shadows undefined.
Childhood daydreams come to mind,
Musing and memories intertwined.

As I paddle with the flow,
The sky above, the water below,
I think of thoughts that I now know,
Thoughts I'm sure will come and go.

Michaela Sanborn, Grade 9
St Thomas More Academy, MI

A Trip to Thailand

I went to Thailand on a vacation
where I met a friend that showed me around Thailand
there we walked to the mountain top to see the sunrise
where it was beautiful and the perfect view of Thailand
We played some game that kept us moving
We sang some songs that help me learn
We have so much fun that it makes me forget
Forget the place I left behind
She cooked some food that tasted so good
When the days were coming
I never thought of leaving
When my days were up
I felt the sadness in my heart
We left to the airport
and we said goodbye
I got in the plane and sat on my seat
I never thought it'll end like this
I fell asleep and started to dream
When I woke back up
I was at home think that it was just a dream
Of having a trip to Thailand.

Kia Xiong, Grade 7
Achieve Language Academy, MN

Betrayed

I lie in bed looking at the ceiling
I only think of that one word
I walk slowly downstairs for dinner
I only think of that one word
With that word you don't know
If you can tell people things
That word could break your heart
When I go to bed at night
I only think of that one word
When I go to school the next day
I only think of that one word
That word could ruin your friendship
That word could ruin your relationship
In each class I go in
I only think of that one word
When I spot my best friends gossiping
I only think of that one word
That word could ruin your whole day
That word could ruin your whole life
That word that can drive you insane is…
Betrayed

Shayna Wykes, Grade 7
Perry Middle School, MI

Shadow

The chair
Sits alone in the corner
Casting shadows on the wall
Rocking back and forth
To the rhythm of it all
I sit down
In the shadow of the chair

Brianna Anderson, Grade 7
Valley View Middle School, MN

Fishing

Cast, snag, set the hook
reeling is harder after
every crank.

You can feel
the fish fighting for
it's life, depending on size.
It's not gonna go down
without a fight.
You can see
the fish jump out
of the water, trying to
spit out the hook.
You can see the end of
your rod bend down.
You can tell that
you'll be eating
some kind of fish tonight.

Jacob Mathews, Grade 7
Ramsey Jr High School, MN

Little Pink Shoes

They fall madly in love
Then there's holy matrimony
Next is the baby with two little pink shoes
Then there's problems, wife is confused
How could this be what did we do?
She stands there in the hospital looking at her baby that cannot be held
Husband doing the best he can to cope with this tragic event
Their own child treated like a medical experiment
Hoping their little one will make it through
They still ask themselves what did we do.

Dana Marshall, Grade 8
Spring Hill School, WI

Pizza

Giovanni's Pizza
The red neon sign flickered outside the shops window
It's the middle of the night and the absence of traffic is unnerving
The wind rustles the green leaves on the trees
A bee buzzes towards the neon sign
Big mistake
Its body fizzes and fries then turns to a crumpled black ball
My heels click as I walk on the sidewalk
I pull open the glass door and enter pizza paradise
I hear hungry stomachs everywhere in the pizzeria, murmuring, waiting to be filled
My stomach joins the other chanting bellies and lets out a little growl
The smell of sizzling cheese and baking bread erupt into my willing nose
The bright lights in Giovanni's are borrowed from heaven
I see Giovanni spinning the golden pizza
The dough flops as it hits his knuckles
I place my order then take a seat
I notice the tiles on the floor are sprinkled with crispy crumbs
I know that I will leave crumbs too

Asma Haidara, Grade 8
Cedar Riverside Community School, MN

Watching and Waiting

I am watching and waiting
I wonder when the world will change
I hear the cry of the unborn
I see children starving and searching for food
I want world peace
I am watching and waiting
I pretend everything in the world is okay
I feel the pain of those hurting
I try to touch the hearts of others but don't always succeed
I worry about not living another day
I cry for those around me
I am watching and waiting
I understand everything in the world won't be perfect
I say not to worry though because God will pull through
I dream about the day we will be in Heaven with no more problems
I try to tell as many as I can about Christ
I hope that I will see those people in Heaven
I am watching and waiting

Lindsay Scanlon, Grade 7
West Suburban Christian Academy, WI

Determined Glory

I'll never forget that awesome night,
As the stadium lights shown so bright.
As me and my men went out to fight,
Like soldiers who never show fright.
A battle it was and battle we did,
Until the time felt just right.
We knew we were destined for glory,
So we put an end to the story.
I ran through the hole, my eyes set to win.
Oh and how I did grin
When my feet passed that line, in the nick of time
To make us win that game.
Oh, how I'll never forget that awesome night.
How the fans jumped up with delight.
Cheering until they could cheer no more,
Now we can sound the victory horn.
Oh, how I'll never forget that awesome night.

Matthew Dessart, Grade 8
Seymour Middle School, WI

Time

Time flies when you're having fun
yet when you're bored
each minute seems like an hour
an hour seems like a year
a year seems like a decade
a decade seems like a century
to end your time of boredom
simply do something you enjoy
whether it's playing your favorite board game
or just sitting down
reading a book or listening to music
time will fly
when you're having fun.

Anita Parce, Grade 7
Necedah Middle School, WI

Them

They tease.
They laugh.
They think they're all that.
They shout and scream, they make me want to screech.
They look and stare as if I'm not there.
I hurt down deep.
They make me want to weep.
I walk and talk and try not to stop.
I breathe in and out, as they look at me and shout.
I walk by and try not to cry.
Because they teased and laughed and thought they were all that.

Kayla Stark, Grade 7
Shakopee Area Catholic School, MN

Spring

Winter has left and spring has come
The thrill of the season has just begun
Flowers blossom and the grass grows green;
The beautiful season, so calm and serene.

The robins approach on a nearby tree;
A homely nest there soon will be.
Life is springing in certain ways.
Such vibrant wealth the earth displays!

The sun beams glow on a carefree face.
An open field, such a lovely place.
The peaceful sun and the sky so clear,
A definite sign that spring is here!

The natural glow on this quiet earth,
A gaze on nature for all it is worth,
Is such a gift that has been shown
From the Creator, God alone!

Kate Prain, Grade 9
St Thomas More Academy, MI

Always and Forever

I said I love you and I always will
When I said I need you I was for real
Always and forever you will be a part of me
We may fight and sometimes cry
But I will love you 'til the day that I die.
Always and forever you and me.

Deborah Canfield, Grade 8
Middle School at Parkside, MI

Patriotism

Patriotism, for the red white and blue
We are proud of our country,
For the old and for the new.
We are proud of the USA.
Red is the color of blood,
Soldiers shed fighting for our country,
Blood that flows through each and every citizen.
Or the color of love,
A feeling that grows passionately for our country.
Blue is the color of Justice,
The freedom we have to live our lives.
And for every man to be treated equal.
Or the color of the cold ocean waters,
That surrounds our country,
Acting as if a shield protecting the United States.
White is the purity of every citizen,
The innocence of each soul,
The chance everyone deserves,
Or the clouds that pass above each state
As we lay on the ground trying to determine their shapes.
Patriotism for the red for the white and for the blue

Katie King, Grade 8
Lake Fenton Middle School, MI

Splash

All day long the water's quiet,
Many love this, but can't buy it.

The water's surface isn't moving,
But watching fish swim, can be soothing.

They swim around all day long,
That is, until dinner comes along.

When they're hungry they make a dash,
After finding their prey…

SPLASH!

Mitch Miklosi, Grade 7
Assumption BVM School, MI

Phantom of the Opera

I am scared
I feel cold
I feel like a bird
Left behind during migration
I am in a dark place
I am lonely
I have goose bumps
Like a mouth full of jawbreakers
I am scared
Phantom of the Opera

Stephanie Sleda, Grade 8
Sandusky Middle School, MI

Two Hours Ago

Here on this spot,
A car bomb went off.
It blew apart this building,
Killing many in its blast.
Two hours ago.

Later the fire department came
And they saved all they could.
Still it wasn't enough.
Many left this planet.
Two hours ago.

Many were left homeless,
Crying in the night.
Wishing they wouldn't have been there
Two hours ago.

For little Tommy B.
Who lost his favorite teddy bear.
Now he needs it more than ever.
Honestly he doesn't care
Because he just lost it all
Two hours ago.

Alex Moe, Grade 7
Springfield School, MN

Happiness Is Joy

Jump for joy. Happiness is a warm bed ready to be slept in.
Happiness is a pair of slippers for cold tired feet.
Jump for joy. Happiness is a bar of chocolate ready to be eaten.
Happiness is a good book ready to be read.
Jump for joy. Happiness is your favorite song playing on the radio.
Happiness is a group of friends laughing at a funny joke you told.
Put a smile on.
It is the time for joy.
Sadness gone
Frowning done
All you need is to JUMP FOR JOY!

Parker Webster, Grade 8
St Andrew's School, MI

Journey

At the birth of time…
Men ascended and climbed up the inevitable stony slope,
to explore untraveled valleys for the land in which promised.
Over hills, through lush green forests.
Unshod, they staggered.
SEARCHING.
The pebble's shadow glimmered in the sun.
And the men kept searching, as the light grew low
and the ball of flame that illuminated their way slowly went down.
SEARCHING
but NOT OBTAINING.
Darkness engulfed them.
Smoke from a flame.
LINGERING.
The light slowly intensified
as the sun ascended into the sky concealing the stars.
They pursued on.
SEARCHING.
DESIRING.
Where would they be if they were
to stop searching now?

Adriana Prada, Grade 9
Clarkston Jr High School, MI

At Day's Rest

Between the valley and the mountain top,
Toward the west,
I examined the beautiful golden sunset as I watch it with awe.
Below the sun,
Off towards the east,
I begin to see the river shimmering off the sun, as I smile and giggle.
Behind the river the sun still setting,
After the wind slowing down,
I welcomed it as my eyes started to water, I was watching the beauty,
I felt safe inside.

Danielle N. Frazho, Grade 7
Beer Middle School, MI

Feast of Seasons

Bright light on the ground,
Flakes of frozen sugar
Frosted on broccoli treetops
Drip, drop
Drop, drip
Cool water drops decorate the apple trees
Buds bloom to life
New existences all around
Grow, strengthen
Strengthen, grow
Air humid as the oven
Sand soft between toes like flour between fingers
Fruity flowers emit sweet fragrances
Bloom, lovely
Lovely, bloom
Cinnamon sugar trees drop their squash leaves
Float softly to the ground
Chilly breezes from the 'refrigerator' above
Cooling, floating
Floating, cooling
Our feast is complete.

Rachel Manssur, Grade 9
Clarkston Jr High School, MI

Character

It's not something you inherit or willed
It's something over time you build
With kindness you will earn respect
Without it you will be someone everyone will reject
To be well-liked takes hard work
Without it you become a jerk
Irresponsible is something you can be
But the opposite is better, trust me.

Brady Myhre, Grade 8
Cedar Grove-Belgium Middle School, WI

Sleeping on Saturdays

Sleep, sleep, sleep.
The thing you do late at night,
When you're in your bed with a fright.
You don't know when you shall awake,
But for sure in the morning you'll have a pancake.

When you wake up and get out of bed,
Your eyes half open and partially red.
You'll go into the bathroom and look in the mirror,
You'll see your saggy eyes and your stuck up hair.
And then you want to comb your hair immediately…
But you remember something,
Today's Saturday you don't need to do nothing.
You eat your pancake and crawl back into bed,
You fluff your pillow and rest your head,
And all you'll think is…Saturday, no school, no work,
no nothing, *sleep.*

Nicholas Schaub, Grade 7
Avondale Middle School, MI

Overwhelming Idiocy

I see America joyously frolicking
in the deep puddles of Incompetence
Choosing not to glance into the light of responsibility
That would diminish the clouds covering Wall Street

I hear America laughing obnoxiously
Uncaringly
At the Inconvenient Truth
Deciding that they deserve the things
and ideas that must be earned
Thinking the Fault should fall on others' shoulders

The demanding reigns of Want overcome and repress
The feelings of one's own Guilt and Error

Alison A. Ross, Grade 9
Clintonville High School, WI

Writing Class

W riting for fun
R eading for ideas
I nspiring others
T hinking of good people for biographies
I deas flowing
N ecessary conference
G iving examples

C razy ideas
L ingering effects on writing
A wesome essays
S cience fiction stories
S upportive editors

John Syswerda, Grade 7
Cedar Springs Middle School, MI

Jor Ge

I went outside through my doorway,
And then it started pouring.
So then I went to Norway,
And realized that it was boring.

Once I went to Norway,
I met a guy named Jor Ge.
I met him while I was touring,
And realized that he was completely boring

So then I went home with Jor Ge,
And realized home too, was boring.
So we went back to Norway,
And we had a blast.

Kyle Garber, Grade 7
Manistee Middle School, MI

Final Last Words

You are my best friend, my hope, my reason for being. You are always there to wipe away all my tears, and defeat all my monsters. You are able to make me forget my problems. Stay with me don't go you always know how to cheer me up and make me better. Mom, I need you, you have to be there, you're my mom, you're all I have.

Kaylee Kiggins, Grade 9
Northwood School, WI

With My Heart in Pain

This pain won't go away. The pain of you. And what you've done to me.
You've left a wound in my heart. Which I've placed a bandage upon.
But a bandage isn't going to heal this wound. You've cut into my heart so deep.
And I cry at night because I'm not sure if you'll come back and finish what you tried to start.
Can't you find another heart to cut? Why do you have to pick mine?
What have I done to deserve this? You told me that you would die without me.
And without my love. If that's true, then prove it.
Because love is just a word until it's proven to you.
I know that you can't prove it, because you don't love me.
And you will never get another chance to again.
Maybe when you get out of jail you'll see. But I'm not gonna be there for you.
'Cause you've put me through so much pain. You've cut into my heart and killed my soul.
Just by what you did. You've cut so deep into my heart.
And I'm bleeding. Bleeding because of everything.
Now my soul is dead. And my body is still alive.
And it kills me inside. To know that you could come back.
And finish what you started. This pain will never go away,
But crying myself to sleep will eventually fade.
The dreams of you and what you did to me. Will remain in my wounded heart.
But the memory of you won't be vague.
It will remain the same. With my heart in pain.

Sierra Pelzer, Grade 8
Manawa Middle School, WI

Royal Dream World

Strong, purple swirls sucking, slurping, touching bare toes
Majestic, shiny, bubbling mess forcing me deeper and deeper
Struggling blindly, searching for the surface vicious waves pulling me away
Stinging my throat burning my nose
My eyes see solid violet
Sudden silence was so still everything simply stopped
My feet found the slimy purple rocks
I pushed my head up through the rubbery surface and stared into the royal dream world
Wading through the deep colored puddle
The liquid gets shallower and shallower flowery aromas hit my nose
I brush my fingers over the velvet blanket of lavender
Lingering sweet tastes fill my mouth
I step into a garden of magenta roses and breathe in the exciting scents
I feel the silky air around me and smell the mouthwatering rose perfume
I see cloudy pools of the soupy paint around me
Again I hear the frightening roar and I see the bright tidal wave
The thick but soft tsunami bowls me over and I am submerged once again
My life flashes before my eyes but it is blurred by the lilac around me
Ghostly whispers echo quietly the rich purple magic retreats
The delicate touch of violet blossoms caress my sore arms
The royal dream world slowly fades to black

Peyton Richardson, Grade 8
Centennial Middle School, MI

Shall I Compare You to a Winter's Night?

Shall I compare you to a winter's night?
You are so chilling yet so very bleak.
Size matters not, but what a scary sight.
Unknown, inside you truly are so weak.
Your deeply cunning ways, so mean and fierce,
Thy hateful mouth with lies and slander sound.
Your efforts my soul and heart do not pierce.
True love and self respect are never found.
By chance or nature challenges begin,
Two strong forces now commence to collide.
What value hast the prize the victor wins?
Matter not the position of each side.
As suddenly as darkness ends the day,
Soon sunrise brings the hope of a new way.

Jennifer Brostowitz, Grade 8
Pilgrim Park Middle School, WI

The Flower Petal

The flower petals are as bright as the rainbow
The garden is a quiet mountain top
The flower is as fragrant as all the fruits in the world
The flowers are warm looking
The flower's stem
The flower's petal
The garden
The flower

Max Marsh, Grade 7
Luxemburg-Casco Middle School, WI

Gone

I'm laying here
Right where you left me
I never understood why you left
Left me here by myself
With the tears that flow
And everyone looking at me
You make me feel so stupid
You strung me along like a puppet
Now I'm alone, all alone
How do you sleep at night?
Not knowing what I'm doing
Not hearing my sweet voice
You never called to say sorry
You never made sure I was ok
I just don't understand
I thought we were one
After everything we've gone through
How could you just walk out?
It's all understood now…you never cared

Sierra Kasee, Grade 8
Seymour Middle School, WI

Dreaming

Dreaming, dreaming
Dreaming of your life
Thoughts away, concerns away
Who you will meet,
When you will start to open your heart into the world,
And where you will go
Building up your life, your future
Everything that you will have to handle
Don't worry, everything will be fine.
Just dreaming,
Softly, to the bright side of your life
As if you are in a movie
Miracles at some point of your life
Something fabulous, something amazing
Will happen, at some point of the life that you dreamed of
Every issue will be precious to you
Dreaming, dreaming
Fly to the sky, to the stars above
Thoughts away, concerns away
Dreaming, dreaming,
Dreams of your life.

Shelby Kang, Grade 7
Abundant Life Christian School, WI

Seth

There once was a was a boy named Seth,
who almost fell off a cliff.
He shouted, "Whoohoo!"
then began to boohoo
because his greatest trepidation was death.

Shavon McSwine, Grade 8
Grosse Pointe Academy, MI

Run

I run away
As I try to hide my fears.
I don't want to share them,
So I keep on running
Into the darkness.
Where did I go?
Where did I go wrong?
What makes me not good enough?
Pushed in second, I thought I was your first.
I don't want you to know,
But yet I think you should.
Not because you deserve to
But because…you're the reason.
I need to blame you.
I don't want to but NEED to.
It hurts.
Everything hurts.
Nothing is the same.
You changed. We changed. Maybe even I changed.
I keep on running.

Alyson Kieckhefer, Grade 8
Washington School, WI

Me and Poems

I can't write poems
'cause they rhyme
They ring around
Through my mind
They twist through time
through all man's minds
I can't write poems
can't you tell
for this time
this is my rhyme

Brooke Wright, Grade 9
Lakeview Christian Academy, MN

A Rainbow in Her Gray Sky

She looked down
With tears in her eyes
There was no hope
She began to realize
Everything was gone
Nothing left to claim her own
No person to love her
No place to call home
Down the rain poured
Atop her small head
She stared at the sky
With her eyes blood red
Her feet began to walk
Down the lonely, dark road
Suddenly she began to run
And started to slow
A rainbow appeared
Painted across her sky
Smiling, she said to herself
I no longer need to cry
There was hope left

Marissa Sinks, Grade 8
St Roman School, WI

Reality

Once there is silence
I can hear
some of the sounds
beyond the ear.
There is so much
of which we are unaware.
Is it that
or do we not care.
In the corners of the house
the flames of imagination
have been doused.
I hear the music being played,
though the musicians have been slain.

Savanah Cass, Grade 8
Adams Friendship Middle School, WI

Talk to Me, January

Cold grips like a vice
Shiv'ring uncontrollably
Huddle in my coat

Moonlight on the snow
See dark shadows thrown askew
Hurry back inside

Look through frosted glass
Fine trees white like spun sugar
Too pretty to eat

Rachel Romens, Grade 7
Core Knowledge Charter School, WI

The Little Cabin in the Woods

I remember the chirping birds,
People talking,
The wind blowing

I miss the green trees,
Glowing campfires,
The little cabin in the woods,
The paintball games in the summer

I remember the wood,
The cold metal of the cars,
The warm blankets,
The wet grass in the morning

I miss the campfire hot dogs,
The smores that melt in your mouth,
The omelets in the morning

I remember the smoke,
The dust,
The pine trees

I miss the little cabin in Ely

Sarah Hochman, Grade 7
Valley View Middle School, MN

War

Once upon a time,
in a far away land
there was a war going on
that no one could stand.
Bombs going off every
night and day
kids crying their pain away,
like standing in the pouring rain.
All we can do is hope and pray
that they will be home someday.

Katie Ludwig, Grade 9
Riverside University High School, WI

Summer

Summer is a runner
That comes by once a year
When it goes it is a bummer
And to some brings a tear

Summer is a holiday
That is enjoyed by all
But does not stay
Because of fall

Michael Keiser, Grade 9
Petoskey High School, MI

Smiles

Waiting for the camera,
To flash to show we're done.
So we can send our smiles,
On our homemade cards.

Happy pictures,
Sent across the country.
So our grandma can receive,
Our smiling little faces.

My grandma calls us on the phone,
Said she got our card.
She put it on her fridge,
And can't wait until the next one.

Kaylyn Zielinski, Grade 8
Necedah Middle School, WI

Tire Tracks

My shell is smooth
To the touch
It is while like a cloud
And orange like an orange
This shell will make
You gasp
At first it may look
Like a shiny stone
But it's actually a shiny shell.
The shiny shell is alive
It could kill you with its looks
You know this shell is living
Because it has a heart monitor
The creature that sued
To live inside this gorgeous
Shell is no longer there
This shell has been run over
Time and time again
But that's what gives
The tire tracks shell
Its gorgeous look.

Lucas Brawdy, Grade 8
Chippewa Falls Middle School, WI

Always There for You

Foolish things can get in your way
Hurtful words can turn you away
Cracks in the sidewalk can make you fall
A darkened hallway can make your back crawl
But you got friends and friends they will be
Who will help you with all your troubles and needs
They will help you make the decisions you plead
And lead you to your destiny
They will keep you safe from the dangers you will face
And help you keep a steady pace
That is why they are called your friends
The ones who you can trust and the ones who can lend
Lend a hand and lift you off the ground

Nancy Vang, Grade 7
Northstar Middle School, WI

Books

Big books little books all lined up in a row.
Books to the right books to the left and books high and low.
Green books red books and blue books too.
Which one is just right for you?

Mystery, fiction, and don't forget adventures.
Books are nice big thirst for adventure quenchers.
We can get books from everywhere.
But please, Oh please be careful not to tear.

Books are found in libraries, school and houses too.
Even books that focus on the animals in the zoo.
There are even very big books that show us how to cook.
Some books on the cover have a very tattered look.

So if you are ever depressed sad or bored.
And entertainment you cannot afford.
Start reading a book and you will see.
That reading is the ultimate key.

Get buried in a book and don't stop until you're done.
Though reading from dictionaries is not so fun.
So I hope books are an interest to you.
So how about a good book review.

Regina Dick, Grade 7
St Thomas More Academy, MI

Robin

Robin:
The horse that I show,
Get her ready and tacked up,
And let's watch her go!

The ride:
We gallop away,
Leaving our problems behind,
Thinking life's O.K.

Mason Herolt, Grade 8
Wheatland Center Elementary School, WI

Ode to My Sister

Who do I see in my little sister Megan?
A best friend
My secret keeper
Someone to talk to
A unique person
The creative thinker
A nimble athlete
My partner in crime
This is whom I see in my little sister Megan

Emily Stidwill, Grade 7
St John Lutheran School, MI

Football Fanatic

Football in the fall
Football in the summer,
Watching everyone cheer for us all
If my friends miss a catch it's a bummer.

I've never missed a catch
And I never miss a tackle,
We never get a challenging match
And we make their bones crackle.

After the game we get cookies
All the girls' eyes turn to us,
We make our opponents look like rookies
And then we just run to the bus.

Cody Carlson, Grade 8
Spring Hill School, WI

Melancholy

A pen, ensnaring you
Bars surrounding just insignificant enough to keep you there
It's not simple
Slander, jests, a completely innocent act.
Longing for joy, hoping for sunshine
Monotony, crying, screaming, unpleasant
Bitter taste, cold chill
It's not simple
Gentle and kind, eating you away
Ragged and fierce, stealing the best of you
Shallow, instant, deep, or forever
What they don't know
It's not simple
The light at the end of the tunnel is small and faint
But still there,
Lingering,
Growing,
Healing

Courtney Villeneuve, Grade 9
Clarkston Jr High School, MI

Together and Forever

Was it even real?
That fantasy of last night?
He said he would be here,
to hold me tight.

We would run away,
away from the world.
I would love him forever,
our hearts would be swirled,
Together, Forever.

But it wasn't a fantasy,
he was right over there.
Walking away from the sunset,
then he rustled my hair.

We will always love each other,
always and forever,
and here we were,
right here,
Forever…Together…

Jordyn Nichols, Grade 7
Cedar Springs Middle School, MI

Sunsets and Trees

The trees are looking gold,
The trees are covered in mold,
The trees are new and old,
The trees are very cold.

I watch the sunset alone,
While the coyotes howl low,
It's just me,
Under this cold tree.

The sunsets looking nice,
the sunsets warm and bright,
It's a masterpiece of art,
The sunsets warm and bright.

It's getting dark,
On this day the sunset made it's mark,
I'm going to leave this tree,
but the sight I will forever keep.

Karli Binder, Grade 8
Jerstad Agerholm Middle School, WI

Water/Fire

Water
Raining, drinking, drowning
River, sea, lava, magma
Blazing, scorching, heat
Burning, boiling
Fire

Sean Pyatt, Grade 7
Edison Middle School, WI

I Will Compare You to a Stone Brick Wall

I will compare you to a stone brick wall.
You are very dark, mellow, cold and frigid.
Rough winds do not shake you; you stand strong and do not fall.
And the stone is built for hard trials, but may look rigid.
Sometimes people vandalize you, but you stay motionless.
And often be strayed by your family and friends.
And often left to stay behind, but still you are emotionless.
Standing alone with nothing beautiful or obscure and it never ends.
And yet you stand strong and do not quake.
You do not wither or even quiver.
You stand still, but sometimes you will be awake.
And you do not blink, cry, shake or shiver.
And for so long as people are still are around.
They look at you and you do not make a sound.

Jack Podewils, Grade 8
Pilgrim Park Middle School, WI

He Is…

He was the boy who was always joking around
He was the boy who you never talked to
He was the boy who gave you a note
He was the boy who you began to like
He said that love lasts forever
He tells you constantly that he loves you
He looks you in the eyes and you know that he's the one
He is the one you'll always love
He is there for you, when you need him the most
He protects you, even if you don't want him to
He can always put a smile on your face
He hates seeing you sad or upset
He listens and tries to understand
He hugs you and your heart stops but only for a moment
He kisses you and your head spins
He holds you in his arms and you listen to his heart beat so steadily and strong
He tells you that he loves you, and says he always will
He is the one you've been waiting for
He is the perfect guy for you, the one you've been dreaming of
He is the guy who will always be there to pick you up when you fall
He is the guy you love

Megan Vandermoss, Grade 8
Seymour Middle School, WI

The Field

The field behind my house is a quiet place.
The weeds sway and sweep.
In the distance you can hear the birds singing.
At your ears bugs buzz.
Crickets, that are out of sight, hum somewhere in the grass.
Nearby, leaves crunch as something steps on them.
Soft squishes come from my feet as I step on the soft ground.
Sticks falling from trees hit the ground with a muted thud.
I can hear the sound of a stream trickling in the background nearby.
It's a peaceful place, here at the field.
That's why I come here.

Cheyanne Schlafley, Grade 7
Manistee Middle School, MI

The Solution

Coming back at you.
Rock hard, strong and tall,
a brick wall.
It's an obstacle, a complication,
using everything in your power to break it.
Achieving, reaching, and finding the solution.
You're in a heavy covered forest,
seeking your way out of it.
You're sitting in a pitch black room,
waiting to see just that speck of light.
And as you see it, hitting your face.
Fascinating, addicting,
drug like,
its blinding, abstract colors,
pulling you towards it.
Don't you understand?
Attempt finding that happy side,
the other end of your rainbow.
Just process it through your intelligence,
it backfires.
Or what do you think?

Amelie Vogler, Grade 9
Clarkston Jr High School, MI

A Broken Heart

Every second of your day,
As time slowly creeps away.
The pain deep, the longing too much,
When all you want to feel is his touch.

All you need to be in his arms,
To lay there and know you're safe from harm.
Flashbacks occur to the day you met,
The connection you felt, you knew it was set.

The moments you shared, so stressless and pure,
You knew it was love, a disease with no cure.
You fell for him hard, as he did you,
He said he meant it, you assumed it was true.

He adored you, would do anything for you,
He stole your heart, and broke it in two,
Maybe you should fix it, just give it a try
A few pieces of tape some glue and let dry.

Yet he's still on your mind, no matter the hurt,
You miss his very scent, it lingers on your t-shirt.
He says he feels stupid, doesn't want you to cry,
You care about him so much, you just can't say good-bye.

Bailey Mumby, Grade 8
Sandusky Middle School, MI

Child at Night

Child why do you cry
Child why do you sigh
Do not scream do not fit
For sadness is only for a little bit
Life is happy don't you see
But for people like you and me it can be very unhappy
So child do not cry
For only listen to the sweet sweet lullaby
Slowly softly to sleep is to you and to me
So child at night do not cry
For you can sleep by your personal lullaby

Felipe Rey Torres, Grade 8
St Stephen Elementary School, MI

Ode to Calculator

I give praise to my dear scientific calculator.
You work wonders for me.
During math,
and during science.
I might just call you blessed.
Praise to you,
oh dear calculator,
you are awesome in many ways.
During that math test
the other day.
The adding, subtracting,
multiplying and all.
I lean on you for support
during all those rough times,
oh dear calculator.
But now I must pack you
away dear calculator,
I cannot wait to see you
another day.

Savanah Beske, Grade 7
St Katharine Drexel School, WI

Life in America

It's difficult to grow up as a kid in this world today,
The scare of global warming,
And the economy plummeting each day,

Life is not as simple as it was years before,
The world is no longer a safe place anymore.

But if we change our ways,
There will be better days.

Bring respect and morals back to the young,
And take the wisdom from your mother's tongue.

Life in America can still be enjoyable,
When we make Americans more employable.

Brielle Ahee, Grade 7
Our Lady Star of the Sea School, MI

Take a Chance and Dance

Dance
You should take a chance
Pick your accessories shirt, and pants
I'm sure you will do just fine
It's not like it's a crime
So pick up your feet
So pick up your feet
Maybe you will go to a meet
Don't think when
You might just get a ten
So take a chance and dance

Mimi Mitrovic, Grade 8
Jerstad Agerholm Middle School, WI

Feelings

How can you look so far and see,
Not one standing close like me?
Though I've been there every day,
You choose to simply look away.

How can it seem like I'm not there?
How can it seem like I don't care?
My love as open as a book,
Is there if you'd only look.

Love is patient, love is kind,
If you'd look at me you'd find,
Someone as special as can be,
Someone as special as…me.

Rebekah Franck, Grade 9
Lakeview Christian Academy, MN

What They Are

They are my weapons.
They are my tools.
They are my sympathy.
They are unusual.
They are diverse.
They are harsh.
They are cruel.
They are power.
They are weakness.
They are pain.
They are anger.
They are words.
Words are everything:
War.
Peace.
Love.
But they are me.
Words are just words,
But make people.
People are the words they speak,
So people must choose wisely.

Allison Canner, Grade 8
West Hills Middle School, MI

War

The blowing of bombs. The shots of guns.
War claims many lives, including our loved ones.

You watched them walk away to get on their plane.
They went for our country, putting you in worrying pain.

You stay up late at night hoping they are okay.
Putting their life on the line, is freedom worth the price we pay?

You want them to come home your heart in one piece.
You're at the airport waiting for them, your mom, dad, brother, and niece.

When you finally see them, your heart begins to race.
You run into their arms before they drop their suitcase.

The time goes by so fast, you don't want them to go back.
Your eyes fill with tears, when you see them begin to pack.

One day you get a phone call, you can't believe what you hear.
Your body starts to shake, you cry more than one tear.

The blowing of bombs. The shots of guns.
War claims many lives, including our loved ones.

Allison von Brevern, Grade 8
Seymour Middle School, WI

My Life

My life is like a roller coaster — it has its ups and downs.
Most days are like the wind that carried me away
And others I still try to believe I'm alive.

I am glad I have my life.
I don't know where I would be without it.
I have a lot of memories that are suddenly disappearing.

This is who I am and the way I live my life.
My parents have given me the courage to live my life to the fullest.
They believe in me and count my scores.

I'm counting my days until I'm free at college.
Do what I want when I grow up
Because I know my parents will be proud of me.

I live my life the way I want.
Nothing will ever change that.
I know that my life will support me with whatever choice I make.

My life is like a roller coaster — it has its ups and downs.
Most days are like the wind that carried me away
And others I still try to believe I'm alive.

Becky Roiger, Grade 8
Springfield School, MN

Aurora Borealis

The Aurora Borealis hangs in the atmosphere
Like smooth colorful waves
Pulsing with great light
Out on the frosted frozen tundra
On the highest mountain summits
It can be sighted
Almost anywhere in the northern hemisphere
The solar gales are responsible
For this astronomical phenomenon
Magnetism is a factor for its radiance
Possible on other planet
Both Saturn and Jupiter
Named after Greek words
The collision of charged particles
From earths magnetosphere
Shifting arcs
Of pink white and green
With many myths that come with this happening
But it all comes back
To the great star in
The center of our system

Samuel Schaefer, Grade 7
Pilgrim Lutheran School, WI

The Flight

A dark stage, excitement blocks the air
The butterflies in my stomach flit their wings
Ready to take flight
All of my hard work has led to this
These few short minutes in which I fly
For that little bit, I'm the center of attention
Nothing can cripple me
Across the stage, adrenaline pumping
The lights blur past as I drift
Then
The stage escapes into darkness, the music's stopped
It's over.
The butterflies had taken flight
The adrenaline withdrawn
A wave of emotions lurches into me,
Foreknowing, but still bewildered by its force
Tears surge in my eyes, why did it have to End?

Geena Kerr, Grade 9
Clarkston Jr High School, MI

The Sail

Wind blowing across my moistened skin
The sun kissing my face lightly
Waves splashing against the body of the boat
The smell of sun screen dancing in the warm air
Sound of laughter filling my heart
The simple pleasure of happiness
Wishing it could last forever

Olivia Parmenter, Grade 7
Ovid-Elsie Middle School, MI

Looking Down

Across the land,
over the ocean,
The smog is obvious and gray.
Through the crowded streets,
over the bridge,
by the hopeless hills of shacks.
Up and down countless hills full of green life.
To the little towns,
dirty and full of stench.
Up the rough mountain,
through the thick trees,
over the bumpy road,
up towards the summit,
where beauty dwells,
peace like no other,
looking down.
Green in so many shades.
A moment there means peace,
no worries,
looking down.

Justina Rinzel, Grade 8
Abundant Life Christian School, WI

Sleeping

Sleeping is like watching TV
you can relax and enjoy it all the time,
you can dream about your feeling,
sleeping is a form of love.
You can fantasize your love,
sleeping is your emotions
like happy, sad or even scared,
sleeping should always be how you want it to be,
sleeping is like spring,
a rainy but satisfying day.

Xavier O. Harris, Grade 8
Middle School at Parkside, MI

Band of Brothers

I think about my brother he's K.I.A.
I don't know how I let him go away
He was a good soldier but now a goner
But at least he got the Medal of Honor
Now he rests in peace in Arlington
I think about it where I live in Washington
I'm still sad to this day
I want him to come back so it will go all away
I think about the last thing I thought about us
in the sea that is blue
I'm standing here and I salute you

Jon Greiser, Grade 9
South View Middle School, MN

Teenage Girls

Teenage Girls —
we're so exciting,
schedules packed,
and nail biting

Picky eaters,
sassing back,
so much homework
we'll break our back

Romance movies,
scary rides,
it's in these things
that we take pride.

Nail biting,
schedules packed,
we're so exciting
and that is that.

Chelsey Knuth, Grade 7
Lake Shore Middle School, WI

Bubble

B low so high
U p in the sky
B uried in the clouds
B urst
L ight as a feather
E nd with a pop

Heather Scherer, Grade 7
Christ Child Academy, WI

Places

Many people many faces.
So little time so many places.
The world out there is really hard.
But try your best and you'll get far.
People come and go.
But what you love the most will show.

Brittany Ruscher, Grade 7
Valley View Middle School, MN

The Sun

The sun begins in the morning.
Coloring the new day sky.
Full of blues, reds, and pinks.
Growing brighter as the day progresses.
Gracing all the Earth with warmness
Then, slowly, again filling the sky
With brilliant colors.
Being replaced by the moon and stars,
Only to begin another journey tomorrow.

Lindsay Hubbard, Grade 7
Otsego Middle School, MI

Rose

Flower
Strong, beautiful
Swaying, growing, blooming
They're soft and prickly
Rose

David Shamblin, Grade 7
Langston Hughes Academy, MI

Swimming

Swimming, swimming in the pool.
Why is the water so cool?

Swimming, swimming really fast.
Why am I having such a blast?

Swimming, swimming, it's so fun.
Why am I not in the sun?

Swimming, swimming, I'm so wet.
Swimming and I have just met?

Niki Breeggemann, Grade 7
Shakopee Area Catholic School, MN

Homeless

The rain is coming down
I seek for shelter for the night
I sit and know I am who I am
A man without a home

Every day I am under your bridges
Every day I am at your home
And every day I wonder
If you will let me sleep in your home,

You know who I am,
A man with only this poem

Ryan Kupietz, Grade 7
Shakopee Area Catholic School, MN

Sweet

A tear drop shows a love so
passionate and rare
Only actions show how much a
person really cares
The words you use to take
Their breath away
Although what you do means more
than anything you say
Sweep them off their feet
And make their heart glow
With a SWEET little poem
and a kiss to make the magic grow

Faith Roberts, Grade 7
Washington Middle School, WI

I Love Him

I love him because he is there
I love him when he is gone
I love him every time I think
I love him when I am at home
I love him when I see his face
I love him because he loves me

Emily Schultz, Grade 7
Centreville Jr High School, MI

Watchful

The ones who stand the tallest
Are always the first to fall
on the battle of the mind.

While the ones who swoon
till the stars are aligned find
they are undeniably successful.

Even the smartest of us are
susceptible to pride and propaganda
the ability to see beyond it is the key.

With a sword of death and daring
One can only go so far
But one can live on forever as a giver

To knowledge and wisdom
Pain usually follows
Like a dog watching you.

For some ignorance is bliss
though to not know always
causes pain for all when the time comes.

Chris Van Hoozen, Grade 8
Seymour Middle School, WI

Love

I love the way you smell soo nice
and your heart is full of sugar and spice
every time I hug you,
I smell the sweet smell of a rose
in my nose
and I hope you know
that you make me feel tingly inside
like my stomach is filled with butterflies
The two of us
are like home skillet biscuits
on a skillet
yes I feel it
the love between us is true
and it is true,
that I love you

Shaprece Nabors, Grade 8
Jerstad Agerholm Middle School, WI

Soccer
Field Fairies freely fluttering,
Soccer balls graciously gliding through the air,
Fans frantically cheering on their teams,
goals that miss but just hit the beams,
games that end with many sad scenes,
intensely interested fans,
goalie's grinding their teeth,
cleats crushing objects in their way,
favorite teams just love to play,
shin guards shielding players' legs,
sweat soaking through the uniforms,
soccer, worldwide favorite sport!
Steven Ambroch, Grade 8
St Roman School, WI

Mustang Pride
Wild horses streak across the plains.
Eluding helicopters whirling after them.

Glittering with sweat, they run on,
Twirling in and out of sagebrush.

Pounding and scoring the dew-covered grass,
And flashing through the water,
Droplets spraying, rich mist flying.

They pop over green-colored,
Peppermint-scented sagebrush,
Bursting onto a hidden trail.

Rocketing away,
Skidding to a halt,
Dripping with water and sweat...
They rest.
Melanie Dubart, Grade 7
Cedar Springs Middle School, MI

Betrayed
I've been betrayed
It's a feeling that never goes away
The feeling that builds up inside you
Something that is awful
You can't really get rid of it
Unless you find the person who caused it
Then you can finally be free from all your hurt
But don't totally let them bring you down
Try to keep away from the frowns
So when you've been betrayed
Try to let it all fade away
Nicole Olson, Grade 7
Perry Middle School, MI

I Who Love My Family
I who love my family
They are very supporting
And loving when I need it
They always give me what I want
In the only way they know how
As if I was an only child, but I am not
Makes them think how well they treat me
When they talk to me, it's helpful to know
Their spirits lift me up, and make them who they are now
Molly Thekan, Grade 8
Central Middle School, MI

Ode to Fire-Belly Newt
O Fire-Belly Newt,
With your slimy skin, your orange belly
Brighter than day, your ink black skin
Darker than night.
Your mouth is wide like a fisherman's net.
Gobbling up food tiny bugs and crawfish eggs.
You live in a canal with ten feet of muck.
Swimming through the green, murky water.
Hopefully with some luck you will find my mom's lost flip-flop.
O Fire-Belly Newt, you seem unafraid
To swim by fish so big they can gobble you up
But you hide behind the lily pads.
O Fire-Belly Newt, didn't you see that frog
Sitting on the lily pad sunning himself.
O Fire-Belly Newt, where did you go?
Liam Acton, Grade 7
Japhet School, MI

Storm and Water
A wisk of air moves slowly across a bright bay.
A calm sun beats down on the soft sand.
Water rushes fast against the shore.
BOOM!
The wind starts to blow.
The sun goes behind a dark cloud.
The water is coming fast, towards the bay.
Drip, drip.
It starts to rain.
The rain hits hard on the ocean water.
The wind picks up even more.
It becomes very dark and cold.
The water has become fierce, crashing on the bay.
Crash, crash.
Lightning lights up the sky like the bright lights of Las Vegas.
The wind starts to push down the trees.
The sky is filled with clouds and thunder.
The water is black and cold.
BOOM, drip, crash.
These are the sounds of a storm,
A fierce storm.
Taylor Baker, Grade 7
Cedar Springs Middle School, MI

The Bright Blue Balloon

A bright blue balloon,
Floating up in the air.
I looked up and knew,
That it was going somewhere.
It traveled the world,
That bright blue balloon,
From Paris to Peru,
And Tokyo, too.
But the balloon got older,
And weaker,
And smaller.
It slowly fell down,
Into a small, little town.
The town where I saw it,
Up in the air,
The town where I knew,
That it was going somewhere.

Veronica Belczynski, Grade 7
Scranton Middle School, MI

Like the Sun

Life is like the sun.
The brightest in the universe.
Shining on everyone.
Making things grow.
Bringing light to the world.
Showing the way.

Life is like the sun.
No sign of going away.
Knowing that it may go
any day.
Not knowing how long
it's been around.

Life is like the sun.
Quiet and gentle.
Loud and rough.

Andrei Georgescu, Grade 8
Washington Middle School, WI

Shattered

The worn down, stingy birch tree
Embedded on the winter slope
With each of its branches
Torn by the snow
Waits for nothing
Promising to come along
Branches like self-confidence
Being shattered because nobody cares
Abandoned, deserted, friendless
The sun smiles and waits for a response

None.

Darcy Knaack, Grade 9
Clintonville High School, WI

Can You Hear It?

There's music everywhere,
Can you hear it?
All you need to do is listen,
There's Bach in the wind, Vivaldi in the stream, Mozart in the sun and
Beethoven in the birds' wings.
Can you hear it? Do you listen?
The violins get their cue from the water reeds,
The piano begins under the direction of the trees.
Can you hear it? Do you listen?
The harp plays in sync with the Lily of the Valley,
The whole meadow is an orchestra, and the wind its director.
Did you hear it?
Stop and listen,
Let the music surround you…can you hear it?

Laura Grunke, Grade 8
Robert J Elkington Middle School, MN

Freedom

The color of freedom is the red blood of our soldiers
The blue of our soldiers' armor, the white stars of all our colonies.
Freedom looks like our flag flying high and proud.
Freedom smells like gunpowder and sweat from winning a battle.
Freedom sounds like our national anthem playing high and loud.
Freedom tastes like a freshly baked apple pie made by Betsy Ross.
Freedom feels like when an eagle flies high and proud, with wind in its wings.

Linda Conaway, Grade 7
Northwood School, WI

My Life Is a Skateboard

The trucks are my grandma that makes me stand
The deck is my brother that balances my life out
The bearing are my nieces and nephew that send me out of control
The hardware are my friends that hold my life together.

Christian Bullis, Grade 7
Manistee Middle School, MI

The Dark Tunnel

Twisting and turning through the dark tunnel
Faster and faster forevermore.
Surcease in the hole, flying through air returning
Home nevermore.
Never to return to see the bright sky
From before.
More and more turning, twisting, and tumbling,
Faster, faster, through the dark and
Dangerous tunnel.
I blow to my God when I see the end of the tunnel.

I can see the end of the dark and dangerous tunnel.
The light at the end is getting
Brighter and brighter.
I fall faster and even faster, hoping to see my
Family some more.
Then I wake up panting, realizing it was just a terrible nightmare.

Abbi Johnson, Grade 7
Bristol Elementary School, WI

A Small Square Mystery

The item on the desk is a mystery
This man's private property that could contain anything
I try to look through as if the casing was clear
The magical wonder that could be inside
Although it could just be paper
But what is on that paper?
Possibly the numerous rough drafts of a story
That will one day be a best seller
But what about?
A prince rescuing a princess from a fire breathing dragon
Or a love story set back in the 1800's
Maybe even a story of a high school bully
And the kids that contend for themselves in the end
I look deep into the man's face
No emotion radiates through giving me hints
About what could possibly be inside
He is a business man probably not writing about
Dragons, love, or bullies
This object is a mystery
A mystery that this man only knows
That I will never find out as I walk away

Olivia Dunn, Grade 9
Clarkston Jr High School, MI

Basketball

It's more than just a game you play
It's a way to relax and get through the day
You work and you work to get things right
Just to walk on the court and be in the spotlight

The game is all about hustle
And how much passion you have and how much muscle
When you look into the crowd
You see your family and want to make them proud

It's not just about you
Get your teammates involved too
You can be the leader of a team
And chase all your dreams

There's 24 minutes of hustle and sweat
And I'm willing to bet
Every player on the court's got the heart
Well I got to go the game's about to start.

Cody Dejewski, Grade 7
St Roman School, WI

Book

A hard covered book
Freshly printed pages
Swift turn of a page
Smooth spine
Tongue bitten words

Kenna Rentmeester, Grade 7
Elkhart Lake Elementary-Middle School, WI

The Darkness

Traveling in the dark,
the mist swirling down in around me.
I miss the warmth of the sun
and hate this feeling of mystery.
I risk everything here,
following my slow beating heart
telling me to come to you,
while my brain tells me to stay
as I have been for a while.
Should I go and risk disappointment,
or stay and save my heart the depression.
My instincts tell me to live my life
boring days and lonely nights as I have been,
but other parts tell me to explore,
to fill the empty hole that burns
dark and deep inside my body.
I travel forward in the dark
the mist swirling down in around me.
I miss my sun.

Alexis Green, Grade 9
Clarkston Jr High School, MI

I'm Gone

My heart pounds as it is grasping for air,
beating as if it is going to fail.
Tears run down my face as I cry for life.
I'm seeing things, things that aren't clear.
I feel as if everything has stopped
As I focus on any image I see…
As everything fades away.
  I'm back to life and everything is different.
  Things that I do not comprehend
  People around me, people I don't know.
  I'm at a place, unknown to my knowledge.
  …I'm Gone.

Autumn Ryan, Grade 7
Sister Academy/Harvest Prep School, MN

What I Learn

I learn don't be nasty
what I learn
no one will come around you
so what I learn
don't be nasty.

Into the world and out the world.
Into the world and out the world
every second and leave every second so many left
so many came into the world and out.

Kanisha Morris, Grade 7
Sherman Multicultural Arts School, WI

Reality

Something that is sometimes hard to face, hard to believe, and hard to take in. Something that is sometimes great, believable, and worth living, but how do you see it. Is it scary, is it happy. What is it? It is a very powerful outlook on life. Whether you are struggling with paying the bills and you see yourself as a gifted and lucky individual or you are one of the richest people in the world and you still want bigger and better things. How could we live without seeing the truth? How could we see without hearing it? How could we live without feeling it, but for me, and how I live, I see reality as just being a theory that is not fully represented.

Joslin Barnes, Grade 8
Middle School at Parkside, MI

Summertime in Duluth

In the morning when I awake, I go for a jog down by the lake
Then I come in and have some brunch, watch ESPN and later have lunch
My friends and I, eat lunch in the sun, you should try it, it's actually quite fun
Then maybe play some sports, with the other kids here in the Twin Ports
That's not all we do, just play sports, we have many activities of all different sorts
I often go biking, others like hiking
Others like to hike on a bike, like my friend, Mike
I go fishing with my friend Neal, at least once a week, we made a deal
Unless it's raining then it's too wet, or night comes too fast and the sun's already set
If that's the case and the sky is in a cry, we go to the Y, my friend Neal and I
Then I go inside for one final meal then it's time to hit the hay, and then do it over again the very next day

Ben Hoven, Grade 9
Lakeview Christian Academy, MN

Not the Perfect One

We've been here together through thick and thin, but I hope we're here until the end.
But if we're not, I just want to say, I'm still going to love you, anyway.
It could have been the way you smiled at me, or how you wore your hair maybe that could be.
I don't know why I even said hello, because now I feel like I'm three million below.
It was great at first, then it came to the worst.
Everyone has their perfect one, their one true love under the sun.
But you must have been too perfect for me, because you said "You're not the one for me."
And I wish I could go all the way back. I know there's so much that I lack.
I hope that our friendship will always be there, as long as we both breathe the same sweet air.
But if it's not, I just want to say, I'm still going to love you, somewhere and someway.
The necklace I gave you has sentimental meaning. It shows everything about us, except my true feelings.

Damian Dagel, Grade 9
Pipestone Sr High School, MN

You Decide

Think of our future, as you normally would. Together or alone? What do you see? Are you really looking? Are you just skimming? Be realistic. Don't imagine bits and pieces, but see it as a whole. What dreams come true? What fears become reality?
What path are you following? What road will you leave? Will you be remembered? Will your name remain unknown? Will you be all that you can be? What will you take for granted? Will you live on your feet? Will you die on your knees?
Will you love and be loved? Will you crave power and be greedy? How much will you help? How much will you hurt? Will you look and really see? What will you over look? Will it even matter?
What will it take to open your eyes? Where will it all go when you blink? What will you risk? Will you regret all or nothing? Will you thrive and flourish? Will you be a culprit of ail? Can you make this lifetime glorious, what generation after generation will envy? Will you make this generation a dirty secret?
What will you become? Are you true to yourself? Will you let one lie fall through the cracks? Two? More? Will you watch the sky turn pink then fade to black? Will you watch others enjoy what you won't work towards? Will you make up your own mind or fall under the influence?
You decide.

Kathryn Snediker, Grade 8
Eppler Jr High School, MI

Summer Is the Best Time of the Year

My favorite season comes once a year
From May through August I'm in the clear,
Come September I will shed a tear
Back to school is what I fear.

Summer brings us nice warm sun
To swim, do activities, and have some fun;
By the end of the day I am done
All the kids go inside and there are none,

The pool is the place I want to be
People in cold places wish they were me
I dive in and open my eyes to see
I'm surrounded by deep blue water.

Eventually, I have to go back to school
One year older, I feel cool
I am ready to learn and apply the rules;
To grow, become smarter, and use the tools.

Summer will eventually be back
I need to make sure I do not slack
My mother makes sure I stay on track
I can't wait for summer so I can kick back.

Marina Bergamo, Grade 7
Our Lady Star of the Sea School, MI

Chaotic

You're the one who's judging me,
yet you're the one who will see
I tell myself,
you're hurting yourself not hurting me.
You're the stinger on the bee
trying to come and attack me.
I won't bet the person
you want me to be
I am who I am and you can't
change me,
this world is big and you pick on someone small
I'm yet here…standing tall.
every day I think about you
wondering what did I ever do,
I'm not growing up too fast
so you need to leave it in the past…
I'm young…and you're trying to make
what I will become…
You have your life, I got mine…
worry about yourself
and it will all be FINE!

Rachel Kutzler, Grade 7
Valley View Middle School, MN

My First Home Run

My First Home Run
It was a fairly cold night
There was a thunderstorm in sight
My bat felt like a feather, it was so light
It was the top of the fifth
We had a comfortable lead of six
Nobody knew what I had in my bag of tricks
The pitch was high and tight
To me, it looked just right
So I swung with all my might
When I hit it, I knew it should
I always knew I could
But, I never thought it would
As I rounded second base
My heart started to race
Wow! It was an amazing feeling when I reached home plate
My First Home Run

Keenan Moehring, Grade 8
Seymour Middle School, WI

It's What We Call Winter

The weather is hushed
By the cool damp air
The leaves have stopped falling
Fields lay in a dead state of life.

Blue jays nest in everlasting evergreens
Maples and oaks sit out naked
The sky is a gloom
Clouds always blocking the shimmery sun.

White has fallen among the still-living wilderness
Flakes of heaven fall from the sky
Tales of men in red suits and reindeer arrive
Soon there will be presents under your tree

Like a sky scraper has fallen from the sky,
The snow lay.
People trying to force the snow away, away
It's what we call winter.

Colton Schenk, Grade 8
Seymour Middle School, WI

Smokey Lake

Where no hate is allowed.
Where people come in with a temper,
and leave as calm as tiny ripples in the water.

Smokey lake is a color of spring,
and people get along as well as root beer and ice cream.

A room of Smokey Lake
is a relaxed room.

Hank Roers, Grade 7
Valley View Middle School, MN

Snow

The snow is so cold
It is beautiful
but it is so fun

Sarah Rice, Grade 7
Centreville Jr High School, MI

A Worthless Day

The classroom is bursting with children
"you kids participate"
choruses the teacher
some hands rise
other stay firmly planted
words sputter off hesitant lips
a correctly answered question
more kids point to the sky
"take a chance,
learn from mistakes"
one kid sits in the corner
hand glued to the desk
afraid of being wrong
doesn't try
doesn't fail
doesn't learn
another worthless hour.

Whitney Kelley, Grade 9
Clarkston Jr High School, MI

The Protectors

We hold our babies in our arms
Waiting for them to fall,
And when they fall,
They have a blanket
To grow tall and strong
But some of us stand alone
And others unprepared.

Joseph Hannay, Grade 8
Zimmerman Jr High School, MN

Bad Company vs Good Morals

It's better
To be alone
Than in
Bad company

When driving
Into Casco
From Luxemburg
You will see a sign

The sign says
"Bad Company Corrupts Good Morals"
This means that bad company
Can ruin you, yourself
As how good you acted before

Emily Hanmann, Grade 7
Luxemburg-Casco Middle School, WI

Ready

I'm crouched down ready to pounce
My body is balanced on my toes
I feel like I weigh an ounce
My claws are extended facing my foes
A fire burns in my eyes
With tense muscles I ready myself under blue skies
I know my job is to protect my turf
My prey lunges through the air, but it cannot escape me.
It's coming my way.
I stare up at it.
Its white skin stands out among the sky blue background.
The words I know all too well escape my throat…"I GOT IT!"
My back bends and I lean back.
My tingling arms and fearful prey collide.
My prey flies back through the sky.
Once again my prey returns, but it is higher in the air.
My clawed hands flatten with my fingers spread apart.
Those same words erupt from my mouth.
My whole arm extends above; my head swings back.
Swishing forward, my hand connects with the ball…and "WHAM!"
It soars over the net and onto the other court's floor.

Andrea Lynaugh, Grade 8
Cedar Grove-Belgium Middle School, WI

Summer Days

Dreary skies won't let me be
Frigid winds rattle me
Ice and mire tempt a groan
I've never felt more alone

For the sun to settle in the sky like an overripe peach
Stretching her warm fingers across the beach
For the periwinkle heavens to never vanish without a trace
Instead to wrap me in a never ending embrace

What would I give
For such a perfect way to live?
More than a mother would convey for her child
I desire this summer's weather to be beautifully mild

I dream of unblemished sand
And gentle breezes swirling across my island
Of azure tides tickling my toes
And the sunlight evaporating my woes

I crave to soak up the glow
That is emitted for everything to flourish and grow
Unfortunately, I will have to wait,
But patience will give me appreciation for what's put on my plate.

Elizabeth Hendra, Grade 8
Sandusky Middle School, MI

Christmas Tree

I woke up to see the snow
There was one thing I had to see
Just what was under the Christmas tree
I got up and went to the floor below

When I crept to the edge of the stairs
My mind was empty and blank
I would get gifts from Mom, Dad and Uncle Hank
I didn't have any worries or cares

I walked up to the Christmas tree
I looked at the presents just for me
Oh that green tree, so very tall
It would be the best Christmas of all

Gavin Griese, Grade 8
Adams Friendship Middle School, WI

Ice Fishing

Weekend weekend to the lake, going to catch that one big fish.
Fishing fishing to the ice. I can smell that one great taste.
Dropping dropping the line of fame.
Waiting waiting for the bit of fame.
Looking looking here's the one.
Reeling reeling so frantically.
Hooray hooray the fish has arrived.
Boohoo boohoo the fish would say.
Cleaning cleaning that one big fish.
Cooking cooking it smells well.
Yummy yummy that was good.

Adam Schuhmacher, Grade 7
Shakopee Area Catholic School, MN

Fallen

From below I watched
As he smiled down at me,
The perfect angel,
Glowing with a brilliant light that warmed my heart.
I continued to look longingly after him,
But I saw him moving farther and farther away.
I was falling, and he was flying,
Drifting higher and higher
As I fell into the dark depths below.
My only hope was the light,
Radiant, just as he was.
Falling and falling,
Helpless to do otherwise,
I watched as he rose farther above me
Until he was gone.
With him he took the wondrous light,
Causing my heart to freeze over.
And still I fell.
For that was me,
The fallen angel.

Andrea EunJoo Scherlinck, Grade 8
Boulan Park Middle School, MI

Team Reptile 2007

The sheer weight
The green shell full of mold emerging from
The darkest recesses
The beast emerged
A behemoth so large, 3 nets, 4 people
Lifted the monstrosity
He hissed like a rattlesnake
Snapped the net and nearly escaped
Twenty minutes of hoisting onto the floating dock
Attacked like lightning
The clenching jaws of the hungry beast
Captured on camera, no doubt there
Sizing him up was a struggle
Neck fully extended beak to tip of tail
Measured five and a half foot long snapper
Bigger than any caught before
In camp the largest I had ever seen
The 189 pound turtle was our biggest catch
Rich, Amy, Courtney, Kourtney, myself, Zach, Lauren
And all the kids were astonished at Independence Oaks
That day, July 17, 2007 Team Reptile ruled.

Max Wolfgang, Grade 9
Clarkston Jr High School, MI

The Beautiful Tetyana

I hear him say her name aloud.
When he sits there and thinks about,
Nothing but, his beautiful Tetyana

I want to see you there with her,
And not right here in the world so hurt,
Please say again "My beautiful Tetyana"

I want you laughing there,
With her all you'll want to share,
The words "My beautiful Tetyana"

To see you catch her when she falls,
In the middle of your high school halls,
And say, "Excuse me, oh my beautiful Tetyana"

When you catch her sight,
You think about the light
That says to you "Your beautiful Tetyana"

I want to see you cry,
And say I lost her because of a small lie,
And say to her once more
"Forgive me, oh my beautiful Tetyana"

Olena Hladun, Grade 8
Spring Hill School, WI

Pain

Pain
Is an angry lion
Limping helplessly
Across the plains
Screaming out at the wound
Leaving behind a crimson trail.

Samantha Gleason, Grade 8
Anderson Middle School, MI

Coco Beach

I sit down on the floor of
The smooth sand
Listening to the rumbling
Crashing waves
Hearing the exciting yelps
Of children
Looking at the swooshing
Movement of the rough
Pattern of waves enjoying
My satisfying summer's day

Casey Mittemiller, Grade 7
Manistee Middle School, MI

Fire and Fear

Fear is like fire
Sometimes you need it then you don't
It can be safe, then it can't
In the one moment of terror
Fire burns through your brains
Erasing your every thought
Fear is like fire

Denisha Montgomery, Grade 7
Valley View Middle School, MN

Baseball

On the top of home plate
With my father's hands over mine
Holding on tight to the bat
Moving our hands together
Swinging at the imaginary ball
He let go of my hands
Picked up the ball
And he swiftly ran away from me
He said
"Keep your eye on the ball"
I watched as he lifted his arm back
And tossed the ball
I watched the ball spin towards me
I gripped the bat tight
And pulled the bat back
And
Swung

Grace Smith, Grade 9
Clarkston Jr High School, MI

Grandpa Al

Why did you have to go
On that dreaded afternoon
You made it through the world war
But not that afternoon
Why
Why did you have to go

Nate Gahler, Grade 7
Shakopee Area Catholic School, MN

Things to Do if You Are the Sun

Be gentle.
Make the world a little brighter.
Kiss my face lightly in the afternoon.
Make the grass green.
Inspire.
Stay here forever.

Eva Meraz, Grade 8
Fairview Charter School, WI

Life...

Life,
life as you know it
you sit, you wonder
what should I do with mine
my life is a roller coaster
it goes
up
down
and goes all around
the life I have is smooth
the life I have gets rocky
so let's get back to reality...

as *life goes on!*

Marshay Kennedy, Grade 7
Valley View Middle School, MN

Motocross

Motocross is a great sport,
Even though it's played off court.
Down dirt tracks and open fields,
Is where the fun is all revealed.

Racing over small bumps,
Hitting huge jumps,
Flying high through the air,
Nothing can ever compare.

All you need is some gear,
A decent bike, and no fear.
And so with all the right stuff,
You will soon be good enough.

Harvey Redman, Grade 8
St Thomas More Academy, MI

Earth

People are killing our Earth!
What is this all worth?
People keep trashing.
And bashing!
People are so mean!
Why don't we try to think green?
Stop wasting paper!
And become a scraper.
That means someone who picks up litter.
And people stop being so bitter!
Don't you see what were doing!
Lots of people are booing.
Why do we do this?
And please don't miss,
The garbage can,
Come on man!
There are a lot of people to blame!
Do they think this is a game?
So stop killing the Earth!
We need our Earth
IT'S THE ONLY PLANET WE GOT!!!!

Brittany Coopman, Grade 8
Washington Middle School, WI

I Do Not Understand...

I do not understand,
Why you have to get toys
Why we have to play outside
Why I am still small

I really don't understand,
Why we have to go to war
Why we fight with our siblings
Why I have to go everywhere

What I understand most is,
Why I have to go to school
Why my family loves me
Why you celebrate holidays.

Cody Fiol, Grade 8
St Mary's School, WI

Spring Is in the Air

The smell of spring is in the air,
the trees are dancing and have no scare,
the birds fly with no direction
because spring is in the air.
Spring tells the flowers to open up
and let the nectar flow,
and let the insects flourish up,
spring, spring, please don't go,
keep this season and never let go.

Joe Randazzo, Grade 7
Our Lady Star of the Sea School, MI

Life

The gift that keeps on giving,
as we continue living,
in this world of grace.

Keeping fear from our face,
and putting fate in its place.

Bringing us joy night and day,
laughing its head off,
when it's no longer time to stay.

In this paradise we call Earth,
which we've torn,
but another is reborn into the cycle of life.

Some say life's a game,
but it will all end the same.

Life, as fragile as glass,
watch where you step or it will break,
like many others who have made the same mistake.

Karry Emretiyoma, Grade 7
Avondale Middle School, MI

Starlight

In the night the stars so bright
And the moon is high in the sky
As the sun rises to begin a brand new day
The stars fade away
But after the day is through the stars come back out to play
And the moon looks down from above

Ashley Thomas, Grade 7
Elkhart Lake Elementary-Middle School, WI

Washington DC

Washington DC is so big and bright
The flowers are blooming
The sky so dazzling
The birds singing their songs of harmony
You can taste the sweet rain upon your mouth
Feel the limestone on all the magnificent monuments
Hear the sound of cars go by and by
Vroom! Vroom! Honk! Honk!
The cherry blossoms blooming so immense and beautiful
Feel the heat on your skin, as your skin soaks it up
The food sometimes tastes weird
See the flashing of cameras
Tourists on every street taking in the beauty of it all
Rain or shine the Beauty of the city always shines

Nichole Sloan, Grade 7
Whitehall Jr High School, MI

Waterfall

I am a high-energy child,
that loves to do things the fun way.

I am a hypnotizer,
that pulls people toward me because of how amazing I am.

I am a sky diver,
that dives from the top of the cliff to the bottom.

I am a singer,
that can be heard for miles around.

I am a beautiful angel,
that dances around showing its rainbows.

I am a spirited horse,
that is happy and free.

Makayla Lakeman, Grade 7
Roosevelt Middle School, MN

Jesus, My Savior

Jesus, oh Jesus, my always shining light,
guide me through this everlasting night.
Guide me to Heaven, show me the way,
take me by the hand so that I never stray.
Let me tell everybody about the things you've done,
let me tell them about how You're God's only Son,
so that they can see that You are our Savior,
and that they see this through my behavior.
Please, help me guide all nonbelievers closer to God.
Oh, God let me show them that they need You God
to bring them closer to Your light,
until Your presence is in their sight.

Sean Larson, Grade 8
Our Lady of Good Counsel School, MI

Music to My Ears

My ears are filled to the brim,
Clogged, stuffed, overflowed,
I need it all,
Every single note and tune,
The music that flows out of the piano,
As I sit there and let my hands feel the rhythm,
They dance across each ivory key,
With a joyous hop.
And when the song comes to an end,
So does that happiness that went along with it.
But then my hands find some new keys,
And begin to play another song
With notes just as joyous,
And my heart begins to soar with each note,
Into the sky, and beyond the clouds,
Farther than we could ever reach.

Jamie Ockner, Grade 8
West Hills Middle School, MI

Caught

The adrenaline rush
is hard to ignore
As you run for the exit,
And push past the door.
Now at full speed,
Your body is shaking,
The rebel inside you
Is fully awaking.
As you see your escape,
Your heart beating quickly
You feel something wrong,
Your stomach all tickly.
A hand on your shoulder,
A cold stare meeting yours,
You know you've done wrong;
A fact you can't ignore.

Rachael Hunter, Grade 8
Perry Middle School, MI

Up to Us

Trying to be green
Helping the environment
For a better world

Morgan Thompson, Grade 7
Prairie River Middle School, WI

Happy

It looks like a warm sunny day
It sounds like a happy child's laughter
It smells like a basketful of flowers
It tastes like a juicy piece of watermelon
It feels like laughing with family
Yellow

Michelle Conklin, Grade 7
West Middle School, MI

Spring Prayer

For the tree's beauty around us
For the wind blowing in the bus
For the animals by our side
For all the animals worldwide
Father all mighty, we thank thee!

For the green grass on the ground
For the dirt that is brown
For the Earth you put us on for so long
For this is where we belong
Father all mighty, we thank thee!

For the water that we drink
For all the colors such as pink
For the sun warms our hearts
For you making us so smart
Father all mighty, we thank thee!

Antonio Presseller, Grade 7
St Andrew's School, MI

friends

friends are flowers something you hold on to
friends are chocolate something you love
friends are your favorite book something you remember about them
friends are a memory that you will never let go
friends are life they are there every part of your life
friends are the sky something you look up to
friends are your diary that you can talk to
friends are friends that make you want to cry

Ellesse Daniels, Grade 7
Valley View Middle School, MN

An Autumn Walk

I took an autumn walk today,
Not knowing where it may have led.
I took an autumn walk today, because something was askew.
I took an autumn walk today,
And saw leaves a gorgeous red.
I took an autumn walk today, and thought of only you.

I took an autumn walk today,
And saw your face in the trees.
I took an autumn walk today, and whistled your song in the wind.
I took an autumn walk today,
And stepped on your fragile hands, the leaves.
I took an autumn walk today, and seeing your hands dance in the air, grinned.

I took an autumn walk today,
Not knowing where it may have led.
I took an autumn walk today, but my mind thought of someone I knew.
I took an autumn walk today,
Attempting to figure out my head.
I took an autumn walk today, and it led me to my heart, to you.

Katelyn Garza, Grade 8
Seymour Middle School, WI

Breath of Spring

It's the end of winter,
The days fresh with the breath of spring.
The sky is as clear as a bubbling stream,
Dotted with fluffy puffs of white cotton.
An evergreen stands tall over everything,
All of its branches reaching toward the sky,
Like little arms stretching when you first wake in the morning.
The branches bounce playfully in the wind,
Happy to be free of the lumbering weight of the crystal white snow.
Its trunk is rough and cracked,
Like chapped lips after a long day in a cold, harsh wind.
Green moss covers the trunk like a furry coat,
Keeping it snug on this brisk morning.
Pine cones are beginning to peak out of their cocoons,
Looking like little brown caterpillars,
Just yearning to burst into spiny brown butterflies.
It's the end of winter.

Andrea Dumais, Grade 9
Clarkston Jr High School, MI

What Will I Become

I sit by the ocean
Reading my book
About dragons and knights
And I think
What will I become
I think of different jobs
I think of different lives
I think of how it will start
And how it will end
I think of life itself
And how bad it can be
Or how good it can be
I think about my childhood
I think about my teens
I think about adulthood and how it will be
I think about all this and more
But I'll just sit
And think of what I am
Instead of what I will become

Rudie Crawford, Grade 7
Centreville Jr High School, MI

Choices

Each and every day
we make choices.
You choose what to have for lunch
or what to wear to school.
But those are the easy choices.
You also make a choice to be a follower
or a leader;
different or similar.
You choose whether or not to let your true colors shine
or to put a mask on.
You choose to either follow the crowd
or to go the other route.
There's only one person who can make those choices
and that person is you.
You have the power to get through all of the choices
that life throws at you, but you also have the power
to make the right ones.
And with a little bit of faith,
you will.

Rebecca Anderson, Grade 8
Iowa-Grant Elementary-Middle School, WI

The Wind

I am greeted by the light and the dark.
I howl and whistle.
I bring on occasion,
The soft drizzle,
Or the harsh worst.
They bring me in and drop me down.
Leaving me knocking at your door.

Brittney Slack, Grade 8
Iowa-Grant Elementary-Middle School, WI

Death Cry

Tell me, why oh why
must our loved ones die?
I hope they go up high,
in our dear beloved sky.
Why oh why
When I look, I miss their crystal eye?
Don't let them see me cry.
Why oh why
Must their eyes close?
My eyes feel like a hose.
Why oh why
Must "they" leave my side?
Now I want to hide.
My friends ask me if I want a ride (to the funeral),
But now "they" aren't by my side.
Why oh why
do I ask myself "Why now?"
instead I wonder how
I bow my head...
and add another...
Oh, why oh why?

Mariah Colburn, Grade 8
River Crossing Environmental Charter School, WI

A Little Lady

Lady is a dog of mine,
We play together all the time.
We run around and play fetch too,
But really she wants to eat my shoe.

Sometimes she barks too much, I know
Does she want me to be her friend or foe?
What could the cause of her barking be?
The rustling of leaves or a bird in a tree?

Lady looks in the pond and sees a goose
And then her energy is let loose.
She chases that goose all day and night.
Finally, it decides to leave and take flight.

Even though she is full of fun
She also likes to lie in the sun.
This proves that she is not only crazy,
But at times she can be lazy.

Lady is a black lab that is for sure
She likes it when I pet her fur.
She likes to have fun and fetch a ball.
Lady is the best pet of all.

Catherine Weisbrod, Grade 7
St Thomas More Academy, MI

One Window Is All I Need

One window is all I need
To see who I am
To see who I will become
To see what I will get into
To prepare for it
And to live my life.

Grant Clementi, Grade 8
West Suburban Christian Academy, WI

Seasons of Life

Time goes by
Real fast, real slow,
And as it flies
We watch the show.

Of hope and love
Despair and pain,
Our lives are lost
In this great game.

Of catching up
And slowing down,
From fall to spring
I write it down.

The boom the burst
The rise and fall,
The joy of life
Is in us all.

Jordan Peyer, Grade 7
St Patrick Elementary School, WI

White

White is the snow
When it falls in the night
White is your fingers
When you're holding on tight
It's the fluffy white clouds,
That float in the sky.
It's the pretty white doves
That go soaring by.
It's the stars that sparkle
And shine so bright
It's the stripes on our flag
That remind us of what's right
It's the teeth in our smiles
On all of our faces,
It's the game of baseball
As they stomp the bases
White's the color
That makes up them all
It's the color of a snowman
That stands very tall
White, the clearest of them all.

Brooke Gow, Grade 8
Lake Fenton Middle School, MI

Three Steps

Violence, screaming, words
Those three things
The only things that can truly hurt me
Nothing else can hurt me, I'll just put my other face back on

Violence is a horrible thing
It should never happen and people should just talk it through
Violence is something that really doesn't need to exist
People use it every day without even knowing it

Screaming really isn't needed either,
When two people scream at each other nobody is listening
Neither of them backs down and they don't even know what they're fighting about
Screaming is the second thing that starts the problem

Words are very hurtful
They hurt everybody no matter what
Words can be used for good or bad
Words are the first thing that starts the problem

Those three things combined
Made me, they chose the way I am
The way I talk and act
These three things I shall never ever do

Jorge Fonseca, Grade 8
Seymour Middle School, WI

My World

I remember sleeping late every morning
And having nowhere to go or nothing to do all day.
I remember being entertained by absolutely everything and anything.
Watching cartoons while coloring and drawing were my hobbies.
I remember every night I was read to before falling asleep with my stuffed animals.
My best and only friends were within walking distance and that was my world.
I remember how my parents dressed me every morning, and that was my world.
Things have changed for me now:
I still enjoy many of the same thrills I did when I was younger, however
No longer do I get to sleep in late
I constantly have somewhere to be or something to do
I still get joy and entertainment from the simplest things
I don't have time to draw, color or watch cartoons.
If I want to be read to before bed, I read to myself
I fall asleep alone without the company of a stuffed animal
My friends don't live nearby
I get up early and get ready for school
I will remember and cherish these teenage days when I'm older
And when I read to my kids every night
Before they fall asleep with their stuffed animals.
This is my world

Markiesa Westphal, Grade 9
Clintonville High School, WI

Mountains

I wander through the mountains,
Up them and back down,
Over their vast feet,
That join them to the ground.

I ascend their legs,
The sun peeks through the clouds.
I can feel the mountain smile,
As it is warmed by the light.

I meander up the mountain,
To a special place I found.
It's peaceful and calm,
I sit down and relax.

The mountain plays me a song.
The rush of a waterfall,
The calls of birds,
The echo of my voice as I sing along.

Along the mighty shoulders of the mountain,
Every step closer to the top.
Soon I'm leaving my footprints,
I've made it to the top.

Erin Cargill, Grade 8
J C McKenna Middle School, WI

Gloomy Morning

I woke up in the morning.
Everything was peaceful and quiet,
not even the birds were singing.
I looked at my clock
and it was very early.
I tried to go back to sleep,
but it was impossible.
I got out of bed
and tiptoed, tiptoed to my window.
I looked outside,
the morning was very dark and gloomy.
Then, I started to hear drip-drop, drip-drop.
I opened my window
and I put my hand out.
Indeed, it was beginning to rain.
I pulled my hand back in,
and took a deep breath.
Then, I closed my window,
went back to bed,
and thanked God
for the world He created.

Fatima Castillo, Grade 7
St Roman School, WI

I Remember...

I remember the hot summer day.
I remember sitting at the picnic table.
I remember the craving I had.
I remember the sweet taste of the half circle fruit.
I remember spitting out one seed at a time.
I remember eating right down to the green outer coating.
I remember how much I love watermelons.

Ashley Garcia, Grade 7
Manistee Middle School, MI

Inspiration

She spins
She leaps
Lights on me, I'm comforted by the words
She speaks like she skates
Graceful and smooth
Russian dancers come to dance
The best of the best
I would never miss the chance
Starting at thirty never to end
Inspires me and my dreams
Inspires my team
That team of hard workers
People watch from the stands
In awe they gasp,
A triple axle she lands
Practice until your feet hurt
Blisters on your hands
To some it's a joke
To some it's all glam
To them it's something else
It's what comes of it at the end

Jessica Jurkiewicz, Grade 8
Fairview Charter School, WI

Big Bear

Skiing downhill for the first time ever
Falling constantly knowing I can only get better

With my skis falling off trying to stand
My mom and dad giving me a hand

Riding up the ski lift way above the trees
Clomping all the snow off of my skis

Time after time down the hill I would go
Faster and faster with my face full of snow

At the end of the day when we were almost done
I was skiing down the hardest run

The skis were so smooth like butter on toast
When I got to the bottom all I had to do was coast

Brianna Messner, Grade 8
Seymour Middle School, WI

Who Am I?

I am one true person that wants to be understood
I wonder how many stars are in the sky
I hear my voice in my mind asking what I am to do
I see different people in the world wondering if we fit in
I want to change things to make them better
I am the one looking around asking myself questions

I pretend to know what is going on
I feel very conscious of the things I do and or say
I touch the deepest part of my heart never wanting to let go
I worry about the people that are lonely and or sad
I cry my self to sleep thinking of the things I have done wrong thinking of how to fix them
I am the uniqueness in this world to myself hoping to stand out

I seem to understand other people's problems
I say things that I might not mean when I say them
I dream of making my life better than what I, my family, and friends expect me to
I try to be not so moody, forgetful, and confusing
I hope that in my life and years I can accomplish all my needs and wants
I am thinking of how I should fix my problems without making any more of them

Diana Gonzalez, Grade 8
St Andrew's School, MI

Fake

Don't you know how to be real, or are you too busy being fake,
Trying to act like someone else, trying to be perfect for someone else's sake.

From the outside, you look happy, but we both know that's not right,
People don't care enough to look closely, to find the real you locked up tight.

Your too caught up in your image, too afraid to actually be you,
Your afraid if you act like yourself, your friends will go find someone new.

Is it tiring acting like someone your not, or is it like riding a bike?
Once you know how, you never forget, deep down you have to know, it's not you they like.

There's no one you can open up to, no one you can confide in,
No one to listen to your problems and help, but if there was, would you know where to begin?

The mask you've put on is just so not you, so how about you stop being so fake
And actually be yourself, do it for yourself, your own sake.

Samantha Gerber, Grade 9
Montgomery-Lonsdale High School, MN

Hamborguesa

Sweet, sweet succulent juices,
how lost I would be without tasting them just once.
The first time my mouth wrapped around this perfect mix of cow and bread my life changed for the better,
I knew then that I shall never stray in the game we call life for I have tasted the food of God Himself.
This wonder that I speak of is of course the majestically edible hamburger.
People call it many a name but no one word can describe the feeling that one gets from taking a bite out of this holy delicacy.
They call you hamburger but to me you are my ever sweet Hamborguesa.

Rich Cieszkowski, Grade 8
Grosse Pointe Academy, MI

Ode to Chocolate

Oh chocolate
so very sweet and tender
you are very flavorful

Some think you're nasty when you are spicy

Oh chocolate
crashing and splashing,
crashing and splashing down my throat.

Oh chocolate
you are like my taste bud smiling
chocolate so smooth and silky

Oh chocolate
the scent and looks of creamy chocolate pie
my, my this is bomb-diggidy good!

Ayishara Ariyachat, Grade 7
Ramsey Jr High School, MN

Ocean Breeze

I felt the cool air of the ocean breeze
And continued to walk on the sandy shore.
It started to get cold and I began to freeze
The beach was fun but soon became a bore.

Jamie Jones, Grade 9
South View Middle School, MN

A Girl

As I look across the room, our eyes meet up,
Mine dark as night,
Hers light as day,
Almost an instant attraction, I would say!

Whenever she walks in the room,
My head sweeps around like a broom,
I went from looking at the ugly walls,
To seeing her sit down beside me
In the desk that's the color of the boy's bathroom stalls.
I don't know what to say,
So I'm just like hey! Hey?!
Man, I could've thought of something better to say!

So while I'm sitting there, taking my test,
All I have on my brain is my stupid greeting, hey!?
I feel so ashamed!
She deserves a better greeting,
I'll get her something good the next day!

So I couldn't get her anything better,
Because there was bad weather.
So I guess hey,
Is just okay!

Kody Gyurina, Grade 8
Washington Middle School, WI

Frustration

Can't think,
Can't stay focused,
Can't be in a good mood,
Can't work

Want to be mad,
Want to smash something,
Want to be able to do something,
Want to punch a brick wall,

Unable to do anything,
Feeling useless,
Wasting time,
In a lose-lose situation

Almost there but then denied,
Reaching but then falling down,
Jumping but being pulled down by gravity,
Getting your hopes up but then disappointed,

Trying over and over again,
Failing over and over again,
Saying I can't do it,
Frustrated

Kaleb Roll, Grade 8
Perry Middle School, MI

A Shoot...And a Miss

Basketball
My favorite past time
I feel like a monster that can't be stopped
dribble, dribble, swish, swish
I can feel the wind on my face as I run
down the court
miss.
that was the half but it doesn't matter
I'll just get right back up
Defense, Dash, Dribble, Dunk.
We catch up
we are only down by two at the start of the 3rd
there's three minutes left in the game and it's tied up
my team has the ball
I pass in.
He passes back to me
I shoot...
the buzzer goes off
We win! We win! We win!
but...then I wake up
A shoot...and a miss

Ampa Garubanda, Grade 7
Ramsey Jr High School, MN

Kids/Adults

Kids
Adventurous, exciting
Growing, napping, laughing
Cute, brat, boring, Dull
Working, rushing, hoping
Intelligent, helpful
Adults

Kasey King, Grade 7
Edison Middle School, WI

Paradise

A crack of thunder
Brings in the mist
On the Caribbean shore
The waves start to twist

Clean, fresh, crisp, air
Streams in through palm leaves
As I lay in my hammock
It begins to tease.

The tropical birds sing above my head
Like angels it's their pride and joy
Fish fly through the warm air
Like a small wind-up toy.

Water from leaves drips
Peacefully on my nose
The water races crazily
Quickly to my toes

Garrett Bular, Grade 8
Sandusky Middle School, MI

Change

In those younger days
I got into trouble
And invaded others bubbles
I picked to fight
And it brought me no light
I chose to swear
And didn't really care

Life must change
Like a nickel or dime
And it may take time
I must stay straight
And change my ways
I want to have light
And not to fight
I want to have love
And to love
I want to change

Cody L. Anderson, Grade 8
Prairie Lakes School, MN

The World Beyond

There is a world beyond,
That holds the freedom,
The freedom to run,
The freedom to flee,
The freedom to cry,
The freedom to laugh,
In the world beyond,
Many mysteries exist,
Mysteries of love,
Mysteries of faith,
Mysteries of feelings,
Mysteries of emotions,
Inside the world beyond,
Dreams come true,
Dreams of young and old,
And Dreams of the middle group,
Oh the wonders,
Of the world beyond.

Sarah Shuman, Grade 7
St John Lutheran School, WI

Eli DeForest Hicks

E very mother's dream
L oves tacos
I ncredible goal tender

D ufus…my dad calls me
E ternal life that's for me
F reakish good looks
O pposite of normal people
R ed Wings are sweet
E lijah isn't my name
S uperb
T ired

H ockey
I 'm a stud
C lark my hero
K ind
S wedish

Eli DeForest Hicks, Grade 7
Pilgrim Lutheran School, WI

Dead and Gone

Just like my sister now she gone in
I am going to miss her hugs and kiss
Came into the world
Gone just like that
Left the state
And never came back
Now she dead and gone
Just like that

Justice Williams, Grade 7
Sherman Multicultural Arts School, WI

Paintball

Paintball
It's always fun to have a paintball war
Crawling through the weeds
Waiting for the perfect shot
Here I come
Watch out below

Cullen Bernetzke, Grade 7
Luxemburg-Casco Middle School, WI

Ordinary Heroes

They never hear a thank you,
But they will help you every day.
They're the ordinary heroes,
You don't think of them that way.

They're teachers and they're coaches,
They're parents and they're friends.
They'll help you through the bad times,
They'll be there 'til the end.

They'll never leave you hanging,
They've always got your back.
You never seem to notice
'Til they're never coming back.

Some only stay awhile,
Some stay for your whole life.
They'll be there when you need them,
They'll help you through your strife.

So next time you're in trouble,
When you're having a bad day,
Just think of your own heroes
And they'll help you find your way.

Alyssa Maxson, Grade 9
Montgomery-Lonsdale High School, MN

Christmas

Christmas is a time of joy
and happiness
friends with you
and families come from all around

All come together
for this special holiday
Christmas tree all decorated
presents waiting to be opened

The fresh falling snow
all having a good time
laughing and happiness
Waiting for Christmas to come

Hunter Windey, Grade 7
Springfield School, MN

I Am

I am the sun that's yellow and bright
I am the moon that shines through the night
I am the fire, the darkness, the day
I am the happy voice that shouts hooray!
I am the past, the future, the moon
I'm that sandwich you eat at noon
I am a bird that soars through the sky
I am your baby who wakes up and cries
I am a man, a girl, a boy
I'm the wrapping paper that covers the toys
I am the colors blue, green, and red
I am the monsters that woke from the dead
I am the girl who rides down the block
I am the hands that move on the clock
I am the shoes you wear on your feet
I am the furnace that warms you with heat
I am the fun that comes from your cat
I am the ball that was hit by a bat
I am a glass that has the most class
I am the sauce on chicken wings
I am the best that's why I'm everything.

Laisha Wells, Grade 7
Ramsey Jr High School, MN

Letting You Go

I'm blinking back all the tears in my eyes
As we're getting close and closer to the place.
I look at you, and I try to smile
Even though this might be the last time I'll see your face

I know you're really ill, and I know you're dying,
But I can't bear to see you disappear and go.
You're my best friend, and you've always been.
I love you too much to let you go.

You're my other half and you complete me,
And I remember all the shared smiles and tears.
We were there for each other though good times and bad,
But now I can't stop looking at you in fear.

You've been strong for me, so I'll be strong for you.
I'll help you survive,
And even if I lose you to eternal sleep,
My dear friend, I'll always remember you alive.

So this is our last goodbye now —
I'm bidding adieu to the other half of me
My dear friend, I love you,
And I'll overcome this grief when you're free.

Eileen Li, Grade 8
Boulan Park Middle School, MI

Lakes

Life is a Lake,
a lake covered with thin ice,
just to know that it might break,
it is as risky as rolling the dice,
You want to pray for God's sake,
If you get off it will be very nice
you wonder why,
it is because risks are what help life pass by.

Kam Friedli, Grade 9
Petoskey High School, MI

Growing Up

Flying through the air, on a silver cloud.
Believing in dreams. Wishing on a star.
Remembering the good times, imagining the sounds.
Wishing they would come back.
That all is what it was. Knowing it could be that way.

Feeling the pain. Hoping it would go away.
Crying for your former friend.
Thinking he was thinking of you too.
Knowing it was all in your head.
You think of him every night and every day.

Riding on a silver cloud is dumb.
Believing in dreams is naîve.
Wishing on a star is for kids
All that comes of remember the good times is pain.

Just do what you're told.
Forget about your dreams.
Stop wishing on a star.
Throw away your memories.

Everyone has to grow up sometime.

Jacquelyn Marion, Grade 8
L'anse Creuse Middle School East, MI

Don't Care

You don't care anymore
You said you'd love me always and forever
You only tell lies and it kills me inside
You enjoy my pain, you see my pain now, and you just laugh
You hate me, but I still love you
You have my heart and my soul

Now I don't care anymore
Now love you always and forever means nothing to me
Now your lies are just words spoken, lies that aren't believed
Your lies don't kill me inside anymore
Now I don't have anymore pain you can't laugh now
Now you want me back and I'm not coming back again
Now you don't have my heart and soul, I took them back!

Stephanie Barrett, Grade 9
St Francis Sr High School, MN

I Cried for Help

I cried for help.
I cried and cried,
as tears flowed by,
but no one helped.
It felt like a dark,
place going on and on,
like an endless maze,
no matter what I did
no matter how much,
I cried for help,
no one can hear me,
no matter how many,
people are in front of me,
they just wouldn't help,
I wish there would be someone,
to hear the voices of,
my cries echoing in the air.

Ying Thao, Grade 7
Achieve Language Academy, MN

I Am

I am
who I am.
There is no way
to change
myself for
it is too
late to
change.
If, I could
I would go
back in time to
change
all of my
actions.

Now in the
present, I
can't even
go to sleep
because of all
the things I've done.
Why, why don't I try harder.

Vincent Vang, Grade 7
Ramsey Jr High School, MN

Tears

Tears are like rain,
It happens when you're sad,
So follow your dream,
Take the right path,
Not the wrong,
Keep on smiling,
Stop crying

Molly Huynh, Grade 7
Valley View Middle School, MN

Turquoise Tranquility

It is night
The crescent moon glows in the blue velvet sky
The lake is calm,
Ripples of waves kiss the cold sand
The majestic forest behind the water fades over a hill into the sky,
Big leaves gently flowing in the soft breeze
A willow dips, bowing to brush the glassy surface of the water
You lay on your back at the water's edge
And gaze up at the pattern of diamond stars across the night sky
A sigh of contentment
A moment
Where everything feels complete
And you understand
The beauty, the rightness of everything
Together
Creating the picture, perfectly flawed
That is painted on the canvas of the earth
For a moment
There is peace

Nadia Torres, Grade 9
Clarkston Jr High School, MI

Life as a Shoe

My leather has gone from white to brown. I am at least one size too small,
But my owner shoves his feet in despite all.

I trudge through thick mud. This has gone from bad to worse.
I am fatigued already. Why am I cursed?

My sole is worn out. My owner starts to run.
It hurts all over. This is no fun.

Now he starts to scale a crag with very jagged rocks.
I wish I were still at the store inside my comfy box.

It seems as if he's been walking forever
This has been a tortuous endeavor.

Finally I am home. I have paid my dues.
I hope it is time for a new pair of shoes.

Aaron Faison, Grade 8
Boulan Park Middle School, MI

Friendship Is There

Friendship has many different personalities.
She lives with her relatives — Love, Peace, and Joy.
She turns bright yellow and can laugh at your most joyous moments,
But she is blue as she cries with your pain.
When your soul feels lonely, Friendship picks you up and listens to you.
Friendship worries for you, but believes you'll go far.
She celebrates all of your victories, yet comforts you when you lose.
No matter your mood, the day, or the weather,
True Friendship will survive.

Olivia Kaiserlian, Grade 7
St Andrew's School, MI

Snowmobiling

I'm going to hop on my snowmobile but first
Should I wear gray or black gloves?
Black snow pants or blue?
Decide, decide, decide…

Where should I ride today?
Should I go through the woods?
Or through some fields?
Decide, decide, decide…

Should I turn my hand warmers on?
Should I go across the street?
Should I head back home?
Decide, decide, decide…

Nate Chitko, Grade 7
St Katharine Drexel School, WI

Do You?

Do you love her?
Do you really?

Don't lie anymore,
She can't take it.

She doesn't want to feel it anymore,
That feeling she hates.

Where she sees nothing but you,
Where her heart goes so fast it skips a beat.

Where she gets butterflies and it hurts.
Where it's hard to breathe and she feels numb.

Manu Sotemann, Grade 8
Spring Hill School, WI

Music…

Who really knows where it all began
It could have started with the creation of man
But if music were to be humanized
Schizophrenic is how he should be classified
One simple beat can change his emotions
From orderly thoughts to those of confusion
His personality can take on many forms
From a quiet rain to a violent storm
His subliminal messages are ever so strong
Hypnotizing you as he sings his song
Changing your mood as he changes his beat
Can be stronger than those of a naval fleet
His rhythm can be heard in many different ways
From one's beating heart to mother nature's play
Tuning him out is sometimes a must
Because his voice is always around us
All you have to do is listen

Kaity Bragan, Grade 9
Clarkston Jr High School, MI

Memories

I used to pay no attention,
I used to think they weren't important,
I used to wonder why we even had them.

But now I know,
When you leave me,
I will still have them.

They stick to me,
Like cherry bubble gum,
To the bottom of a shoe.

Memories are personal treasures.
You don't need to care about mine!
I don't want you to!
They are mine and only mine to care about.

Arika Kujawa, Grade 8
Lake Fenton Middle School, MI

The Sky

Where air is a fine-spun silk
A blessing to the skin
And clouds are pillows stuffed with cotton fields
That cushion the deadened limb
Where infinite blue is a sea of salvation
To the starved lip, parched with thirst
And rainy rivers course atmosphere canyons
To where droughts are thriving the worst
Soul-slicing thunder is born to rumble
Heaven's regrets from it do tumble
Emotion ablaze in wild spears of fire
Lightning igniting, secretly private desires
And sun's luminosity, mother of our stars
Shines all-healing warmth to our cold, grounded hearts

Angela Como, Grade 8
Central Middle School, WI

4th Quarter

Tic toc, tic toc went the clock
An idea came into my head and it didn't knock

It was 4th and long, far and scary
As I told my team, were going for the hail Mary

I snapped the ball, threw it to the man
Number 81 leaped, and caught it with one hand

From the 40 to the 30, from the 20 to the 10
They scored a touchdown and 6 points for the win

Phil Lynch, Grade 8
Washington Middle School, WI

Writer's Block

Yesterday I got on my computer
I felt like writing a poem
So I opened up Word and surprise
This topic wouldn't leave me alone

It was eating me up inside
I couldn't help but write
And finally Word uploaded
And my topic slipped out of sight

It left my poor brain completely
Never to be seen again
So now I'm writing something different
It's not what it had been.

I've got a topic-less poem now
And it's a pitiful sight
And I'm sure I would delete it
If that wasn't so impolite.

So today on my computer
I sat down and was quick to think
That I had better be careful
'Cause topics can disappear in a blink.

Victoria Riley, Grade 9
Vassar Sr High School, MI

We All Feel That Way

We all feel that way
We all feel tired
We all feel stressed
We all feel unhappy
We all feel happy
We all feel grateful
We all feel victorious
We all feel exotic

We all feel that way

Owen Hauser, Grade 7
West Middle School, MI

Time

Tick tick tick went the clock
Trying to snooze by the clock
Then I heard a bell
Ran and almost fell
Got on the bus
Almost lost the race
Time never ending
Like water folding
Time is always there
To guide you in despair
Time is fast steady
Me slow, but ready

Dhiraj C. Surapaneni, Grade 7
Detroit Country Day Middle School, MI

Snow Day

Fluffy snow everywhere
School is closed today
Because of the snow like the Sahara but white
Kids across town are happy

School is closed today
Kids are having fun
Kids across town are happy
Because today is going to be a funny fantastic and awesome day

Kids are having fun
Because they are building snowmen 100 ft high
Because today is going to be a funny fantastic and awesome day
Parents and teachers fill with fright

Krishan Patel, Grade 7
Manistee Middle School, MI

Miracles Can Happen!

In the hospital lay the man,
whose room was spick and span.
He had no family but his cat,
who had died three months back.
He did not know up from down,
but he knew no one was around.
In came a little boy,
with his brand new favorite toy.
The boy walked up to the man,
and said, "Take my hand."
They walked to the hospital café,
where they played with the toy the whole day.
When the doctor saw the man sitting down,
he turned as white as a clown.
You see, the man was paralyzed from his waist to his feet,
so how was he supposed to get there without defeat?
The doctor ran to the man and said, "Are you okay?"
The man looked at the doctor and said, "I am just here to play."
The boy then said "Yippee hooray! Today is my favorite day!"

Ashley Pitrof, Grade 7
St Roman School, WI

Spinning Swirling Chilling Changes

The beautiful time is here, its swirling gallantly suffocating around me.
Its chilling, prickling feeling brings spirits out, and reminds us of love.
The power is strong far beyond decorations and trees,
It's about believing and not seeing,
It's about what's inside of you and how you give it to others.
Worries seem to fade and being together is what is important.
Laughs and hugs are shared,
The feelings are expressed and illuminate the air.
Unity is created and explored.
the bond between all of us becomes powerful and unbreakable.
Loving overcomes fate and fiction overcomes fact,
And the fantasy's live and lives in a world where it all transcends.
The spirit lives its swirling gallantly suffocating around all of us.

Alyssa Spytman, Grade 9
Clarkston Jr High School, MI

Being Me

Childhood memories race through my head;
Forever remembered with words unsaid.
The dim light still cast from my young days
Will always be here, for me, to stay.
My favorite color went from purple to blue.
I had a cat, and I watched *Blue's Clues*.
"Mom, I want a cookie! Maybe two?
But I need them! I need them! Please?! I love you!"
Now, I am older and don't have to cry
Because soon I will be in senior high!
Now, I read Twilight, and eat cookies, galore,
And I love to take naps; I do more and more.
Not only do I read and sleep,
But I write stories, too, and I've written a heap!
I look back on my childhood days
And laugh at all those silly ways
That I messed up and cried and watched my TV,
And fell down a lot; I was so clumsy.
As one door opens, another's uncovered to me,
But that's okay; I'll just keep
Being Me!

Kelli Trester, Grade 8
Golda Meir Middle School, WI

The Game

To be or not to be is the question,
Can I avoid this storm safe from collision?
Are we meant to be for eternity?
Or are we the tools of our own calamity.

Because when I see your face,
My heart disappears without a trace.
And When I hear your voice,
My stomach vanishes bereft a choice.

Some call it love, some call it lust,
Some call it a game made purely of trust.
Some say it won't happen, it cannot be,
Please come help me, from this cage I cannot free.

I would walk through a valley of nothing,
And I would walk across a sun.
If we could start a new beginning,
If our two could become one.

But "we" I'm afraid cannot be,
For it is a choice we made too late.
We cannot deal our own cards you see,
And my cards have been played by fate.

Keegan Stitt, Grade 9
Flushing High School, MI

My Haven

This place has sounds of music filling the air,
snores of the beagle at the end of the bed

This place has sights of colors,
from posters to pictures,
CD's of my favorite bands

This place has touches of warm blankets in the wintertime,
and light sheets in the summer

This place has a delicious taste of buttery popcorn
for me and my friends

This place is full of good smells and bad
the delightful smell of mango madness spray,
the smelly fish food for my goldfish, Willy

This place is my haven.

Ellie Smith, Grade 7
Valley View Middle School, MN

What Am I?

I am a special invention helping many people
I am the machine moving quickly to get the job done
I am an important tool always humming as I work
I need electricity and I have a foot and an eye
I love working with colorful things
I am used to piece things together

What am I?
I am a sewing machine.

Kathryn Koller, Grade 7
Washtenaw Christian Academy, MI

A Perfect Game

A perfect game!
It was a Thursday night,
All ten pins were in my sight.
It was my first turn for the day,
Bowling is a great game to play.
I went nine frames with all strikes,
No other feeling was quite alike.
It was then the tenth frame,
If I didn't get a strike I would feel shame.
I stepped up to the line,
Knowing that this strike was going to be mine.
Just as I released the ball,
I heard a bang and saw all of the pins fall.
I was never more proud,
I just wanted to scream aloud.
I finally bowled my first perfect game,
Now I have tons of fame.
A perfect game!

Tiffany Fameree, Grade 8
Seymour Middle School, WI

Cat a Log

Skeeter
Lumpy and round like an old couch
Wraps his arms around you
With a purr of content.

With a loud meow
Like an engine's roar
He demands his cat food.

Slurp, slurp, slurp,
He sips up his milk
Orange flaming fur
Burning to be touched.

Shining bold eyes
Begging to be held
With a sigh of happiness
He starts to dream.

A loud crash
He's awoken
His yawns as big as a hole
A complaint left unspoken.

Hannah Bogema, Grade 8
Paw Paw Middle School, MI

Not Eating

Hurts me.
Scares me.
Damages me.
Ruins me.
Starves me.
Affects me.
Kills me…

Catherine Rigby, Grade 7
Centreville Jr High School, MI

In the Turkey's Head

In the turkey's head,
some magical things are going on,
because in the turkey's head,
so many things have come and gone.

In the turkey's mind,
he never listened to his friends,
and in the turkey's mind,
he knows his life won't end.

In the person's thoughts,
he knows that something will be caught,
in the person's thoughts,
well that's not what the turkey thought.

Noelle Gartzke, Grade 7
Washington School, WI

sad

every day it's hard to say
that i am fine or nothings wrong
nails on a chalkboard is what i hear
but no one knows this because i fear

we are all in a waiting
innocent but waiting to die
i see across the room
a dying flower, it has no food

being depressed is like this
every day it feels as if
i am being punched in the face
it's not fair, that life is this way

most people smell cupcakes;
and dream of flowers
but me i dream of moldy cheese
and death and pain
i don't know why i feel this way

sometimes i'm happy
but mostly i am sad
i can't help that i feel this way

Aubrey MacDonald, Grade 8
Lake Fenton Middle School, MI

Lake

My feet reach her surface.
I'm falling into her.
Her breath is cold,
But she has a warm feeling.

I open my eyes,
She is all around.
Slowly and calmly,
She slithers past.

I don't know why,
But when you're beneath her,
It no longer matters,
What goes on above.

I've run out of air,
And break her surface.
I swim to her shore.
It's time to leave.

The waves kiss my feet,
They're saying goodbye.
I wish for her secrets to not be forgotten,
And that I will see her again.

Monica Tessman, Grade 8
J C McKenna Middle School, WI

Thunderstorm

Crash! Flash!
Lightning brightens the sky
Wind wildly whips
Rolling thunder
Rain rushing rapidly
Wind wildly whips
Drip! Plop!
Mother Nature calms
All is still
Storm slowly ceases

Amanda Milquette, Grade 8
Suring Elementary/Middle School, WI

Flight 802 Sacrifice for the US

On a plane to Florida
We see people this day
That gave people horror
For the rest of their lives
I tell the story of flight 802

We see about 40 people
from New York going on a plane
to Florida what they did is an act
of bravery

When the plane starts to leave
They have no idea what is going
To happen to them
When terrorists or strangers get on
The disaster begins
When the strangers start to
Hijack the plane, disaster strikes
Then the passengers start to fight
back the terrorists on the plane
When the terror stops, the plane crashes

Let the US honor the people who fought
to keep our country safe on 9/11

Chazz Casarez, Grade 8
Fairview Charter School, WI

Lifeless

Our life in which we try and live,
isn't always as we see.
We cry, we hurt and we try to forgive,
then what comes to be?
People step in and people walk out,
but with God, that is never a doubt.
So with life we try and give it all,
but how can we live if we never fall?

Stephanie Weller, Grade 9
Lakeview Christian Academy, MN

Strange World of Mine

Strange creatures swimming in slime,
And a moon is as green as grass, is rising in the sky,
To sing a sweet, sweet lullaby,
On this strange world of mine.

The great pink ocean loves to rhyme,
This is why the fishes sing,
And the plants swing,
On this strange world of mine.

The creatures are awake playing in slime,
Until I wake they play,
Until the yellow sun says it's day,
On this strange world of mine.

Lennon Churchill, Grade 7
Valley View Middle School, MN

Home

I miss the breeze of summer at home
I miss your face when I'm alone.
I miss the times we spent together.
Times I could dream of forever
I miss the people I once called family.
The people that used to care for me.
I miss the sounds you used to make.
Now I know missing you is what I can't take.
My nightmares are gone when I'm with you.
I have a question, did you miss me too?

Saadia Hassan, Grade 7
Valley View Middle School, MN

A Weathered Lesson

It begins far away,
Ignited by a single flame.
Stories told of battered lands,
Time has come for new landfall.
A wind picks up, clouds roll in,
Anger stands feet from the shore.
Waiting to charge,
Weathermen salivate over the storm.
A nation watches in awe,
Scared with excitement.
Predictions made,
Who knows if land can hold out.
Storm swings first, winds rage with little rest,
No stop in its eyes.
Land digs in, trying to hold on,
Stamina pulls land slowly along.
Land eventually overpowers, but not without toll.
Relief rushes in, to heal the wide wounds
No one wants to look, yet they can only stare
A lesson learned, and precautions secured.
No more storms dare come around.

Spenser Pawlik, Grade 9
Clarkston Jr High School, MI

How Would You Feel?

You're standing there,
As everyone pushes their way to class,
And stands at lockers, talking,
Your books fall, and you see everyone bypass.

You wish someone would help,
But they ignore you on their way to class,
They just walk away,
some even laugh as they pass.

You pick up your books,
Your emotions are clear,
Because someone ran into you,
You wish you could just disappear.

You wish someone would do something,
Just to help your miserable day,
But they just walk on by,
Without even one glance your way.

Miranda Wilkins, Grade 8
Sandusky Middle School, MI

Hidden in the Jungle

The mask is a human camouflaged
Everything is quiet but the chirping birds in the sky
It is a football
Which can be thrown very high

The mask is like the jungle
Different shades of green
The mask is like trees hiding
So it won't be seen

You could hear everything in the jungle
Staring with its human eyes
When it comes out
All of the sound dies

Dakota Bremness, Grade 8
Chippewa Falls Middle School, WI

Existence

Empty hours
Empty days
Fill our lives
Every day
Until that day
That you have
Full hours
And full days

Alex Phelps, Grade 8
Iowa-Grant Elementary-Middle School, WI

Tic Toc

The clock's hands are ever spinning. The secretive language of Tic Toc.
The sound everlasting slow but never stopping.
Time is quick but never silent the evil Tic of coming the worry some departure of Toc.
The clock will not stop.

Stephen Schulte, Grade 7
Manistee Middle School, MI

Summer Days

Summer days are like a batch of fresh homemade cookies;
You never want to stop having them and they're so warm.
In the morning you wake up to the smell of fresh orange juice and
French Toast and bacon sizzling on the fryer, just waiting to be eaten!
Later going outside, swinging on a rope and gently falling into the beautiful cool water,
Then going inside for some sandwiches and lemonade.
Glancing at the sun glistening in the lake after a good swim.
After that you roast sticky marshmallows over the big, crackling, bright fire;
Then gaze at the beautiful, twinkling, numerous stars in the sky,
Without a cloud in sight, knowing you're going to sleep peacefully tonight…

Bethany Highman, Grade 7
Abundant Life Christian School, WI

Cupcake Satisfaction

I had a dream I was a giraffe eating delicious mouthwatering cupcakes.
There were so…many different flavors
There was Chunky Monkey Chocolate,
Slurping Slipping Strawberry,
Luscious Lingering Lemon,
Outrageously orangey orange, and last but not least, there was Fuzzy Fluffy Cotton Candy.
Each was divinely unique.
Chunky Monkey Chocolate had a funky cream icing with dark chocolate shavings.
Luscious Lingering Lemon had lots of licking lime,
Fuzzy Fluffy Cotton Candy had puffy fussy pink punch icing.
Such Fantastic cupcakes are creating magnificent bursts of flavor
As they touch the tip of my tongue and slide down my gangly throat
to my strapping stomach.
Aww…the satisfaction is like sunshine shining on my golden body,
While my brown spots shiver.

Courtney Fabick, Grade 8
Abundant Life Christian School, WI

Martin Luther King Jr.

Born on January 15, 1929, to Martin Sr. and Alberta King, he was their sunshine.
In Atlanta, Georgia he lived with his family. Encountered racism and unfair treatment — they longed to be free.
His Grandfather and his father worked as a Baptist minister. They never were happier.
Graduated when he was twenty five. On a mission to be holy, he would thrive.
In 1953 he married Coretta Scott. Together they would boycott.
Had four children Yolanda, Denise, Martin Luther III, Dexter and Bernice Reese. Hoping one day they would all bring peace.
He wanted to be a leader of civil rights. This task would not happen overnight.
Also famous for a speech called I have a dream. Many people think he was supreme.
He won the Nobel Peace Prize in 1955 in Chicago. This seems like so long ago.
Assassinated on April fourth, 1968. Many African Americans would retaliate.
Assassinated in Memphis Tennessee, Martin Luther King Jr. would be a forever memory.

Jacob Jimenez, Grade 7
Lakeview Middle School, MI

Yellow Sunbeams

Her sizzling sunlight blossoms in the early morning.
She glides along the canary beaches, drizzling her heat on the silky ground.
Her chirping, calming sensations fly past as her gold fire burns mighty.
A color of countless shades, from light to dim.
Her chirping, friendly, cheerful personality pouncing through the forest.
Sweet and salty splashes flutter, through the air.
Flying about she dances in all of her topaz and sulfur glory.
Yelling playfully, she pounces onto the rosemary scented flowers.
Her bright waves splash against the hot, damp, soft shore of light.
By evening the sunlight disappears, dissolving into the sunset.
Only leaving the dismal array, to wait until the next dawn.

Nicole Fredericks, Grade 8
Centennial Middle School, MI

Mailman

Dear Mailman,
I would just like to say
That the other day
When you were dropping off a box
Couldn't you have just knocked?
You didn't need to ring the doorbell two times
I could hear you the first time just fine
Ringing the doorbell makes the dogs go crazy
Even when they are lazy
And did I really have to sign that sheet?
Because you are someone my dogs would love to meet
And they were trying to get past my feet
Honestly I know my dogs can destroy
Now I think you should have a protector; a convoy
Because my dogs think of you as a toy
Now I think you should give me the box and go away
Because you look like you don't even want to say
"Have a nice day!"
You brought it on yourself that the dogs barked
Next time don't put your truck in park.

Megan Warfield, Grade 7
St Katharine Drexel School, WI

Questions

Have you ever wondered why chipmunks store up nuts?
Or have you ever pondered what holds up little huts?
Why the lightning strikes?
Or how the flowers grow?
How 'bout what your teacher thinks.
That I do not know.
Why are oceans blue, and why do tigers kill?
Maybe you have questioned why the earth has hills.
Questions, Questions, Questions: I ask them every day.
Why does snow come, how does dust form?
My questions never go away.
And I cannot help but wonder why I am this way.
And why I have these questions each and every day.
Is my curiosity a curse?
I ask; with much dismay.
Can it be taken from me?
How much need I pay?
This life is full of questions, some that have no end.
If you don't have the answer, I'll just ask a friend…
or Google it.

Rachel Russell, Grade 7
Abundant Life Christian School, WI

Index

Abbott, Angelica 139
Abdi, Mohamed 69
Abolt, Ellen 205
Abosi, Kalu 118
Acosta, Jose 210
Acton, Liam 241
Adams, Abigail 124
Adams, Terrance 116
Addison, Ian 130
Afdahl, Aaron 92
Agnew, Drew 192
Aguzzi, Natalie 163
Ahee, Alexis 50
Ahee, Brielle 237
Ailport, Lucas 32
Ait Daoud, Imane 124
Aleck, Katie 141
Alexander, Brandon 127
Ali, Ismahan 22
Ali, Muna .139
Ali, Sahaam 161
Alonso Razo, Wendy 113
Ambroch, Steven 241
Ambrosius, Theo 115
Amdahl, Brooke 174
Anderson, Brianna 228
Anderson, Cody L. 256
Anderson, Emilee 87
Anderson, Erika 33
Anderson, Mikayla 168
Anderson, Rebecca 251
Anderson, Samantha 51
Andonoff, Addison 55
Andrade, Cyanni 51
Angel, Zachary 215
Angrabright, Donald 112
Aqel, Haleemah 69
Archie, Yvonne 136
Arend, Grace 58
Ariyachat, Ayishara 255
Arndt, Logan 48
Arndt, Preston 171
Arnold, Allison 145
Arradondo, Gabriel 215
Ashe, Amishade 178
Auclair, Jesse 71
Avila-Lopez, Cris 214
Aviles, Alex 42
Bablitch, Nicole 159
Backes, Emily 160
Bacon, Mayce 127
Baez, Angeles 189
Baker, Jacob 134
Baker, Megan 216
Baker, Taylor 241
Balcom, Josh 224
Baldeshwiler, Kyle 26
Baldry, Cody 203
Ballough, Kristina 63
Banks, Gabrielle 183
Barajas, Marcos 138
Baranczyk, Sara 189
Barnes, Bradley 213
Barnes, Cara 201
Barnes, Joslin 244
Barnes, Justine 202
Barrett, Katie Lynn 98
Barrett, Stephanie 257
Barrone, Bryce 175
Barton, Allison 155
Bashi, Alaijah 173
Bass, Amani 181
Bates, Hallie 42
Baum, Dylan 149
Baysdell, Chase 171
Beal, Aaliyah 103
Becher, Sean 202
Bechler, Amanda 43
Belczynski, Veronica 242
Belinky, Katherine 63
Bell, Jenn .220
Bemis, Taran 47
Bemis, Taylor 160
Bennett, Kurt 111
Benser, Danielle 58
Benson, Mary 142
Benzik, Lizzie 24
Berg, Alexandra 191
Berg, Hannah 67
Bergamo, Marina 245
Berggren, Joseph 109
Bergmann, Jessica 136
Berndtson, Jackie 144
Bernetzke, Cullen 256
Berns, Courtney 165
Bertrand, Justin John 128
Beske, Savanah 237
Bettcher, John 121
Bhullar, Amy 30
Biggs, Tony 33
Binder, Karli 236
Bindon, Brittany 125
Bing, Caris .38
Birch, Leah .94
Birkley, Dennis 34
Birt, Isabelle 147
Birt, Nathaniel 123
Bjorkquist, Lilly 90
Blackdeer, Calvin 97
Blackford, Alexis 185
Blanco, Jhony 122
Blank, Kara 177
Blondin, Alan 129
Blondin, Mary Kate 54
Blust, Kathleen 118
Boeve, Tricia 213
Bogema, Hannah 262
Bohrer, Sam 144
Boll, Abigail 65
Booker, Chris 68
Booth, Ashley 12
Bork, Rachel 170
Bornbach, Kellen 211
Boucher, Joe 108
Bougie, Mathew 145
Bouret, Claire 86
Bouret, Laure 28
Bower, Megumi 160
Bowles, Kevin 171
Bozeman, Andrea 118
Brady, Ellie .98
Bragan, Kaity 259
Brand, Nikie 130
Brawdy, Lucas 234
Breeggemann, Niki 240
Bremness, Dakota 263
Brennan, Robert 48
Breuer, Andy 52
Brey, Madeline 161
Brick, Kayty 119
Brisse, Shannon 213
Broman, Ethan 218
Brostowitz, Jennifer 233
Brown, Eric 201
Brown, Jesse 218
Brown, Kaylynn 182
Brown, Lauren 128
Brown, Taylor 227
Bruce, Trudie 58
Buchanan, Kelsea 45
Bucio, Isis .151
Buerkle, Austin 56
Bular, Garrett 256

Bull, Sydni .195
Bullis, Christian .242
Bullock, Morgan .196
Bumstead, Angela .13
Burke, Jacqueline .108
Burks, Dontae .47
Burks, Shay'Toya .66
Burmesch, Sarah J. .95
Burnette, Austin .63
Burnham, Stephanie .75
Busch, Eric .80
Bush, Diamond .102
Buskirk, Melanie .122
Buss, Colyn .50
Buttweiler, Nellie .161
Byrne, Daniel J. .34
Byrnes, Hannah .14
Cagney, Katlin .29
Cameron, Ashlynn .217
Cammack, Hunter .125
Campbell, Christie .96
Campbell, Sueann .74
Canfield, Deborah .229
Canner, Allison .238
Caracci, Anthony .96
Cargill, Erin .253
Carl, Hailey .48
Carlson, Cody .235
Carlson, Keanna .111
Carnagie, Alyssa .216
Carril, Olivia .109
Carroll, Tania .145
Carter, Ahkeel .182
Carter, Alicia .223
Carter, Emily .155
Carter, Kayla .130
Carter, Victoria .51
Casarez, Chazz .262
Cass, Savanah .234
Castillo, Fatima .253
Castillo, Tyler .121
Castillo Canedo, Adolfo .90
Castle, Alex .40
Cecconi, Nick .94
Cerniglia, Nicholas .188
Cevigney, Marissa .195
Chambasian, Cody .114
Chan, Jessica .198
Chappell, Abbey .165
Chappie, Amanda .157
Charpenter, Cheyanne .218
Chase, Chelsea .167
Chavez, Eric .182
Chen, Allen .143
Chen, Helena .102
Chen, Lily .210
Chen, Marshal .100
Cheng, Micah .57
Chennault, Courtney .147
Chitko, Nate .259
Chiu, Alexa .110
Chmelka, Abbie .79
Chorey, Allison .219
Chouinard, Tanner .97
Christensen, Cody .129
Christensen, Hunter .138
Christensen, Janice .175
Christensen, Tyler .133
Chroscicki, Monika .92
Church, Kira .196
Churchill, Lennon .263
Cieszkowski, Rich .254
Clark, Chelsey .42
Clementi, Grant .252
Clements, Lindsey .108
Cline, Keith .170
Colburn, Mariah .251
Cole, Dane .131
Colvett, Jacqueline .195
Colvin, Quinn .224
Combs, Kylie .81
Como, Angela .259
Conaway, Linda .242
Congdon, Courtney .197
Conklin, Michelle .250
Conner, Rachael .66
Contreras, Desirae .216
Coon, Elle .106
Cooper, Autumn .26
Cooper, Sarah .137
Coopman, Brittany .248
Copa, Alexander .104
Cory, Camille .124
Coutier, Brooke .132
Coutier, Lucian .219
Couturier, Justin .86
Craig, DashaNette .57
Crain, Kristen .211
Crawfis, Cierra .69
Crawford, Rudie .251
Crowe, Ashley .206
Crowley, Anne .82
Culver, Michael .43
Currao, Alyssa .188
Czuprynko, Monica .40
D'Alessio, Dani .188
DaaJa-Ra, Kamau .43
Dagel, Damian .244
Dahl, Nick .138
Dahlberg, Julian .196
Dailey, Alexia .64
Dalebroux, Hope .34
Daniels, Ellesse .250
Dapaah, Rhema .158
Darwin, Brieana .187
Dauterman, Leah .226
Davidson, Ian .29
Davis, John .56
Dawley, Shannon .199
Day-Williams, Hugh .170
De Jardin, Julie .91
Deaver, Jessica .122
Dechant, Maria .108
DeForest, Amanda .78
Deitrick, Daniell .46
Dejewski, Cody .243
Dekhne, Mihir .35
DeLeeuw, John .130
Delmore, M.J. .64
DeLong, Elishia .99
Denny, Demetri .152
Densmore, Destiny .134
Denton, Jordan .176
Deprey, Evan .139
Derenne, Dana .70
Dessart, Matthew .229
DeVaney, Michaela .46
DeWeerd, Aaron .207
Dick, Regina .235
Dickinson, Nicolas .174
Dickman, Kathryn .119
Dickman, Mike .68
Dindorf, Ashley .32
Dixon, Gabrielle .192
Dobbs, Cody-James .141
Donskey, Lisa .32
Dooley, Alyssa .144
Dotson-Baird, Marques .141
Downard, Katy .107
Downs, Justin G. .73
Doxtator, Brandon .131
Drewery, Rico .57
Drozdowski, Hannah .177
Dubart, Melanie .241
Duczak, Adrian .84
Dumais, Andrea .250
Dumas, Kendall .206
Duncan, Mariah .120
Dunlap, Jordyn .153
Dunn, Olivia .243
Duru, Kelechi .67
Earl, Stephanie .74
Eason, Brandon .164
Eberle, Lindsey .114
Ebert, Steven .173
Ecklor, Jazmine .34
Edenburn, Caitlan .146
Edwards, Allison .87
Effa, Hunter .220
Eggerichs, Marissa .143
Egizi, Dominic .165

Eick, Makayla 39
Eisenhut, Christiana 184
Elbe, Luke 226
Eliason, Sheyanne 207
Elliott, Amanda 183
Ellithorpe, Dakota 182
Ellsworth, Harlan 204
Elrich, Kerilyn 79
Elwood, Tyler 35
Emerson, Franclyn L. 174
Emretiyoma, Karry 249
Enrique, Josiah 123
Erickson, Charlie 218
Ertman, Sydney 156
Escobar, Carlos 133
Estacio, Amanda 191
Estes, Austin 100
Etienne, Samantha 215
Evans, Christopher 99
Ewulomi, Samuel 91
Fabick, Courtney 264
Fairbanks, Kim 50
Faison, Aaron 258
Falicki, Lauren 72
Fameree, Tiffany 261
Fantin-Yusta, Enzo 202
Fantin-Yusta, Ettore 131
Fantozzi, Gabriella 63
Farnam, Victoria 29
Farrier, Courtney 158
Fasching, Laurelanne 139
Fassett, Tyler 39
Fawcett, Christopher 123
Feest, Helen 74
Feldmann, Ryan A. 93
Felton, Tonya 149
Feltson, Taylor 110
Feng, Kelly 219
Ferge, Katherine 206
Ferguson, Shayla 37
Fernholz, Abby 134
Ferri, Jon Austin 75
Fettig, Trevor 172
Fiegel, Haley 149
Filipiak, Faith 125
Fillmore, Antonio 181
Finley, Janice 117
Fiol, Cody .248
Fiol, Ryan 90
Fisher, Maria 106
Fjerstad, Andrew 196
Flamang, Jennifer 59
Flannigan, Tiffany 113
Flory, Samantha 199
Flowers, Kyra 73
Foley, Conor 218
Fonseca, Jorge 252
Foote, Tina .48
Forcier, Christina 66
Ford, Alison 39
Ford, Charmane 94
Forner, Victoria 176
Fortune, Kevin 67
Foster, Matthew 32
Fouks, Allison 139
Foust, Seth 183
Frailey, David 226
Frame, Hannah 49
Francis, Michael 15
Franck, Rebekah 238
Frazho, Danielle N. 230
Frazier, Laci 93
Fredericks, Nicole 265
Freedman, Sydney 146
Fricke, Alyssa 114
Fricke, Tyler 101
Friedli, Kam 257
Frinak, Aryanna 54
Frisbey, Lizzie 169
Fritsch, Vanessa 206
Fritz, Katie .93
Fritz, Marissa 141
Frohmader, Alisha 53
Froman, Michelle 103
Frommann, Nicole 64
Fryatt, Alexis 178
Fuhr, Alex .96
Gaber, Hunter 195
Gabrich, Rachel 148
Gabris, Dalton 71
Gahler, Nate 248
Gallenberger, Olivia 187
Gander, Colin 96
Garber, Kyle 231
Garcia, Ashley 253
Garcia, Elishia 91
Garcia, Liz .83
Garland, Allison 69
Garlock, Troy 90
Garten, Natalie 122
Gartzke, Noelle 262
Garubanda, Ampa 255
Garza, Katelyn 250
Garza, Marisol 68
Gates, Alexandria 223
Gates, Meckeal 78
Gauthier, Jessica 164
Gavrilovski, Jessica 112
Gayan, Parker 46
Gearig, Carolyn 28
Gehling, Emily 129
Geis, Paige 201
Geister, Jordan 212
George, Gaby 22
Georgescu, Andrei 242
Gerber, Samantha 254
Gergen, Anna 78
Gerndt, Stormy 114
Gerry, KateLynn 152
Geydoshek, Ryan J. 42
Gibson, Kari 133
Gilmore, J.C. 26
Gilmore, Lulu 82
Gjonaj, Prishtina 153
Glaser, Sammy 170
Gleason, Samantha 248
Glinski, Tricia 204
Glyzewski, Stephanie 85
Goddard, Anna 54
Godsey, Taylor 188
Goitz, Dylan 204
Golembiewski, Elizabeth 101
Golliher, Jenna 170
Golson, Mixon 109
Gomez, Leonardo 203
Gomez, Reina 41
Gong, Jason 108
Gonsior, Madison 72
Gonzalez, Diana 254
Goodell, Rachel 196
Gordon, Carley 16
Gorectke, Alesha Marie 118
Gorgas, Evan 59
Gorski, Isaiah 176
Gorun, David 71
Gossett, Joshua 185
Gow, Brooke 252
Gransee, Kealie 160
Grant, Shane 17
Grawe, Sterling 71
Gray, Devin 118
Gray, Erin .198
Gray, Revin 98
Green, Alexis 243
Green, Brian 93
Green, Dondre 114
Green, Rayshell 177
Green, Tyara 92
Greene, Kianna 167
Greiser, Jon 239
Grenlin, Jaclynn 74
Grieman, Luca 159
Grieman, Mackenzie 152
Griese, Gavin 247
Grieser, Louden 102
Grimme, Alexandria 223
Grinn, Alex 24
Grinnell, Quarteney 120
Grittinger, Harrison 23
Grodi, Nate 70
Groebner, Elizabeth 219

Grossholz, Matthew .116
Grosu, Ioana .86
Groth, Sarah .33
Gruebnau, Kyle .42
Grunke, Laura .242
Gudipudi, Rachana .135
Gumieny, Clinton .154
Gunderson, Kailee .193
Gyurina, Kody .255
H., Patrick .193
Haack, Zach .64
Haag, Friederike .30
Hackett, Kaitlin .119
Hagenow, Brooke .124
Hagert, Colin .67
Haidara, Asma .228
Hakim, Ali .126
Hall, Abbey .226
Hall, Taylor .105
Hall, Zhané .166
Hamilton, Sierra .151
Hammond, Megan .217
Hanek, Allison .181
Hanmann, Emily .246
Hannay, Joseph .246
Hannon, Michael .116
Hannosh, Mary .25
Hansen, Haley .172
Hanson, Molly .185
Harbottle, Dustin .98
Harder, Andrew .214
Harenda, David .157
Hargas, Joanna .194
Harley, Sarah .46
Harman, Emily .156
Harrington, Anna .151
Harris, Shantae .103
Harris, Xavier O. .239
Hart, Michael .113
Hart, Tim .49
Hasenbank, Robert .174
Hasenberg, Jordan .99
Hassan, Abdirashid .36
Hassan, Saadia .263
Hau, Ethan .88
Haughie, Abigail .34
Hauser, Owen .260
Havens, Rachel .182
Havey, Colton .199
Hawkins, Emily .68
Hawkins, Tré .178
Hayes, Aaron .92
Hayes, Jenna .34
Hearst, Clara .60
Hefko, Stormy .97
Hefty, Taylor .187
Heiden, Alex .138
Heiden, Brian .77
Heintz, McKenna .197
Heinzen, Alleck .113
Heise, Robert .50
Helland, Megan .76
Henderson, Megan Elaine .192
Hendra, Elizabeth .246
Hendricks, Alisha .42
Hendricks, Korina .107
Hendrickson, James .60
Hendrix, Matt .184
Henney, Jordan .187
Her, Jenny .142
Herbold, Madeline .209
Herdic, Lori .100
Herkness, Jenna .215
Herman, Savannah .173
Hernandez, Nina .214
Herolt, Mason .235
Herrmann, Leah .70
Hersey, Grace .193
Hertel, Kim .33
Hertzner, Lynnzee .80
Hervat, Graham .130
Hester, Ashley .134
Hicks, Ahmad .26
Hicks, Eli DeForest .256
Hiddings, Jonathan .141
Higgins, Parker .48
Highman, Bethany .264
Hightower, Jamila .118
Hilbert, Dalton .110
Hitchner, Dakota .25
Hladun, Olena .247
Hlavaty, Becca .92
Hmielewski, Ryan .218
Hochman, Sarah .234
Hoey, Dylan .53
Hoffman, Brittany .44
Hoffman, Tory .153
Holden, Matthew .184
Holden, Max .53
Holme, Koree .92
Holmes, Jeff .141
Holmes, Kayla .85
Holtz, Cody .66
Holtze, Maddie .75
Hopkins, Josh .140
Hoskins, Jake .199
Houbeck, Patricia .178
Hovell, Megan .155
Hoven, Ben .244
Hubbard, Dakota .123
Hubbard, Lindsay .240
Hubregsen, Abbey .150
Huebler, Samantha .172
Hughes, Anna .160
Hughes, Ayla .115
Hughes, Becca .166
Hughes, Chris .49
Hughes, Troy .224
Huiras, Alexis .225
Humbach, Kahyil .104
Hunt, Alexandra .74
Hunt, Summer .85
Hunter, Rachael .250
Hussein, Nasra .58
Huwatcheck, Taylor .36
Huynh, Molly .258
Idzikowski, Emma .89
Iftekhar, Raika .127
Igo, Kayla .117
Illes, Kevin .174
Insteness, Nathan .48
Iroha, Nneka .91
Isenberger, Elijah .96
Jackson, Ariel .198
Jacobs, Miranda .148
Jahnke, Samantha .147
Jakubowski, Katelyn .170
Jansen, Dylan .206
Janz, Renee .56
Jaskolski, Brian .80
Jeans, Alexa .45
Jensen, Maggie .103
Jensen, Max .92
Jimenez, Jacob .264
Jogodka, Emma .61
Johnson, Abbi .242
Johnson, Bethany .163
Johnson, Charles .216
Johnson, Gabrielle .23
Johnson, Hannah .28
Johnson, Kalena .89
Johnson, Mariah .138
Johnson, Najah .186
Johnson, Nick .119
Johnson, Sarah .181
Johnson, Stephen .216
Jones, Dominique .78
Jones, Jamie .255
Jones, Jordan .83
Jones, Rio .178
Jorgensen, Thea .163
Jorstad, Charles .172
Jost, Michael .145
Jungbluth, Rachel .50
Jurcich, Hannah .88
Jurkiewicz, Jessica .253
Kabaka, Daisy .221
Kahnke, Nina .70
Kaiser, Tyler .101
Kaiserlian, Olivia .258
Kallestad, Megan .174

Kang, Shelby .233
Karinen, Tayler .24
Karow, Nick .49
Kasee, Sierra .233
Kasinger, Jacob .104
Katzenmeyer, Morgan .183
Kawak, Rita .144
Kay, James .58
Keeley, Eagen .227
Keiser, Michael .234
Kellen, Jake .188
Keller, Kaitlyn .99
Kelley, Amber .198
Kelley, Whitney .246
Kelly, Kristina .126
Kendzierski, Kimmy .24
Kenfield, Tisha .63
Kennedy, Marshay .248
Kenney, Catalina .26
Kenney, Mark .115
Keohen, Jen .163
Kerr, Geena .239
Keryluk, Zacary .147
Kettlewell, Payshence .154
Kidder, Rebecca .142
Kidrowski, Dana .114
Kieckhefer, Alyson .233
Kieckhefer, Andy .109
Kiesling, Chelsea .136
Kiggins, Kaylee .232
Kilbourn, Courtney .28
King, Kasey .256
King, Katie .229
Kinzer, Sandra .134
Kirchman, Cole .176
Kirchner, Rachel .45
Klaas, Dustin L. .201
Klabunde, Bobby .35
Klaetsch, Bergindy .77
Klavekoske, Connor .117
Kleczka, Mallory .163
Klein, Reva .91
Klemme, Aryanna .136
Klomp, Madeline .166
Klusman, Jacob .84
Kmecheck, Kristin .189
Knaack, Darcy .242
Knapp, Jessica .113
Knoll, Michelle .102
Knuth, Chelsey .240
Koch, Dana .88
Kociszewski, Hailey .61
Koenig, Jackie .53
Kolbeck, Austin .182
Kollath, Chris .99
Koller, Kathryn .261
Koronka, Morgen .217
Koschtial, Lexi .143
Kosewski, Nathan .137
Kosterman, Alison .66
Kotcher, Kendall .197
Koukal, Cody .191
Kowalis, Matthew .206
Kozlowski, Autumn .127
Kraemer, Taylor .150
Krause, Heidi .55
Kremers, Alli .38
Krenzer, Ashley .107
Kromanaker, Mariah .214
Krstic, Danijela .78
Krueger, Kelli .128
Krueger, Tim .197
Kruemmer, Joseph .86
Krull, Jack .65
Krumenauer, Kali .76
Krupa, Taylor .132
Krus, Stephanie .204
Kubiskey, Garrett .72
Kudwa, Daniel .41
Kuehn, Savannah .213
Kuehnl, Shalyn .84
Kuhn, Emerson .85
Kujawa, Arika .259
Kujawa, Zack .210
Kuntz, Sophie .30
Kupietz, Ryan .240
Kusmierz, Paige .186
Kutschke, John .110
Kutzler, Rachel .245
LaBarge, Katie .207
Lafavre, Trevor .179
Laidler, Christina .83
Lakeman, Makayla .249
Lallensack, A.J. .217
Lamar, David .178
Lana, Luke .176
Lang, Anna .183
Langolf, Kimberly .179
Langreder, Matthew .117
Lanning III, Raymond Lee .222
Lapczynski, Jessi .92
Larson, Sean .249
Larson, Thomas .111
Lattery, Mariah .218
Law, Sarah .169
Lawler, Ethan .200
Laws, Emily .222
Lay, Mariya .122
Leatherwood, Candice .70
LeBlanc, Molly .83
LeDuc, Bennett .39
Lee, Kasia .194
Lee, Rachel .160
Lee, Shia .90
Lee, Walker .205
Leisgang, Emily .212
Leja, John .86
LeMay, Sammy .79
Lemmen, Alexandria .116
Lendvay, Megan .121
Leong, Christine .193
Lesha, Anne .171
Lester, Ross .100
Lett, Fred .68
Lewis, Donielle .65
Lewis, Harleigh .164
Lezama, Andrea .27
Li, Eileen .257
Liang, Alice .135
Liddell, Austin .202
Liebeck, Jessica .179
Lightfoot, Madison .188
Linak, Ryan .49
Lindeen, Marisa .65
Linsenmeyer, Cecily .43
Litz, Bree .155
Lively, Ellen .218
Long, Jasmine .79
Long, Lee .111
Lopez, Maritza .48
Loschen, Sarah .133
Loudermilk, Jordan .155
Lovelace, Taylor .189
Lovell, Caleb .204
Loza, Alejandro .112
Lucas, Amber .38
Ludwig, Katie .234
Luedtke, Madalynn .124
Luna-Walker, Alexis .72
Lunak, Anna .160
Lupient, Lisa .92
Lutes, Kirsta .145
Lutz, Kellie .151
Lutzke, William .57
Lynaugh, Andrea .246
Lynch, Phil .259
Lynn, Bre'Ana .196
Lynn, Kaitlyne .61
Lyons, Jordan .203
Mabee, Nick .64
MacDonald, Aubrey .262
Mackley, Stephanie .70
Mackowiak, Anne .26
MacLellan, Colin .38
Mader, Beth .111
Maenke, Joshua .104
Majeski, Tyler .73
Malecki, Eric .205
Malecki, Kayla .54
Manker, Nathan .64
Manssur, Rachel .231

Marani, Stephanie 76
Marion, Jacquelyn 257
Marsh, Max 233
Marshall, Dana 228
Marshall, Dezarae 54
Marshall, Heaven 226
Martens, Rachel 89
Martin, Max 128
Martinez, April 196
Martinez, Kimberly 218
Martinez, Valeria 64
Marvin, Kevin 49
Massart, Cassie 140
Mathews, Jacob 228
Mathews, Neena 133
Mathieu, CharLee 31
Matteson, Paige 210
Matthews-Peace, Maurice 162
Mattson, Emmie 81
Matusik, Travis 36
Maurer, Hannah 175
Mauritz, Trevor 100
Mauthe, Cody 208
Maxey, John 153
Maxson, Alyssa 256
Maxwell, Hampden Meade 23
Maxwell, Malena 140
Mayer, Lisa 100
Maynard, Carissa 25
Maznio, Jacqueline 62
Mazur, Erin 167
McCallum, Kelli 59
McCambridge, Anna 166
McCarty, Lindsey 220
McClenton, Danielle 156
McCloskey, Luke 216
McCright, Tareya 153
McDonald, Kierra 125
McGowan, Victoria 179
McGuire, Meg 42
McLain, Abigail 87
McLaughlin, Seth 152
McMahon, Makenzie 146
McManus, Angela 61
McMurray, William 169
McMurtry, Armond 160
McShane, Cody 24
McSwine, Shavon 233
McWilliams, Jeremiah 27
Mefferd, Riana 47
Meier, Anna 18
Meine, Baily 61
Meinen, Manny 122
Melby, Haley 210
Meleski, Ben 46
Meling, Elizabeth 27
Menge, Christine 56
Menke, Alex 154
Mentch, Travis 38
Meraz, Eva 248
Mermuys, Abby 105
Meshew, Katie 19
Messner, Brianna 253
Metcalfe, Briana 173
Metoxen, Mariah 164
Meylor, Becky 211
Micek, Logan 209
Michalak, Sarah 184
Michielutti, Emily 114
Michielutti, RJ 36
Miesler, Nick 91
Mijnsbergen, Danielle 131
Mikita, Abby 144
Miklosi, Mitch 230
Milender, Merra 162
Miley, Monica 203
Miller, Austin 138
Miller, Chaz 67
Miller, Justin 69
Miller, Kachay 78
Miller, Paige 226
Miller, Trelijah 140
Milquette, Amanda 262
Minard, Taylor 73
Minea Jr., Charles 115
Miracle, Quinn 75
Mitrovic, Mimi 238
Mittemiller, Casey 248
Mocol, Joe .34
Moe, Alex .230
Moehring, Keenan 245
Mohamed, Hamdi 159
Mohamed, Muhubo 90
Mohle, Jennifer 226
Monahan, Dan 34
Montgomery, Denisha 248
Moon, Steven 138
Moore, Margeaux 175
Morency, Renee 82
Moreno, Jessica 215
Morgenstern, Rachel 208
Morin, Tommy 44
Morris, Kanisha 243
Morrow, Anthoni 71
Mott, Alex .51
Moua, Melody 152
Mox, Mitch 152
Mudri, Dane 135
Mueller, A.J. 144
Mueller, Courtney 59
Mueller, Megan 31
Mulder, Megan 219
Mullen, Patrick 190
Mumby, Bailey 237
Munn, Elaine 97
Murrell, Dominque 89
Myhran, Jordyn 41
Myhre, Brady 231
Nabors, Shaprece 240
Nagel, Megan 138
Nagle, Samantha 76
Napier, Colleen 62
Negrete, Gabriela 130
Nemetz, Cecelia 167
Ness, Kylie 100
Neuhauser, Mariah 197
Neuman, Alicia 125
Neumann, Devin R. 56
Nghiem, Emily 77
Nguyen, Kevin 137
Nguyen, Phuong Trinh 100
Nguyen, Rebecca 223
Nguyen, Tina 87
Niccum, Kayla 34
Nichols, Jordyn 236
Niebauer, Kaitlin 186
Nier, Sadie .53
Nierzwicki, Alyse K. 162
Niezgoda, Angela 173
Niles, Rae Lynn 211
Nitka, Debbie 33
Nix, Elysia 106
Nogalski, Alex 175
Norman, Caitlyn 32
Nourse, Michaelle 65
O'Brien, Meaghan 39
O'Driscoll, Sarah 110
O'Leary, Patrick 153
O'Loughlin, Alexis 184
O'Mara, Logan 177
Oakes, Tia .56
Ockner, Jamie 249
Officer, Jordan 186
Okoroh, Chidimma 47
Oldenberg, Brooke 145
Olson, Chloe 210
Olson, Kaitlyn 98
Olson, Nicole 241
Olson, Sarah 220
Ore, Brian 113
Ormsby, Nick 157
Osborne, Callie 180
Osterman, Briana 197
Osweiler, Tori 115
Oteman, Quinn 82
Otto, Truth 188
Paglia, Danny 220
Pajur, Amber 80
Parce, Anita 229
Parmenter, Olivia 239
Particka, Andrew 152

Paschke, Jessica 31
Passint, Mike 42
Patel, Krishan 260
Patel, Rishi 161
Paton, Justin 218
Patterson, Andrea 200
Patterson, Quilon 157
Paulson, Kyle 165
Paulson, Laura 203
Pavlik, Melissa 88
Pawlik, Spenser 263
Pederson, Mary 142
Peers, Brienne 152
Pelky, Emily 37
Pelzer, Sierra 232
Penn, Shelby 132
Peoples, Amber 157
Peplinski, Sarah 96
Perales, Ana 149
Perion, Karri 168
Peronto, Nicole 108
Perry, Kimber 74
Perry, Tannon 62
Peters, Carli 23
Petruska, Danielle 194
Peyer, Jordan 252
Peynetsa, Carlos 205
Pham, Tracy 209
Phan, Rithdaro 76
Phelps, Alex 263
Philippon, Emily 101
Phillipi, April 72
Phillips, Bailey 74
Phillips, Braxton 152
Piotrowski, Justin 22
Pipe, James 144
Pitrof, Ashley 260
Pitrof, Danielle 129
Pitts, Aniyah 26
Placzek, Andrew 190
Platz, Kelsey 203
Ploeckelman, Emily 188
Plys, Hannah 78
Poddig, Maddi 132
Podewils, Jack 236
Poe, Vincent 58
Poisson, Eric 144
Politowicz, Alex 182
Pollard, Jonah 44
Polonis, Samantha 42
Pompeo, Kara 108
Pompura, Jalen 161
Poole, Molly 55
Portillo, John 60
Portner, Alex 27
Portz, Grace 93
Posada, Anthony 205
Potts, Keagan 220
Poulose, Solomon 225
Prada, Adriana 230
Prain, Kate 229
Prastitis, Rachel 185
Pratte, Kylie 194
Presseller, Antonio 250
Prieur, Gabe 152
Pritzl, Lucas 105
Proper, Zachary Scott 42
Puglie, Olivia 119
Pupi, Stacie 171
Pyatt, Sean 236
Pytel, Rachel 166
Quigley, Hannah 22
Quirk, Shaun 71
Rabideau, Zachary 146
Rader, Jonathan 204
Rahi, Ashley 157
Rajchel, Anthony 119
Rajewski, Samantha 51
Ralston, Ashley 32
Ramnarine, Orissa 95
Randazzo, Joe 248
Rasmussen, Beth 112
Ratajczak, Andy 120
Ravet, Blake 130
Reau, Zach .93
Redman, Harvey 248
Redman, June 188
Reece, Sierra 195
Reed, Ashley 103
Reedy, Robin 86
Reikowski, Jarid 155
Reimann, Laura 196
Reiner, Luke 86
Reiners, Jessica 76
Reiners, Joanne 55
Reis, Sami .131
Reitz, Aubrey 59
Rentmeester, Kenna 243
Reyes, Maria 223
Rezac, Katie 71
Rhode, Hattie 208
Ribbens, Joseph 108
Rice, Lee 81
Rice, Sarah 246
Richardson, Peyton 232
Rickard-Lindner, Miranda 95
Rienstra, Rachael 95
Rigby, Catherine 262
Riillo, Rocio 23
Riley, Victoria 260
Rinehard, Sadie 162
Rinzel, Justina 239
Rios, Uriel .70
Robart, Noah B. 26
Roberts, Amanda 209
Roberts, Faith 240
Roberts, Tori 29
Robertson, Laura 165
Robertson, Sarah 129
Robinson, Jay 211
Robinson, Kian 169
Rodewald, Lauren 52
Rodriguez, Alyssa 186
Roers, Caroline 183
Roers, Hank 245
Roffers, Darcie 132
Roggenbuck, Lauren 147
Rogotzke, Amanda 64
Roiger, Becky 238
Rolka, Kate .33
Roll, Kaleb 255
Romens, Rachel 234
Ronsman, Becca 198
Rosario, Alexis 148
Ross, Alison A. 231
Ross, Nathan 107
Rousso, Megan 189
Rueckl, Noah 140
Ruiz, Alexandria 48
Rumbold, Tyler 107
Runft, Kelsey 102
Ruscher, Brittany 240
Russell, Destinee 80
Russell, Diamond 180
Russell, Matthew 81
Russell, Rachel 265
Rutherford, Ethan 75
Rutkowski, Bryan 227
Ryan, Autumn 243
Rybar, Macauley 162
Rydzewski, Nicole 47
Saccoman, Vannessa 45
Sadiq, Izzy .58
Salawater, Amanda 166
Salerno, Jordyn 25
Sanborn, Michaela 227
Santos-Braceros, Alfred 41
Sartin, Jordan 40
Saukas, Connor 188
Saulog, Minette 194
Sawyer, Shelby 191
Scanlan, Maddie 212
Scanlon, Lindsay 228
Schaefer, Samuel 239
Schamens, Bekah 44
Schanke, Jenna 117
Schaub, Nicholas 231
Schaut, Kassidy 146
Schenk, Colton 245
Scherer, Heather 240
Scherkenbach, Jocie 31

Scherlinck, Andrea EunJoo 247
Schieber, Abigail 29
Schirber, Frannie 154
Schlafley, Cheyanne 236
Schleif, Kaitlyn 114
Schlichting, Sabrina Mary Marie ...213
Schliesman, Sara 140
Schmiedeknecht, Sarah 176
Schmitt, Alyssa 44
Schneider, Rachel 101
Schooler, Charles 48
Schroeder, Austin 204
Schuchardt, Mercedes 125
Schuhmacher, Adam 247
Schulner, Heather 210
Schulstrom, Brooke 142
Schulte, Stephen 264
Schultz, Becky 77
Schultz, Emily 240
Schultz, Will 77
Schumacher, Grace 83
Schwantes, Grace 130
Schwark, Jacquelyn 214
Schwartz, Cody 127
Schwartz, Eli 44
Schwartz, Mike 64
Schwarzkopf, Kelsey 171
Scobie, Lauren 128
Scorpio, Grace 225
Scott, Sarafina 89
Seaman, Hannah 63
Sedano, Alexandra 180
Seegert, Taylor 22
Sego, Morgan 37
Seidel, Jamie 208
Selbee, Elizabeth 219
Setting, Alyssa 179
Settler, Tapanga 112
Seymour, Dayna 220
Shah, Shalin 149
Shamblin, David 240
Shands, Stormie 121
Shang, Alice 165
Shannon, Brandon 70
Shawn, Kaitlyn 111
Shearer, Courtney 36
Shepard, Jenna 88
Sheppard, Reanne 56
Shirley, Elizabeth 146
Shong, Alexis 193
Shovan, Jake 43
Shuman, Sarah 256
Sibley, Brenna 88
Sibley, Jonah 150
Silvers, Aisha 222
Simmons, Anna 114
Singhi, Pooja 156
Sinks, Daniella 57
Sinks, Marissa 234
Sippel, Miranda 169
Skibbe, Kayla 70
Skluzacek, Tyler 191
Skone, Tyler 177
Slack, Brittney 251
Slagle, Awbreigh 57
Slattery, Ben 161
Sleda, Stephanie 230
Sledge, Cali 78
Sloan, Nichole 249
Small, Elijah 137
Smart, Natalia 120
Smeriglio, Rylee 24
Smith, Darian 222
Smith, Ellie 261
Smith, Grace 248
Smith, Kelsey 81
Smith, Kendra 221
Smith, Makaiah 79
Smith, Na'chelle 154
Smith, Nicole 167
Sneath, Destini 169
Snediker, Kathryn 244
Snider, Andy 79
Solberg, Rachel 106
Sorenson, Zack 109
Sotemann, Manu 259
Spencer, Elexus 61
Spencer, Molly 44
Spleas, Rebecca 47
Springer, Paige 43
Spryszak, Andrew 100
Spytman, Alyssa 260
Stackus, Tianna 65
Staeglich, Jennifer 70
Stampfli, Cierrah 105
Stanislawski, Colton 187
Stapleton, Olivia 186
Stark, Gabrielle 126
Stark, Kayla 229
Stauche, David 123
Stawara, Allison 130
Stecker, Amelia 52
Steffeck, Liza 63
Steffens, Rachel 75
Stegeman, Laura 117
Steinmetz, Kegyn 60
Stember, Adam 209
Stephens, Brianne 106
Stephenson, Winston 149
Stevens, Nathan 112
Stevens, Stephanie 164
Stevenson, Kelsey 185
Stewart, James 102
Stidwill, Emily 235
Stigall, Sarah 224
Stiles, Kevin 151
Stippich, Robert E. 39
Stitt, Keegan 261
Stock, Nicole 160
Stoiber, Rachel 95
Stoloff, Hannah 167
Stone, Shannon 41
Stoner, Leah 154
Stordahl, Sydney 55
Stout, Brian 135
Stowers, Kassie 68
Strachan, Mackenzie Jade 54
Strampp, Mackenzie 129
Strand, Sarah 123
Strasser, Brett 122
Street, Kelsie 200
Strehlow, Lacey 102
Strelecki, Danielle 207
Stroud, Najalie 153
Sturm, Samson 182
Suarez, Emiliano 29
Suprise, Alex 210
Surapaneni, Dhiraj C. 260
Sutherland, Emma 25
Sutherlund, Nic 144
Sweeney, Thomas 67
Sweeter, Brittany 82
Syswerda, John 231
Szopinski, Caleb 60
Szymusiak, Michelle 222
Tanton, Lea 217
Tarté, Daniel 109
Tavierne, Zach 45
Taylor, Daleshon 66
Taylor, Sarah 190
Taylor, Starsha Nicole 22
Tenor, Taylor 174
Terrian, Sara 135
Tesch, Kaylee 95
Tesch, Lizzie 133
Teslow, Austin 65
Tesnow, Steph 192
Tessman, Monica 262
Tessman, Yvonne 174
Thao, Ying 258
Thekan, Molly 241
Thelen, Grace 172
Thill, Brooke 226
Thiry, Roger 45
Thomas, Ashley 249
Thompson, Angelic 191
Thompson, Kirsten 105
Thompson, Morgan 250
Thorpe, Ian 53
Thull, Ivan 96
Thundercloud, Brennan 106

Tibbetts, Zach 77
Tibbits, Jonah 122
Tilkens, Christen 87
Tily, Conor 103
Timm, Hannah 159
Tinajero-Espinoza, Karla 99
Tindall, Ashley 26
Tlachac, Mitchell 139
Toenjes, Nathan 208
Toledo, Nohemi 185
Tomaszewski, Ashley 208
Tomczak, Taylor 28
Topci, Stephanie 154
Torres, Felipe Rey 237
Torres, Nadia 258
Tran, Rebecca 31
Trautmann, Lauryn 56
Trester, Kelli 261
Trinidad, Adrian 182
Tubbs, Hannah 192
Turner, Alexis 23
Turner, Alissa 204
Tylka, Angelika 150
Tysinger, Tori 50
Urban, Rosemarie 82
Urso, Alyssa 151
Uselmann, Trent 56
Valdez, Yasmin 137
Van Berkom, Anna 127
Van Hoof, Alex 225
Van Hoozen, Chris 240
Van Slyke, Alicia 87
Van Weelden, Sara 181
VanBeek, Reba 166
Vanden Avond, Kaitlin 184
Vanderhoff, Sanorraine 114
Vanderhoof, Breanna 205
Vandermoss, Megan 236
Vandermuse, Kayla 201
VanDerWal, Allison 207
Vang, Nancy 235
Vang, Vincent 258
VanPay, Jocelyn 20
VanSchoyck, Kevin 181
Vargas-Alva, Francisco 60
Varno, Rebekah 73
Vaughan, Danny 48
Veal, Rakiya 206
Veenstra, Heidi 86
Veeser, Trevor 172
Viegut, Tanner 37
Villagran, Alejandra 132
Villeneuve, Courtney 235
Vo, Laura .187
Vogel, Jordan 174
Vogler, Amelie 237
Volz, Robbie 34
von Brevern, Allison 238
Voss, Max 69
Vue, Joe 37
Vue, Ka 199
Wack, Chelsie 190
Waggoner, Trevor 162
Wagman, Jen 124
Wagner, Eric 80
Wagner, Nicholas 115
Walburg, Jason 28
Walczak, Adam 166
Walde, Bridget 179
Walker, Brittany 182
Walker, Kyle 226
Walker, Makenzie 168
Wallace, Allison 98
Wallace, Emily 73
Wallace, Sarah 173
Wallander, Emma 36
Waller, Caylin 27
Wallis, Taylor 214
Walz, Megdalena 163
Wang, Alex 134
Warfield, Megan 265
Warren, Chandler 217
Washington, Melina 25
Washington, Safiyyah 168
Watkins, Jon 198
Webster, Emily 101
Webster, Parker 230
Weisbrod, Catherine 251
Weiss, Suzannah 158
Weisz, Laura 97
Welch, Courtney 89
Welch, Julie 180
Welch, Rachel 202
Weldy, Trinity 188
Weller, Stephanie 262
Wells, Laisha 257
Wendt, Cody 224
Wersal, Dylan 221
Wesseling, Jason 97
Weston, Stevie Lee 110
Westphal, Markiesa 252
Weyrauch, Claire 159
White, Aidan 172
White, Joey 166
White, Raelon 59
White, Sabrina 196
Whiteaker, Nikki 55
Wiard, Rachelle 204
Wichert, Chris 90
Wiedel, Sean 120
Wilczynski, Emily 135
Wilczynski, Erica 38
Wilkins, Miranda 263
Wilkinson, Madeline 156
Williams, Justice 256
Wilquet, Trisha 194
Wilson, Aaron 210
Wilson, Avyonne 55
Wilson, Jaelen 21
Wilson, Tabitha 37
Wilton, Courtney 85
Windey, Hunter 256
Winfield, Amie 35
Wing, Casey 210
Winn, Brandon 68
Wojciechowski, Michael 51
Wojewoda, John 175
Woldt, Bryanna 193
Wolf-Dixon, Greyson 35
Wolfgang, Max 247
Woo, David 131
Woodward, Katherine 71
Woolstrum, Jeff 35
Wright, Brooke 234
Wright, Melissa 143
Wusthoff, Emily 105
Wyckoff, Matt 192
Wykes, Shayna 228
Xiao, Annie .86
Xiong, Kia .227
Xiong, Mary 143
Xiong, Sia .150
Xiong, Tracy 27
Xiong, Xinxy 201
Yang, Kazoua A. 82
Yim, Angela 41
Yoder, Taylor 225
Yoeckel, Terah 108
Young, Angela 122
Young, Julia 46
Young, Paul 107
Zahran, Denise 78
Zich, Brianna 138
Zielinski, Kaylyn 234
Zimmerman, Tyler 100
Zoller, Nerissa 31
Zurfluh, Danielle 58

Author Autograph Page

Author Autograph Page

Author Autograph Page

Author Autograph Page

Author Autograph Page

Author Autograph Page